To Judy and Al —

SILENT VOICES
OF **WORLD WAR II**

Nancy R. Bartlett

2-17-07

SILENT VOICES
OF WORLD WAR II

When
SONS of the LAND of ENCHANTMENT
Met
SONS of the LAND of THE RISING SUN

Everett M. Rogers
and
Nancy R. Bartlit

SANTA FE

On the Cover: Patriotic New Mexicans Volunteered for Military Service Early in World War II. During the Santa Fe Fiesta in 1942, military bands played and young men were inducted in this ceremony on the city's Plaza, at the Palace of the Governors. (See Figure 2-1. page 39).

© 2005 by Everett M. Rogers and Nancy R. Bartlit.
All Rights Reserved.

No part of this book may be reproduced in any form or by any electronic or mechanical means including information storage and retrieval systems without permission in writing from the publisher, except by a reviewer who may quote brief passages in a review.

Sunstone books may be purchased for educational, business, or sales promotional use. For information please write: Special Markets Department, Sunstone Press, P.O. Box 2321, Santa Fe, New Mexico 87504-2321.

Library of Congress Cataloging-in-Publication Data:

Rogers, Everett M.
  Silent voices of World War II : when sons of the Land of Enchantment met sons of the Land of the Rising Sun / Everett M. Rogersand Nancy R. Bartlit.
       p. cm.
  Includes bibliographical references and index.
  ISBN 0-86534-423-X (hardcover)   ISBN 0-86534-472-8 (softcover)
 1. World War, 1939–1945—New Mexico. 2. World War, 1939–1945—Participation, Indian. 3. Navajo Indians—New Mexico—History—20th century. 4. Los Alamos Scientific Laboratory—History. 5. Atomic bomb—New Mexico—History. 6. Hiroshima-shi (Japan)—History—Bombardment, 1945. 7. World War, 1939–1945—Prisoners and prisons, Japanese. 8. Bataan Death March, Philippines, 1942. 9. Japanese Americans—Evacuation and relocation, 1942–1945. 10. Japanese Americans—New Mexico—History—20th century.
 I. Bartlit, Nancy R., 1936- II. Title.

D769.85.N33R64 2004
940.53'789—dc22
                                  2004025033

WWW.SUNSTONEPRESS.COM
SUNSTONE PRESS / POST OFFICE BOX 2321 / SANTA FE, NM 87504-2321 /USA
(505) 988-4418 / *ORDERS ONLY* (800) 243-5644 / FAX (505) 988-1025

CONTENTS

PREFACE / 11

1 JUMPING INTO THE FRAY / 19

    AIMING AT AIOI BRIDGE / 22
    NEW MEXICO / 25
    WORLD WAR II / 27
        European Fascism / 27
        Spreading Japanese Aggression / 30
        The Tide Turns / 32
        Culture Clash / 33

2 THE BATAAN DEATH MARCH / 36

    OLD TWO HUNDRED / 37
    THE JAPANESE ATTACK / 40
        Bombing Clark Field / 40
        A Cat in a Bag / 43
    FIGHTING ON BATAAN / 44
    THE DEATH MARCH / 47
        Violating the Geneva Convention / 50
        Japanese Atrocities / 51
    IMPRISONMENT / 54
        Camp O'Death / 55
        Cabanatuan Prison Camp / 58
        News from the Philippines / 61

THE DEATH SHIPS / 62
    Horror Ships to Japan / 62
    Sabotage / 64
COMING HOME / 65
    Coming Alive / 66
    A Bataan Veteran's Love Story / 72
    Manuel Armijo / 75
HONORING THE BATAAN SURVIVORS / 80
THE 1999 CONFLICT OVER THE INTERNMENT CAMP MARKER / 81

3 NAVAJO CODE TALKERS / 83

SECRET CODES IN WORLD WAR II / 84
DECIDING TO USE NAVAJO CODE TALKERS / 85
    The Code Talker Demonstration / 86
    Recruiting the First 29 Code Talkers / 87
    Navajo Distrust of the U.S. Government / 90
    Enlistment / 90
BOOT CAMP / 92
DEVELOPMENT OF THE CODE / 95
    Military Equivalents in *Diné* / 97
    Wollachee-Shush-Moasi / 98
    A Code-within-a-Code / 100
    Recruiting Bill Toledo / 101
    Reasons for Enlisting / 105
    Torturing Joe Kieyoomia / 107
    The Army's Code Talkers / 109
THE CODE TALKERS IN ACTION IN THE PACIFIC / 110
    Guadalcanal / 110
    Bougainville / 112
    Saipan / 115
    Guam / 118
    Peleliu / 119
    Iwo Jima / 119
    Mount Sunovabitchi / 119
        Rooting Out the Japanese / 121
        Proving the Value of the Code Talkers / 122
        Having Coffee with Uncle Frank / 123
    Okinawa / 125

GOING HOME / 127
    Nightmares / 128
    Impacts / 130
ACHIEVEMENTS AND RECOGNITION / 132
    Lack of Public Understanding / 134
    Attitudes toward the Japanese / 137

4 THE JAPANESE AMERICAN RELOCATION/INTERNMENT CAMPS / 139

THE GOVERNMENT DECISION ON RELOCATION / 140
THE LOYALTY OF JAPANESE AMERICANS / 143
    The Munson Report / 143
    Issei, Nisei, and *Sansei* / 146
    The Media as Guard Dogs / 150
THE RUTH HASHIMOTO STORY / 151
THE RELOCATION PROCESS / 155
    Internment Camps / 155
    Where Were the Relocation Camps? / 157
    Camp Facilities / 160
    Racialization / 162
EFFECTS OF THE RELOCATION CAMPS / 164
    Research on the Relocation Camps / 164
    The Agony of the Two Questions / 165
    The Purple Heart Regiment / 166
THE INTERNMENT CAMPS / 167
    The Santa Fe Internment Camp / 171
    The Internment Process / 175
    Mutual Accommodation / 180
    Minor Revolts / 183
    The Lordsburg Army Camp / 189
RESTITUTION / 192

5 LOS ALAMOS / 194

BACKGROUND OF THE ATOMIC BOMB / 195
    The Discovery of Fission / 196
    The Race to the Atomic Bomb Begins / 201
    Einstein's Letter / 202
    The Italian Navigator / 203

    The Manhattan Project / 205
J. ROBERT OPPENHEIMER / 208
    Perro Caliente / 208
    Oppenheimer's Academic Career / 210
    A Pull to the Left / 211
    Oppenheimer's Selection as Director / 212
SELECTION OF LOS ALAMOS / 214
INSIDE BOX 1663 / 215
    Recruiting Scientists / 221
    Richard Feynman / 222
    Military/Scientist Relationships at Los Alamos / 224
    Censorship / 225
    Oppenheimer's Crisis / 226
    Compartmentalization Versus Cross-Fertilization / 227
FAT MAN AND LITTLE BOY / 230
    Designing the Bombs / 230
    The Race with Time / 232
    Uranium and Plutonium / 233
    The Unsung Role of the SEDs / 235
    The Cowpunchers / 239
SELECTING TRINITY / 240
    Constructing the Base Camp / 241
THE TEST / 243
    The Countdown / 245
    The Explosion / 246
    Effects of the Bomb / 248
THE POTSDAM CONFERENCE / 249
JAPAN AS A PUNCH-DRUNK FIGHTER / 251
    B-29s Over Japan / 251
    The Cost of Invading Japan / 253
HIROSHIMA / 254
    Engineering the Bomb / 256
    Tinian / 258
    Dropping Little Boy / 259
    Hiroshima as a Military Target / 261
    Pumpkins from the Sky / 261
NAGASAKI AND SURRENDER / 262
    Japan Surrenders / 264
WINNING THE RACE / 265

6 CONCLUSIONS / 266

    AFTERWARDS / 267
        In the Matter of Robert Oppenheimer / 267
        The Future of Los Alamos National Laboratory / 269
        The Soviet Union Gets the Bomb / 270
        Los Alamos National Laboratory Today / 274
    HEROES / 276
    THE QUALITY OF POLICY DECISIONS / 278
    NETWORKS / 280
    PARADOX / 281
    THE ROLE OF RELIGION / 282
    THE ROLE OF WOMEN / 283
    TRAMPLING INDIVIDUAL LIBERTIES / 284
    CONSCIENCE / 284
    INTERSECTIONS / 285

ADDENDUM A: FURTHER RESOURCES AND POINTS OF INTEREST / 289

ADDENDUM B: COMPARISON OF MAIN EVENTS 1941–1945 / 291

ADDENDUM C: WORLD WAR II TIME-LINE / 292

LIST OF ILLUSTRATIONS and TABLES / 293

NOTES / 297

REFERENCES / 309

NAMES INDEX / 324

SUBJECT INDEX / 330

PREFACE

In December 1941, Everett Rogers was a ten-year-old farm boy in Iowa. As a sixth-grader, he listened to the "Day of Infamy" radio broadcast on Monday, December 8, in which President Roosevelt, speaking in somber tones, asked Congress to declare war on Japan. Rogers also recalls the humid August day in 1945 when his family learned of the news of Hiroshima. A neighboring farmer, driving home from the county seat town of Carroll, Iowa, stopped alongside the Rogers' family car, which was headed in the opposite direction. During this middle-of-the-road conversation, the neighbor exclaimed: "We dropped a new bomb on Japan today, and it wiped out an entire city. The War is over!" The head of the Rogers family took this news quietly. After some seconds, father Rogers asked, "Well, do you think it will rain tonight?"

Thus the American public received the spectacular news of a scientific breakthrough, developed at a remote site in New Mexico, in creating an awesome weapon that ended the war in the Pacific. Other key events in the Pacific War also involved New Mexicans and the Japanese. The American public in mid-August 1945, lacked knowledge of the Navajo Code Talkers, and few knew about the Bataan Death March survivors, or the Japanese American relocation and internment camps.

The purpose of this book is to describe the important role of New Mexico in the conduct of World War II. Despite its small population size, New Mexico and New Mexicans played crucial roles in military intelligence and secrecy, and in the scientific success that ended World War II in the Pacific. The United States government recognized the special potential of this sparsely-settled state for certain wartime activities. New Mexico provided an ideal site for the highly secret development and testing of the atomic bomb. New Mexico's tri-ethnic culture included Navajo Indians, whose language, *Diné*, was only understood by 28 non-Navajos (none of them Japanese). The Navajo language provided the basis for an undecipherable code in the Pacific War with Japan.

New Mexicans participated in the first ground warfare of World War II involving Americans. They were then involved in the Bataan Death March, as a New Mexico National Guard unit, the 200th Regiment, was stationed in the Philippines in 1941, where they were the first to fire on the Japanese attackers. Finally, an internment camp for some 4,455 Japanese Americans was located in Santa Fe, in part because of its relatively isolated location, at great distance from the West Coast states where the internees had lived. The stated purpose of this massive relocation and internment of 110,000 Japanese Americans was to prevent espionage and sabotage of West Coast military facilities in case of a feared Japanese invasion.

This book focuses on issues of intercultural communication, mainly the difficulties between New Mexicans and Japanese when they came in contact, often at the opposite ends of a weapon or through the barbed wire of a prisoner stockade. Their markedly different cultures led to mutual misunderstandings, heightened prejudice, and violent acts, with both the United States and Japan violating the Geneva Convention (such as by killing prisoners).

Many publications are available about the topics included in the present volume. There are more than 300 books about the development of the atomic bomb at Los Alamos. Several dozen books have been written about the camps in which Japanese Americans were held during World War II, and more than 50 books have appeared about the Bataan Death March. However, to our knowledge no other book connects such events as the Navajo Code Talkers, the Bataan Death March survivors, Japanese American internees, and the atomic scientists at Los Alamos. Here we show the intersections between these actors and events. For example, several thousand Japanese Americans classified by the FBI as "dangerous enemy aliens" were interned in Santa Fe, the gateway to Los Alamos, America's most secret scientific laboratory, where the two atomic bombs were produced. This book is filled with paradoxes and strange turns of history.

Because World War II ended so long ago, many of the participants in the events chronicled here are no longer available to tell their story. However, we found key informants who told us of their experiences. Their voices help to humanize the events of history which form the backbone of this book. We seek to provide voice to the quiet individuals, such as the Army enlisted men who actually fabricated the atomic bombs at Los Alamos, the troops of the New Mexico National Guard in the Philippines, and the Marine privates who were Navajo Code Talkers. These people on the ground experienced World War II up close and personally. Their stories have not been fully told.

We utilize the extensive historical record that is available in the National Archives in Washington, D.C., and College Park, MD; the U.S. Library of Congress in Washington; the Niels Bohr Library, Center for History of Physics, American Institute of Physics, College Park, MD; the Japanese American National Museum in Los Angeles; the Bradbury Science Museum in Los Alamos; the Los Alamos Historical Museum; the Bataan Memorial Military Museum and Library in Santa Fe; the Museum of Northern Arizona, Flagstaff; the Doris Duke Collection at the University of Utah's J. Willard Marriott Library; the National Cryptographic Museum at Ft. Meade, MD; the Marine Corps Historical Center, Washington Naval Yard, Washington, D.C.; and the Oral History Archives at California State University Fullerton.

The authors wish to thank the following individuals for their help with this book: Joe Ando, Albuquerque, NM, a retired Air Force officer whose father was in the Santa Fe Internment Camp; Dorothy Cave Aldrich, historian of the Bataan Death March, Roswell, NM; Manuel A. Armijo, Bataan veteran, Santa Fe, NM; Dr. Fred Begay, Los Alamos, NM; Jimmy Begay, Navajo Code Talker, Window Rock, AZ; Jim Bergey of Albuquerque, NM, whose computer knowledge assisted us many times; Joe Bergstein, Bataan veteran, Los Alamos, NM; Sam Billison, President, Navajo Code Talkers Association, Window Rock, AZ; Fred Billey, Navajo Code Talker, Farmington, NM; Larry Campbell, Alamos, NM; Guy Claus Chee, Navajo Code Talker, Window Rock, AZ; Nick Chintis, Bataan veteran, Silver City, NM; Rebecca Collinsworth,

Archivist, Los Alamos Historical Museum, Los Alamos, NM; Jean Dabney, former WAC master sergeant and laboratory technician, Manhattan Project, Los Alamos, NM; Master Sergeant Winston Dabney, retired, former SED (Special Engineering Detachment), Manhattan Project, Los Alamos, NM; Hedy Dunn, Director, Los Alamos Historical Museum, Los Alamos, NM; Tom Foy, Bataan veteran, Bayard, NM; Professor Miguel Gandert, Department of Communication and Journalism, University of New Mexico, for his photograph of Manuel Armijo; Evans Garcia, Bataan veteran, Albuquerque, NM; the late Mary Gorman, Gallup, NM, wife of Carl Gorman, one of the First 29 Navajo Code Talkers; Michael Anaya-Gorman, grandson of the late Carl Gorman, for his photograph of four surviving First 29 Navajo Code Talkers in Washington, D.C. in 2001; Zonnie Gorman, Gallup, NM, daughter of the late Carl Gorman; Edward F. Hammel, Jr., Manhattan Project Research Leader in Plutonium Metallurgy and Metal Physics, and a longtime employee of Los Alamos National Laboratory, now retired, Los Alamos, NM; Ruth Hashimoto, Alliance for Transportation Research, University of New Mexico, Albuquerque, NM, whose father was in the Santa Fe Internment Camp; George R. Hawthorne, Lieutenant Colonel (Retired), U.S. Corps of Engineers, Santa Fe, NM; Susan Jack and Thomas McLaughlin of Black Dog Computer Consulting, LLL, Santa Fe, NM; Tomas Joehn, Director, Fray Angelico Historical Museum and Archive, Santa Fe, NM; Jack Jones, Navajo Code Talker, San Juan Pueblo, NM; Gordon Knobeloch, former SED, Los Alamos, NM; Keith Little, Navajo Code Talker, Window Rock, AZ; Bill Nishimura of Gardena, CA, for his remembrances of the Poston and Tule Lake Relocation Camps, and the Santa Fe Internment Camp; Michael O'Hara, Archivist, Museum of Northern Arizona, Flagstaff, AZ; Vicente R. Ojinaga, Bataan veteran, Santa Fe, NM; Rick Padilla, Director, Bataan Memorial Museum and Library, Santa Fe, NM; Mollie Pressler, scholar of the Lordsburg POW Camp, Lordsburg, NM; Aurelio Quintana, Bataan veteran, Santa Fe, NM; Tony Reyna, Bataan veteran, Taos Pueblo, NM; John Rhoades, Director, Bradbury Science Museum, Los Alamos, NM; Ralph Rodriquez, Jr., Bataan veteran, Albuquerque, NM; Albert Smith, Navajo Code Talker, Gallup, NM; the late Arthur Smith, Bataan veteran, Santa Fe, NM; Allen Stamm, former developer,

Santa Fe, NM; Frank Thompson, Navajo Code Talker, Gallup, NM; Randy Thompson, Trails and Open Space Planner, Planning Division, City of Santa Fe, NM; Bill Toledo, Navajo Code Talker, Laguna, NM; Benjamin T. Wakeshige, State Librarian, New Mexico State Library, Santa Fe, NM; Steve Wallace, Navajo Code Talker, Gallup, NM; and Jay Wechsler, a former SED and laboratory engineer, Manhattan Project, Los Alamos, NM.

We thank Andy Rubey for his role in creating the maps and other work. Special thanks to Everett E. Rogers-King and Jim Bergey for their help with the indexes for this book.

Certain individuals' personal experiences, such as Bataan survivor Manuel Armijo, code talker Bill Toledo, and Japanese American Ruth Hashimoto, are particularly featured in our chapters. We especially thank these individuals for sharing their life stories.

We acknowledge the assistance of several individuals who contributed their expertise by critiquing certain of our chapters: Dorothy Cave Aldrich for reading Chapter 2 on the Bataan Death March; Ruth Hashimoto for reviewing our draft Chapter 4 on the Japanese American relocation/internment camps; and Ed Hammel, John Bartlit, and Rebecca Collinsworth for reacting to our chapter dealing with Los Alamos.

Many readers of the present volume are not old enough to remember the events of the 1940s described here. In order to convey a greater sense of reality, we have included several dozen photographs that help convey the spirit of the World War II period.

The coauthors of this book have resided in New Mexico for a total of 54 years. Author Nancy R. Bartlit is a longtime resident of Los Alamos, serving the community in various leadership positions. Her father was a chemical and civil engineer who worked on the Manhattan Project, although not at Los Alamos. She married John Bartlit, with a Ph.D. in chemical engineering, and a career employee at Los Alamos National Laboratory. After her BA degree in history from Smith College, Nancy Bartlit taught in Japan, and then moved to Los Alamos. In July 1961, when Bartlit and her husband arrived at 109 E. Palace Avenue in Santa Fe, where all new employees of the Manhattan Project had reported before being sent up the Hill to Los Alamos, they were greeted by Dorothy

McKibbin, the so-called First Lady of Los Alamos, who retired the following summer. By a coincidence, McKibbin and Nancy Bartlit were both alumnae of Smith College. Bartlit later became "mayor" of Los Alamos (her actual title was Chair of the Los Alamos County Council). She is President of the Los Alamos Historical Society. Bartlit's Masters thesis in Communication at the University of New Mexico analyzed visitors' reactions to the Bradbury Science Museum's display of the two atomic bombs and to an alternative display of Little Boy's consequences on Hiroshima. This controversial display was featured in 1995, on the 50th anniversary of the end of World War II. It elicited thousands of written comments by visitors to the Bradbury Science Museum, some justifying, and others attacking, uses of the atomic bombs on Japan.

Everett M. Rogers's last position was Distinguished Professor in the Department of Communication and Journalism, University of New Mexico, in Albuquerque, NM. He had previously written *A History of Communication Study* (1994) and published several articles about the role of Edward T. Hall of Santa Fe, NM, in the history of intercultural communication. Rogers grew up on a family farm in Carroll County, Iowa. After earning a degree in agriculture from Iowa State University, he served for two years in the Korean War. His doctorate is in sociology and statistics from Iowa State University, although he made his career as a professor of communication, specializing in intercultural and international communication. Professor Rogers wrote 31 books, this being the last, and hundreds of articles during his 47-year career as university professor, author, researcher, and health education proponent that took him around the globe. Worldwide he is best known for developing a communication theory, called "Diffusion of Innovation," that offers an explanation of how new ideas are incorporated into a culture. His 1962 book on the topic is in its fifth edition, and is still widely used by educators and researchers. In 2002, Rogers was selected by the University of New Mexico as its 47th Annual Research Lecturer–the highest honor UNM bestows on its faculty."

In recognition of the many voices who speak through this book, we share its royalties with the Bataan Memorial Military Museum and

Library, the Japanese American National Museum, the Navajo Code Talkers Association, and the Los Alamos Historical Society.

We enjoyed writing this book, a process of peeling back the layers of history to understand the events of the 1940s. Our search was like a treasure hunt, pursued through chains of interpersonal networks, sometimes leading to surprise endings. Fortunately, New Mexico is a "small world" of dense networks linking individuals over long distances, an ideal system in which to pursue the trail of history. For example, many New Mexicans call their U.S. senators "Jeff" and "Pete." In such a thoroughly networked system, gathering historical materials is made easier by tracing through interpersonal links. For example, Nancy Bartlit learned that Abner Schrieber had been an administrator of the Santa Fe Internment Camp in the early 1940s. Nancy had known Schrieber, who later practiced law in Los Alamos. She contacted his widow through a mutual friend. The end result of this chain of interpersonal relationships was a box of invaluable photographs and other historical materials about the Santa Fe Internment Camp. Several of these pictures appear in our book, and our account of this camp draws on Schrieber's memoirs. When the May 2000, Los Alamos fire threatened Nancy Bartlit's home, she was evacuated, and the cardboard box went with her.

❖ ❖ ❖

We hope you enjoy learning more about the important events of 1941–1945, when the freedom of the future world was uncertain, and when New Mexico, in its unique way, helped determine that future.

—Everett M. Rogers, Albuquerque
—Nancy R. Bartlit, Los Alamos

1

JUMPING INTO THE FRAY

"Sixteen hours ago an American airplane dropped one atomic bomb on Hiroshima, an important Japanese Army base. That bomb had more power than 20,000 tons of TNT. It is a harnessing of the basic power of the universe. The force from which the sun draws its power has been loosened against those who brought the war to the Far East. If they do not now accept our terms, they may expect a rain of ruin from the air, the like of which has never been seen on earth . . . ."
—(U.S. President Harry S. Truman, 11:00 A.M., on August 6, 1945, quoted in Knebel & Bailey, 1960, pp. 178–179.)

Just before their take off on August 6, 1945, from Tinian, the Pacific island located 2,000 miles from Hiroshima, Lieutenant Colonel Paul Tibbets and each of his B-29 crew members were handed a cyanide capsule to swallow in case they were captured. The U.S. Marines had invaded Tinian a year previously in order to provide a bomber base within striking distance of Japan. The *Enola Gay* took off in the darkness at 2:45 A.M., clearing the end of the two-mile runway with only 100 feet to spare (Russ, 1984). While taking off, the B-29 passed the burned remains of four B-29s that had crashed the previous night; the wreckage had been bulldozed to the side of Runway A. The *Enola Gay* weighed 65 tons at take off, eight tons overweight. It carried a single bomb, nicknamed Little Boy, which weighed five tons. This gun-type uranium bomb, developed by Dr. J. Robert Oppenheimer and the Manhattan Project scientists at Los Alamos, New Mexico, contained batteries which had to be kept charged during the long flight. Also, the bomb could not get too cold. At 7:30 A.M., Navy Captain Deak Parsons inserted the red plugs in Little Boy. Now the weapon was fully armed. It rode in the B-29's bomb bay, glistening black.

An hour before the *Enola Gay's* departure, another B-29, *Straight Flush*, a weather plane, had taken off from Tinian for Hiroshima. The weather plane radioed a coded message to the *Enola Gay*, identified as "Dimples 82," that the skies were clear over the target. This signal was the death sentence for Hiroshima (Knebel & Bailey, 1960). The lengthy flight from Tinian to Hiroshima, requiring six and some half hours of flying time, was uneventful. The *Enola Gay* arrived over the target at 8:15 A.M. plus 17 seconds, almost precisely on time (their ETA was 8:15). The B-29 flew at 30,000 feet, an almost unprecedented altitude for bombers at that time. This height reduced the danger from enemy planes, which was important given that the bomber's machine guns had been removed in order to save weight.

The pilot of the *Enola Gay*, Paul Tibbets, was 29 years old (Figure 1-1). He had proven his skill as a bomber pilot on missions in North Africa and over Germany. Then he had a year's experience in testing the B-29 Superfortress, when he worked with the Physics Department at the University of New Mexico to determine how well the new bomber could defend itself against fighter attack at high altitudes (Rhodes, 1986). General Leslie Groves (1983, p. 258), Commander of the Manhattan Project, selected Tibbets because: "He was a superb pilot of heavy planes, with years of flying experience, and probably was as familiar with the B-29 as anyone in the service." Tibbets named his plane after his mother's first and middle names; she had encouraged him to pursue his love of flying despite his father's resistance.

Figure 1-1. The Crew of the *Enola Gay* on Tinian with their B-29 in the Background.

Lieutenant Colonel Paul W. Tibbets, Jr., pilot of the *Enola Gay*, is standing in the center. On his left is Major Tom Ferebee, the bombardier, who took over the controls of the plane during its final 12-mile bombing run at the T-shaped Aioi Bridge in Hiroshima. Tibbets then took back the controls and put the plane in a violent diving turn to escape the explosion 45 seconds later. When the B-29 returned to Tinian and the photographs taken by the plane's fixed cameras were developed, the roll of film showed nothing of the mushroom cloud, due to the violent dive and turn. The only photographs were taken by the plane's tail gunner, Sergeant George R. Caron from Brooklyn, squatting above, who wore a Brooklyn Dodgers' cap for good luck.

Source: Used by permission of Johnny J. Marks, Unisearch Antiques, Lakewood, CO.

AIMING AT AIOI BRIDGE

Hiroshima means "broad island" in Japanese, as the city lies on a delta bisected by seven rivers that run down from the mountains into the Seto Inland Sea. Hiroshima was a perfect target for the atomic bomb. It was flat, with no point more than 15 feet above water level. Unlike most other Japanese cities, Hiroshima had been spared from previous destruction. Hiroshima's officials had anticipated a fire bombing with incendiary bombs, the fate of 66 other Japanese cities, and on the morning of August 6, school girls were clearing fire lanes through the city to contain the spread of the expected conflagration. They looked up, unalarmed, at the single B-29 flying overhead.

The city was a military target, a major port of embarkation for the Japanese Army, and a convoy assembly port for the Imperial Navy. There were 43,000 military personnel in the city, along with 280,000 civilians, including 25,000 Korean laborers. A prisoner-of-war camp in Hiroshima contained several soldiers from the New Mexico National Guard who had been captured earlier in the war on Bataan, in the Philippines. They labored under Japanese guards in railway yards, on shipping docks, and in industrial plants.

The aiming point for the *Enola Gay's* bomb run over Hiroshima was the distinctively T-shaped AIOI Bridge, situated over the intersection of the Motoyasu and Honkawa Rivers, near the center of the city. The *Enola Gay's* bombardier, Major Tom Ferebee, got the Aioi Bridge in the crosshairs of his Norden bombsight. When the five-ton bomb was released over Aioi Bridge, the B-29 suddenly lightened. Years later, in a 1999 interview, Colonel Tibbets recalled that on the bomb's release: "The seat slapped me on the ass" (Greene, 1999, p. 1). Once the crew heard the bomb bay doors click shut, their next thought was to escape the forthcoming blast of the explosion.

Little Boy would detonate 45 seconds after release, at a height of 1,902 feet over Hiroshima, an altitude ideal for its maximum effect. The bomb formed a thin layer of condensation on its surface, as it dropped swiftly from the cold air of 31,000 feet into the humid, 80 degree air over the city. The first odd buckling of the metal surface began to suggest what was going on inside. A single neutron started the chain reaction. A millionth of a second later, there were two neutrons, then four, eight, sixteen, and so on. Mass was disappearing inside the bomb, converted to energy by the speeding neutrons, according to Einstein's formula of $E = mc^2$. The chain reaction inside Little Boy went through 80 generations of doubling as it dropped through the skies over Hiroshima. Tremendous heat was created, with the temperature shooting up to several million degrees Celsius, similar to that at the center of the sun (Bodanis, 2001).

Tibbets put the huge plane in a diving, 156 ½ degree turn to the right in order to increase its speed. The *Enola Gay* had to be eight miles from Ground Zero in order to withstand the shock waves. The epicenter for Little Boy was above the courtyard of Shima Hospital, missing the Aioi Bridge by only 550 feet (Rhodes, 1986). Tibbets and his crew felt the concussion waves in their plane, and knew that Little Boy had exploded. When pressed by Tibbets, Robert Oppenheimer had estimated the chances of Little Boy being a dud at only one in ten thousand. "A bright light filled the plane," Tibbets (1985) remembered. "The city was hidden by that awful cloud . . . boiling up, mushrooming. For a moment, no one spoke."

On the ground in Hiroshima, it was a sunny morning. At 7:31 A.M., the all-clear had sounded after the B-29 weather plane passed over the city, so no one was in the bomb shelters. Sarugaku-cho, the neighborhood near Aioi Bridge, was an area of *noh* actors, artisans, doctors, and shops. All were obliterated by the blast. The atomic bomb would completely destroy an area of four square miles, leveling 60 percent of Hiroshima's 76,000 buildings. First response was a brilliant flash of intense light ("*pika*"), followed by a gigantic boom ("*don*"). Kengo Nihawa's watch, stopped forever at 8:15 A.M., is now in the Hiroshima Peace Museum, located near Ground Zero. Nihawa died of radiation poisoning two weeks after the explosion.[1]

The concrete Aioi Bridge was tossed up by the force of the bomb, but was repaired after the war. The shadow of a man who had been crossing the Bridge was marked onto the concrete by the extreme heat of the *pika-don*, which vaporized the man's body. The solidly-built Hiroshima Prefectural Industrial Promotion Hall, located 160 yards from Ground Zero, was heavily damaged but only partially destroyed. The steel frame of its dome was melted and fused, but remained in place. Today it is called the Atomic Bomb Dome, and is the only bomb-damaged building that remains in Hiroshima.

Tibbets flew the *Enola Gay* in a semicircle around the awesome mushroom cloud which was rising violently to a height of about nine miles. Finally, tail-gunner Robert Caron noted that the radioactive cloud was blowing toward their bomber, and Tibbets wheeled the plane toward Tinian. The crew could see the mushroom cloud for 363 miles of their return flight. When they arrived in Tinian, a welcoming party of top military brass and Los Alamos scientists celebrated the successful mission, and a Distinguished Flying Cross was pinned on Tibbets.

Within minutes after the explosion, black rain began to fall on Hiroshima, caused by the dust and debris in the air, which was highly radioactive. In addition to the some 100,000 people killed instantly, 40,000 individuals died over the following four months, suffering from vomiting, diarrhea, fever, and burns. Radiation poisoning caused their hair to drop out, and gamma rays affected the ability of their bone marrow to replace their white cells. Radiation sickness led to anemia and internal bleeding. Men became sterile and women miscarried and stopped menstruating. Later, keloid tumors formed over the burns; these deep layers of pink, rubbery tissue developed in crab-like growths, disfiguring the survivors (Hersey, 1989). By the end of five years, 200,000 had died in Hiroshima.

Japan surrendered a week after the destruction of Hiroshima, and Nagasaki, on August 14, 1945. The sudden end of World War II, celebrated as V-J Day on August 15, saved the lives of an estimated one million men who were expected to die in the invasion of the Japanese home islands, scheduled a few months later, in November. Benefitting from the unexpected, sudden peace was 100,000 American POWs, whom the Japanese planned to kill before they were liberated by the invading forces.

The scientific achievement of creating the atomic bomb had occurred at a secret laboratory in New Mexico, as the world learned the day after the explosion on August 6, 1945, [2] when U.S. President Harry Truman announced the destruction of Hiroshima. The Manhattan Project was so secret that even the people of Santa Fe, the nearby gateway to Los Alamos Laboratory, were completely surprised.

NEW MEXICO

In 1940, just before World War II, New Mexico had a total population of only 531,815 people, this in a land area so large that the state was ranked fourth-largest in the U.S., after only Texas, California, and Montana. Much of the state's population was concentrated in the city of Albuquerque. So New Mexico had vast areas that were sparsely settled, ideal for secret military operations like developing and testing a new weapon. For a variety of planned and unintended reasons, New Mexico played a role in World War II far out of proportion to its rather meager population.

New Mexico claims to be the oldest state in the United States in the sense that a permanent Spanish colony was established in 1598, nine years before English colonists arrived at Jamestown and 22 years before the Pilgrims landed at Plymouth Rock. Further, Santa Fe is the oldest capital in the United States. Long before the Spanish arrived in what is now New Mexico, Native American settlements existed, as many still do today. A major area of the state comprises the Navajo Nation, two Apache reservations, and 19 Indian pueblos.

Nuevo Mexico was at the extreme reaches of the Spanish Empire, 1,400 miles from Mexico City, which in turn was thousands of miles across the Atlantic from the King of Spain in Madrid. This physical isolation, coupled with intermarriage with native people, meant that New Mexico's Hispanic culture developed in a distinctive way. New

Mexico attracted individuals, like Jewish refugees from the Inquisition in Spain, who wanted the safety of living in an isolated place.

New Mexico was ruled by Spain, then Mexico, and finally was transferred to the United States in 1848 by the Treaty of Guadalupe Hidalgo that ended the U.S./Mexican War. For a brief period, the Confederate flag flew over the territorial capital in Santa Fe, and three Civil War battles were fought in New Mexico. The state also furnished many of Teddy Roosevelt's Rough Riders, who fought in the Spanish American War (in 1898). The state's sons fought in France in World War I, and during the 1940s New Mexico played a key role in the Pacific War.

New Mexico is a uniquely tri-cultural state with a population today that is 9 percent Native American and 42 percent Hispanic; most of the remaining people are "Anglos" of European American stock. New Mexicans tried ten times over a 62-year period to achieve statehood, until they were finally successful in 1912 when New Mexico was admitted as the 47th state. Easterners perceived the New Mexico Territory as a heavily Spanish-speaking area and as a barren desert that was not suitable to become a state. New Mexicans feel they are misunderstood by other Americans yet today. A popular story in Albuquerque concerns a New Mexican who made a purchase in Macy's, to be told by the New York salesclerk that she would have to pay in dollars, as pesos were not accepted.

WORLD WAR II

In order to understand the role of New Mexico in World War II, we here recount certain of the main events of this historic conflict.

European Fascism

The roots of World War II grew out of World War I, mistakenly called "the war to end all wars." The peace terms that Germany was forced to accept in the Versailles Peace Treaty in 1919 were harsh. Huge chunks of German territory were reassigned to neighboring nations, large reparation payments were assessed, and the German military was shrunken to a token police force. Germany was forbidden to rearm. Europe was thrown into a prolonged economic depression after World War I, accompanied by a high rate of inflation and massive unemployment.

In the decades after the end of the war, many German people believed that they had been deceived by their leaders. Out of this political and economic chaos rose Adolf Hitler, a leader who promised the German people that he would lead them back to greatness. His brand of political ideology was called National Socialism, or Nazism. Hitler attracted a growing number of followers, although never a majority of the German people, often using violent means to advance his cause. Finally, he was named the German Chancellor in 1933 (Table 1-1).

Table 1-1. Time-Line of the Main Events in World War II.

Date	Event
1933	Adolf Hitler becomes Chancellor of Germany.
1938	
March	Germany annexes Austria and the Sudetenland of Czechoslovakia.
November	Nazis attack Jews and their property on *Kristalnacht*.
1939	
March	Germany occupies Czechoslovakia and stops uranium exports.
September 1	World War II begins with the German invasion of Poland.
1940	
April	Germany invades Denmark and Norway.
May	Germany invades the Netherlands, Belgium, and Luxembourg.
June	Germany conquers France.
September	The London Blitz begins.
1941	
June	Germany invades Russia.
December 7	Japan bombs Pearl Harbor, and the United States enters World War II.
1942	
January	Roosevelt and Churchill agree to defeat Germany first and then Japan.
March	U.S. government begins relocating and interning Japanese Americans living on the West Coast.
April 9	American military forces on the Bataan Peninsula in the Philippines surrender to the Japanese, and the Bataan Death March begins.
June	The Japanese Navy is defeated in the Battle of Midway, a turning point in the Pacific War.
August 7	Marines land on Guadalcanal, beginning the island-hopping campaign in the Pacific towards Japan.
October	The British defeat Germany's Afrika Corps in the Battle of El Alemain in North Africa.
November 8	Allied forces land in Morocco and Algeria.

1943
January	The German Sixth Army in Stalingrad surrenders, a turning point on Front.
July	Allied military forces land in Italy.
September	Italy surrenders.

1944
June 6	D-Day landing on the Normandy beaches of France.
July 24	Japanese soldiers on Saipan surrender, and nearby Tinian is invaded.
October	The United States invades the Philippines.
November	B-29s begin bombing Tokyo from bases in Saipan.
December	Battle of the Bulge in Europe.

1945
January	Soviet troops liberate Auschwitz.
February	U.S. Marines invade Iwo Jima.
March 9-10	American B-29s firebomb Tokyo, killing 125,000 people in one night.
April 12	Roosevelt dies and Harry Truman becomes U.S. President.
May 8	Germany surrenders.
June 23	Okinawa is captured.
July 16	First atomic explosion at Trinity Site.
July 24	Potsdam Declaration demands the unconditional surrender of Japan.
July 28	Japan rejects the Potsdam Ultimatum.
August 6	Little Boy is dropped on Hiroshima.
August 8	USSR declares war on Japan.
August 9	Fat Man is dropped on Nagasaki.
August 15	End of World War II, which killed 55 million people.
September 2	Formal surrender of Japan on the USS *Missouri* in Tokyo Bay.

Hitler immediately began building up Germany's army, navy, and air force. From 1936 to 1939, the German Luftwaffe (air force) fought in the Spanish Civil War, supporting dictator Francisco Franco and gaining military experience. In 1938, Hitler's army marched into Austria and the Sudetenland, a Czechoslovakian province with a predominantly Germanic population.

Hitler blamed the Jews for Germany's social and economic problems, and German anti-Semitism, already formidable, was fanned to violence. One night in November 1938, government-inspired mobs throughout Germany and Austria broke the windows of Jewish-owned stores and looted their contents. After this so-called *Kristalnacht*, an increasing number of European Jews began to flee, with thousands coming to America. Many Jews, some six million, did not escape from Germany and German-occupied Europe. They were systematically eliminated in German concentration camps.

Until September 1, 1939, when Hitler's army invaded Poland, France and Britain had pursued a policy of appeasing Hitler's demands, thus hoping to avoid warfare. But when the "blitzkrieg" (or lightning war in which motorized troops and tanks advanced rapidly, supported by the Luftwaffe) was unleashed on Poland, the Allies declared war on Germany. For the next several years of World War II, the conflict went disastrously for the Allies. In quick succession, Hitler invaded Denmark and Norway, and then the Netherlands, Belgium, and Luxenburg. German tank columns wheeled on into France. In a month-long blitzkrieg in May/June 1940, Hitler conquered France, leaving Britain alone against Germany's further expansion.

Hitler began the invasion of Russia in June 1941. At first, the German blitzkrieg gobbled up huge areas of the USSR, pushing through the Ukraine, surrounding Leningrad, and advancing to the suburbs of Moscow. But as the fierce Russian winter of 1941/1942 took its toll, the German advance slowed and was then thrown back.

Spreading Japanese Aggression

In Japan during the 1930s, military officers began to dominate the national government. They pursued an increasingly aggressive policy of territorial expansion for the Land of the Rising Sun, invading Manchuria, and then, after 1937, China (Figure 1-2).

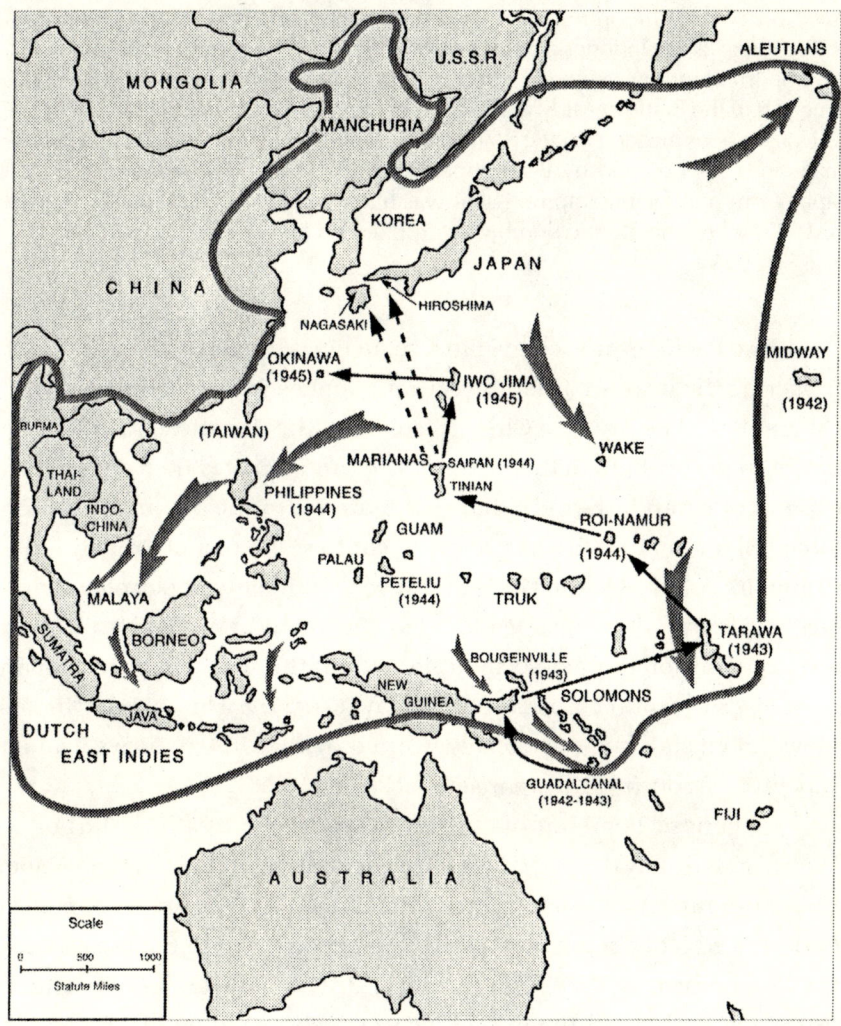

Figure 1-2. The Farthest Advance of the Japanese Empire in Mid-1942 (heavy arrows), and the Main Island-Hopping Battles with the United States (lighter arrows).

The Pacific War began in July 1937, with Japan's invasion of China, followed by expansion into Indo-China in 1941. (Japan refers to World War II as "The 15 Years War" because they count from an incident they provoked in Manchuria in 1931, for which they justified controlling all of Manchuria.) United States involvement in World War II began with the Japanese attack on Pearl Harbor, Hawaii (not shown here). This event was rapidly followed by the Japanese invasion of the Philippines, British Malaya, Thailand, Burma, the Dutch East Indies (present day Indonesia), the South Pacific islands, and Attu in the Aleutians. An important turning point occurred in June 1942, when the Japanese fleet was defeated in the Battle of Midway. Thereafter, the Japanese were on the defensive, as U.S. Marines invaded Pacific islands, including Tinian, from which the Japanese mainland was bombed by B-29 Superfortresses. U.S. naval superiority cut off Japan from her Pacific empire. Japan was like a punch-drunk fighter by August 6, 1945, when the atomic bomb was dropped on Hiroshima.

The Pacific War escalated in a sequence of events with each action triggering the next. In order to prevent supplies from reaching General Chiang Kai-shek and his Chinese soldiers, the Japanese invaded the northern part of French Indo-China. The United States then embargoed exports of scrap iron and other war material to the Japanese, which forced them to push further south to capture the rest of French Indo-China. In July 1941, the U.S. embargoed shipments of petroleum and steel to Japan. Japanese leaders felt they could only maintain their war economy for another six months without these vital imports. Japan needed the resources of British Malaya and the Dutch East Indies (now Indonesia), but was sternly warned by the United States against this further southward expansion.

Japanese bombing of the U.S. naval base at Pearl Harbor in Hawaii essentially destroyed much of the American Navy in the Pacific. The two-hour attack sank or heavily damaged 21 U.S. ships, damaged or destroyed 323 aircraft, and killed 2,388 people. The Japanese invaded the Philippines, an American territory, British Malaya, and the Dutch East Indies. These initial successes were celebrated by the Japanese, although the nation's leaders knew they were hopelessly outmatched by the United States. By April 1942, when the American forces in the Philippines surrendered, Japan ruled most of East Asia.

The Tide Turns

Then, in three crucial engagements, the tide of World War II was reversed, and thereafter the Allies were everywhere successful. A key factor in this reversal of previous Axis victories was the industrial resources and manpower of the United States, fighting in conjunction with Britain and Russia. The three important turning points of World War II were (1) the Battle of Midway in June 1942 in the Pacific, in which the Japanese Navy suffered heavy losses; (2) the Battle of El Alamein in North Africa, on October 23-24, 1942, in which British armored forces turned the tide of battle against the German Afrika Corps; and (3) Stalingrad, in which Russian forces cut off the German Sixth Army, which surrendered on January 31, 1943.

In June 1944, Allied forces landed on the Normandy beaches of France, and began pushing the Germans back toward the Rhine. Russian troops overcame the German army on the Eastern Front, forcing it back into Germany, and captured Berlin. On May 8, 1945, Germany surrendered, following Hitler's suicide.

The Pacific War initially received only secondary attention from the Allies, as President Franklin Delano Roosevelt and Prime Minister Winston Churchill felt that Nazi Germany represented a more global danger than did Japan. The war in the Pacific consisted of an island-hopping campaign starting from Australian bases, and moving through Guadalcanal, Bougainville, Guam, Tinian, Saipan, Iwo Jima, and Okinawa. The main American strategy was to secure airbases from which U.S. planes like B-29 Superfortresses could bomb Japanese cities. This bombing, especially with incendiary bombs, essentially obliterated most Japanese cities, while the U.S. Navy destroyed Japanese shipping. Nevertheless, Japan remained a formidable foe in mid-1945 when atomic bombs were dropped on Hiroshima and Nagasaki. Emperor Hirohito agreed to unconditional surrender, and World War II ended officially on September 2, 1945.

Culture Clash

Americans and Japanese at the beginning of World War II had very little experience in dealing with each other. Most Americans had never met a Japanese person face-to-face before the fighting began, unless they were in a West Coast state or the territory of Hawaii. The Pacific War brought Japanese and Americans into direct contact, often at the opposite ends of a gun. For the Bataan veterans in Japanese POW camps and for the Japanese Americans in the U.S. relocation and internment camps, this intercultural communication took place through the strands of a barbed wire fence.

Both participants in the Japanese/American conflict thought of the other as inferior. To the Americans, the Japanese soldiers were "little yellow men." The Japanese army's success in sweeping through the Pacific in the first months of World War II convinced the Japanese of their superiority over white men. The extreme ethnocentrism of the Americans toward the Japanese was expressed by words like "Japs" and "Nips." Often the noun "Jap" was preceded by adjectives like "dirty" or "yellow." Americans considered the Japanese to be "tricky." After all, the Pacific War began with a Japanese "sneak" attack on Pearl Harbor. The Japanese had not even declared war! Much was made of the fact that the Japanese had little regards for human life. For instance, they fought to the death on Guadalcanal and on other Pacific islands. Some Americans felt that killing Japanese prisoners and violating the Geneva Convention in other ways were justified.

Brutality was the essence of Japanese military training, and Japanese soldiers were trained to fight to the death. So, for example, the Japanese who took the New Mexico National Guard troops captive on Bataan regarded them as cowards. Many New Mexicans said afterward that if they had known what their lives were going to be like as prisoners of the Japanese, they would never have allowed themselves to be surrendered (Cook & Cook, 1992).

Only 100 Japanese prisoners were captured by the U.S. Marines from the 4,700 defenders of the Pacific Island of Tarawa (Cook & Cook, 1992, p. 340). Generally, only about one Japanese soldier surrendered in the Pacific War for every 100 killed. In Europe, it was generally considered that if one-fourth to one-third of an army were casualties, the rest would surrender (Cook & Cook, 1992, p. 520). The fanatical nature of the Japanese soldiers was demonstrated by their *banzai* attacks, a headlong massed advance with the soldiers yelling "*Banzai! Banzai!*" (Hurray! Hurray!) as they rushed forward.³ The Marines often mowed down the Japanese attackers in these frontal charges.

Japanese soldiers firmly believed that their fighting spirit could overcome all odds (Gilmore, 1998). Thus it did not really matter that Japan was totally outmatched in the Pacific War by the industrial resources and manpower of the United States. The Japanese believed that what ultimately mattered was spirit. Here the *bushido* (which means "the way of the gentry of the sword") code of Japanese warriors (*samurai*) provided inner strength for the Imperial Army. The aversion to surrender was so strong in the *bushido* code that Japanese soldiers were not instructed in how to behave if they were captured. Thus Japanese POWs seized in the Pacific fighting often provided pertinent military information to their captors (Gilmore, 1998). By socially defining the Japanese as a race apart from themselves, the Americans felt more justified in firebombing Japanese cities in 1945, which meant killing hundreds of thousands of civilians and destroying the homes of 15 million people. Ultimately, the American perspective on their Japanese enemies helped them decide to use the two atomic bombs on Japanese cities.

❖ ❖ ❖

Now we describe how New Mexicans became involved early in World War II in the Pacific, on the Bataan Peninsula of the Philippines.

2

THE BATAAN DEATH MARCH

"We're the Battling Bastards of Bataan,
No mama, no papa, no Uncle Sam;
No aunts, no uncles, no cousins, no nieces,
No pills, no planes, no artillery pieces.
And nobody gives a damn.
And nobody gives a damn."
—(Poem written by journalist Frank Hewlett, popular among the New Mexicans on Bataan, quoted in Cave, 1996, p. 130).

The New Mexico National Guard was already in the Philippines in 1941, several months before the attack on Pearl Harbor. The New Mexico National Guard's 200th Coast Artillery had been ordered to the Philippines, then an American territory, because they were named as the best antiaircraft regiment in the U.S. Army (Jolly, 1964), and many of the New Mexicans (about one-third) were Hispanic (Takaki, 1993). The Pentagon thought that cultural similarity would help the American troops get along well with Filipinos.

The U.S. government anticipated the threat to the Philippines, which lay directly in the path of Japan's southward expansion toward the oil and other resources of South Asia. In 1940, General Douglas

MacArthur felt that the Philippines could be defended by the United States, thus denying the Japanese use of the South China Sea. American troops began to arrive in the Philippines, and the Filipino Army was greatly expanded through the training of recruits. MacArthur hoped to prepare an adequate defensive force by April 1942. Unfortunately, the Japanese did not cooperate with this time schedule.

By December 7, 1941, the defensive preparations were completely inadequate. Only about 25,000 U.S. troops had arrived in the Philippines. These soldiers were considered expendable, and were neither reinforced nor supplied. Calling themselves the "Battling Bastards of Bataan" and fighting under extremely difficult conditions, they held up the Japanese advance for four months. This crucial delay helped save Australia and New Zealand from a planned Japanese invasion. Thus General Douglas MacArthur and his American troops were provided with a springboard, and the time to prepare for their island-hopping advance toward Japan after the tide of the Pacific War turned in mid-1942. But the New Mexicans paid dearly for being surrendered to the Japanese.

OLD TWO HUNDRED

The 200th Coast Artillery, a regiment of the New Mexico National Guard, originally was cavalry, but was converted to an antiaircraft unit by the U.S. Army in the months before World War II. They were equipped with one battery of 50-caliber machine guns, twenty-two 37-mm guns (seven of which were defective), and a dozen 3-inch guns. The regiment also had a primitive radar system, although it did not function properly under battle conditions.

Due to a shortage of ammunition in the prewar Army, the New Mexicans were not allowed to fire their guns in training (Jolly, 1964). The seals on their ammunition cases were not broken until the first wave of 54 Mitsubishi bombers attacked Clark Field in the Philippines on December 8, 1941, simultaneous with Pearl Harbor Day (the Philippines were on the other side of the International Date Line from

Hawaii). To their dismay, the New Mexicans found that many of their shells were duds (Ojinaga, 2000; Aldrich, 2000). Machine gun ammunition, made in 1918, was issued to the New Mexicans in 1941. They had to polish the corrosion off of the bullets before they would fit into the machine gun belts (Cave, 1996).

The 200th Regiment included many Hispanics and Native Americans from the pueblos and the Navajo Reservation. There were cowboys, medical doctors, a newspaper editor, a lawyer, college students, and high school students who had lied about their age. New Mexico was a very patriotic state. The Regiment had a strong feeling of solidarity, in part because most had known each other for several years. As First Sergeant Manuel Armijo (2000) explained: "We were *amigos*." This esprit de corps was important when they fought on Bataan, and later when they sought to survive the Japanese POW camps and the Death Ships to Japan. Tommy Foy joined the National Guard unit in Silver City to be "with people that I knew" (Foy, 2000). In fact, he was already acquainted with every one of the 78 others in Battery B at Silver City when he enlisted.

When General Douglas MacArthur first saw the youthful New Mexicans, he remarked, "I asked for soldiers, not Boy Scouts" (Thomas & others, 1994). Later, when the General got to know them better, he called them his "New Mexico horse thieves." Perhaps he knew that the New Mexicans, while fighting on Bataan, ate his personal mount. Aurello Quintana (2000), recalling the event years later, rubs his stomach with pleasure.

The New Mexicans joined the National Guard for various reasons. The pay was low ($18 a month for a private, plus one dollar for each weekly training meeting attended), but this meager wage was enough to attract volunteers (Figure 2-1). When Private First Class Aurelio Quintana joined the National Guard, he was only 15 years old. Quintana won sharpshooter trophies, and soon he was rated a master shooter, an even higher level of excellence than sharpshooter. Vicente Ojinaga (2000) grew up in Santa Rita, New Mexico, and when the winds of war began to blow, he wanted to volunteer for military service, but his mother was opposed. He was drafted and sent to Fort Bliss in March 1941. Ojinaga was assigned to the 200th, thus joining his fellow New Mexicans; shortly he shipped out with them for the Philippines. He became a bugler and earned a sharpshooter ranking. At Clark Field, he was a fuse cutter for the antiaircraft shells.

Figure 2-1. Patriotic New Mexicans Volunteered for Military Service Early in World War II.
During the Santa Fe Fiesta in 1942, military bands played and young men were inducted in this ceremony on the city's Plaza, at the Palace of the Governors.
Source: New Mexico State Records Center & Archives, Santa Fe, New Mexico.

Nick Chintis was playing tailback for 300-student New Mexico State Teachers College (now Western New Mexico University) in Silver City. He came from Hammond, Indiana, and was dubious on his arrival in bleak southern New Mexico when he saw the mine tailings on the rocky hillsides. Then he met "the prettiest girl I had ever seen;" she was working at a drive-in restaurant, wearing a white cowboy hat and white boots.[1] Suddenly, Silver City looked quite good to him (Chintis, 2000). He heard that the National Guardsmen could take their girlfriends horseback riding on Sundays. So he signed up, along with eleven of his football teammates. The New Mexico National Guard was federalized on January 6, 1941, as the U.S. government began to prepare for the forthcoming War. After the 200th was trained at Fort Bliss, they were shipped to the Philippines, arriving in Manila Bay in September 1941. In November 1941, wives and dependents were sent home, as the Americans prepared for the coming war.

THE JAPANESE ATTACK

Japanese military forces struck at the Philippines as soon as World War II began in the Pacific, on December 8, 1941, simultaneously with the attack on Pearl Harbor. Japanese troops landed in both the north on Luzon and the south on Mindanao. A first priority in the Japanese attack was to knock out the U.S. Far East Air Force in order to prevent American planes from bombing the Japanese troopships approaching the Philippines.

Bombing Clark Field

The 200th was posted to Fort Stotsenberg, adjoining Clark Field, which the New Mexicans were assigned to defend from attack. Clark Field, located about 60 miles north of Manila, was the main American air base in the Philippines. The 35 B-17 bombers based at Clark Field flew a fruitless mission over the Philippines on the morning of

December 8, and were refueling at midday. The B-17s were lined up like sitting ducks.[2]

The war began for the New Mexicans when the Mitsubishi bombers attacked Clark Field at 1235 hours (shortly after midday); the Japanese bombers could not take off earlier from their airfield in Taiwan, which was socked in with a heavy fog. The New Mexicans were the first unit in the Philippines to fire at the enemy (Figure 2-2).

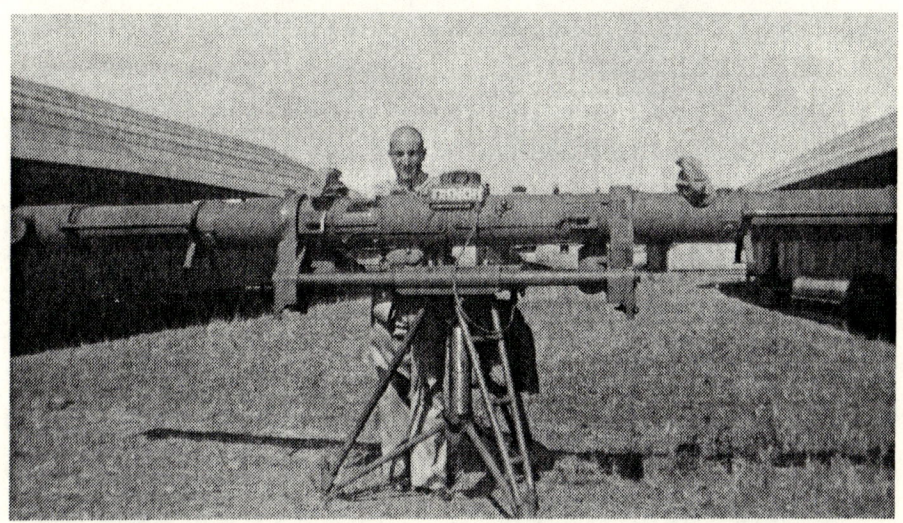

Figure 2-2. Private Art Smith with "Frenchy," the Range Finder, at Fort Stotsenberg, Near Clark Field, in the Philippines.
Frenchy, named after Sergeant Manuel Armijo's wife, Frances, was an aiming device used by the 200th Regiment to direct their antiaircraft weapons. Armijo and Smith became so fond of their range finder that they cried when they were ordered to destroy it in preparation for the April 9, 1942, surrender on Bataan.
Source: F. Manuel Armijo, Santa Fe, New Mexico.

The Japanese bombers flew at 23,000 feet, just above the height of the U.S. antiaircraft fire. The 200th's antiaircraft guns, equipped with obsolete powder train fuses, were effective to only 20,000 feet.

The Mitsubishis were followed by 170 Zero fighters, who strafed Clark Field. An American B-17 that got airborne was shot down by a Zero over Clark Field. Manuel Armijo (2000) watched with horror when the Zero machine-gunned the B-17 crew members as they parachuted to the ground. The Japanese obviously fought with different rules than did the Americans.

Master shooter Aurelio Quintana (2000) claims to have shot down the first Zero, firing a BAR (Browning automatic rifle) from his trench. By the end of the attack on December 8, the New Mexicans had shot down five Zeros with their ancient guns (Jolly, 1964). Private Ralph Rodriguez (2000) had gone to a special mass that morning. After church, someone told him that Hawaii had been heavily bombed. At 1227 hours, Rodriguez stepped out of the mess hall at Fort Stotsenberg and began counting the Japanese bombers overhead. When the first bomb exploded, Rodriguez dived under a cot near the door of his barracks. Then a buddy yelled at him to help carry ammunition belts to their machine guns. As they staggered under the weight of the ammo, a Zero came in low, strafing. Rodriguez noticed little puffs of dust that were kicked up near his feet. Only later did he realize that the puffs were made by the Zero's machine gun bullets.

That evening, 500 of the 2,000 New Mexicans were split off of the 200th, to form another unit, the 515th Regiment, which was ordered into nearby Manila to help defend the city and nearby Nichols Field from Japanese bombers. It was pointless for the New Mexicans, who constituted the largest single military organization in the Philippines, to continue defending Clark Field, which no longer had any operational aircraft (Jolly, 1964).

Nick Chintis had set up his 37mm. antiaircraft gun behind a copra plant near Clark Field. The American and Filipino workers at the copra factory were concerned that he had no protection from strafing by the low-flying Zeros when he was firing at them. They fabricated two large metal plates and mounted these shields on his artillery piece. Later, in Bataan, Americans eyed his unusual equipment, looked at each other in puzzlement, and asked "What kind of gun was *that*?"

(Chintis, 2000; Cave, 1996, p.87). Chintis sent a cheeky cable to his family that December: "Jerry Christmas and a Jappy New Year."

After the war was several weeks old, by Christmas Eve,1941, many of the New Mexicans fought as infantry on the Bataan Peninsula. They dug pits to depress their antiaircraft guns so as to enable them to fire at Japanese tanks. The U.S. strategy in the Philippines at this time was to try to hold out until reinforcements arrived from the United States. American and Filipino troops were outnumbered and overwhelmed. The Filipino Scouts, who were well-trained, forged an outstanding fighting record. But the main body of Filipino soldiers, draftees who had inadequate arms and little training, simply melted away when they came into conflict with the veteran Japanese troops who had previously fought in China (Daws, 1994).

A Cat in a Bag

General MacArthur planned to retreat into the nearby jungles of the Bataan Peninsula, across the bay from Manila (Figure 2-3). The Bataan Peninsula, 25 miles long and 20 miles wide at its base, was mountainous jungle, ideal for fighting a defensive war. MacArthur planned an orderly retreat into Bataan, where he could hold out with the remainder of his American and Filipino troops. According to plan, reinforcements were to arrive within six months. Despite MacArthur's pleas, President Roosevelt was committed to a "Europe First" policy. American tanks, troops, and planes were shipped across the Atlantic to aid England and Russia. Nothing could be spared for the Battling Bastards of Bataan.

The New Mexicans hauled their antiaircraft guns from Manila and Clark Field in order to defend two vital river bridges from Japanese air attacks. These bridges were key passageways for the Americans and Filipinos retreating into the Bataan Peninsula. There was no escape from the Bataan Peninsula. The only choice was to die fighting or to surrender. A Japanese general, observing the Americans and Filipinos pouring into the Bataan Peninsula, said it was like watching a cat going into a bag (Daws, 1994). Further, MacArthur had not moved enough food and medicine into Bataan to provision his soldiers for an extended defense (Daws, 1994). Almost from the time they arrived on Bataan, the New Mexicans were put on half rations, and then half of that. As Ralph Rodriguez (2000) stated, "Daily rations were actually anything you could find to eat." Tropical diseases began to take a toll, as the Americans had little medicine.

By New Years Day, 1942, the 200th had 23 confirmed hits on Japanese planes, and the 515th had 13. The final count, at the time of surrender in April, was 51 confirmed hits for the 200th and 35 for the 515th (Cave, 1996, p. 152). The New Mexicans were so heavily attacked from the air that they had plenty of Japanese planes at which to fire. In the week or two before the April 9, 1942, surrender, Japanese bombing and strafing of the Americans was almost continuous.

FIGHTING ON BATAAN

One of the priorities of the New Mexicans on Bataan was to defend a small jungle airstrip from which seven remaining P-40 fighters operated. Eventually, all of the P-40s were destroyed in dogfights with Zeros. The American troops suffered from malaria, beriberi, dysentery, and dengue fever. The lack of ammunition and the food shortage became ever more severe as the months on Bataan went by. The Americans ate their horses, their mules, and then local carabaos. They ate an officer's polo pony. Then they resorted to eating monkeys and iguanas, and finally jungle insects, roots, and plants.[3] They went without adequate sleep due to almost constant Japanese shelling and bombing.

On March 11, 1942, General MacArthur, his wife, and son, on direct orders from Washington, slipped out of Corregidor, the fortified island in Manila Bay, in a PT boat, and then flew to Australia. MacArthur announced by radio, "I shall return." He did, on October 12, 1944, when the Americans re-conquered the Philippines. But at the time, the New Mexicans left behind on Bataan thought that MacArthur's rhetoric sounded rather vain.

The Americans and Filipinos fighting on Bataan defended a series of battle lines across the Bataan Peninsula that had been planned by MacArthur. The Japanese attacked with tanks, troops, and artilliery, and the defenders fought and then fell back to the next defensive line. Gradually, the Americans and Filipinos were forced into a smaller and smaller space, near the bottom of the Peninsula. The "sack" of Bataan was being drawn tight. The 250,000 Japanese soldiers had a strong numerical advantage.

On April 7, after several weeks of heavy fighting, Japanese tanks and infantry broke through the final defensive lines on Bataan. The New Mexicans, now positioned on the front lines, had nothing left with which to stop the enemy tanks. Major General Edward P. King, the U.S. commanding officer, realized that further resistance would be suicidal for his troops. Against the orders of General MacArthur in Australia and General Jonathan Wainwright on Corregidor, King sent a surrender message to the Japanese commander, Lieutenant General Masaharu Homma. The American troops were ordered to stack their rifles, display white flags, and surrender.

At the time of their surrender in April, the Americans were eating less than one thousand calories per day, a diet that barely kept them alive (2,000 calories per day is considered minimal for an active adult). Inadequate nutrition increased the Americans' susceptibility to various diseases. Malaria was endemic on Bataan, and supplies of quinine were exhausted. At the time of their surrender, one-third of the Americans and Filipinos were either sick or wounded (Knox, 1981).

The 200th's Battery C was bombed continually on April 8, 1942, the last day before the American troops were surrendered on Bataan. Japanese bombers dropped 15 bombs on Battery C that day, but the New Mexicans kept on firing back with their remaining antiaircraft weapons, and they shot down four Japanese planes (Cave, 1996).

Ralph Rodriguez (2000) made a large white flag out of a bed sheet at the field hospital to which he was assigned. An officer ordered him to burn the American flag, prior to surrender. That act brought home to him that he was surrendering. Nick Chintis destroyed his customized

37 mm. cannon (with the two metal plates) on April 8, and was walking to a surrender point when he encountered a Japanese jeep painted with the rising sun symbol. A Japanese lieutenant said in perfect English: "It will be a long time before you get home." Chintis' heart sank (Chintis, 2000).

On April 9, 1942, the Americans and Filipinos on Bataan were surrendered to the Japanese. A handful of New Mexicans managed to get to Corregidor, where they fought on for another month until the last remaining American resistance collapsed. The Bataan surrender was the heaviest numerical reversal ever suffered by an American military force in a single engagement (Knox, 1981). The Bataan defeat received much less attention from the U.S. public than did Pearl Harbor. However, in New Mexico, the 1,800 members of the 200th represented one soldier for every 200 men, woman, and child in the state (Thomas & others, 1994).

For the next several years, the American captives and their Japanese conquerors would be in close contact. Few of the prisoners-of-war had the slightest idea of what the Japanese were like, and vice versa. During the first six months of World War II in the Pacific, the Japanese had captured 320,000 prisoners, one-third of them white Europeans (mainly Dutch and English), Australians, or Americans. The Japanese lost only 15,000 dead or wounded (Daws, 1994). As the Japanese in 1942 reflected on their victorious battles, they concluded that they were superior fighting men. They felt their prisoners were inferior, doubly so because they had surrendered, a cowardly act to the conquerors.

The New Mexican survivors felt guilty about the surrender. They were surrendered; they did not surrender. But for some, which was a moot point, as they were nevertheless prisoners-of-war. Some say that had they known how they would be treated, they would have tried to escape into the jungles of the Philippines.

THE DEATH MARCH

Amazingly, only about 20 of the 1,800 New Mexicans had been killed during the previous four months of fighting. But thereafter, during the Death March, in the POW camps in the Philippines, on the Hell Ships to Japan, and in POW camps there, about half of the New Mexicans died.

The Bataan Death March began with the victorious Japanese herding their prisoners into groupings of about 500 prisoners, who were then marched in long columns of fours and sixes. Corporal Joe Bergstein was already in bad physical shape when the Americans on Bataan were surrendered. His legs were swollen with beriberi. On the second morning of the Death March, he could not stand, and was resigned to being killed by the Japanese guards. Then an American stood over him and insulted him by calling him a "little yellow bastard." Bergstein was so angry that he got up and started walking. But the March was an agony. He counted his steps in order to keep going. Then he simply resorted to putting one foot in front of the other. Somehow he dumbly trudged on. He knew that death was certain if he fell or lagged behind.

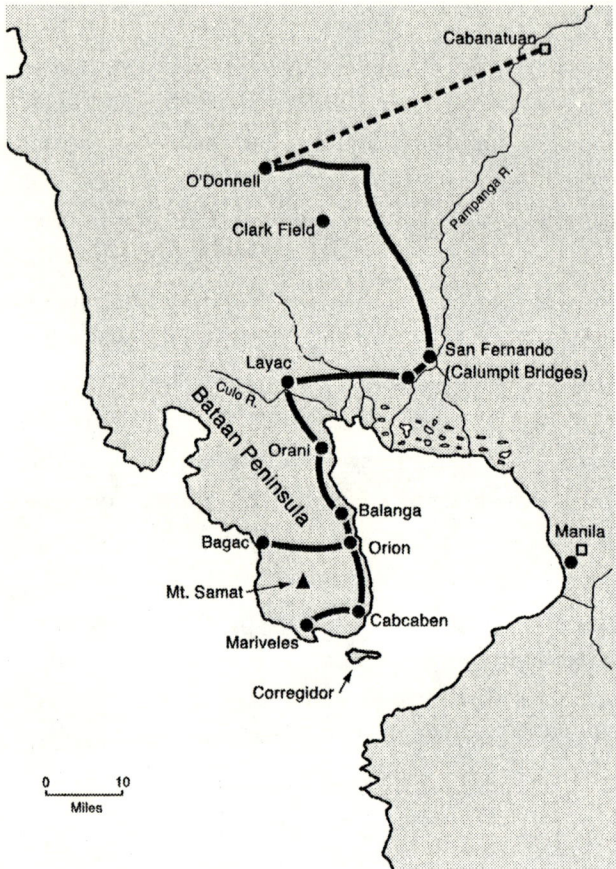

Figure 2-3. The 75-Mile Bataan Death March from Various Surrender Points in Southern Bataan to the Railhead at San Fernando, Where the 75,000 Prisoners, Including 12,000 Americans, Were Transported to Camp O'Donnell.

The American/Filipino surrender on April 9, 1942, occurred after Japanese infantry and tanks broke through the final defensive line across the Bataan Peninsula at Mount Samat. Many of the Allied troops were sick and undernourished after several months of jungle fighting. The Japanese rushed to remove their prisoners from Bataan, so they could attack Corregidor, which commanded Manila Bay. About 10,000 individuals died on the Bataan Death March; many were bayoneted or shot by the Japanese guards. After several months in Camp O'Donnell, most of the New Mexicans were moved to the POW camp at Cabanatuan.

Source: Based on Cave (1996) and an Associated Press graphic.

Some 75,000 soldiers, 12,000 of them Americans including 1,800 New Mexicans, were marched by their Japanese captors the 75 miles from Mariveles, on the southern tip of Bataan, to San Fernando (Figures 2-3 & 2-4). The Japanese were already far behind their time schedule in conquering the Philippines. Tokyo put intense pressure on their commander, General Homma, to attack Corregidor. First they needed to get the prisoners out of the way by moving them off of the Bataan Peninsula. The march to San Fernando took up to seven days for some prisoners. The Japanese bayoneted those who did not keep up with the march. The U.S. government estimated that 5,000 of the 12,000 Americans on the Bataan Death March died. That works out to an average of one corpse every 20 yards of the 75-mile Death March (Sides, 2001). From San Fernando, the survivors were transported in cramped railroad cars to Camp O'Donnell, a former Filipino training base near Clark Field.

Figure 2-4. Three American Prisoners-of-War on the Bataan Death March Rest Briefly En Route to Camp O'Donnell.

A Japanese guard stands over these POWs, whose hands are tied behind their backs. One New Mexican in the 200th Regiment dropped from 160 pounds to 118 pounds during four days on the Bataan Death March. About 150 of the 800 prisoners in his group of marchers died or were killed on the march to Camp O'Donnell.

Source: Washington, D.C., National Archives, War and Conflict #1144.

An American medical doctor, Paul Ashton (1985, p. 159), who was on the Death March, described it as follows: "Numerous emasculations, disembowlings, decapitations, amputations, hundreds of bayonetings, shootings, and just plain bludgeanings to death of defenseless, starved, and wounded soldiers were common on the march, in full view of their helpless comrades, and one documented by the outraged survivors."

Violating the Geneva Convention

The Japanese military took their prisoners watches, rings, and cigarettes. This shakedown was a warning of the treatment that the American prisoners of war would receive over the following three and one-half years. They would be beaten, tortured, starved, and demeaned in every possible way. Many were killed, some in particularly inhumane ways. The Japanese military system was brutal, and the guards on the Death March were sadistically cruel. They forced the prisoners to stand at attention in the midday sun until many dropped from heat exhaustion.

Early in the war, on January 1942, the U.S. government, through the Swiss as neutral intermediaries, inquired of Japan as to whether they would abide by the terms of the 1929 Geneva Convention, the international agreement dictating how prisoners of war should be treated. Japanese Foreign Minister Hideki Tojo informed the United States that his nation was a signatory to the Geneva document, and, although the Japanese government did not ratify it, Japan would "strictly observe the Geneva Convention." As the experience of the Bataan prisoners shows, Japan did not live up to the Geneva Convention. Japan had not done so during the previous decade of fighting in China, in which the Japanese used poison gas. Japanese troops went on a binge of raping and killing when they conquered Nanking, the capital city.

The Japanese military code of *bushido* stressed the shame of surrender. Death was preferred to the dishonor of surrender, and

Japanese soldiers were taught to fight to the death. This abhorrence of surrender on the part of the Japanese explains in part why they mistreated the American POWs.[4]

The Americans also violated the Geneva Convention in the Pacific War, particularly in regard to killing prisoners. One reason so few Japanese troops surrendered was because many were killed by American servicemen. The unofficial American practice was to take only a few Japanese prisoners for interrogation. *Life* magazine published a photograph of an American girl whose boyfriend had sent her a Japanese skull. The Japanese, who were scrupulous about the bones of their ancestors, regarded this act as an ultimate barbarism (Daws, 1994).

Japanese Atrocities

One New Mexican on the Death March, Bill Evans, remembers the sound of a bayonet entering a body, "an exhalation of air such as when a guy gets punched in the gut. Then, there is the unreal sound of a blade passing through bone and gristle . . . ." (quoted in Cave, 1996, pp. 182-183). The sadistic Japanese guards tempted the Americans with food and water. The marchers would be halted near an artesian well, but if the POWs drank the water, they were killed.

Luther Ragsdale recalled that whenever an exhausted marcher dropped out of the line due to exhaustion, the Japanese "gathered like a pack of coyotes around a carcass . . . . The first bayonet usually found the testicles; then a couple through the upper arm muscles; then a bayonet through each calf. Each Jap tried to outdo the others in inflicting pain without killing the man . . . . Very few who died on the Death March were lucky enough to be shot and die quickly" (quoted in Cave, 1996, p. 184).

A sick American soldier was staggering and barely able to keep up. As the prisoners met a column of Japanese tanks heading toward Corregidor, a Japanese guard threw the sick American onto the road, in front of the lead tank. As the tanks drove over the body, it completely disappeared. The prisoner's paper-thin uniform was imbedded in the cobblestones of the road (Knox, 1981). Joe Bergstein remembers the "games" that the Japanese played with the POWs on the Death March. Trucks traveling in the opposite direction swerved into the marchers, killing several. One Japanese truck driver beckoned to an American to come closer for a proffered cigarette. When the prisoner approached the truck, a soldier on the truck bashed in the POW's head with his rifle butt.

Ralph Rodriguez (2000) stopped on the Death March to help a wounded American who was crying out for help. A Japanese guard bayoneted the wounded man, and then kicked the body. Rodriguez considered suicide during the Death March, but prayer carried him on. One night, while sleeping on the ground, a bump under his body kept him from sleeping. He thought it was a rock, but when he dug it up, it turned out to be a large turnip. It was his only food on the five-day march.

Guards who found Americans with anything Japanese assumed the objects were taken from dead Japanese soldiers. The punishment was death. Captain William C. Schultz from Albuquerque had traded cigarettes with a guard for a small Japanese fan when he was feeling very hot. Later, when he arrived at Camp O'Donnell and was shaken down, the guards found the fan. He did not know Japanese and could not explain how he had acquired the fan. He was promptly executed (Foy, 2000; Olson, 1985; Knox, 1981).

The lack of a common language caused many problems between the prisoners and their captors.[5] As Art Smith (2000) explained, "We couldn't speak Japanese, and were not allowed to speak English. When we couldn't answer a question in Japanese, the guards beat us." Under these conditions, some Americans eventually learned a good deal of Japanese. One POW explained: "I began to learn Japanese on the *Tattori Maru* [a Death Ship]. When you get bumps on your head and then the bumps beaten off because you don't understand the language, it behooves you to learn, doesn't it? I started by listening for words, by using my ears. If you're paying attention and if they say something enough times, you begin to pick it up" (Knox, 1981, p. 375). Most of the prisoners, however, refused to learn any Japanese, other than numbers, which they had to know in order to count off at the roll calls, which took place daily: *Ichi, ni, san, shi, go, roku*, etc. Bataan survivors like Vicente Ojinaga remember many Japanese words today, 60 years later: *Gunso* (sergeant), *benjo* (bathroom), *kempeitai* (police), and *senso owari* (the war is over).

Filipinos standing along the Death March route tossed rice balls and bananas to the POWs over the heads of the Japanese guards. Some guards allowed Filipino children to give water to the prisoners from artesian wells along the route. They might leave a pail of water on the road, which the prisoners would pick up as they walked past. But the Japanese guards often kicked over the buckets (Ojinaga, 2000; Cave, 1996).

Finally, the New Mexicans reached San Fernando, and were loaded into steel boxcars, which were as hot as frying pans (Figure 2-5). Four Americans died in Manuel Armijo's boxcar during the 45-mile trip. Then the New Mexicans were marched the final eight miles to Camp O'Donnell. The diminutive Japanese commander, Captain Yoshio Tsuneyoshi, whom the Americans nicknamed "Cherry Blossom" or "Baggy Pants," stood atop a table and addressed the prisoners: "You are guests of the Emperor!" (Ojinaga, 2000). Then he shouted at them, "We will work you to death!" (Armijo, 2000). The New Mexicans thought it was a rather strange welcome.

Figure 2-5. Manuel Armijo (with blanket ends tied) on the Bataan Death March.
   This photograph was taken by a Japanese Army photographer and later captured by American Forces. It was taken on the first day of the Death March, April 9, 1942, somewhere between Mariveles and Cabcaben. Some 1,800 New Mexicans were on the Death March, then imprisoned in Camp O'Donnell and Cabanatuan in the Philippines, and later transported on Death Ships to POW camps in Japan.
   Source: Santa Fe, New Mexico, Bataan Memorial Military Museum and Library, Photo #6.

IMPRISONMENT

   The Japanese prison camps for the POWs were similar to the Nazi concentration camps, but with one important difference. The German camps were equipped with death chambers, so as to kill large numbers of the Jewish prisoners. The Japanese camps killed slowly, through overwork, starvation, and disease. Prime Minister Tojo said that a POW who did not work should not eat. This order was essentially a death sentence for the many POWs who were sick or wounded (Daws, 1994).

Camp O'Death

Most American POWs reacted to their imprisonment by banding together with their fellow prisoners. This action typified most of the New Mexicans, who looked out for each other. Nick Chintis helped a buddy, Steve Alex, who could hardly stagger in through the gate of Camp O'Donnell, he was so dehydrated from the Death March. Chintis dripped water in Alex's mouth for several days until he came back to life (Cave, 1996).

As Chintis explained: "We were all in the same kettle . . . . The quickest way to gauge a man's character is through his stomach. Hunger brings out the best or the worst in him. I saw some who just couldn't cope. And some, who were really noble, were still part of the human race" (quoted in Cave, 1996, p. 205). Prison life became a process of fighting to survive, both physically and mentally (Figure 2-6). The number one concern was food. The regular diet consisted of *lugao*, a watery rice gruel with little nutritional value. Sometimes the gruel contained small fish heads or vegetables. The rice was dirty and discolored, and had inch-long weevils in it. Most prisoners in Camp O'Donnell, including Ralph Rodriguez (2000), ate the weevils; he figured that they were a source of protein. Some Americans regarded the rice as tasteless, and could not force themselves to swallow it. A company cook was rather fat when the Americans arrived at O'Donnell. Due to not eating the daily ration of rice, he soon became very thin. A few weeks later, he was dead (Bergstein, 2000).

Figure 2-6. Vicente Ojinaga (the POW wearing the Hat) in Camp O'Donnell.
The prisoners had much time on their hands. Mainly, they struggled to stay alive under the difficult conditions of starvation rations, work, disease, and beatings by the Japanese guards.
Source: Santa Fe, New Mexico, Bataan Memorial Military Museum and Library, Photo #5.

One of the prisoners' special joys was to make a prison stew, called a *quan*, a mixture of anything edible. A particular *quan* might contain some turnips that were stolen by a prison work detail, a rat or two that had been caught in the camp, and some crude sugar that friendly Filipinos had given the prisoners. All of this material would be cooked together and eaten by the POWs who had contributed to it. *Quan* played an important role in keeping the prisoners alive. Aurelio Quintana (2000) says that "The camp was very clean. We ate rats, mice, cockroaches, anything that moved."

One day when Joe Bergstein returned to his barracks at Camp O'Donnell, his friends told him that a prisoner with pyrexia, who was losing his teeth, had stolen a drink out of Bergstein's canteen. He was furious. "That canteen was my life!" (Bergstein, 2000). He disinfected the canteen with potassium permanganate, and then boiled the canteen in water.

Bergstein was on the burial detail at Camp O'Donnell (Figure 2-7). He tried to pay a certain degree of respect to the dead. For instance, he would put a handful of grass over the crotch and on the eyes. Some bodies had an arm or a leg sticking up, erect from rigor mortis. Bergstein disapproved when some prisoners in the work detail clubbed the erect limb with their spade, as they tried to fit the body into a shallow grave.

Figure 2-7. The Daily Burial Detail at Camp O'Donnell.
This photo, captured from the Japanese, shows the POWs carrying their deceased comrades in blankets to be buried near Camp O'Death, as it was nicknamed. The prisoners were provided little food and many died of starvation and illness.
Source: Washington, D.C., National Archives, War and Conflict #1145.

In mid-1942, the Japanese dispersed the POWs from Camp O'Donnell to other sites, mainly Cabanatuan. By this time, two months after their surrender, some 1,800 (22 percent) of the 8,000 Americans imprisoned in Camp O'Donnell (nicknamed Camp O'Death by the New Mexicans) were dead (Ashton, 1985). The death rates for the Filipino prisoners in Camp O'Donnell were even higher, estimated at 50 percent of the 55,000 POWs (Olson, 1985; Ashton, 1985). During World War II, one in every 25 American prisoners of war died in German prison camps. But for American prisoners of the Japanese, this rate was one in three.

Cabanatuan Prison Camp

When the New Mexicans arrived in Cabanatuan, the Japanese formed the prisoners into ten-man "blood brother" groups. If one escaped, or attempted to, the other nine were shot (Bergstein, 2000). Dysentery and starvation continued to take their toll. After a few weeks in Cabanatuan, Nick Chintis "looked around at my blood-brother group, and there was only me and one other guy alive" (quoted in Cave, 1996, p. 224).[6]

The American prisoners pleaded with their officers to demand more food. The response by a Japanese mess sergeant was to order any POWs who were not happy with his cooking to take two steps forward. Joe Bergstein and his fellow prisoners reasoned that the Japanese would not beat everyone, so they all took two steps forward. They were wrong. The Japanese promptly beat all of the prisoners. When they were lined up again, the Japanese mess sergeant repeated his question, "Now, is anyone unhappy with my cooking?" No one stepped forward. That episode ended the prisoners' attempt to get more food (Bergstein, 2000).

When Private First Class Aurelio Quintana (2000) was in Cabanatuan Prison Camp, he weighed only 60 pounds, and had several illnesses: malaria, dengue fever, and dysentery, among others. He got appendicitis, with the operation performed in the prison "hospital." An American doctor cut a six-inch incision with a sharpened spoon, and removed his inflamed appendix without the benefit of anesthesia. After the operation, his doctor remarked, admiringly: "This son of a bitch just won't die!" Quintana spent two months in Zero Ward (for patients with zero hope), but finally recovered. Later, when Quintana was working on a farm outside the prison, a Japanese guard beat him with a stick for getting a drink of water. The guard hit him so hard that Quintana's arm was broken. As a result, Quintana was given three days of rest. Then it was back to work. Fortunately, a friend of his did some of his farm work when the guards were not looking.

Quintana (2000) describes the "water treatment" by which the guards punished prisoners. They rammed a garden hose down a POW's throat or up another orifice, until the prisoner's belly was swollen with water. Then the Japanese jumped on the individual's stomach, which nearly always resulted in death.

When a prisoner became so sick or injured that he could not fend for himself, he could go to the prison hospital. But there were little or no medicines, and the American prison doctors could do little to help. The hospital at Cabanatuan had a large "Zero Ward" for prisoners who just lay there and died, then to be hauled off for burial by a work detail.

Camp #1 in Cabanatuan was composed of Death March survivors. Camp #3 contained POWs from Corregidor and was commanded by a Marine Corps officer, a Colonel Besher. Camp #3 had almost no deaths. Camp #1 lost so many prisoners that the two camps finally were combined. The Marine colonel convinced the Japanese commandant to provide some lumber, so that the Americans could construct a latrine with seats. Two cigarettes were offered for each can of dead flies, which was a serious health hazard in spreading diseases. Prisoners constructed makeshift flyswatters, put out a grain of rice for bait, and killed flies. Fly killing became a perverse pleasure for the prisoners, and the disease rate at Cabanatuan began to drop.[7]

On Christmas Day, 1942, the Americans were allowed to receive Red Cross packages containing cheese, chocolate, canned meat, and other high-protein foods. The death rate at Camp Cabanatuan suddenly dropped to zero (except for one prisoner who gobbled all of the rich food at once, and died of overeating). Joe Bergstein made his Red Cross package last for almost six months. The prisoners' health improved due to consuming protein, which was missing from their rice diet. The psychological lift of a message from home was also important.

One of the most destructive behaviors by the American prisoners in the Japanese POW camps was gambling. Among the prisoners were a number of "sharpies," soldiers who before the war organized barracks card games. When these dishonest gamblers arrived in a POW camp, they made packs of marked playing cards. Evans Garcia (2000), who loved to gamble, had a pair of small red dice in Cabanatuan that he was able to hide from the guards. Instead of dollars or pesos or yen, which the Japanese would not let the prisoners have, the POWs used cigarettes or rice rations as money units. Three cigarettes were equivalent to the rice ration for one meal. Prisoners who went into debt were charged two rice rations the next day, four the following day, and so forth in an exponential process. Soon, some of the losers in the barracks card games were as much as 50 rice rations in debt. Then they realized that they were on a straight track to Zero Ward, and death.

Gambling in the prison camps could be dangerous in another way. The Japanese forbade gambling, with serious punishment for anyone who was caught. Joe Bergstein was shooting dice with eight friends one evening in their barracks at Cabanatuan. They had posted a lookout, but somehow a Japanese guard caught them. They were beaten with pick handles all night. When one set of guards were worn out from beating the nine POWs, another set of guards took over. A wooden 2 x 4 was placed behind their knees, and they were forced to kneel. By morning, they could not walk, and had to crawl on their stomachs from the jail back to their barracks. A few years ago Bergstein had to have a knee operation to relieve the constant pain.

What kept the New Mexicans going during the hellish experience of the POW camps? For Manuel Armijo (2000), it was his intense desire to be reunited with his wife and baby daughter back in Santa Fe, and his faith in God. Vicente Ojinaga (2000) had been an altar boy in the Catholic Church while growing up in Santa Rita, New Mexico. He says, "I was in love with the Church," and feels that his strong religious conviction helped carry him through his prison experience. He prayed the rosary every Sunday during the war. Art Smith (2000) kept thinking of his girlfriend in Santa Fe, Bessie Pacheco. Luck was a big factor in survival. Happening to volunteer for a certain work detail, being assigned to a certain Death Ship, and other random factors often determined life or death.

Why didn't the prisoners try to escape? The prison fences consisted only of several strands of barbed wire, with wooden guard towers at regular intervals. It was not difficult to get out, especially at night. But most prisoners were so lethargic and weakened by their starvation diet that they had no energy for escaping. The 10-man shooting squads were also a strong deterrent; if all ten prisoners in a blood brotherhood escaped together, the larger group of 100 prisoners to which the ten were assigned was executed. Further, the American prisoners did not know the countryside or the local Filipino languages. They would need the help of Filipinos if they were to escape Japanese patrols. It was 9,000 miles to Australia, the nearest haven from the Japanese. "Any white captive was a prisoner not only in a Japanese camp, but in Asia. His skin was a prison uniform he could not take off" (Daws, 1994, p. 100).

News from the Philippines

In April 1943, three Bataan survivors did escape and eventually found their way to General MacArthur's headquarters in Australia. News of the Bataan Death March appeared in the U.S. media. Of the some 1,800 New Mexicans stationed in the Philippines in 1941, approximately 900 returned home at the end of the war.[8] Many of these did not survive their first year of freedom after release from Japanese POW camps, dying from the effects of their starvation and illnesses. The Bataan Death March created a strong anti-Japanese attitude on the part of the American people.

The U.S. government actually knew about the Japanese atrocities in the Philippines, but kept a fairly tight lid on this information until January 1944. Perhaps the government feared that a horrified America would demand a shift in priorities from Europe to the Pacific. President Roosevelt argued that if news about the Japanese brutality toward POWs were released to the public, the Japanese might treat the American POWs even worse than they did.

Nevertheless, limited information about the Death March filtered back to New Mexico, whose citizens began demanding that the U.S. government give more attention to the Pacific War. In March 1942, a Bataan Relief Organization (BRO) was formed, and began to flood the U.S. War Department and the White House with letters demanding that help be sent to the Philippines. The BRO led a War Bond drive in 1943, raising half a million dollars, enough for two bombers. One was named "The Spirit of Bataan." New Mexicans demanded that it be sent to the Pacific War, but the government was evasive on this point.

THE DEATH SHIPS

As the war progressed, it became obvious to the Japanese that General MacArthur's troops intended to invade the Philippines (which they did, in October 1944). Determined to prevent the liberation of the POWs, the Japanese began transferring the prisoners to Korea, Manchuria, and, especially, to the Japanese mainland, in order to meet labor shortages in Japanese factories, mines, and dockyards.

Horror Ships to Japan

A variety of cargo and troop ships, each overloaded with POWs, carried the Americans from the Philippines north to Taiwan, Yokohama, and Moji harbor (on the south coast of Kyushu in Japan), and to Pusan, Korea. Fourteen unmarked Death Ships were sunk. The *Arisan Maru*,[9] carrying 1,800 American POWs, was torpedoed by a U.S. submarine on October 24, 1944. The Japanese locked the hatches before the ship went under. Only eight Americans survived, one of whom was Master Sergeant Calvin Graef from Carlsbad, New Mexico. Luckily, he and his fellow prisoners found a small boat while swimming around their sinking ship. The following day they encountered two small barrels of water and a sail. They traveled 200 miles to the coast of China, where Chinese fishermen helped them escape Japanese patrols. Disguised as Chinese, the eight Americans then walked 1,500 miles across China to a U.S. airbase. They were flown to Washington to report on the Bataan Death March and the prison camps.

All of the Death Ships followed a circuitous and zigzag route in order to avoid U.S. ships, submarines, and planes, which by this stage of the war practically owned the sea routes off the coast of China. The Death Ships sailed in convoys with other Japanese ships; they carried no markings to indicate that they carried American prisoners. The passage often required a month or sometimes two, even though a direct trip by sea only required six days. About 11,000 American prisoners died en route on the Death Ships.

When Joe Bergstein was marched onto Pier 7 in Manila Harbor on October 1, 1944, two ships waited at the dock. Arbitrarily, the Japanese guards forced him into the hold of the smaller ship. The larger ship was torpedoed at sea a few days later by an American submarine. Bergstein's ship was an old coal freighter, partly filled with coal dust. Its 40 by 50 foot hold was crammed with prisoners. Each individual had two square feet of space, hardly enough to sit down. Planks were placed over the hatch with a two-inch gap for air; the prisoners gasped for oxygen. Each POW was given a splash of water in their canteen each day, and a bucket of rice was lowered into the hold twice each day. The trip began with two sweltering days at anchor in Manila Harbor. When the convoy finally went to sea, the ships were continually zigzagging, so forward progress was very slow. The prisoners listened apprehensively to the pinging of submarine radar. After 38 days at sea, the ship docked in Taiwan, only 600 miles from Manila.

Bergstein and his fellow POWs worked in a stone quarry for several months, and then were shipped to Japan. They landed at Moji in January 1945; it was freezing and the prisoners were wearing only their shorts and tattered shirts from the Philippines.

Nick Chintis and four of his buddies, in order to get out of the prison camp at Cabanatuan, claimed that they were mining engineers and airplane mechanics. With 1,200 other POWs, they sailed on the *Tottori Maru* in October 1942. The prisoners were locked in holds, short of oxygen, starving, and desperately thirsty. Finally, after stops in Taiwan, Pusan, and Moji, the *Tottori Maru* arrived in Osaka. Chintis had a bad case of scurvy, and his tongue and scrotum were swollen. A friendly Japanese guard gave him six limes to eat. He promptly recovered (Chintis, 2000; Cave, 1996). Chintis was ordered to repair ships in Yokohama harbor. The *Tottori Maru*, on which he had spent 35 days at sea, soon came back into Yokohama harbor for repairs after being torpedoed. The ship's crew was not eager to sail again. Two days later, the ship was back again, after being hit by another U.S. torpedo (Cave, 1996).

Chintis was assigned to live in an unheated barracks, which got so cold at night that by morning, his canteen was solid ice (Cave, 1996). The Americans were being systematically starved. Chintis was caught smuggling food, and was punished by solitary confinement in a bamboo cage, naked and shoeless in the February cold. But the Japanese guards were kindly, and moved their charcoal brazier close to his cage. That is how Chintis spent Valentine's Day, 1943 (Chintis, 2000; Cave, 1996).

Sabotage

The American POWs engaged in ingenious acts of sabotage, to prevent the industrial work they were forced to do from contributing to the Japanese war effort. They put fine sand in bearings, dropped tools like wrenches in the water or in a cement foundation they were pouring, and removed the firing pins from rifles that they manufactured (Ojinaga, 2000). Art Smith (2000) remembers that while loading bombs on a ship, he and his fellow prisoners bent the fins, so that the bombs would miss their targets when they were dropped.

Vincente Ojinaga (2000) says: "We got very good at stealing things." While assigned to stevedore work in a Japanese port, "Oji," as he was nicknamed, slipped cans of food into his sleeve. The guards beat the POWs unmercifully for "liberating" food supplies or engaging in sabotage. To the Japanese, the Americans all looked alike, and they had difficulty identifying a suspect. Ojinaga today has the photograph that he was required to carry in Japan, on which is written "8-9-'44" and "537-ID." For minor (or imagined) acts, the Japanese might force two of the POWs to strike each other in the face until both were bloody. A major "crime" (as defined by the Japanese), was punished by slow torture, beheading with a *samurai* sword, or shot by a bullet.

Of the approximately 12,000 American military personnel in the Philippines on December 8, 1941, only an estimated 1,200 survived at the end of the war in the POW camps in Japan. Many were killed on the Bataan Death March and on the Death Ships sailing to Japan. New Mexico had the highest per capita casualty rate of any U.S. state during World War II.

COMING HOME

Most of the New Mexicans were so isolated in the POW camps in Japan that they did not know how the war was progressing. But they were aware that American B-29s were bombing Japanese cities. Evans Garcia (2000) was working in the coal mine at Fukuoka Camp 17 where the prisoners' *bento* lunch boxes were wrapped in Japanese newspapers. One American could read Japanese. The prisoners did not believe the official news of American "defeats" in the Pacific. They noticed that the "defeats" were moving closer and closer to the Japanese home islands. But the end of the war came as a complete surprise to the POWs.

Manuel Armijo in Fukuoka Camp 17 was close enough to Nagasaki to see the smoke from the explosion of Fat Man. The camp guards suddenly became very bitter (Knox, 1981, p. 439). A prison guard told Nick Chintis (2000), "A little bomb killed many people in Hiroshima." News of the atomic bombs began to circulate in the POW camps in Japan. A few days later, all the guards disappeared.

One American prisoner-of-war, who took a train ride into Hiroshima after his release, described the devastated city: "It was just like the ripple effect you get when you drop a stone into water. First there were leaves. Then the leaves were missing. As you got closer, branches were missing. Closer still, the trunks were gone and then, as you got in the middle [of the city], there was nothing. Nothing! It was beautiful. I realized this was what had ended the war . . . . I believe the end probably justified the means" (Knox, 1981, pp. 451-452).

The Japanese were determined that the planned American invasion not be allowed to free the POWs. They would kill the prisoners of war before they could be freed by American forces. On August 1, 1944, the war Ministry in Tokyo had issued a directive to the commanders of POW camps regarding the final disposition of prisoners. "The August 1 Kill-All Order" demanded the annihilation of all POWS (Sides, 2001). Only the dropping of the atomic bombs and the unexpectedly rapid end of the war saved the lives of American prisoners. As a result, the Bataan survivors have understandably favorable attitudes toward the Manhattan Project, and toward President Harry Truman for his decision to drop atomic bombs on Japan.

Tommy Foy (2000) was in a POW camp in Japan in August 1945. The American prisoners were forced to dig deep trenches near their barracks, where 50-caliber machine guns were set up to kill the prisoners when the invasion of the home islands began. In Aurello Quintana's POW camp, barrels of gasoline were stacked near the trenches, ready for action when the American invasion of Japan began (Bartlit, 1998).

Coming Alive

For several weeks after the bombing of Hiroshima and Nagasaki, even after Japan agreed to unconditional surrender on August 14,

1945, most of the POWs remained in, or around, their camps. The guards departed after destroying camp records. Then the skies began raining food, clothes and medicine (Daws, 1994, p. 338). Supplies were dropped from B-29s and other U.S. planes to the 69,000 POWs held in 158 camps in Japan. Prisoners marked their camps with blankets or rocks to spell out "POW." At one camp a note tied to a wrench was dropped from an American plane, instructing the POWs to write a "1" if they needed medicines, "2" for food, and "3" for clothes. The POWs painted all three numbers on the roof of their prison barracks (Weintraub, 1996). The B-29s dropped supplies in 55-gallon oil drums, each attached to a parachute. One drop hit a building, and the POWs rushed to letter on their barracks roof: "DROP OUTSIDE. THANK YOU" (Weintraub, 1996, p. 660). Nick Chintis found Hershey bars scattered all over a hillside from a parachute drop. He sat down in the midst of them, and took one bite out of each of several dozen (Chintis, 2000; Cave, 1996).

Joe Bergstein was in a POW camp in northern Honshu when the war ended. On August 15, the Japanese guards stopped the prisoners' work day at noon without explanation. As they walked back from the factory to their barracks, an Australian prisoner obtained a Japanese newspaper and read that the war was over. Then their guards just melted away. The prisoners spelled out "PW" with lime in the yard outside of their barracks. The prisoners' first thought was of food. Two days later, a Navy scout plane flew over, and dropped a message in a small bag of sand: "Food coming." Next, two B-29s came over to drop 55-gallon drums of food. The barrels were so heavy that the parachutes ripped off, allowing the barrels to plummet to earth, burying themselves in the ground. Unfortunately, one barrel fell through the roof of a barracks, killing two POWs. Bergstein (2000) thought this event was particularly sad, given what the two POWs had gone through over the previous three and one-half years. A month later, the American prisoners were transported to Sendai, where they boarded a Navy destroyer. Then, home.

Art Smith, who weighed 168 pounds before the war, had plummeted to only 72 pounds by the time he was freed. Vicente Ojinaga, who weighed 140 pounds prior to the war, dropped to only 90 pounds by August 1945 (Figure 2-8). Then, in the three weeks that it took his hospital ship to reach San Francisco, Ojinaga put on an amazing 55 pounds! The ex-POWs were allowed to eat anything they wanted, and at any hour of the day. Military doctors gave them massive shots of vitamins. On one Navy troop ship across the Pacific, the ex-prisoners were served rice. They promptly erupted, in protest, throwing the rice all over the ship.

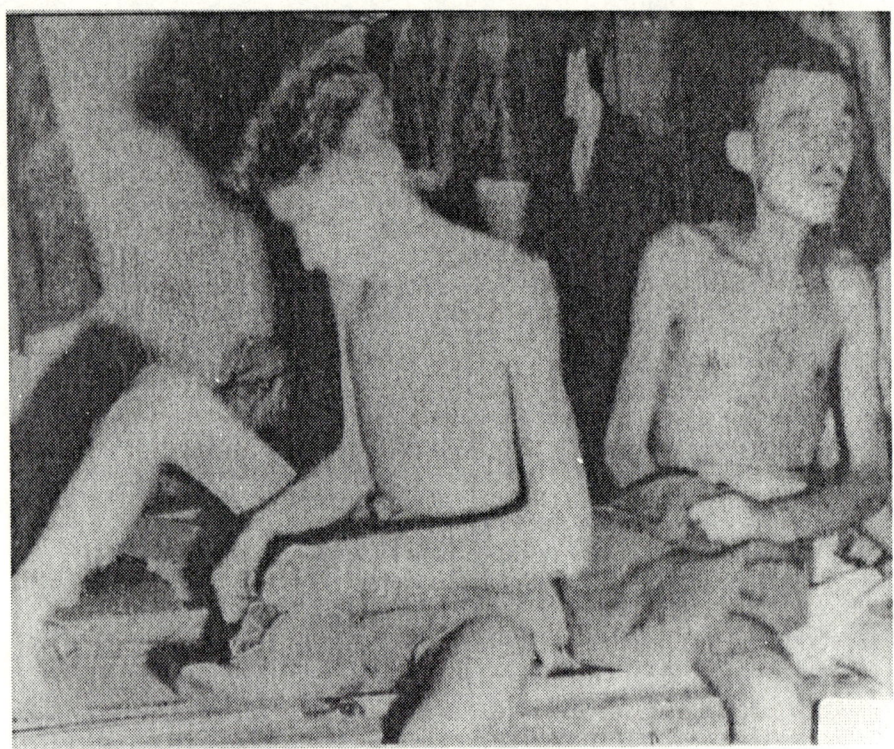

Figure 2-8. Two Americans Liberated from a POW Camp in Japan.
These emaciated prisoners are typical of the Bataan survivors after three and one-half years in Japanese POW camps. Most New Mexicans lost about half of their body weight during their imprisonment.
Source: Santa Fe, New Mexico, Bataan Memorial Museum and Library, U.S. Navy Photograph #138-19.

As soon as Evans Garcia landed on U.S. soil, he telephoned his girlfriend in Santa Fe. Garcia told her how much he loved her, and how he had missed her for the past three and one-half years. After an awkward pause, she told him that she was married to a big Marine who then came on the line and threatened Garcia (2000). Garcia downed a beer, and decided to forget her. Garcia's "Dear John" experience was not uncommon for the returning New Mexicans.

Aurelio Quintana (2000) was hospitalized in a Denver hospital for several months after the war. One day he simply walked, going AWOL for 260 days. He returned to Santa Fe, got a job, and played a lot of baseball. He married the sister of Ramon Apodaca, his buddy who was killed on Bataan. Finally, the Army located him, and he was discharged in 1947.

After living in a kind of limbo for three and one-half years in POW camps, the New Mexicans had many surprises when they were liberated. When Manuel Armijo and Evans Garcia arrived at a U.S. military base in Nagoya, they saw GIs wearing a new kind of helmet (U.S. soldiers had worn World War I-style helmets in the Philippines in 1941-1942). They met their first WACs, another big surprise (they had never seen some women in uniform). They saw, or were told about, other strange new objects: bazookas, radar, flamethrowers, jet planes, DDT, and penicillin.

When he was finally freed, Nick Chintis turned down the opportunity to fly home. He preferred a slow boat, so that he could "gain some weight and look presentable" (Cave, 1996, p. 387). He stuffed himself on milk, ice cream, and other foods, like eggs and bacon. Chintis did not know that his wife Winifred had enlisted in the Marines. She learned that he was recovering in Letterman General Hospital in San Francisco. Someone told Chintis that his wife had arrived in the hospital, so he "slipped out, and I came up behind her, and I tapped her on the shoulder, and said, 'Looking for somebody?'" (Chintis, 2000; Cave, 1996, p. 395). Staff Sergeant Nicholas Chintis was soon discharged, and returned to live in Silver City, New Mexico.

When Ruben Flores of Las Cruces arrived back in New Mexico, he scooped up and ate a handful of soil. At the time, it seemed like the right thing to do, after being gone so long, and with such uncertainty of ever returning. Gap Silva had been injured in a coal mine accident at Camp 17, and was in a military hospital after the war when his family came to see him. He learned that his father had gone blind several years previously (Silva, 1999).

Many of the New Mexicans were sent to Bruns General Army Hospital in Santa Fe for a period of recovery. Most returnees had difficulties in readjusting to civilian life after their years in the prison camps. Some began to drink heavily. The doctors at Bruns told the Bataan survivors they had only ten years to live and that they could not have children. The medics were wrong, on both counts (Cave, 1996). Gap Silva, 83 years old in 2002, has seven children and 13 grandchildren (Silva, 1999).

Despite the beatings, abuse, starvation, and overwork in the Japanese prison camps, many of the surviving Bataan veterans today are amazingly fit. Aurelio Quintana, who was 84 years old when the present authors talked with him in 2000, leads an active life. Quintana (2000) goes hunting or fishing year around, sometimes out of season. He is still a crack shot with a hunting rifle. Army doctors classified him as 100 percent disabled in 1947, when he was discharged. Instead of living on his veteran's pension the rest of his life, Quintana worked as a prison guard at the New Mexico State Penitentiary in Santa Fe for a number of years, and then formed his own security business. When asked why he chose to work when he did not have to, Quintana (2000) replied that "A lifetime of watching TV all day would have killed me!" He is a heavy smoker, two packs a day, and yet has had few health problems. Quintana lives alone in a modest adobe house just off Old Pecos Trail in Santa Fe.

Tommy Foy of Bayard, New Mexico, weighed 165 pounds before the war, but only 74 pounds when he was liberated. After a year in Brooks General Hospital in Texas, Foy returned to his hometown to practice law, and served in the New Mexico Legislature for many years (Foy, 2000). Ralph Rodriguez of Albuquerque, 84 years old in 2000, is trim and healthy in appearance, looks more like a 60-year-old. However, as a consequence of having beriberi in the Philippines, his hearing and eyesight have suffered. Evans Garcia, a spry 87-year-old in 2000, serves as a patient representative in the Veterans Hospital in Albuquerque, and pursues his gambling interests at nearby gaming casinos. Nick Chintis, today a retired administrator at Western New Mexico University in Silver City, has had two knee replacements, two hip joint replacements, and open heart surgery. Yet he leads an active life.

Manuel Armijo has almost constant pain from his knuckles, which were crushed by a Japanese guard at Camp O'Donnell when Armijo was caught eating an onion while on a gardening detail. Armijo also suffers from the back injury that he received when a Japanese soldier struck him on the Bataan Death March.

Vicente Ojinaga (2000) used the GI Bill to complete an accounting degree at the University of New Mexico. Then he was employed by the Internal Revenue Service in their Santa Fe office. Joe Bergstein (2000) used the GI Bill to attend college, where he majored in physics, an academic interest that he did not know he had until his release from the Army. After completing graduate work at Vanderbilt University, he was hired by Los Alamos National Laboratory. Today Bergstein lives in retirement in Los Alamos. He drives a Japanese car.

As Paul Ashton (1985, p. xi), an Army medical doctor, stated, "Practically all of the survivors have become, to some degree, physically disabled." It seems amazing that any of the Bataan veterans could be alive today, given their physical mistreatment during World War II. The three and one-half years as a POW translates approximately to aging a man physically by 10 to 15 years (Daws, 1994). By this reckoning, a Bataan veteran born in 1915 would be 97 to 102 years old in 2004.

A Bataan Veteran's Love Story

The late Arthur Smith grew up in Santa Fe, and, at age 17 in 1939, enlisted in the New Mexico National Guard. Jobs were scarce, and Smith needed the extra money that he received from participating in the Guard. When the 200th Regiment was federalized and sent to El Paso in January 1941, Smith was separated from his high school sweetheart, Bessie Pacheco. He kept an 8 x 10 photograph of her on a little table next to his Army bunk at Fort Bliss. His fun-loving buddies in the 200th regularly stole the photo, and hid it in various places. Once he returned to the barracks to find the photo in the latrine, propped over the shower.

Bessie persuaded her father to drive her to El Paso, but they arrived just as Smith's troop train was pulling out for San Francisco and points beyond. She spotted Smith in the train, and got her father to race along the road paralleling the train tracks. Bessie saw that Smith tossed something out of the train window. It was a copy of *Life* magazine. Smith had scrawled on the cover: "Bessie, wait for me. I love you." She did wait, but after the surrender on Bataan, there was no news from Smith for several years. She wrote to him every day during the war, although he received none of her letters. His parents received a postcard, written from his prison camp, and sent via the International Red Cross in Geneva, Switzerland (Figure 2-9). Today, the card is so yellowed with age that it is almost brown. Smith was allowed to dictate a brief message to a Japanese typist: "Love to all."

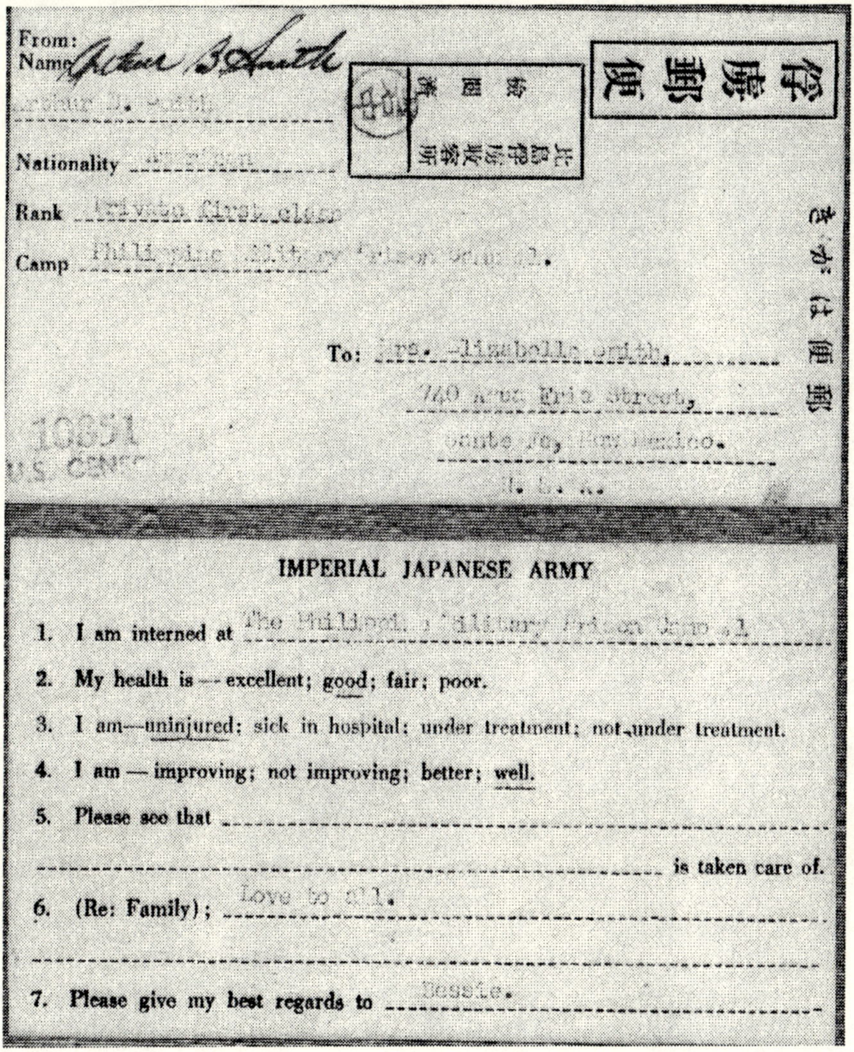

```
From:
Name  Arthur B. Smith
      Arthur B. Smith
Nationality  American
Rank  Private First Class
Camp  Philippine Military Prison Camp #1

                    To: Mrs. Elizabelle Smith,
                        740 Avus Eric Street,
                        Santa Fe, New Mexico.
                        U. S. A.
```

IMPERIAL JAPANESE ARMY

1. I am interned at The Philippine Military Prison Camp #1
2. My health is — excellent; **good**; fair; poor.
3. I am — **uninjured**; sick in hospital; under treatment; not under treatment.
4. I am — improving; not improving; better; **well**.
5. Please see that _____ is taken care of.
6. (Re: Family); Love to all.
7. Please give my best regards to Bessie.

Figure 2-9. POW Art Smith Sent a Postcard Home that Contained a Code Word Indicating He Was Alive.

A postcard dictated by Smith to a Japanese typist in a prisoner-of-war camp was sent through the International Red Cross in Geneva, to his parents in Santa Fe. The words "Love to all" contain a key word that Smith and Bessie Pacheco had worked out before the war to indicate that he was alive.

Source: Art Smith, Santa Fe, New Mexico.

Figure 2-9a. When Smith returned to Santa Fe after the war, he married Bessie, shown here wearing the parachute-wedding dress made for her by her mother.
Source: Art Smith, Santa Fe, New Mexico.

A Navajo friend from Gallup told Smith to put a pebble in his mouth on the Death March, so he would not feel so thirsty. A Japanese guard grabbed the chain on which Smith's dog tags were fixed, along with a crucifix that Bessie had given him, and broke it with a jerk. So Smith made a new "dog tag" out of a 1 x 2 inch strip from his metal mess kit, on which he punched his name and Army serial number with a nail. Bessie has these mementos, 60 years later.

Smith was very sick in Cabanatuan Prison Camp. When Manuel Armijo encountered him, he exclaimed, "Why Art, is that you?" He carried him to the prison hospital. Armijo was a cook, and he gathered the burned rice on the sides of the cooking caldrons, which he fed to Smith. This charred rice seemed to have some medicinal quality, and Smith's health began to improve. Armijo also fed him guava leaves. Smith's dysentery got better, and soon he was sent to Japan on a Death Ship, the *Mati-Mati Maru*. In Japan, the food was somewhat more plentiful. While working on the docks of Kobe, Smith was able to surreptitiously grab a fish off a drying rack. He was only wearing a G-string, and so he hid the fish in the only possible place. Fortunately, the Japanese guards did not spot it. Smith feels that the support of his New Mexico friends and his love for Bessie pulled him through the POW experience.

Smith was in a prison camp about 70 miles from Hiroshima on August 6, 1945, and could feel and hear the explosion of Little Boy, the uranium-type atomic bomb. On August 15, the prison guards did not take the POWs to their work site. The following day, the guards gave the prisoners some clothes and extra food. Something was certainly up, but the New Mexicans could not imagine that the war was over. Soon, Smith was liberated, hospitalized, and sent back to the United States. Unfortunately, the Army mistakenly sent him to El Paso, but he immediately grabbed a Greyhound bus to Albuquerque and then on to Santa Fe.

Smith brought home a white satin parachute from a B-29 food drop on his prison camp in Japan. Bessie's mother made her wedding dress from the material (Figure 2-9a). After waiting six years, they finally were married and raised two sons. In 2001, they celebrated 56 years of marriage. Later that year, Art Smith passed away.

Manuel Armijo

Perhaps Manuel Armijo's experiences in the New Mexico National Guard were typical of Bataan veterans. He grew up in Truth or Consequences (then called Hot Springs), New Mexico, and moved to Santa Fe where his job pumping gas in a service station earned Armijo one hamburger each day. He was allowed to sleep at night in a car parked behind the gas station. So he needed the extra income from enlisting in the National Guard. He married his love Frances.

By late 1941, when First Sergeant Armijo was stationed with the 200th in the Philippines, he was more than 28, the upper age limit. He applied to go home because his wife had given birth to a daughter. Armijo was scheduled to depart the Philippines on December 10, and had already packed his bags when the Mitsubishi bombers arrived over Clark Field at noon on December 8. Armijo would not get home to hold his daughter for four more years (Armijo, 2000).

Armijo remembers: "Around 12:30, Arthur Smith and I were playing around with the height finder [a sighting device used to aim the antiaircraft guns]. We turned the height finder north and saw a big wave of airplanes. There had been rumors that the U.S. Navy was sending us a whole bunch of airplanes . . . . I said to Arthur, 'Hey, Art, here comes those darn Navy bombers we've been expecting'" (Engles, 1985). When Smith looked through the device, he said: "Sure enough, but they've got big red balls painted on their wings" (Smith, 2000).

Armijo, instead of going home to his wife and baby daughter in Santa Fe, was promoted to First Sergeant in early January 1942. While the 200th was withdrawing into the Bataan Peninsula, he was ordered by the U.S. Army to sign up every New Mexican for national service insurance. Many did not want to buy the insurance, but Armijo insisted, as he was ordered to do, completing the paperwork while they were under Japanese attack. After the war, Armijo felt obligated to his New Mexican buddies to ensure that the $10,000 insurance policies were honored by the Veterans Administration. This process was difficult, given the lack of military records for a three and one-half year period of World War II. Back home, Armijo was appointed Director of the New Mexico Veterans Service Commission (Armijo, 2000). So an unwanted responsibility on Bataan eventually led to Armijo's postwar occupation.

On April 8, 1942, just before the surrender on Bataan, a bomb dropped directly on Armijo's battery. The blast blew him about 40 feet from his foxhole. When he came to, "My helmet was gone, and I was bleeding through my mouth, my nose, my ears - and I was scared" (Armijo, 2000; Cave, 1996, p. 145). By the time that Armijo got to the medics, he was shaking badly. They handed him a glass of alcohol, and then another. By the time the bleeding stopped, Armijo was almost drunk, and feeling brave again. He said, "Hell, I'm going back to my outfit" (Armijo, 2000; Cave, 1996, p. 145).

As the time for surrender approached, Armijo and Art Smith were ordered to destroy their height finder. Armijo had named the height finder "Frenchy," after his wife, Frances. He and Smith took a hammer and broke up the sights and the lens. Armijo, the tough First Sergeant, was crying. They were near Cabcaben Airport, a small field at Mariveles, near the tip of Bataan, when they were ordered to surrender. Thousands of white sheets, handkerchiefs, shirts, and other signs of surrender were waved by the American troops.

Armijo's Bataan Death March began on the morning of April 9, when he was awakened by a kick in the backside from a Japanese soldier who stood over him. Along with thousands of American and Filipino soldiers, Armijo was herded into a long column of threes and fours. They passed two young Americans beside a stream. They had been bayoneted while filling their canteens. The lesson was perfectly clear. By the third day of the march, Armijo was desperately thirsty. He stumbled and fell. Immediately, a guard hit him in the lower back with his rifle butt, crushing a disc (he cannot lift heavy loads to this day). A New Mexico friend, Eddie Martinez, helped Armijo stand up, and he staggered on, in great pain.[10]

Later, Armijo scooped up some water while passing a small fountain. When the prisoners were allowed to rest for the night in a field, Armijo found a big turnip, which he devoured, along with some grass and weeds. Then he saw a guard bayonet a red-haired American prisoner. The horror of this senseless act made Armijo so sick that he threw up what he had just eaten.

Once Armijo arrived at Camp O'Donnell, he found that the latrines consisted of slit trenches which were dangerous if an individual slipped in. Armijo and his buddy, Paul Roessler, both sick, would help each other to the latrine. One would faint and the other would keep him from falling into the trench (Armijo, 2000; Cave, 1996).

Manuel Armijo and Art Smith were included in a group of 500 prisoners from their POW camp to be transported to Japan in mid-1944. Their Death Ship, nicknamed the *Mati-Mati Maru* (the Wait-Wait Ship), required 66 days for the relatively short trip, due to its zigzag course to avoid submarine attack. The POWs were crammed into the ship's hold, and a bucket of rice was lowered to them each day. On arrival in Japan, Armijo's head was shaved (as a delousing measure), and he was assigned identification number 1137 (which he can still rattle off in Japanese today).

Armijo was assigned to Fukuoka Camp 17, near Omuta, on the island of Kyushu. Along with the other 1,721 POWs in Camp 17, he worked in a coal mine owned by the Mitsui Coal Company. They worked 12-hour days, with one day off every ten days. The POWs stood in water up to their waists, while they chipped coal out of underground seams. They were covered with black dust. The mining was backbreaking labor, and dangerous. The mine had been closed for safety reasons several years before the war, but was reopened in 1943 because the Japanese were desperately short of fuel, due to the tightening naval blockade. The New Mexicans went a mile underground in order "to rob the pillars," that is, to remove the columns of coal that held up the mine roof, replacing the coal with log props (Rodriguez, 2000). Sandy Sandoval of Albuquerque had a leg amputated as the result of a mine accident. Bernie Montoya had a leg broken in a cave-in. Such accidents were everyday occurrences. Some prisoners intentionally broke an arm or leg, in order to escape working in the mine.

After being injured in a mine explosion, Manuel Armijo was assigned to the blacksmith shop, sharpening picks for the coal miners.[11] On Christmas Day, 1944, an elderly Japanese blacksmith gave Armijo a baked sweet potato and a bottle of sake. Unfortunately, a guard caught him eating, and beat the blacksmith for feeding a POW. The blacksmith was actually the guard's father.

Armijo was thirsty one night at Camp 17, and went outside of his barracks to fetch some hot water to make tea. The "One-Armed Bandit," Sergeant Omoru, a Japanese guard who had lost his left arm, caught Armijo. The guard forced Armijo to kneel, and count to 100 in Japanese. Then Omoru hit Armijo on the side of the head with his Nambu pistol, knocking him over and sending his brain reeling. The Japanese guard said: "I will kill you if you go out after the 7:00 curfew again." Then Omoru spilled the pail of hot water on the ground. When the war ended in 1945, the Japanese guard reluctantly "traded" his pistol to Armijo for a pack of Camel cigarettes.[12] Today, the One-Armed Bandit's pistol is one of Armijo's prized possessions (Armijo, 2000) (Figure 2-10).

Figure 2-10. Master Sergeant (retired) Manuel Armijo in Santa Fe, in 2001.
Armijo, aged 90, holds the Luger-style Nambu automatic with which he was pistol whipped by a Japanese guard, the One-Armed Bandit, in Fukuoka Camp #17 in Japan. At the end of the war, in August 1945, Armijo "purchased" the weapon from the One-Armed Bandit, who was executed in 1946 after a War Crimes Trial.
Source: Miguel Gandert, Albuquerque, New Mexico.

Manuel Armijo and his fellow prisoners in Camp 17 learned about the atomic bomb and the end of the war from an American war correspondent, who unexpectedly walked into the camp one day. This news set off a wild celebration (Armijo, 2000). The Japanese guards simply vanished, leaving the American prisoners on their own for several weeks until they were liberated by U.S. troops. Armijo craved chicken, so he went door-to-door in the town of Omuta until he found two chickens, for which he bartered all his clothes, including his "long johns." Then he and his buddy Evans Garcia (2000) cooked and ate the chickens. American B-29s dropped food packages into the POW camp. The food was a welcome sight to the emaciated Armijo, who weighed only 88 pounds (he weighed 140 pounds before the war). By the time he reached Santa Fe, a month after the Japanese surrender, Armijo had regained 20 pounds.

Armijo and Evans Garcia did not wait for the arrival of American troops. They forced their way onto a Japanese passenger train and traveled for two days until they reached an air base at Nagoya where American planes had landed. They took showers, exchanged their prison rags for Army uniforms, and enjoyed eating American food. When Armijo finally got home to New Mexico, after recovering for two months in Letterman General Hospital in San Francisco, his wife, daughter, and other family members were at the railroad station in Lamy to meet him. His mother prepared a big welcome-home dinner of green chile stew, turkey, and his other favorite foods. Unfortunately, she had prepared rice, which he simply could not face. Armijo's mother had kept a candle burning for him all during the war. Just before the meal, she led him to the corner of the living room, and asked him to blow out the candle. In 2000 Armijo sobbed while describing this homecoming scene to the present authors.

HONORING THE BATAAN SURVIVORS

The former New Mexico state capital building in Santa Fe is named the Bataan Memorial Building, in honor of the New Mexicans who fought in the Philippines in World War II. An eternal flame burns outside the building in memory of the New Mexicans who did not return. A few blocks along Old Pecos Trail from the State Capital is the modest Bataan Museum, housed in the former National Guard Armory in Santa Fe. All of the New Mexicans from the Santa Fe area took their physical exams in this building, and weekly drills were conducted there.

April 9, the surrender date on Bataan, was designated as "Bataan Day" in 1947, and is celebrated each year with a National Guard band, speeches, and a reception. The high point of the annual ceremony is the raising of an unadorned white satin flag. This banner was the idea of Manuel Armijo in 1947 when he was president of the Bataan Veterans Association. Every year at the April 9 ceremony, one or more additional individuals come forward to disclose that they were with the 200th Regiment. At the 2000 ceremony, Alexander Matthews, who served in H Battery during World War II, received 12 medals that he had earned 58 years earlier.

THE 1999 CONFLICT OVER THE INTERNMENT CAMP MARKER

Many Bataan veterans in 1999 violently opposed a proposal to construct a marker in the Frank S. Ortiz Park, overlooking the site of the Santa Fe Internment Camp during World War II, to recognize the Japanese Americans who had been imprisoned there during World War II. After several months of debate and attempts at mediation between the opposing groups, the Santa Fe City Council voted 5 to 4 in favor of the marker, with Mayor Larry Delgado's vote breaking the tie.

The highly emotional nature of the debate was reflected by Clarence "Porky" Lithgow, son-in-law of Manuel Armijo, who rose in the Council chambers to state: "You just kicked the Bataan veterans in the teeth, in the twilight of their years" (Hummels, October 28, 1999, p. 1). One irate individual, in support of the Bataan veterans, stated that he intended to defecate on the marker, once it was erected. In order to attempt to placate the Bataan veterans group, the City Council voted unanimously in favor of the construction of a monument to honor military veterans in Santa Fe.

Not all of the Bataan survivors in Santa Fe opposed the marker for the Japanese Americans. Vicente Ojinaga was asked whether he objected to a Japanese family moving into a neighboring home. Ojinaga (2000) said: "These are not the same people who mistreated me as a POW 55 years ago." When he returned from Japan to Santa Fe in 1945, Ojinaga noticed the striking similarity between the guard towers at the Santa Fe Internment Camp, and those at Camp O'Donnell in the Philippines.

Some ex-prisoners-of-war remain bitterly anti-Japanese. For example, Victor Lear insists: "Anyone who buys a Japanese automobile is as un-American as a traitor" (quoted in Knox, 1981, p. 465). Most New Mexican Bataan veterans that the present authors interviewed used the term "Japs." An exception is Vicente Ojinaga, who carefully refers to the "Japanese people," even when he describes his wartime experiences. Ojinaga and his wife still live in the area of the Santa Fe Internment Camp and attended the dedication in April 20, 2002.

The text of the marker in Ortiz Park states: "This marker is placed here as a reminder that history is a valuable teacher only if we do not forget our past."

3

NAVAJO CODE TALKERS[1]

"The Navajo Code Talkers gave us history's most historic lessons of the power of communication. And they showed that our cultural diversity can be our greatest strength."
—(U.S. President Bill Clinton, April 18, 2000, addressing an audience of 20,000 Navajos at Shiprock, New Mexico.)

After tough fighting on Iwo Jima, in which U.S. troops suffered 33 percent casualties, the Marines raised the United States flag atop Mount Suribachi on February 23, 1945. News of this most celebrated event in Marine Corps history was transmitted in code to the USS *Eldorado* and thus to the world as follows: " . . . *Gah tse-nill yeh-hes dibeh dzeh be Shi-da Klesh chuo ah-jad be-la-sana ah-tad do ye-dzeh-al-tsisi-gi Tsin-tliti a-kha no-da-ih a-chin d-ah Dibeh dzeh bi-so-dih ne-zhoni wol-la-chee ah-di neeznaa taa ashdla be-la-sana na-as-tso-si*" (Raised U.S. flag and secured Mount Suribachi at 10:35 A.M.). The capture of Mount Suribachi was a key victory in the Iwo Jima campaign, which cleared the way for the planned invasion of the Japanese home islands.

Harold Foster (1992), a Navajo Marine, transmitted this news in *Diné*, the language of the Navajo people ("*Diné*" means "The People" in

Diné). An unusual chapter in World War II history concerns the Navajo Code Talkers, who protected U.S. radio transmissions from being broken by the Japanese in the Pacific War.

SECRET CODES IN WORLD WAR II

A partial explanation of why one side or the other was winning at various points during World War II was the antagonists' success in cracking their enemy's secret code. Early in the war, the Germans broke the code with which radio exchanges were transmitted between U.S. President Roosevelt and British Prime Minister Winston Churchill. The United States cracked both the Japanese "Purple" code and British broke the German Enigma coding system, to the advantage of the Allies in conducting the war.

The British captured one of the Enigma machines from a German submarine early in the war, in 1941. Alan Turing used a prototype computer at the British cryptographic center at Bletchley Park, near London, to try millions of possible combinations on the machine until the code was cracked. After the British broke the German Enigma coding system, they knew in advance the actions of German troops, ships, and aircraft. This broken German code gave the Allies a major advantage in the Battle of Britain, the Battle of El Alemain, and in other key engagements.

The United States cracked the Japanese "Purple" cipher machine through a process called "Magic" in August 1940, more than a year before the U.S. entered World War II. "Purple" was broken when the U.S. constructed an analog of the Japanese cipher machine, which was created over an 18-month period by analyzing hundreds of Japanese diplomatic messages. The Japanese Navy hoped to finish off the U.S. Navy in 1942 by luring American forces to Alaskan waters, and then invading Midway Island, a key base in the mid-Pacific. In June 1942, the Americans deciphered a message in the Purple code indicating that the Japanese would fake an attack on Attu in the Aleutian Islands, off of Alaska, in order to draw American ships away from Midway Island. Admiral Chester W. Nimitz, Commander-in-Chief of the American forces in the Pacific, thanks to "Magic," knew the location of the Japanese ships. U.S. planes caught the Japanese aircraft carriers in the midst of refueling and rearming their planes. The outcome was an especially sweet victory because the carriers sunk at Midway had the previous December attacked Pearl Harbor.[2]

During the U.S. Marines' island-hopping offensive in the Pacific (see Figure 1-2), the American code was virtually unbreakable because the messages were coded in *Diné*, the language spoken by the Navajo people. Japanese code-crackers were stymied by the Navajo code, although they broke the U.S. Army, Navy, and Air Corps codes (Thomas, 1998). This story of the Navajo Code Talkers was an official U.S. government secret for several decades. Finally, in 1968, the code talkers were allowed to disclose the key role they had played in shortening the Pacific War.

DECIDING TO USE NAVAJO CODE TALKERS

At the beginning of World War II, only 28 non-Navajos knew how to speak *Diné*. One of them was Philip Johnston, whose parents had led the Presbyterian Mission at Leupp, Arizona, 35 miles northeast of Flagstaff. He grew up playing with Navajo children, and as a result possessed a certain fluency in *Diné*, what the Navajo commonly call "trading post *Diné*," meaning an ability that was adequate for business transactions at trading posts (in fact, Johnston worked at various trading posts for several years). Johnston was capable enough in *Diné* to serve as the translator for two Navajo tribal leaders and his father when they met with President Teddy Roosevelt in the White House to plead for fair treatment. Johnston was only nine years old at the time, 1901 (Johnston, 1970).

The *Diné* language was unwritten, and the Navajo discouraged *bilagaana* (non-Navajos) from learning their tongue. The 28 *bilagaana* who understood *Diné* were mainly American anthropologists and linguists. Navajos like to say that speaking *Diné* is like painting pictures in the mind. There were very few such painters, other than the Navajo themselves.

The Code Talker Demonstration

Johnston left the Navajo Reservation, served in the Army in France during World War I, graduated in civil engineering from the University of Southern California, and was working as a city engineer in Los Angeles at the time of the Japanese attack on Pearl Harbor. He knew that a few American Indian code talkers (not Navajos) had been used in the trench warfare in France during World War I. In early 1942, shortly after Pearl Harbor, Johnston read a newspaper article about the U.S. Army experimenting with American Indian code talkers during training exercises in Louisiana. Johnston took the idea of Navajo Code Talkers to the Marine Corps at Camp Elliott, located just north of San Diego.[3] Major James E. Jones was skeptical of Johnston's idea at first, but then Johnston spoke to him in *Diné*, leaving Jones dumbfounded. Even when Johnston spoke a word very slowly, the major could not draw any meaning from it. Jones arranged for Johnston to give a demonstration to a very high-ranking Marine officer, Major General Clayton B. Vogel, Commanding General, Amphibious Corps, Pacific Fleet. The Marines had been practicing amphibious landings for a dozen years before World War II, anticipating the forthcoming conflict with Japan. General Holland M. ("Howlin' Mad") Smith, who led these landing exercises, felt that a Pacific War would offer the Marines their moment on the world stage (Bradley, 2000).

Johnston located four Navajos who were working in the Los Angeles area, and on February 25, 1942, drove with them to Camp Elliott. The next morning, one pair of Navajos were given six military commands by General Vogel, in English, which they were asked to transmit over a field telephone to the other two Navajos, who were in a distant office (Johnston, 1970). Each message went from English into *Diné*, and then was transmitted verbally by telephone to the other Navajos, who then translated the contents back into English. Among the messages were: "Begin withdrawal at 2000 today," and "Enemy expected to make tank and dive-bombing attack at dawn" (McClain, 1994, p. 26). The transmission was almost immediate, requiring only a few minutes, much quicker than the several hours that would have been required if the military commands had been encoded with a coding machine and the Navy's Shackle cipher. However, the four Navajos had difficulty with certain military words for which there were no equivalents in their language, such as tank and dive-bomber.

General Vogel was very favorably impressed, foreseeing how useful the Navajo Code Talkers would be in the amphibious landings and jungle warfare that lay ahead in the Pacific. Vogel recommended to the Commandant of the Marine Corps in Washington that an initial batch of 200 Navajo Code Talkers be recruited. He anticipated assigning 100 Navajo Code Talkers to each of the two Marine divisions. However, Washington decided to begin with a pilot project of 30 code talkers, one platoon.

Recruiting the First 29 Navajo Code Talkers

The first batch of code talkers were signed up on the "Big Res," the huge Navajo Reservation that covers much of northwestern New Mexico and northeastern Arizona, and a part of southern Utah. In 1942, some 50,000 Navajos lived in this physically isolated and economically depressed land. Most Navajos resided in traditional hogans, heated by burning wood or coal, with no piped water, electricity, or telephones. Most Navajo families were sheep farmers who exchanged homegrown wool or homemade woven rugs for necessities at a local trading post in one of their few contacts with *bilagaana*.

When Marine recruiter Sergeant Frank Shinn parked his mobile trailer at the Indian Health Service Hospital in Fort Defiance, Arizona, in April 1942, no one came forward to volunteer as a code talker (Figure 3-1). He played martial music, which blasted from the big speakers on top of the recruiting trailer. This John Philip Sousa strategy had worked in previous recruitment efforts. But in Fort Defiance, Navajos walked past the trailer with puzzled expressions (M. Gorman, 1999). After several days without snaring a recruit, Shinn approached Henry Chee Dodge, Chair of the Navajo Tribal Council, in Window Rock, Arizona. Dodge agreed to help the Marine recruiter, and the tribal leader then spread the word that Shinn was looking for a few able men. His message went out by shortwave radio to every trading post on the Big Res, and some Navajo young men dropped by Shinn's trailer. But the Sergeant recruited most of the first batch of code talkers out of government boarding schools in Fort Defiance, Arizona; Fort Wingate, New Mexico; and Shiprock, New Mexico.

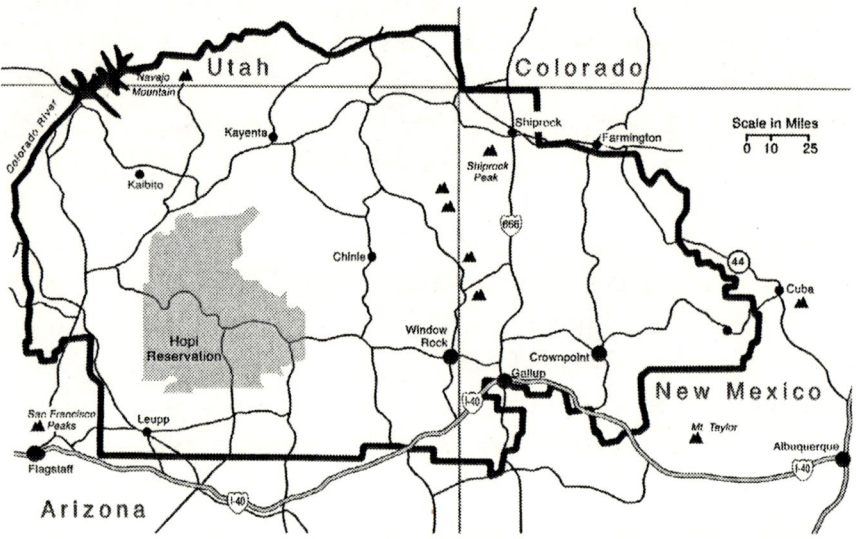

Figure 3-1. Map of the Navajo Nation in Arizona, New Mexico, and Utah.
The Navajo Nation, headquartered in Window Rock, Arizona, includes northeastern Arizona, northwestern New Mexico, and a portion of southeastern Utah, with the exception of the Hopi Reservation. Few of the highways shown here were paved in 1941 (the famous Route 66 is now I-40). The total population of the Navajo Nation, presently 250,000, was 50,000 in 1941. The assimilationist policy of the U.S. Bureau of Indian Affairs (BIA) at that time included sending Navajo children to distant boarding schools, such as at Ganado, Gallup, Albuquerque, and Santa Fe (north of Albuquerque), where only English language was allowed. The First 29 Code Talkers were mainly recruited from boarding schools at Fort Defiance (just north of Window Rock), Fort Wingate (near Gallup), and Shiprock.

Navajo students were generally forbidden to speak *Diné* by the Bureau of Indian Affairs, the U.S. government agency operating the schools that Navajo youth were required to attend. Before the 1940s, the United States government pursued an official policy of trying to break down Navajo culture by discouraging use of *Diné* by Navajo students. The government's forced Americanization policy was brutal. The Bureau of Indian Affairs insisted that Navajo children be sent to boarding schools far from their homes, so that the children would have little contact with their parents during the school year.[4] Teachers in the boarding schools often scrubbed out students' mouths with harsh brown soap when they caught them speaking *Diné*. One of the First 29 Navajo Code Talkers, Carl Gorman, was chained to an overhead pipe in his school's four-foot high basement for a week after he spoke *Diné* to a school teacher (Z. Gorman, 2002).[5] Some Navajo students were whipped with a belt or strap; others were forced to kneel for several hours facing a blank wall (Toledo, 1999).

The BIA boarding schools followed a military model. Students typically lived in two-story wooden barracks. Male students wore uniforms on certain days of the week, had inspection, did daily calisthenics, and drilled on a parade ground. Students in the Indian schools marched in formation to church and to other events, and were served an army diet (Greenberg & Greenberg, 1996, p. 41). Only in 1974, years later, did the Bureau of Indian Affairs drop its assimilationist policy, and the BIA schools were eliminated, with responsibility for the schooling of Navajo children turned over to local school boards. They promptly began teaching *Diné*, instead of discouraging its use.

In the 1940s the Navajo Marine recruits thought it was humorous that the same government that had forbidden them to speak their language in school was now begging them to join the Marine Corps in order to speak *Diné*.

Navajo Distrust of the U.S. Government

The Navajo, the largest Native American tribe in the United States, had suffered a long history of conflict with the U.S. government. This confrontation began in the mid-1800s when the Navajos resisted the American frontier movement that was pushing them off their tribal lands. In the Long Walk of 1863-64 Colonel Kit Carson and his U.S. Army troops pursued a scorched earth policy to drive the 8,000 Navajos 350 miles from their homelands to Fort Sumner, New Mexico. Many Navajos died during the privation of the Long Walk, which was something like an earlier, American version of the Bataan Death March, with soldiers killing stragglers, including women and children. After four years at Fort Stanton, the Navajo were allowed to return to their grazing lands in Arizona and New Mexico. But the Long Walk is still remembered bitterly by the Navajo today.

In the 1930s, the federal government decided that the Navajo pasture lands were over grazed and were becoming eroded. So, federal officials destroyed more than one-third of the Navajos' beloved sheep, cattle, and horses. Government compensation for taking the animals was minimal. This government Livestock Reduction Program lingers on in Navajo stories relayed by tribal elders. All Native Americans were granted U.S. citizenship in 1924, but the Navajos did not have voting rights in New Mexico and Arizona until several years after World War II. Young Navajo men in 1942 had several very good reasons *not* to enlist in the U.S. Marines.

Enlistment

The patriotic young Navajos did enlist, however, and in large numbers. Eventually some 3,600 served in the U.S. armed forces during World War II (a relatively high proportion of the 50,000 Navajo people), with about 420 assigned to be Navajo Code Talkers.

In order to be accepted as a code talker, a young Navajo man had to be between 17 and 30 years of age, be educated through the tenth grade, and be fluent in both *Diné* and English. Sergeant Shinn, the Marine Corps recruiter, also assessed the degree to which each enlistee spoke in a clear voice. He knew they were to serve as code talkers, although the young Navajos were only told that they were volunteering for some kind of special service. Many code talkers today believe that the First 29 were also selected, as well as Sergeant Shinn could gauge such abilities in personal interviews, for their intelligence and understanding of Navajo culture. Perhaps for this reason, several older Navajo were selected, along with the majority of 17 and 18-year-olds (some were even younger). Sergeant Shinn selected the First 29 out of 200 applicants, so he could be very selective (Z. Gorman, 2002).

Many of the patriotic volunteers were underage, teenagers of only 15 or 16 when they joined the Marines. One volunteer among the original 29 code talkers, Carl Gorman, had just been laid off as an interpreter and timekeeper for the government's Stock Reduction Program. Gorman and his friend John Benally traveled all night from Kaiberto, Arizona, to Fort Defiance, in order to volunteer (M. Gorman, 1999). Gorman was actually 34 at the time, well over the age limit for joining the Marines. He told Shinn that he was 28.[6] Given the lack of official birth records, a Navajo's age was whatever he said it was.

One of the First 29, in a 1977 speech, introduced himself in the traditional Navajo way: "My name is Cozy S. Brown . . . . My clan is the Deer Spring, which is the same as the Bitter Water Clan [his mother's clan]. I was born for the Red Running into Water People, which is the same as the Tobacco People [his father's clan]" (Brown, 1977, p. 52). Brown was raised by his grandmother, who was born at Fort Sumner, after the Long Walk. He had only a Navajo name until he was six years, when his father enrolled him at the BIA Boarding School at Chinle, Arizona. His father gave him the first name of "Cozy," after his boss at a trading post. Brown was at Shiprock High School in 1942, in the same class with Dean Wilson. They both volunteered for the First 29 when Sergeant Shinn visited their school. "They gave us two weeks to think about it. I did my own thinking; I didn't inquire of my parents" (Brown, 1977, p. 53).

BOOT CAMP

The initial group of 29 future code talkers assembled at Fort Wingate, New Mexico. The Marine Corps had assigned 30 serial identification numbers for the first batch, but at the last-minute one individual was not present, leaving 29. This volunteer, with serial number 358518, has never been identified by name by the Marine Corps and remains a mystery to this day (Z. Gorman, 2002). Shortly, the 29 Navajos departed by bus on the 1,200 mile trip to San Diego.

The Marine Corps brass decided that the Navajo Code Talkers should be Marines first, and communication specialists second. Under combat conditions in the Pacific, a code talker would also serve as a rifleman, a message runner, and perform all other duties expected of a Marine. So the Navajo Marines were taught to use a carbine, to assemble and fire a machine gun, throw grenades, and use other weapons in the two months-long Basic Training course. Boot camp was a very demanding experience, with a usual attrition rate of five to 10 percent.

Carl Gorman, one of the oldest of the First 29, became the most respected code talker. He was born near Chinle, Arizona, where his father operated a trading post. When his father had arrived as a child at the Fort Defiance Army Station to be assigned to a BIA boarding school, the Army sergeant could not pronounce his Navajo name. So the sergeant arbitrarily selected a name, Nelson Carl Gorman, from the Army Station's roster, wrote it on a tag, and hung it around the child's neck (Greenberg & Greenberg, 1996). Thus Carl Gorman, although born a Navajo, inherited a German name (many other Navajo names have similar etiology). Carl Gorman attended a private Christian school in Gallup, and then the Albuquerque Indian School, where he was a football star and an excellent boxer.

One day during boot camp in San Diego, a drill sergeant explained that he would give the all-Navajo 382nd Training Platoon a boxing lesson. The sadistic sergeant threw a punch at each recruit, sending each Navajo reeling as the sergeant moved down the line of trainees. Gorman was tenth in line. He ducked the sergeant's fist, and hit him with a one-two punch, knocking the sergeant down. The Navajos laughed. Word about this incident soon spread throughout the training camp (Greenberg & Greenberg, 1996, p. 59). Gorman could have been court martialed, but he was not. He was on his way to becoming a leader of the First 29.

Boot camp consisted of rigorous physical exercises and a punishing experience in military discipline (Figure 3-2). Heads were shaved. The Marine Corps strategy was to break the recruits down, and then to build them up as Marines. One of the 29 future code talkers, Eugene Crawford, had been in the Reserve Officer Training Corps (ROTC), and told his colleagues on the long bus ride to San Diego what to expect in Basic Training.

Figure 3-2. The First 29 Navajo Code Talkers at the Completion of their Boot Camp Training in San Diego.

The 382nd Platoon, an all-Navajo training group, had no washout during boot camp. Following boot camp, the First 29 were involved in creating the code of 250 words for military terms that did not exist in *Diné*. After formulating their code and gaining proficiency in its encoding and decoding, the First 29 shipped out for Guadalcanal, except for two individuals (John Benally, second row, fifth from left, and Johnny Manuelito, top row, third from left) who remained behind to serve as instructors for future batches of code talkers. Carl Gorman is sixth from the left in the top row. Three non-Navajo drill instructors are in front row center.

Source: Salt Lake City, University of Utah, J. Willard Marriott Library, Special Collections, Marine Corps photograph.

The First 29's training platoon, the 382nd, was the first all-Navajo batch in the history of the Corps. The young Navajos were already toughened by herding sheep, by chopping wood, and by participating in other physical activities needed to survive in their harsh environment on the Reservation. They endured the physical rigors of basic training with relative ease, laughing at the *bilagaana* in the other training platoons who could not keep up on a 30-mile hike carrying full combat gear. The tough discipline of boot camp reminded the Navajos of their boarding school experiences. One Navajo Marine said, laughingly, "This Marine stuff is nothing compared to the hell we had to take in the boarding schools" (Greenberg & Greenberg, 1996, p. 58).

Most of the young Navajos had never been off the Reservation until their trip to San Diego. Training methods were direct. For instance, one Navajo who did not know how to swim was simply pushed into a pool by a drill instructor. The Navajo recruits were a boisterous, playful bunch. For example, during smoke breaks, they practiced self-styled "drills" with mounted bayonets. The wooden stocks of their rifles were nicked by bayonet thrusts. Several Navajo trainees were also nicked. Training officers ordered an immediate halt to these informal bayonet drills. Then the trainees invented a new game, in which several Navajos would unexpectedly pile on top of one of their surprised instructors when he come outside the door of the training center during break time. After the pile-on-an-instructor game was prohibited, the Navajos found it was great fun to plunge their 14-inch bayonets through the walls of the training buildings, which were made of light material.

Despite such unruly behavior during their breaks, the Navajos were serious students in the classroom training sessions (McClain, 1994).

All 29 Navajo Code Talkers completed boot camp, which was amazing, given the usual rate of attrition. Accordingly, Colonel James L. Underhill, commanding officer of the Marine training base, in his address to the all-Navajo platoon on their graduation day, June 27, 1942, told the initial 29 code talkers: "Yours has been one of the outstanding platoons in the history of this Recruit Depot and a letter has gone to Washington telling of your excellence . . . . As a group you have made one of the highest scores on the Rifle Range." The Marine officer concluded: "You are now to be transferred to a combat organization where you will receive further training. When the time comes for you to go into battle with the enemy, I know that you will fight like true Navajos, Americans, and Marines" (quoted in McClain, 1994, pp. 45-46).

DEVELOPMENT OF THE CODE

After completing Basic Training, the First 29 Code Talkers were enrolled in a communication course at the Field Signal Battalion Training Center (at Camp Pendleton, near Oceanside, north of San Diego) in which they learned Morse Code, semaphore flags and blinker signals, and how to operate field radios. Then the Navajos were sent to the special code talkers' school at nearby Camp Elliott, before shipping out for the Pacific (Table 3-1). Both the actual development of the code and intensive training in its use were responsibilities of the First 29 themselves. So the first code talker training school was essentially self-taught.[7]

Table 3-1. Time-Line for the Navajo Code Talkers.

Date	Event
1941	
December 7	Japanese bomb Pearl Harbor.
December 8	United States enters World War II.
1942	
February 25	Philip Johnston and four Navajos demonstrate the Navajo code to U.S. Marine Corps General Vogel.
April	Sergeant Frank Shinn arrives in Fort Defiance to recruit 30 Navajo Code Talkers.
June	The "First 29" finish boot camp in San Diego, and begin creating the code at Camp Elliott.
August 7	Invasion of Guadalcanal by the 1st and 2nd Marine Divisions, and the code talkers soon engage in their first combat.
October–November	John Benally and Johnny Manuelito recruit a second batch of code talkers.
1943	
June	An *Arizona Highways* article about Navajo Code Talkers is published.
November 1	Marines invade Bougainville, in the Solomon Islands.
1944	
June 15	Invasion of Saipan.
July 21	Marines invade Guam.
July 24	Invasion of Tinian.
September 15	Marines land on Peleliu Island in the Palaus.
1945	
February 19–March 26	Invasion of Iwo Jima by the 3nd, 4th, and 5th Marine Divisions.
April 1–June 21	Invasion of Okinawa by the 1st, 2nd, and 6th Marine Divisions.
August 6	An atomic bomb is dropped on Hiroshima.
August 9	An atomic bomb is dropped on Nagasaki.
September 2	Peace Treaty is signed.
1969	
June	Chicago reunion of 4th Marine Division in Chicago; several Navajo Code Talkers participate. Navajo Code Talkers Association is formed.

1971
July 9-10   First reunion of code talkers at Window Rock, Arizona.

On the first morning of the code talker training school, a Marine officer told the 29 Navajos that they were to serve as code talkers in *Diné* in the forthcoming Marine invasions of Pacific islands. This announcement was the first they knew of their special mission. Then the officer ordered them to get to work on developing the code, wheeled, and left the classroom. For several minutes, there was silence as the young Navajo Marines realized the gravity of their responsibility. They were immensely pleased, as Ken Etsicitty, a code talker in the 3rd Marine Division, was later to state: "We, the Navajo people, were very fortunate to contribute our language as a code for our country's victory" (quoted in McClain, 1994, p. v).

Constructing the code was a very difficult task, and the effective cipher that resulted is one reason why the First 29 are held in such high esteem by other code talkers today. Building the code required fluency in *Diné* and in English, a thorough grasp of Navajo culture, and considerable creativity. The major task facing the code talkers was cerebral (Little, 1999).

Military Equivalents in *Diné*

The 29 Navajo Code Talkers created a lexicon of *Diné* words for untranslatable English words, such as submarine, bomb, cruiser, and other military terms. It made sense to the Navajos to memorize familiar words for military terms (McClain, 1994). They decided to name ships after fish, planes after birds, and land objects after animals. So "bomb" became the *Diné* word for "egg" (*ayeshi*), "submarine" became *besh-lo* ("iron fish"), and "dive bomber" was coded as *gini* ("chicken hawk"). Hand grenades were called "potatoes" (*nimasil*). The Navajo chose words in *Diné* that were standardized in voice inflection, and that had distinct sounds, in order to avoid possible mistakes under combat conditions (Toledo, 1999).

Some 211 military code-words had to be memorized plus 26 *Diné* words for the letters of the alphabet (the code grew to 619 terms by the end of World War II). The Navajo trainees were not allowed to take notes, as security precautions prevented taking a code book into combat. Actually, a code book was developed, for purposes of standardization of the code during the later training sessions, but it was not taken overseas.[8] Fortunately, the Navajo Marines had a special advantage in remembering the code, as the memorization of elaborate songs, prayers, and religious ceremonies is part of Navajo culture. Nevertheless, the task of the Navajo trainees was daunting. As Philip Johnston said, "The code talkers presented a phenomenal feat of memory, and I don't know to this day how they could react so quickly to the substitute words in Navajo in a fraction of a second" (quoted in Paul, 1973, p.45).

Training classes typically consisted of an instructor reading out a list of words, which the trainees then wrote down in translation, either English-to-*Diné*, or vice versa. Fluency and skill in the code was developed until it became almost automatic. In the barracks at night after lights-out, the Navajos whispered "*wol-la-chee*," "*shush*," "*moasi*," "*deeh*," etc. They practiced the code over and over, until fatigue finally overcame their enthusiasm (McClain, 1994). Amazingly, the First 29 developed, and memorized, the code in only eight weeks (Johnston, 1970; Singh, 1999).

Wollachee-Shush-Moasi

Words like place-names in English, say "Guadalcanal" or "Iwo Jima," were spelled out letter by letter in *Diné*. The Marines' phonetic alphabet (Able-Baker-Charlie-etc.) became *Wollachee-Shush-Moasi* (Ant-Bear-Cat). The 29 original code talkers worked out the following alphabet:

A	*wol-la-chee*	ant
B	*shush*	bear
C	*moasi*	cat
D	*be*	deer
E	*dzeh*	elk
F	*ma-e*	fox
G	*klizzie*	goat
H	*lin*	horse
I	*tkin*	ice
J	*tkele-cho-gi*	jackass
K	*klizzie-yazzie*	kid
L	*dibeh-yazzie*	lamb
M	*na-as-tso-si*	mouse
N	*nesh-chee*	nut
O	*ne-ahs-jah*	owl
P	*bi-so-dih*	pig
Q	*ca-yeilth*	quiver
R	*gah*	rabbit
S	*dibeh*	sheep
T	*than-zie*	turkey
U	*no-da-ih*	Ute
V	*a-keh-di-glini*	victor
W	*gloe-ih*	weasel
X	*al-an-as-dzoh*	cross
Y	*tsah-as-zih*	yucca
Z	*besh-do-gliz*	zinc

These code words were written without accents or the guttural sounds that characterize spoken *Diné*. The Navajo Marines figured that the instructors who would teach the code to later batches of code talkers would know how to correctly pronounce each word. That was a safe assumption, given that the instructors were always Navajos. *Diné* is unintelligible to anyone who is not a Navajo.[9]

A basic strategy in code-breaking is word-counts ("the" is the most commonly-used word in English, for example) and letter-counts. To confuse the Japanese code-breakers, the Navajos created two additional *Diné* words for the six most commonly-used letters, also one additional *Diné* word for another six letters.[10] So the English letter "a" could be translated as either the *Diné* word for "ant" (*wol-la-chee*) or "apple" (*belesana*) or "axe" (*tsenill*). The letter "e" could be translated as the *Diné* word for "elk" (*dzeh*), as "ear" (*ahjah*) or "eye" (*ahnah*). These multiple *Diné* words meant more memorization and mental dexterity for the code talkers. Thus, "Guadalcanal," originally coded as "Goat-Ute-Ant-Deer-Ant-Lamb-Cat-Ant-Nut-Ant-Lamb" became "Goat-Ute-Ant(*Wol-la-chee*)-Deer-Apple(*Be-la-sana*)-Lamb-Cat-Axe(*Tse-nihl*)-Nut-Axe-Leg(*Ah-jad*).

In order to spell out names and other words in English, a code talker had to be an excellent speller of difficult words. For example, think of coding words like "bivouac" or "strafing" into *Diné*. Accuracy was crucial. The code talkers were told that "a mistake could cost someone their life" (Toledo, 1999). Imagine an order to bomb Position X at a distance of 1,000 yards from the front lines. If it were mistranslated as 100 yards, the result would be "friendly fire" on one's own troops, and perhaps oneself.

A Code-within-a-Code

In order to further complicate the task of Japanese code-breakers, the Navajo played humorous word-games. "District" became "deer-ice-strict," and "belong" became "long-bee." "Bulldozer" became "bull sleep" in *Diné*, and "dispatch" was translated as "dog is patch" (Bixler, 1992, p. 53). "Not" was translated as "no turkey" (*ni-dah-than-zie*), and "that" became "turkey hat" (*than-zie-cha*). "Capitol" was *tkah-chae* ("sweat house") (Paul, 1973, pp. 27-29). "Detail" became *be-beh-sha* (deer trail). "Anti-tank" became "turtle-shooter," *chay-ta-gahi-be-wol-doni*.

The Navajo Code Talkers were certain that the Japanese could not decode their radio transmissions. Navajo sounds are very difficult for *bilagaana* to understand. Vowels rise and fall, changing meaning with pitch. Indeed, the Japanese could not break the code, although they eventually determined that the radio transmissions were in *Diné*. Unless the Japanese could obtain a code book (none were taken overseas) or a Navajo Code Talker (the code talkers *were* the code books in this case), the Japanese could not break the code. No Navajo Code Talkers were captured by the Japanese during the Pacific War, although eleven code talkers died in combat.

The intense effort by the initial 29 code talkers resulted in an elaborate code-within-a-code. Despite transmitting thousands of commands during the Pacific War, the Navajo Code Talkers made few known mistakes. They were fast, consistently able to run circles around the U.S. Navy's mechanical coding machines using the Shackle cipher. In many situations, speed was essential, as Japanese artillery often targeted on the source of radio transmissions. So the Navajo Code Talkers would send their message, and then quickly move out.

Finally, when the initial 29 code talkers had worked out their code and memorized it, 27 shipped out to Guadalcanal, in order to test the use of the code under combat conditions. Two of the code talkers who were particularly effective in using the code, John Benally and Johnny Manuelito, were assigned to serve as instructors at Camp Elliott for the next batch of Navajo Code Talkers. First, Benally and Manuelito returned to the Reservation with Sergeant Shinn for four months to recruit the next batches of code talkers. They toured the Big Res in a recruiting trailer, giving talks in high schools and at community functions. The two Navajo recruiters wore their snappy Marine dress uniforms, which made a big impression on their tribal brothers.

Recruiting Bill Toledo

The story of how one young code talker joined the U.S. Marines illustrates the experience of many others. Bill Toledo was home from boarding school in the summer of 1942. Toledo lived with his grandparents, his aunt, and her husband on a small sheep farm near

Torreon, New Mexico, in the eastern part of the Reservation, some 25 miles southwest of Cuba, New Mexico. He was raised in the traditional Navajo way, with his grandfather teaching him how to pray, to experience the sweat house, and to begin each day by running toward the sun while shouting. Toledo's grandmother would give him one bullet for his short-barreled .22 caliber rifle, and tell him to bring home a rabbit or a prairie dog (his accuracy with a rifle would later help Toledo win an expert marksmanship badge in U.S. Marine Boot Camp).

His grandfather urged him to enjoy physical exercise. So while Toledo herded his family's sheep, he jumped across arroyos, zigzagged around juniper bushes, and climbed trees. In wintertime, Toledo was taught to roll naked in the snow, and to bathe with ice water. In the extreme heat of the sweat lodge, Toledo's grandfather taught him about the meaning of life, tribal history, and how to live in harmony with nature. It was a Spartan, vigorous lifestyle. Yet, while herding sheep, Toledo often "wondered what was on the other side of the mountain" (Toledo, 1999). He had never been off of the Reservation.

One evening in late August 1942, Toledo herded the sheep into the corral behind his grandfather's house. The next morning, he left for nine months in boarding school, which turned out to include three years of fighting the Japanese in the Pacific. He washed carefully, rounded up the family's team of horses, and his uncle-in-law drove him in their wagon to a local elementary school, several miles away. Around noon, the young Navajos climbed aboard two flatbed trucks and rode the 80 miles to the Indian School at Crownpoint, New Mexico.

Toledo was in his senior year of high school. One day in early October, a young Marine in a dress uniform, Johnny Manuelito, one of the First 29, visited the school. All of the 18-year-old Navajos were sent to the school auditorium, where Manuelito talked to them for a half hour about the Marine Corps. He stressed the positives, failing to mention the rigors of boot camp. Manuelito said that the Marines wanted Navajos who could speak both English and *Diné* fluently and who were in good health. Bedazzled by Manuelito's Marine dress uniform, Bill Toledo enlisted on the spot, along with his uncle, Frank

Toledo; a cousin, Preston Toledo; and two other classmates, Herbert and Ralph Morgan (Figure 3-3). The young Navajos were attracted by the promise of travel, and by the opportunity for employment (Toledo, 1999).

Figure 3-3. Private First Class Preston Toledo and His Uncle, Private First Class Frank Toledo, Relay Military Orders Over a Field Radio in *Diné*.
 These two Navajo Code Talkers were in training in Ballarat, Australia, on July 7, 1943, prior to going into combat with their Marine artillery regiment on Guadalcanal. Frank would later meet his other nephew, Bill Toledo, under combat conditions on Iwo Jima. All three Toledos were enrolled in a BIA boarding school, and enlisted in the Marine Corps on the same day.
 Source: Salt Lake City, University of Utah, J. Willard Marriott Library, Special Collections, Marine Corps photograph.

A few days after enlisting, the five young Navajos from Crownpoint Indian School were transported to Fort Wingate for physical examinations. Bill's cousin Preston weighed only 119 pounds, underweight by three pounds. During lunch, Bill Toledo suggested to Preston that he put rocks in his pockets. Uncle Frank suggested instead that Preston drink a lot of liquids, and he did, about a gallon of water. When he was re-weighed that afternoon, Preston passed the physical, weighing 123 pounds. The five recruits were transported to San Diego. "Boot camp was a shock to all of us" (Toledo, 1999). The Navajos felt small, compared to the other Marine recruits, some of whom had been basketball or football players. The Marine Corps in World War II had a reputation that attracted big, tough men. Bill Toledo has a photograph of his unit; the other five Marines in the photo are at least a foot taller.

The stamina and toughness of growing up on a sheep farm on the Reservation was valuable to Bill Toledo during boot camp. After Basic Training and Communication School, Toledo and his fellow Navajos were separated from the other Marines in their training platoon,[11] and assigned to the code talker training course. They were not asked if they wanted to be code talkers; all Navajos were automatically assigned to this specialty. Nor were Toledo and his fellow Navajo Marines even told that they were going to Code Talker School; on the first morning at Camp Elliott in the training center, the instructors simply began teaching them the code in *Diné*.

Bill Toledo went to the Code Talker Training School about six months after the First 29 (who were already fighting on Guadalcanal). At this time, the code was well developed and the training curriculum was standardized. Security was very tight. There were guards around the training center, and bars on the windows. The trainees could not take notes. They were required to take an oath never to reveal the code. The final two weeks of training consisted of field experience with the radio equipment, rapidly translating messages in the face of the noise and other distractions encountered in simulated combat. Toledo passed the practical test at the conclusion of the code talker course. Trainees who failed the test were assigned to Marine Corps infantry units (by the end of the war, 30 of the 450 Navajos who were recruited as code talkers had failed to qualify).

Toledo finished the eight weeks of code talker training in late January 1943, and was immediately assigned to the 3rd Marine Division. His troopship, the USS *Mount Vernon*, raised anchor the next morning, departing from San Diego harbor for New Zealand. There Toledo would undergo further drills, followed by jungle training in the summer of 1943 on Guadalcanal. Thereafter Toledo would be in the thick of the Pacific War, landing on Bougainville in November 1943, and experiencing further action on Guam and Iwo Jima.

While herding sheep back in New Mexico, Toledo had wanted to see what lay on the other side of the mountain. He got his wish.

Reasons for Enlisting

Why did the Navajos enlist in the blood-and-guts Marine Corps? The reasons were somewhat different for each individual, but certain common themes emerge. Carl Gorman, one of the First 29, had been laid off by the Stock Reduction Program and needed a job. On the Big Res, where unemployment was high, being a Marine looked like an attractive job. Some Navajo men knew that they would be drafted into the Army if they did not enlist in the Marines (Billey, 2000).

Many young Navajos enlisted out of patriotism. Albert Smith (1999) did not want "Our Mother Earth being dominated by foreign countries." America was regarded as "Our Mother" (*Nihima*), an illusion to the Navajo belief about the beginning of human life. Smith felt that "Japan wanted to take Mother Earth from us." He was only 15 years old at the time, an eighth grader at the Fort Wingate Indian School. Smith had two uncles in the 200th Regiment, the New Mexico National Guard unit in the Philippines. Smith followed the progress of the war closely, and was crazy to enlist. When his older brother joined the Marines, in spring, 1943, Smith's father agreed to sign the forms certifying that Smith was 17 years old, so that the two brothers could go into the Marine Corps together. However, due to the Pentagon's

"Sullivan Brothers" policy,[12] the two Smith brothers were separated after bootcamp in San Diego. Only Alfred Smith became a code talker.

Jimmy Begay was studying in a BIA school when he turned 17 on November 7, 1942. He and two school friends decided to join the military. They chose the Marine Corps because its insignia of a globe and anchor combined the Army and Navy functions. Today Begay feels that their choice as to which military branch to join was arbitrary and frivolous. They were young and patriotic and wanted adventure. The three boys were sworn in on November 15, a week after Begay turned 17 (Begay, 1999).

Sam Billison, President of the Navajo Code Talkers Association in 2002, was a high school student at the Indian School in Albuquerque in 1943. He had been impressed by John Wayne movies glorifying the U.S. Marines, and also by a radio commercial urging young Navajos to enlist in "The Few, the Brave, the Marines." But when Billison went to the Marine recruiting office, the sergeant told him to go back and finish high school. Billison had played football, basketball, and run track in school; he actually *enjoyed* boot camp, seeing it as another physical challenge (Billison, 1999). He had no intention of volunteering as a code talker, and had no idea that this specialty even existed. But when he completed boot camp in San Diego, a drill instructor asked him, "Are you an Indian?" Billison responded that he was a Navajo. Did he speak the Navajo language? "Yes." "English?" "A bit," Billison replied laconically. The DI said, "Do we have a program for *you*! Get your seabag." Thus Sam Billison became a Navajo Code Talker.

Keith Little was attending Ganado Mission School, operated by the Presbyterian Church, on December 7, 1941. "The school served pretty bad food, and several of us were down in a wash [ravine] behind the school, cooking a rabbit that we had shot, along with some vegetables that we had taken from the school garden. About 4:00 or 5:00 P.M., we realized that we needed salt, so one guy went to the school kitchen. He came running back. He said, 'Hey, the U.S. has been bombed!' We asked, 'By whom?' He said: 'By Japan.' 'What city?' 'Pearl Harbor.' We were angry because it was a 'sneak attack;' in fact, we were too angry to eat our food. We swore that we would all join the military" (Little, 1999). The Pentagon soon lowered the minimum age requirement from 18 to 17 years with parental permission. Little tried to enlist on March 4, 1943, his 17th birthday, but the Marine recruiter told him to finish the school year. Later in the spring Little was inducted, and sent to boot camp in San Diego.

Frank Thompson was graduated from the Albuquerque Indian School one day in spring, 1942, and volunteered that same afternoon at the Albuquerque recruiting station. He had listened regularly to a Marine Corps radio program, "To the Shores of Tripoli," and he was gung-ho about the Leathernecks. He lied to his parents, telling them that every young man had to go into military service. They reluctantly signed his enlistment papers (Thompson, 2002).

Jack Jones was 21 years old and working in a shipyard in Sausalito, CA, while waiting for his draft call. He had met some Marines in San Francisco and admired them, so he enlisted, and was sent to San Diego for boot camp. One day a drill instructor asked him the name of his tribe. Jones replied, "I'm a Navajo." He was assigned to the Code Talker School, where he knew Johnny Bernally, an instructor. They had attended the Santa Fe Indian School in 1937 (Jones, 2000).

Torturing Joe Kieyoomia

Of the 3,600 Navajos who served in World War II, about 420 became code talkers (Kawano, 1990). A Navajo, who knew *Diné* but who had not been trained in the code, could not break it. For example, consider the following two messages, both translated from *Diné* into English, the first as a Navajo untrained in the code would hear it, and the second as a trained code talker would hear it (McClain, 1994):

    1. "Ask for many big guns and tortoise fire at 123 Bear tail drop Mexican ear mouse owl victor elk 50 yards left flank ocean fish Mexican deer."

    2. "Request artillery and tank fire at 123B; Company C move 50 yards left flank of Company D."

Evidence of the crucial role of the code-within-the-code is provided by the experience of Joe Kieyoomia, a member of the New Mexico National Guard unit that was stationed in the Philippines in 1941 (see Chapter 2). He was on the Bataan Death March, and then was held for 1,240 days as a POW at Camp O'Donnell in the Philippines and later in Japan. He was tortured in order to force him to tell the Japanese the Navajo code, which he did not know. Kieyoomia believed that he was moved to Japan because his guards at Camp O'Donnell thought that he was of Japanese ancestry. "Key-oh-me" indeed sounded like a Japanese name. When interrogated, Kieyoomia insisted that he was an American Indian. Angrily, his questioners shouted "You are American Japanese! Why are you fighting against your own people?" An interpreter, appropriately named Goon, hit Kieyoomia with a club, breaking his ribs and then his wrist. Later, the Japanese made Kieyoomia listen to taped radio broadcasts. He says," . . . I couldn't believe what I was hearing. It sounded like Navajo, just not anything that made sense to me. I understood my language, but I could not figure out the code they were using. That made the interrogators very angry!" (McClain, 1994, p. 120). For instance, Kieyoomia recognized *chay-da-gahi* as "turtle," but he did not know that turtle meant "tank."

The Japanese guards removed Kieyoomia's clothes, and threw him outside. It was very cold, and his feet soon froze to the ground. When they clubbed him back inside, his feet were bleeding from being torn away from the ground. Still he could not, and would not, help the Japanese understand the radio broadcasts. The guards pounded a nail into his head (Fred Begay, 2002). Torture and daily beatings continued, and Kieyoomia believes that he was kept alive by the Japanese desire to break the code. Hearing the radio broadcasts in *Diné* gave him hope that American forces were getting close to Japan.

Kieyoomia was transferred to a POW camp 60 miles south of Nagasaki, just before this city was destroyed by the second atomic bomb, Fat Man. Shortly thereafter, when Japan surrendered, Kieyoomia was sent home in a hospital ship. While he spent four years recovering in military hospitals, the nail was removed from his head. He finally arrived back home in Shiprock, New Mexico (McClain, 1994).

The Army's Code Talkers

The U.S. Army learned about the Marines' Navajo Code Talkers from Philip Johnston, and in 1944 inquired about the feasibility of using a similar approach. Due to inter-service rivalry, the Marine brass discouraged the Army from further consideration of using Navajo Code Talkers (McClain, 1994).

In 1999, 55 years after the event, the Pentagon disclosed that 17 Comanche code talkers played a role in transmitting U.S. Army commands during the June 1944, landings in Normandy. The only survivor, Charles Chibitty, was honored by the Military Intelligence Corps Association in 1999 for his role as one of the Comanche who were recruited to serve in the Army Signal Corps. Training of the Comanche code talkers started in August 1941; they developed a special vocabulary of 250 words because their language, like *Diné*, did not contain words for military terms.

But the U.S. Marines were the only branch of the military services that used Navajo Code Talkers, and that used code talkers on such a large scale.

The growing acceptance of the code talkers in the field, and the expansion of the Marine Corps through the creation of four additional divisions, led to a need for many more code talkers. Marine Corps commanding officers requested 632 code talkers, but only 420 could be recruited and trained by the end of the war.[13] In October 1942, Philip Johnston enlisted for a two-year tour of duty with the military rank of staff sergeant.[14] He was 50 years old. Sergeant Johnson did not teach the code, but served as the school's director, and as a liaison between the Navajos and the Marine officials.

By fall 1943, the Marine Corps wanted to recruit 50 code talkers per month, but could only attract about 25. Johnston tried new means of recruiting code talkers. For instance, he contacted local draft boards and recruiting offices in New Mexico and Arizona, alerting them to the need for Navajos in the Marine Corps. Even then, the expanded demand for more Navajo Code Talkers could not be filled.

Every effort was made to keep the code talkers a secret. During their training in San Diego, the Navajos were told never to disclose their actual function, but rather to tell people that they were "radio operators," which was true. The code talkers were instructed that even if they went to Los Angeles and slept with a woman, they should not say that they were code talkers (Toledo, 1999). Later, under combat conditions in the Pacific, neither their code nor the code talkers were ever identified as "Navajo," but rather as "New Mexico" or "Arizona," as when a commanding officer would say, "Get me a New Mexico" (Little, 1999).

THE CODE TALKERS IN ACTION IN THE PACIFIC

Initially, many United States military commanders in the Pacific were skeptical of using the Navajo Code Talkers. They had not been previously informed about the code talkers, because of the top secret nature of the project. It struck many commanders as a rather hair-brained idea. Most were eventually convinced by the Navajo Code Talkers' performance under fire. Some commanders had only certain of their orders transmitted in *Diné*, while other commanders sent almost all of their orders through the Navajo Code Talkers. The first combat involving the code talkers was on Guadalcanal, where the Marine brass sent only a few messages via the Navajo Code Talkers. But it was a start, and use of the code talkers grew. Eventually even Admiral Chester Nimitz, the Commander-in-Chief in the Pacific, used the Navajo Code Talkers (M. Gorman, 1999).

Guadalcanal

Guadalcanal, a 25 x 90 mile island in the Solomon Islands chain north of Australia, marked the most southeasterly point of the Japanese advance in the Pacific. In summer, 1942, the Japanese were building an airfield on Guadalcanal, from which their bombers could destroy Allied shipping on the sea routes from the United States to Australia. Invading Guadalcanal was the first step in the three-year American island-hopping push north across the Pacific toward the Japanese homeland (Figure 1-2). The 1st Marine Division landed on the beaches of Guadalcanal on August 7, 1942, and the six-month struggle for control of the island began. When it was over, 24,000 Japanese soldiers lay dead. Some 5,600 U.S. casualties included 1,500 dead.

The battle of Guadalcanal was an important turning point in the Pacific War, proving that American Marines could push back entrenched Japanese troops. The strategic importance of Guadalcanal lay particularly in its Henderson Field, which the United States needed as an airbase for its fighters and bombers. Bulldozing and other preparation of Henderson Field began as soon as the Japanese defenders were forced from that part of the island. Guadalcanal also represented the first evidence that the Navajo Code Talkers could be an effective means of secure communication under combat conditions. At first, their commanders did not understand exactly what the code talkers were capable of doing. So they were used mainly as runners (messengers) or as Marine riflemen.

The 27 code talkers arrived on Guadalcanal in October 1942, as part of a fresh Marine unit some two months after the initial landings. They were assigned to the fighting around Henderson Field. Navy and Marine commanders transmitted certain of their orders, especially those that were "urgent" or "secret," in *Diné* (McClain, 1994). But many of the military orders on Guadalcanal were transmitted by the Navajo Code Talkers in coded English. Obviously, many of the top brass were not yet sold on the Navajo coding system. The breakthrough came with Carlson's Raiders, an elite Marine fighting force, whose officers understood the full potential of the Navajo Code Talkers. A particular advantage was speed in encoding and decoding the messages, a crucial quality in an island invasion. Soon, a second contingent of 83 code talkers arrived in the South Pacific. They were used to convey radio messages in *Diné*.

Bougainville

Bill Toledo was in the second batch of code talkers in the Pacific. After recovering from malaria that he contracted on Guadalcanal during jungle training, Toledo landed on Bougainville in early November 1943. There were high waves and his landing craft got stuck short of the beach. After wading ashore, he was strafed by Japanese Zeros. The fighting on Bougainville was particularly rough, and the jungle was swampy and mosquito-infested, even worse than on Guadalcanal (Figure 3-4).

Figure 3-4. Two Navajo Code Talkers on Bougainville in December 1943.
Corporal Henry Blake (left) and Private First Class George Kirk operate their portable radio in a clearing hacked in the jungle just behind the front lines.
Source: Salt Lake City, University of Utah, J. Willard Marriott Library, Special Collections, Marine Corps photograph.

On November 11, 1943, Toledo was asked to transmit the following message: "To all units: Japanese are booby-trapping personal equipment, installations, and bivouacs. Over." He received and relayed this message in less than 30 seconds. Then Toledo experienced a narrow escape from Japanese retaliation. "I had received the warning message and passed it along to the rear units, shut off my radio, and only moved about 10 yards when a Japanese mortar hit the exact spot from which I had just sent the message. One of the first things they teach you in the field training exercise is to send, receive, 'Roger' the message, and move!" (Toledo, 1999). This close call was the first of five that Toledo would experience during his combat in the Pacific. The Japanese had excellent tracking equipment that could pinpoint the source of radio signals. The code talkers learned not to stay on the radio a second longer than absolutely necessary.

The experienced Navajo Code Talkers taught the rookies to carry their radio in front of them for protection from enemy bullets (the TBX radio issued to most code talkers weighed about 80 pounds).[15] They should carry their rifle in the "ready" position, with their combat pack on their back, so as to be prepared if they were jumped on a jungle trail. The newly-arrived code talkers were also told never to touch anything that had belonged to the enemy, like a flag or sword or weapon, as the Japanese often attached explosive devices.[16] Even the Japanese dead were often booby-trapped (McClain, 1994).

In amphibious landings, the code talkers typically worked in pairs, with one Navajo on board a Navy ship and his partner going ashore with an advance landing party. The Marine Corps discovered that pairing up Navajos who were close friends made for the most effective communication team. A special hazard facing the code talkers was that they were often mistaken for Japanese by American troops. Both had dark hair, dark eyes, and nonwhite skin. Indeed, a number of Navajos were "captured" by U.S. soldiers. This mistaken identification was one reason why the Marines assigned bodyguards to some code talkers. The other reason was to maintain the secrecy of the code. The bodyguards were ordered to stick to their code talker like a leach, even accompanying him to the latrine (M. Gorman, 1999).

One day, Bill Toledo was startled to feel a gun muzzle in his back, and was ordered to put up his hands (Toledo, 2000). He was "captured" by a Marine, who mistook him for a Japanese infiltrator. Thereafter, a non-Navajo Marine, Richard Bonham, was assigned by their commanding officer to be Toledo's bodyguard. Toledo did not realize that he had had a bodyguard until several decades after the war, when he met his "foxhole buddy" at a Marine reunion. Toledo stated, "I was happy to be alive and have the privilege of Richard's friendship and company in the foxhole every night. We watched out for each other like good Marines should, and I always felt safe when he was around. I didn't learn until 1968 that he had been assigned to be my bodyguard, and frankly I was a little surprised when he told me" (Toledo, 1999; quoted in McClain, 1994, p. 107).

Bonham remembers when several Marines brought Toledo at gunpoint to battalion headquarters. "They were saying, 'He says he is a Marine, but he doesn't look like one to us . . . . Is he for real, or do we shoot him on the spot?' Colonel Walter Asmuth, Battalion Commander, affirmed that Bill was indeed 'for real' and then turned to me and said, 'Bonham, he is yours'" (Bonham, quoted in McClain, 1994, p. 103).[17] Bonham remembers a specific instance that convinced him of the value of the code talkers. On Bougainville, on the fourth day of the Marine invasion, a 19-word order was transmitted to his unit: "Jump off at 0600; move 50 yards left flank of C Company. Proceed 200 yards and report your position." These orders were transmitted in the old Shackle cipher in the middle of the night. It took Bonham, skilled and experienced in the Shackle code, four hours to decode the order. "What a mess! It had been poorly relayed, poorly transmitted, and I could not get the full context of the message" (Bonham, quoted in McClain, 1994, p. 105). Bonham woke up Bill Toledo and asked him for help. Toledo requested and received the order in *Diné*, and transcribed it by flashlight in a blackout tent, all in a few minutes. Before daylight, the Marine unit had its orders.

The U.S. government maintained strict security concerning the Navajo Code Talkers. The Marine Corps censored the V-mail letters written home by the code talkers. Eventually, the code talkers' family members became puzzled and apprehensive about their sons. The parents contacted school officials, who in turn contacted Philip Johnston, for news about the young Navajos. He explained to the school administrators that the Navajo Marines were code talkers, a disclosure that violated military secrecy policies. An article, "Navajo Indians at War," was published in the magazine *Arizona Highways* in June 1943. The Pentagon investigated, copies of the magazine were destroyed, and Johnston was reprimanded by military authorities (Smith, 1999). He blamed a Marine recruiting officer in Arizona for the leak (Johnston, 1944).

Saipan

The invasion of Saipan, in the Marianas, began on June 15, 1944 (Figure 3-5). The Japanese retreated several hundred yards from the shore and the Marines advanced into the previous positions the Japanese had occupied. Then a salvo of U.S. artillery shells exploded close by. The Marines radioed their new position to the artillery, and requested a halt to the friendly fire. But the next round dropped even closer. The Japanese had been imitating Marine messages in English (the Japanese could even mimic a Texas drawl or a New York accent), and so the artillery did not stop firing. Headquarters requested that Navajo Code Talkers transmit the message to cease fire, and the friendly fire stopped immediately (Watson, 1993). A few minutes later, a cloud of smoke and dust arose from the Japanese positions, as the American artillery bracketed the enemy.

Figure 3-5. These Three Code Talkers Were in the First Wave of Marines to Fight their Way Ashore in Saipan in June 1944.
Code talkers also served as infantrymen in the invasion of Saipan and other Pacific islands. Here three of the First 29 (left to right), Corporal Oscal Iithma of Gallup, New Mexico; Private First Class Jack Nez of Fort Defiance, Arizona; and Private First Class Carl Gorman, Chinle, Arizona, dig in as the Marines gain control of Saipan, an island just five miles from Tinian, which became an important air base for B-29s bombing Japan.
Source: Salt Lake City, University of Utah, J. Willard Marriott Library, Special Collections, Marine Corps photograph.

A Navajo transmitted the following order to all Marine units who had just landed on the beaches of Saipan: "*Tses-nah tlo-chin tsah ha-ih-des-ee ma-e ne-ahs-jah gah ne-tah al-tah-je-jay. Le-eh-gade do who-*

neh bihl-has-ahn" ("Be on the alert for *banzai* attacks. Dig in and report positions"). The *banzais* were suicide attacks, usually at night, with the attacking Japanese shouting "*Banzai! Banzai!*" That night, when the *banzais* came, the Marines were ready and threw them back (McClain, 1994). By providing effective, secure communication transmission, the Navajo Code Talkers proved their worth in the fighting on Saipan (Figure 3-6).

Figure 3-6. Marines of the 2nd Division, 3rd Battalion, 6th Regiment on Saipan, Resting behind the Front Lines, Just after Fighting Off a Japanese *Banzai* Attack.
  Navajo Code Talker Frank Thompson is the dark-haired Marine near the top of this photograph. He feels he was the 30th of the First 29.
  Source: Frank Thompson, Gallup, New Mexico.

Guam

Bill Toledo landed with the 3rd Marine Division on Guam on July 21, 1944. He came ashore in an amphibious landing craft, which ran up on a coral reef. His captain gave Toledo an American flag to carry onshore and to plant on the beach. It was a dangerous mission.

In a nighttime *banzai* attack, Toledo's radio and field telephone were lost. So he was ordered to carry a message as a runner from a forward position back down to headquarters on the beach. A Japanese sniper fired at Toledo as he crossed an open area (later, he learned that the sniper had picked off several Marines earlier that day). So Toledo ran in a zigzag fashion, until he fell down in the mud. A group of Marines, crouching under a bank, laughed and hooted at him, "Hey Chief, where did you play football?" (the Navajos were commonly called "Chief" by their fellow Marines). Later, Toledo noticed a rather neat bullet hole through the corner of his dungaree jacket flap (Toledo, 1999). This close call was number 2 (the first was the mortar round that dropped in his just-vacated foxhole on Bougainville).

Number 3 also occurred on Guam. Toledo walked into a field of land mines, which had not been roped off. A Marine yelled for him to freeze. Then Toledo walked backwards, carefully putting his feet back into his previous footprints.

The Navajos referred to the Japanese as *na-as-tso-si* ("mice") because of the quiet way they could steal through the jungle without detection. Their commanders told the Marines not to move after dark because of the Japanese soldiers' skills in nocturnal fighting. Often Japanese soldiers came down from the hills at night to steal food. Sometimes they even joined the Marines' chow lines (Toledo, 2000). One night Toledo was manning a machine gun with another Marine, when they heard strange noises near their position. They were about to start firing when the "Japanese soldier" squealed, and they realized it was a little pig. The fresh pork was particularly tasty the next day.

Peleliu

Peleliu is a seven-mile-square coral island located 500 miles east of the Philippines. Its conquest by the Marines protected General MacArthur's flank when he attacked the Philippines. Some 16,000 Marines landed on Peleliu, expecting to conquer the Japanese defenders in a few days. The fighting lasted for 68 days, and the Marines suffered heavy casualties.

Jack Jones was in the second wave of Marines to hit the beaches of Peleliu on September 15, 1944. Heavy Japanese fire pinned the Marines down on the beach the first day. The next morning, Jones' platoon had advanced 150 yards when a bomb exploded about 50 yards from his foxhole. The concussion knocked him down and he lost consciousness. He awoke several days later in a Navy hospital tent on Guadalcanal, unable to remember the code. Jones spent several months in military hospitals, and gradually much of the code came back to him, but he was assigned to guard duty at Puget Sound Navy Yard, near Seattle, for the rest of the war (Jones, 2000).

Iwo Jima

Iwo Jima was a particularly prized objective in the American advance north across the Pacific Ocean toward Japan. The volcanic island was only 660 nautical miles south of Japan. It was an obstacle on the main flight patterns of the Marianas-based B-29 Superfortresses to and from their Japanese targets, with swarms of Japanese Zeros rising to attack the American bombers. Also, Iwo gave Tokyo advanced warning of air raids.

Mount Sunovabitchi

Iwo Jima was defended by a dense cluster of antiaircraft guns mounted atop Mount Suribachi. Air Force pilots referred to the mountain as "Mount Sunovabitchi" (McClain, 1994, p. 157). Iwo Jima had two completed airfields and a third was under construction. Their use by B-29s would cut the American bombers' flying time from the Marianas in half (Wheeler, 1965). The Pentagon decided that Iwo Jima would have to be conquered prior to the main attack on the Japanese home islands.

The fighting for control of Iwo Jima was especially fierce, and its conquest became the best-known battle of World War II. Led by General Tadamichi Kuribayashi, a talented military strategist, the Japanese defense was formidable. The island was only two and one-half by 5 miles in size, and was composed of volcanic rock and sand. When they landed, the beaches were steeply sloped and composed of loose volcanic sand. The Marines took a step forward and slipped right back. Crawling was the only effective way to move forward. Bill Toledo recalls that when he dug a three-foot deep foxhole on Iwo Jima, the ground was so hot from volcanic activity that he had to line it with his blanket (Toledo, 1999). A nasty sulfuric smell hung over the island; indeed Iwo Jima means "sulfur island" in Japanese.

Iwo Jima was subjected to daily bombing for six months prior to the Marine landing on February 19, 1945, and an intensive Naval bombardment from battleships and cruisers immediately preceded the invasion. But the Japanese had dug 16 miles of deep tunnels into the volcanic rock, connecting 5,000 pillboxes and fortified caves. Once the bombing and shelling stopped, the defenders promptly resurfaced. The Naval bombardment proved inadequate, with only 200 of the 915 main defensive installations silenced (Ross, 1985). The Japanese emplacements were carefully designed so as to provide crosscutting fields of fire, so that attack from any angle was equally lethal.

General Kuribayashi, the shrewd Japanese commander, allowed the first several waves, about 6,000 Marines, to land on the beaches. Then the Japanese shelling began, directed from atop Mount Suribachi, the highest point in the island at 560 feet. Artillery, mortars, and machine guns let loose from pillboxes, caves, and trenches. Japanese artillery that was dug into the mountain attacked landing ships with

U.S. reinforcements. The first objective for the Marines was to capture Suribachi. The fighting consisted of rooting the Japanese defenders out of their underground bunkers and tunnels. Progress was often measured only in 100 to 200 yards gained per day, with each yard achieved at a high cost in human life.

The news that Mount Suribachi had been captured, transmitted in *Diné* (as described at the top of the present chapter), was a very welcome event for the Marines. It meant the end of murderous fire by Japanese artillery, machine guns, and snipers that had pinned the Marines on the beaches. Instead, Marine gunners could now accurately rain fire down on the Japanese defenders. A photograph of five Americans raising the U.S. flag atop Mount Suribachi became the classic image of World War II. It was taken by Joe Rosenthal, an Associated Press photographer, and is described as "a masterpiece of instantaneous composition and lighting that captured the mood of the unfolding drama on Iwo Jima" (Ross, 1985, p. 102). Rosenthal was awarded the 1945 Pulitzer Prize for the photograph, and it is reproduced as a famous bronze statue in Arlington National Cemetery, across the Potomac River from Washington, D.C.

A B-29 named *Dinah Might* made an emergency landing on Iwo Jima on March 4, 1945, while returning from a raid on Japan. This event occurred only two weeks after the initial landing on the beaches, while Marines were still killing Japanese defenders at the other end of the island. Eventually, more than 2,000 crippled B-29s made emergency landings on Iwo, preserving the lives of 27,000 crewmen (Cave, 1997).

Rooting Out the Japanese

Once Suribachi was captured, the tough task of overcoming the dug-in Japanese forces from the remainder of the island began. First the Americans would call in a massive Naval bombardment and air strikes to soften up a Japanese defensive position. Then it was up to the Marines to attack on the ground, with rifles, grenades, satchel charges, and flamethrowers. At sunset, the Marines fell back to a defensive line. During the night, the Japanese would reinforce their positions through underground tunnels. Some Japanese soldiers were in "spider traps," a tunnel ending on the surface with a hinged metal lid. A Japanese soldier could fire at the advancing Marines, disappear, and later emerge to attack the Americans from the rear. With morning would come a repeat of the previous day, with bombardment of the next Japanese position. Then the Marines would slug it out on the ground again.

Iwo represented the fiercest resistance that the American forces had yet faced in the Pacific War. General Kuribayashi prohibited his troops from making senseless *banzai* charges; instead they concentrated on defending their dug-in positions. Among the thousands of American deaths on Iwo were three Navajo Code Talkers. Overall, the U.S. casualty rate on Iwo Jima was 33 percent, but it was 60 percent for combat units (Ross, 1985). These sobering figures would haunt Pentagon military planners, who were beginning to lay out the scenario for the invasion of the Japanese mainland. Such fighting would be costly, very costly.

Proving the Value of the Code Talkers

Iwo Jima was a high point in proving the value of the Navajo Code Talkers. Sam Billison remembers being one of the eight code talkers on the command ship with a Navy admiral and the Marine generals commanding the three divisions that were going ashore. One of the Marine divisions was led by Holland M. (Howlin' Mad) Smith, a legendary character. Iwo was the biggest Marine landing to date in the Pacific War, and Billison and his fellow Navajos were drowning in a flood of messages. Just as Billison would doze off from fatigue, someone would shout, "Hey Chief, here's another message!" Speed was of the essence. The code talkers could process a message in two minutes that took the Navy code experts two hours to decode. Finally, on Day 3, Billison went ashore. He actually felt relieved to escape the constant pressure of the command ship (Billison, 1999).

Iwo was such a small island that there was no rear echelon. "The ocean was the rear echelon" (Billison, 1999). His platoon leader, a lieutenant, was killed. Along with code talker Paul Blatchford and an Anglo sergeant, Billison was considered for field promotion to second lieutenant. The Anglo sergeant got the job, presumably because Billison and Blatchford were needed as code talkers (Billison, 1999).[18]

Bill Toledo had his fourth close call while on a transport ship just off Iwo Jima, where his 3rd Marine Division was held as a floating reserve while the 4th and 5th Marine Divisions were fighting on shore. One day in the late afternoon Toledo came up on deck after eating chow. While standing in the shade of a .50 caliber antiaircraft turret, Toledo spied a tiny speck on the horizon. It was closing fast. He yelled to a sailor manning the machine gun, who looked at the speck with his binoculars, and then sounded an alarm to the entire convoy. The Japanese plane flew just above the waves, and released a torpedo which headed directly for Toledo's transport. It missed by a few feet, and hit another ship nearby. Then the torpedo plane was downed by American antiaircraft fire.

Merril Sandoval, a code talker with the 5th Marine Division, recalls how the Japanese on Iwo Jima attempted to interfere with the Navajo radio transmissions between ship and shore. "The Japanese would try to jam our radio all the time. They would shout, sing, or bang pots in order to disrupt our rhythm, but they never succeeded. Our message went through because we knew each other's voices and the code so well that we could do it without any repeat or mistakes" (quoted in McClain, 1994, p. 175). When the Japanese were interfering with their transmission, the code talkers would yell "Flip," and both sender and receiver would change quickly to another, predetermined channel.

Having Coffee with Uncle Frank

Bill Toledo recalls: "One of the guys in my unit came over to my foxhole and asked me if I had a cousin or uncle because he was on the radio asking for me. Frank Toledo was my uncle, I told him, and he said to get over to him and find out what he needed." Bill Toledo was with the 3rd Marine Division, and his uncle was a code talker with the 5th Marine Division, stationed a half-mile away on the other side of an airfield. "I made my way over to Frank's foxhole and he fixed me a cup of [instant] coffee. Actually, they were heat tablets, and we just started catching up on news from home, telling stories about what we had seen. He knew Ira Hayes [a Pima Indian from Arizona who had helped raise the flag atop Mount Suribachi], and he told me about what happened the day the flag was raised" (quoted in McClain, 1994, pp. 190-191). Bill Toledo and his uncle snuggled down in the foxhole and drank coffee, while bullets zinged overhead. The war went on around them while they talked about their family members back in Torreon, New Mexico (Toledo, 1999). Then Bill Toledo returned to his unit. He would not see his Uncle Frank again until after the war.

The Navajo have a well-developed sense of humor, and the code talkers today enjoy telling war stories. One of the authors invited Bill Toledo to tell about his experiences as a code talker to a doctoral seminar in intercultural communication at the University of New Mexico. Toledo described a B-29 bomber flying over Iwo Jima en route from Guam to bomb Japan. The plane's crew picked up Navajo code talk on the military radio band. A Navajo crew member on the bomber, hearing the code for "bomb" ("egg" in *Diné*) and for "pig" (*bi-so-dih* for the letter "p"), said on the plane's intercom, "Captain, those are my people down there! I think they are preparing breakfast."

By 1945, the Navajo code as taught in San Diego had changed enough that the Navajos fighting on the Pacific islands were out-of-date. So the Marine Corps transported five code talkers from each Marine division back to Hawaii for three weeks of refresher training. These trainees then returned to their units in order to retrain the other code talkers (Paul, 1973). Here we see that the code as a living, ever-changing system, flexibly adapted to new situations. For instance, the original code did not contain a word for "rocket," which was developed late in the war. The *Diné* code word became "whistling bullet."

When the code talkers were given a period of rest and relaxation, they often packed their combat fatigues, unwashed, and sent them home. Their relatives then used the clothing in protection ceremonies conducted by Navajo religious leaders (McClain, 1994). Many of the Navajo carried a small buckskin pouch of sacred corn pollen. At dawn, they placed a small amount on their tongue, atop their head, and made an offering to the sun in the east (McClain, 1994). They believed that this ritual helped give them clear thought and a safe path.

Okinawa

The invasion of Okinawa by the 1st, 2nd, and 6th Marine Divisions, also four Army divisions, took place on Easter Sunday, April 1, 1945. Some 110,000 Japanese troops defended Okinawa to the death, and U.S. casualties were high: 31,000 wounded and 7,200 dead. The Pentagon promptly raised the number of American casualties expected in the forthcoming invasion of Japan.

Most World War II correspondents stayed well back from the front lines, participating in news briefings by commanding generals, and writing their accounts of the fighting from a safe distance. Not Ernie Pyle. He insisted on covering the war up close, taking chances with his life, and living in fear. Pyle, shortly before his death on April 18, 1945, interviewed two Navajo Code Talkers with the 1st Marine Division (Figure 3-7). One was Alex Williams, who had landed with Pyle on Okinawa in the seventh wave. They moved inland about a quarter mile and dug foxholes. Pyle asked, "Where are you from?" and told Williams that he was from Albuquerque. Williams (1971) related to Pyle how the code talkers had held a ceremony on Pavuvu, in the Russell Islands, just prior to the invasion of Okinawa, in order to weaken the Japanese defenders (Paul, 1973). The six Marines did a war dance (*Yeibichai*) in which they stabbed photographs of Hitler and Tojo (King, 1971). They ended the ceremony by singing the Marine Corps hymn in *Diné*.[19] Then Pyle told Williams goodbye, because he was going to land with the Marines on the island of Ie Shima.

Figure 3-7. Ernie Pyle, the Famous War Correspondent, at Home in Albuquerque.
Pyle lived with his wife, whom he called "that girl" in his daily newspaper columns, in this small house at 900 Girard Boulevard, in Albuquerque. Due to his frontline reporting from North Africa and Europe, Pyle became *the* war correspondent of World War II. He was killed by a Japanese sniper in the invasion of Okinawa in 1945, shortly before the end of the war.
Source: New Mexico Palace of the Governors, Santa Fe, New Mexico, photograph by Ferenz Fedor.

Pyle was killed by a Japanese sniper on Ie Shima, a small island three miles from Okinawa that was valued because it had three long runways which could accommodate American heavy bombers. Capturing Ic Shima was not easy, costing 1,155 Americans killed, wounded, or missing out of the 6,100 who were engaged. The U.S.

troops placed a marker on Ie Shima. It said "At this spot the 77th infantry division lost a buddy Ernie Pyle, 18 April 1945." It is still there.

The general pattern for the disposition of the Marine divisions in the Pacific War was for each period of heavy fighting (the invasion of an island) to be followed by time to regroup, train replacements, and relax on Maui in the Hawaiian Islands, or in some other rest area. Following their heavy combat on Iwo Jima, the three Marine divisions pulled back to Maui in April 1945. There they were trained for the first time in street fighting. They knew what that meant: Their next assignment would be the invasion of Japan (Little, 1999).

One night in August 1945, a Marine dressed in just his underwear ran through the barracks area on Maui, shouting that the war was over. Doubtful, some Marines got partly dressed and went to the radio shack, where the news was confirmed. Then the yelling and celebration really began (Little, 1999).

GOING HOME

Bill Toledo had earned enough points for discharge by late spring, 1945, after the fighting for Iwo Jima. In May, he packed his duffel bag and was shipped to San Diego. Toledo received a 30-day furlough, and left immediately on the Superchief train to Gallup, and then on to Albuquerque. He took a bus to Bernalillo, and hitchhiked to San Isidro. There he spent all day waiting for a ride. The next morning, Toledo caught a bus to Cuba, and then got another ride to a small post office near his home. He waited a few hours until his aunt and uncle-in-law came to pick up their mail. Then he jumped out from behind a door, surprising his family members. Toledo was home at last, after three years in the Pacific. His family did not ask him questions about his wartime experiences, which was convenient, given that he was sworn to secrecy. Jokingly, the next morning his aunt told him: "You can let the sheep out of the corral, where you left them last night" (Toledo, 1999). Indeed, Toledo went back to herding sheep after his October 1945, discharge from the Marines.

With the help of the GI Bill, he completed his high school diploma, and then two years of college. Toledo got married and settled down in Laguna Pueblo, New Mexico (his late wife was a Lagunan), where he lives today in a comfortable house with his daughter and her children. Toledo worked for uranium mining and milling companies near Grants for 40 years until he retired, about the time that the uranium industry went into decline with the end of the Cold War (Toledo, 1999). Today, he actively participates in the Code Talkers Association, has a large garden, and gives occasional talks about his wartime experiences. At age 80 in 2002, Bill Toledo's short, wiry frame still looked quite fit.

Nightmares

Like many code talkers, Bill Toledo had bad dreams after the war. In a repetitive nightmare, Toledo saw Japanese soldiers coming down a mountain slope toward him (he actually had seen them through his binoculars when he was fighting on Guam). Then the enemy would charge his position, shouting "*Banzai!*" and he would wake up screaming. Finally, in 1970, Toledo had a Blessing Way ceremony performed by a traditional Navajo medicine man, a *Yataalii*. Toledo was dressed in clean clothes and a Navajo necklace, belt, and bracelets. His relatives and close friends attended the three-day ceremony. Thereafter he slept more soundly. Today, the bad dream still returns occasionally, but he no longer wakes up screaming (Toledo, 1999).

Before Jimmy Begay (1999) went off to the San Diego Marine Corps Recruit Depot in November 1942, his grandfather, a Navajo medicine man, conducted a religious ceremony to protect him. Begay describes it as being like a protective shield. Later, in combat on Guadalcanal, a Marine with a flame thrower was shot. When the Marine fell, his flamethrower went off and burned the backs of Begay's legs. He was hospitalized for the next 18 months, until his discharge in 1945. Like many other code talkers, Begay had nightmares when he returned to living on the Big Res. His grandfather conducted an Enemy Way Ceremony, in which he made a sand painting on the floor of Begay's hogan. The prayers and singing continued all night. At sunrise, Begay threw up, to cleanse himself. His grandfather sprinkled sacred corn pollen on Begay's head and used an eagle feather to sprinkle him with water and herbs. Thereafter, he felt considerable relief, although he still has an occasional bad dream.

A special problem for the code talkers was that Navajos feel particularly uncomfortable around dead bodies. They believe that the *chindi,* the evil spirits of the dead, remain in the area when someone dies. So when Navajo Marines were assigned to burial details, it was very difficult for them to handle the bodies. The memories of fallen buddies is one reason why many code talkers today say they do not want to return to visit the battlefields of Guadalcanal, Saipan, Iwo, and Okinawa. Dean Wilson (1971) recalled one morning on Tarawa when he was assigned to burial detail. He helped gather 500 bodies of fallen comrades, and then bury them in a huge trench. It was extremely unpleasant, but he was ordered to do it.

Cozy Stanley Brown (1977), one of the First 29, experienced a great deal of combat, often involving dead bodies. In December 1943, Brown arrived in New Guinea where he encountered the body of Kee Bahe, his in-law and an Army soldier. Shortly thereafter, Brown's buddy Rod Morgan was killed when a Zero dropped a "daisy cutter" bomb near him. In 1944, when Brown arrived on Peleliu, he looked up his cousin Roy Begay, only to find him in a body bag. Brown carried Begay's personal effects home to his mother. These several encounters with the dead had a profound impact on Brown.

His worst combat experiences were killing Japanese soldiers with his machine gun as they charged his position. On Cape Glouster in the New Britain Islands, the Japanese overran the Marines' frontline in a *banzai* charge. Brown's buddy was grappling with two Japanese soldiers. Brown grabbed one of them by the hair: "I used a knife to cut his head off . . . . The Squaw Dance was performed on me for the enemy scalp that I brought home" (Brown, 1977, p. 59). These bloody experiences caused Cozy Brown severe mental problems. In late 1944, Brown came back to the Big Res on a 35-day furlough. An all-night Blessing Way chant was performed for him, as well as a Squaw Dance. "From there, my mind began to function well again" (Brown, 1977, p. 60).

Impacts

Service in the U.S. Marine Corps was a liberating experience for the code talkers; it took them out of the confined life on the remote Navajo Reservation, and showed them the world. Sometimes they learned that the world was not a pretty place. Keith Little encountered racial prejudice when he was in boot camp in San Diego in 1943. His training platoon included many Texans, one of whom asked Little if he were a "nigger-lover." Little was so surprised by this query that he could not answer. The Texan said: "Aha, so you *are* a nigger-lover!" A drill instructor overheard this exchange and threatened the Texas Marine with a court martial if he continued to incite prejudice. The DI made it clear that the U.S. Marine Corps did not tolerate such racial intolerance. This incidence deeply impressed Keith Little (1999). The Marine Corps was unlike the BIA schools in which all Navajos were made to feel inferior.

The Navajo Code Talkers thought it was bizarre to be addressed as "Chief" by their fellow Marines. This title conjured images of B movies, and of the Lone Ranger and Tonto. When Fred Billey (2000) was called "Chief" on Saipan, he jokingly replied: "If I were the Chief, we wouldn't be *here!*"[20] The code talkers began to understand that the "Chief" title was not an expression of racial hostility. In fact, they were treated with growing respect by other Marines. In the Pacific island battles, many Marines observed the code talkers performing a valuable role as secure communication specialists. Many Marines, however, did not understand that the code talkers in their midst were sending and receiving messages in *Diné*. They perceived them as just ordinary radio communication operators.

During the war, the Navajos experienced equality for the first time. When they returned to civilian life, they expected to be treated by the *bilagaana* as equals, and, gradually, over many years, they were.

After the war, Dean Wilson (known as William D. "Bill" Yazzie in the Marine Corps), one of the First 29, returned to a boarding school to finish high school. He was told by school authorities that he could not speak *Diné*! In protest, he quit school, and rejoined the Marines. Later, he became a judge in the Navajo tribal court system. The Navajos were finally able to end the Bureau of Indian Affairs' boarding schools in 1974. In recent years, emphasis has been placed in elementary schools on teaching in both *Diné* and in English, so that the Navajo tongue is continued into future generations. The Navajo Nation has its own legislature, courts, tribal police, and economic development activities. Many World War II veterans rose to leadership positions in their tribe, and one code talker, Peter McDonald, became President of the Navajo Nation. Another former code talker, John Pinto, served in the New Mexico state legislature for many years.

Frank Carl Todecheenie (quoted in Kawano, 1990, p. 89) stated: "I remember my visit to the Great Wall of China; I thought at the time, 'I can't believe I'm here'." Code talker Guy Claus Chee (1999) said: "The Marines taught us manhood." Many code talkers grew up fast in the Marine Corps. Albert Smith was only 15 years old when he entered the Corps, so in 1945 when he was discharged, he was still only 18! But he felt that he was much older in terms of life experiences.

Fred Billey was stationed in Nagasaki for a month after the war ended. He and his fellow Marines walked over Ground Zero, oblivious to their exposure to radiation. "No one told us about radioactivity," says Billey (2000). After his discharge in 1946, Billey earned his BA and MA degrees at the University of New Mexico, and worked as a teacher, counselor, and school principal for 40 years.

Many social changes began to occur in Navajo society after World War II. Some changes were triggered by the wartime experiences of the code talkers and other returned servicemen. For example, many Navajo veterans were not willing to go back to sheep farming. Improved roads (the only paved road on the Navajo Reservation prior to 1941 was Route 666 between Gallup and Shiprock) and vehicle ownership made it possible to live in a hogan on the Res and commute daily to an urban job. Many Navajos migrated to cities, especially Los Angeles, in the years following the war. Further, some returned servicemen married outside of the Navajo people, such as to Pueblo Indians, Hopis, or Anglos. When a group of the code talkers visited Saipan and Guam a few years ago,[21] they were surprised to encounter several Navajos who had married local women and settled down on the Pacific islands. The high point of the code talkers' visit to the South Pacific (the 50th anniversary of the end of World War II) was meeting Paul Tibbets, the pilot of the *Enola Gay* (Begay, 1999).

Some code talkers had drinking problems when they returned to a bleak future after the war. Unemployment rates were high on the Reservation. One code talker, in great pain from his World War II wounds, committed suicide. Most of the code talkers got jobs, raised families, got ahead. Jimmy Begay worked as a logger, and eventually built up his own business, selling and servicing chainsaws. He is also "a little bit of a medicine man" (Begay, 1999). Keith Little made a career in logging. Sam Billison earned a doctorate in education at Arizona State University, and pursued a career as a school administrator. Albert Smith was a teacher and adult educator. Carl Gorman worked for the Navajo tribal government, taught at the University of California at Davis, and became a noted painter. So the Marine Corps' experience, and the GI Bill, gave these individuals a boost in occupational and social status.

ACHIEVEMENTS AND RECOGNITION

The Navajo Code Talkers stormed ashore in every Marine assault in the Pacific War from 1942 to 1945: Guadalcanal, Bougainville, Rabaul, Saipan, Tinian, Guam, Peleliu, Iwo Jima and Okinawa. The Navajo Code Talkers as a cryptographic system fit naturally and easily with the Marine-based, island-hopping strategy of the Pacific War. Unlike the more landlocked fighting in Europe, the Pacific war was characterized by fluid movement over vast distances of water and by jungle fighting. Secure lines of fast, but efficient military communication, provided by the Navajo Code Talkers, were essential for victory. The distinctive nature of combat in the Pacific explains, in part, why Navajo Code Talkers were used there but not in Europe.

Commanding officers in the Pacific wrote official memoranda in which they praised the Navajos as fighting men and for their contributions to secret communication. For example, Major Howard Conner, the Signal Officer of the 5th Marine Division in Iwo Jima, stated: "During the first 48 hours, while we were landing and consolidating our shore positions, I had six Navajo radio networks operating around the clock. In that period alone, they sent and received more than 800 messages without an error." Connor concluded that "Were it not for the Navajos, the Marines would never have taken Iwo Jima" (quoted in Greenberg & Greenberg, 1996, p. 186). Philip Johnston, who originally proposed the idea of the Navajo Code Talkers, said: "The Marine Corps just thought it was a miracle. They were more than delighted with it" (Johnston, 1970).

The Navajo Code Talkers were an important secret weapon for the United States, contributing directly to the eventual American victory. When the Navajos were discharged to return to the Big Res, they were required to take an oath of secrecy about their role in the Pacific War (Little, 1999). Albert Smith (1999) was told, when he was discharged: "Leave the War behind you." The Pentagon classified their contribution as Top Secret.

After 23 years, in 1968, the Pentagon acknowledged the existence of the code talkers, and declassified the code. At the reunion of the 4th Marine Division in Chicago in 1969, the code talkers were honored with a special medal by their fellow Marines (McClain, 1994, p. 230). Each bronze medallion was about three inches in diameter and was suspended around the neck by a rawhide thong with red, white, and blue beads. One side of the medallion shows the Mount Suribachi flag-raising, with Ira Hayes on horseback. The other side is the logo of the 4th Marine Division (Paul, 1973). At the convention, the ever-irascible Philip Johnston disclosed that he had "liberated" a copy of the official documents concerning the code talkers, when he was released from the Marine Corps in 1944. This act was a strict breach of military security. He donated these materials to the code talkers, and they are now available in the Philip Johnston Collection at the Museum of Northern Arizona, Flagstaff, a lasting testimony to Johnston's devilish nature.

Following the 1969 convention, the Navajo Code Talkers Association was formed. The first code talkers' reunion was held in July 1971 at Window Rock, with 60 code talkers in attendance (Greenberg & Greenberg, 1996, p. 159). A code talking demonstration was provided, using Marine Corps radios. The code talkers ate C-rations for lunch. The Navajo Code Talkers Association has continued as a strong organization to this day. Its functions are largely ceremonial and social. The aging code talkers look forward to telling their "war stories" at the monthly gatherings in Gallup, NM. Each year, the number of code talkers grows ever fewer. In 2002, only some 100 of the 420 code talkers were left, including only five of the First 29.

In 1973, the Navajo Code Talkers Association designed a logo, flag, and a dress uniform consisting of a red cap, gold velveteen shirt, and khaki trousers (McClain, 1994). The code talkers then began to march in parades and to make other public appearances. A memorial was erected in their honor at Window Rock, Arizona, headquarters of the Navajo Nation, in 1995. Belatedly, the code talkers received kudos for their contributions to World War II. President Ronald Reagan designated April 14, 1982, as National Code Talkers Day.

Lack of Public Understanding

After the war, Keith Little, the logger, eventually became President of the National Inter-Tribal Timber Council, a responsibility that often took him to Washington, D.C. On one such trip, Little visited the Pentagon in order to observe the photographs, plaques, and exhibits commemorating American military accomplishments. Little was incensed to observe that almost no credit was given to American Indians, and the Navajo Code Talkers were not even mentioned (Little, 1999).

The Navajos had noticed that very few of their number received the Congressional Medal of Honor, perhaps, they reasoned, because during the war their contribution to victory was secret. A few code talkers received Purple Hearts for being wounded in action. Nevertheless, it bothered the code talkers in the 1970s and the 1980s that their role in World War II went largely unrecognized. Finally, in 2001, President George W. Bush belatedly awarded a special gold Congressional Medal to each of the First 29 and heirs in Washington, D.C., and a special silver Congressional Medal to all other code talkers (Figure 3-8).

The code talkers feel that the public is uninformed, or at least poorly informed, about the contributions made by the Navajo cryptographers to victory in World War II. Understandably, the code talkers are touchy about mistaken notions that have been promulgated by the media. For example, a pulp novel, *The Code Talkers*, concerns a Native American Rambo named "Johnny Redhawk," who leaves the Navajo Res to become America's secret weapon in the Pacific. A song, "Code Talkers," sung by Vincent Craig, son of code talker Bob Craig, received relatively little attention.

In 2000, Hasebro, the huge toy company, announced a "Navajo G.I. Joe" as the newest of 22 classic G.I. Joe figures (which included a female helicopter pilot, Japanese American soldiers, and President John F. Kennedy as a PT boat commander). If one lifts Navajo G.I. Joe's arm, he says seven *Diné* phrases, each followed by an English translation: "Request air support," "Attack by machine gun," etc. Sam Billison, President of the Navajo Code Talkers Association, provided the phrases and the voice for the foot-high toy. Hasebro donated $5,000 to the Association, and gave a Navajo G.I. Joe to each of the surviving code talkers in 2000.

Figure 3-8. Four of the Five Surviving Members of the First 29 Code Talkers, Who Received Gold Congressional Medals in Washington, D.C., in 2001.

This photograph was taken by Michael Anaya-Gorman, grandson of code talker Carl Gorman, with his grandfather's Leica camera. Shown here (left to right) are Allen Dale June, Chester Nez, Lloyd Oliver, John Brown, Jr., and a uniformed U.S. Marine. Joe Palmer, the fifth surviving member of the First 29, could not attend the ceremony due to poor health. The U.S. government belatedly awarded a special Congressional Medal to each of the 420 Navajo Code Talkers or their survivors.

Source: Michael Anaya-Gorman, Gallup, New Mexico.

Several documentary films have been made about the Navajo Code Talkers. Then, in 2000, two Hollywood films about them were announced. "Darkwind" by Red Horse Productions and backed by Gayle Heard involved the code talkers as consultants in reviewing the script. The other film, "Windtalkers," a $100 million action/drama by MGM, starred actor Nicholas Cage playing a code talker's ("Carl Yahzee") bodyguard in the battle for Saipan (this John Woo-directed movie was filmed in Hawaii). Code talker Albert Smith served as a language consultant for the film, and attempted to prevent inauthenticities in the production (such as by explaining that Japanese *Banzai* charges only took place at night). Smith's suggestions were rebuffed, with the explanation that "This is Hollywood" (Smith, 2002). "Windtalkers" was released in June 2002, and became a modest hit.

Attitudes toward the Japanese

Do the Navajo Code Talkers continue to hate the Japanese? The Navajos strongly value harmony, living in peace with nature and with other humans. Japanese culture also emphasizes *wa* (harmony). So in the years since 1945, Japanese and Navajos have grown to understand each other in a genuine way.

Back in the mid-1970s, Carl Gorman picked up a young Japanese photographer, Kenji Kawano, as he walked along an Arizona road. Out of this chance encounter grew a strong friendship. Gorman learned that Kawano's father, Yukio Kawano, had been trained in the Japanese Navy to be a "suicide torpedo" (a *kamikaze* one-man submarine operator). Soon the young photographer was accompanying Gorman to Navajo traditional ceremonies and to meetings of the Navajo Code Talkers Association. Kawano became the code talkers' official photographer, publishing a 1990 book, *Warriors: The Navajo Code Talkers*. Kawano married a Navajo, and became a U.S. citizen, with Gorman sponsoring his citizenship application (M. Gorman, 1995). Kawano's *Warriors* book contains photos of some 70 code talkers. They universally like him, and call him by his first name.

Another telling experience about Navajo/Japanese relationships involved Bill Toledo. His daughter, a school teacher, was selected to travel to Japan for three weeks in 1993, in order to describe Native American cultures to Japanese school children. She took Navajo rugs and pottery, and a miniature hogan. Toledo was invited to accompany his daughter to Tokyo, but was apprehensive about whether he would be welcome (as a former U.S. Marine and code talker). Eventually, he did accompany his daughter to Japan. The presentations to Japanese school children were a big success. Toledo was able to visit Hiroshima, which meant a great deal to him. The Japanese were welcoming and gracious, and quite frank in talking with him about World War II. What really touched Bill Toledo's heart was a little Japanese girl who asked: "May I call you 'Grandfather'?" (Toledo, 1999).

❖ ❖ ❖

So this is the story of 420 Navajo Code Talkers who were proud to call themselves *Washindon be Akalh B-kosi-lai*, or, as the Japanese could never understand, "the United States Marines" (Thomas, 1998). Their encryption system may have been the only truly unbreakable code in military history. The code talkers' contribution to winning control of the Pacific islands allowed U.S. planes to bomb Japanese cities, leading to Japan's surrender.

4

THE JAPANESE RELOCATION/INTERNMENT CAMPS

"I am interned at Santa Fe. Rights and freedom are restricted, so I am having an awful time. All the Caucasian officials in here are big and seem strong. But they are good for nothing. They are useless. Also the censors in here are all damn fools . . . .We are the people of great Imperial Japan, from the beginning to the end, we are all faithful to our nation."

—(Letter from Henry Hideo in the Santa Fe Internment Camp, dated August 10, 1945, to Sashima Itow. This section of the letter was deleted by a Camp censor, and Hideo was sentenced to 20 days in the stockade for writing it.)

World War II was fought in order to save the world from Adolph Hitler's concentration camps, ruthless Gestapo, and the Nazis' inhuman treatment of conquered people, as well as from Japanese aggression. How paradoxical that in fighting to prevent such barbaric behavior, the United States itself imprisoned 120,000 Japanese-Americans,[1] two-thirds of them U.S. citizens, in "concentration" camps during the war.

This unfortunate chapter in American history, when viewed from today, seems unbelievable. But in 1942, during the months immediately after Pearl Harbor, there was widespread panic in the U.S. about possible attacks on the West Coast. The disaster at Pearl Harbor was blamed by many Americans as due to espionage by Japanese Americans, rather than on the lack of preparedness by American military forces. Actually the U.S. government knew that Japanese Americans were not a serious threat. "Not a single documented act of espionage, sabotage, or fifth column activity was committed by an American citizen of Japanese ancestry or by a resident Japanese alien on the West Coast" (Commission on Wartime Relocation and Internment of Civilians, 1982, p. 3).

Removal of all Japanese Americans from the West Coast struck some observers as not only illegal, a violation of their Constitutional rights, but also as a futile waste of national resources in a time of great scarcity. Perhaps the most telling comment came from Norman Thomas, the Socialist Party crusader. Thomas said that putting Japanese Americans in relocation camps was "a good deal like burning down Chicago to get rid of gangsters" (Weglyn, 1976, p. 111). Nevertheless, very few Americans spoke out at the time against the West Coast deportation. The prevailing mood, especially in California, was one of seething racial prejudice against the Japanese Americans. A windshield sticker on a pickup truck stated, "Open season on Japs" (Spicer & others, 1946, p. 7).

THE GOVERNMENT DECISION ON RELOCATION

The White House decision about relocation represents several paradoxes. For example, why were Japanese Americans relocated while German and Italian aliens[2] were left relatively free? Further, why were the 160,000 Japanese Americans living in Hawaii (40 percent of the Islands' population), who was much closer to the Pacific War, not relocated in camps? The U.S. Army, which in 1942 insisted on relocation of Japanese Americans from the West Coast, a year later sought to recruit volunteers from the relocation camps for combat duty. They hoped to attract an entire division of Japanese American soldiers, some 15,000 men.

Immediately after the Japanese attack on Pearl Harbor, President Franklin Delano Roosevelt told the American people: "We will not under any threat, or in face of any danger, surrender the guarantees of liberty our forefathers framed for us in the Bill of Rights" (Weglyn, 1976, pp. 69-70). But during the early months of 1942, a policy conflict arose among Roosevelt's Cabinet officials as to what came to be called the "Japanese problem." On one side of this struggle was the U.S. Department of War (presently the U.S. Department of Defense), led by Secretary Henry Stimson, and the U.S. Department of the Navy, led by Secretary Frank Knox. Opposed was the U.S. Department of Justice, headed by Attorney General Francis Biddle, who was concerned about the violation of individuals' Constitutional rights. Eventually, Roosevelt deferred to Stimson and the war Department, and on February 19, 1942, signed Executive Order 9066. The result was the West Coast deportation of all Japanese Americans.

The Executive Order was drafted by a 35-year-old Stanford University law school graduate, Major Karl R. Bendetsen, who was a Washington staff member in the Aliens Division of the U.S. Army's Provost Marshall (essentially the Army's police force). Bendetsen created the formula for removing Japanese Americans from the West Coast: The Presidential executive order authorized the Secretary of War to designate military areas from which certain persons could be excluded as a military necessity. The western half of California, Oregon, Washington, and the southern half of Arizona were promptly designated as Military Area 1 (Figure 4-1), commanded by Lieutenant General John L. De Witt. Bendetsen was promoted to Lieutenant Colonel and, ten days later, to full Colonel and placed in charge of implementing the Executive Order as Director of the Wartime Civil Control Administration (WCCA), a new military agency that was established to implement the President's decision. Public Law 503 was then passed by Congress and signed into law by the President on March 21, 1942, which made it a federal offense to violate any order issued by the commander of a military area.

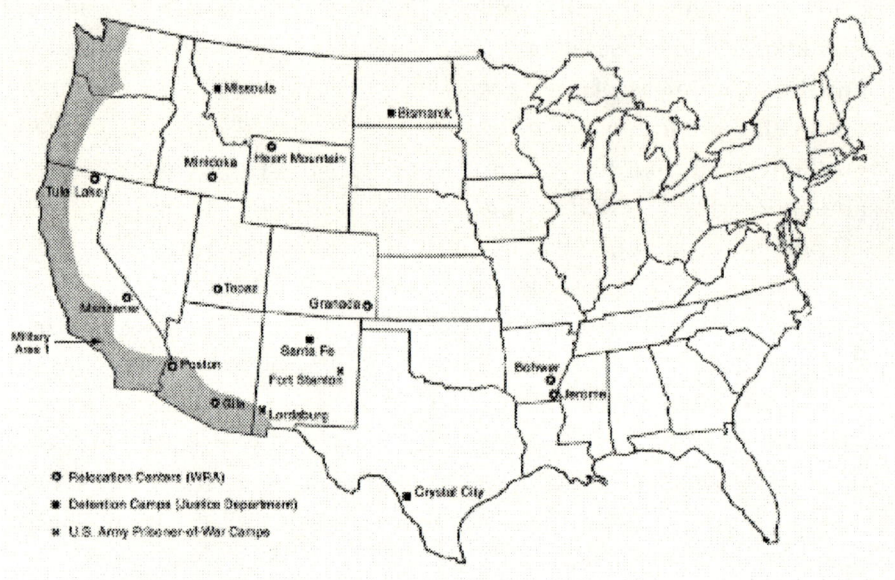

Figure 4-1. Location of the Ten WRA Relocation Camps and the Four U.S. Department of Justice Internment Camps.

Japanese Americans were uprooted from their homes in Military Area 1 on the West Coast (where almost all Japanese Americans lived) in early 1942, gathered in 16 assembly centers, and relocated to ten WRA camps. In addition, on or soon after December 7, 1941, some 7,000 Japanese-born *Issei* who were classified as dangerous enemy aliens, were seized by the prisoner-of-war camps, at Fort Stanton, New Mexico, and at Lordsburg, New Mexico, in which certain of the *Issei* were interned, separate from the German and Italian POWs. All of the 14 relocation/internment camps were located in bleak surroundings with unpleasant climates.

The relocation process got underway with the Army's WCCA in charge. When the Japanese Americans reported to WCCA centers, in response to orders posted in the areas where they lived, they came under the control of soldiers with rifles and bayonets. Sixteen assembly centers were established to which all West Coast Japanese Americans were transferred.[3] They were allowed only what they could carry, typically a single suitcase. Many of these temporary detention compounds were in California, as 80 percent of Japanese Americans on the West Coast lived in that state. The largest of the 16 assembly centers, with 18,000 residents, was created at the Santa Anita Race Track in the Los Angeles area. The Japanese Americans were moved into horse stalls that had vacated their previous tenants only a week previously.

Meanwhile, a civilian agency, the War Relocation Authority (WRA), was established to handle the relocation process, when the federal government realized how many soldiers would be required (an entire army division) to staff the relocation camps. The WRA began construction of ten relocation centers at remote sites in California, Arizona, Idaho, Wyoming, Colorado, Utah, and Arkansas. The WRA built military-style barracks, strung barbed wire, and erected guard towers and searchlights. Each camp would be a prison.

THE LOYALTY OF JAPANESE AMERICANS

As may occur in any policy decision made under conditions of uncertainty and hysteria, the real facts of the case were not seriously considered by policymakers. Racial prejudice against the Japanese was heavily involved in the government's decision.

The Munson Report

Not considered in the relocation decision was a 25-page report entitled *Report on Japanese on the West Coast of the United States*, prepared by Curtis B. Munson, a Chicago businessman who served as a special representative of President Roosevelt. Munson's Report was submitted to the White House on November 7, 1941, a month before the Japanese attack on Pearl Harbor. It had become evident during 1941 that war with Japan was imminent, and the United States government needed to gauge the loyalty of Japanese Americans, many of whom lived near Navy bases, Army installations, and aircraft and other key manufacturing plants. Munson toured the Pacific Coast states and Hawaii, interviewing Army and Navy intelligence officers, military and city officials, and the Federal Bureau of Investigation (FBI).

Munson concluded that Japanese Americans were loyal to the United States. He stated, "There is no Japanese problem on the West Coast." Instead, he pointed to "a remarkable, even extraordinary degree of loyalty among this generally suspect ethnic group." Munson stated that the *Nisei* (American-born individuals) "show a pathetic eagerness to be Americans," while the *Issei* (individuals born in Japan) may be "loyal romantically to Japan," but their decision to make America their home guaranteed their loyalty to the United States.

The Munson Report was circulated among several Cabinet members, including Stimson, Knox, Biddle, and Cordell Hull, U.S. Secretary of State. On February 5, 1942, shortly before Executive Order 9066 was signed, Stimson sent a copy of the Munson Report to President Roosevelt, with an accompanying memo stating that the top officials in the U.S. Department of War had carefully studied the document (Weglyn, 1976). Perhaps Roosevelt only read the memo, and not the report.

Top government decision-makers had even "harder" data than that provided by the Munson Report on which to base their policy decision. During World War II, and for months before the war, American cryptographers had broken the Japanese "Purple" code through which diplomatic cables were encrypted. These decoded messages showed clearly that an espionage network of Japanese Americans on the West Coast did not exist. Further, Tokyo told its agents to recruit *non*-Japanese in preference over Japanese Americans.

Then why did U.S. officials decide to relocate 120,000 Japanese Americans? One explanation is the prejudice against the vegetable farmers and small shopkeepers on the West Coast. Japanese Americans were physically distinguishable from the majority population of European Americans. The Japanese Americans were hardworking and financially successful,[4] and other Californians resented them for their achievements. The Japanese Americans were concentrated in Los Angeles, San Francisco, San Jose, Portland, and Seattle in *Nihonmachi* ("Japantowns"), in part because they were not allowed to live in other areas (Figure 4-2).

Figure 4-2. The U.S. Army Ordered Japanese Americans to Report to Assembly Centers in 1942.
This order was posted at First and Front Streets in San Francisco on April 1, 1942, demanding that all persons of Japanese ancestry evacuate by noon on April 7. The Japanese Americans were gathered in assembly centers operated by the U.S. Army, and then transferred to the ten relocation camps operated by the War Relocation Administration (WRA). Note the air raid shelter announcement. In early 1942, the West Coast of the United States was prepared for attacks by Japanese bombers.
Source: Washington, D.C., U.S. Library of Congress, WRA Collection, Dorothea Lange, LC-USZ62-34565.

Forty years after the war, a United States government commission, in its report *Personal Justice Denied*, concluded: "The promulgation of Executive Order 9066 was not justified by military necessity, and the decisions which followed from it . . . were not driven by analysis of military conditions. The broad historical causes which shaped these decisions were race prejudice, war hysteria, and a failure of political leadership. Widespread ignorance of Japanese Americans contributed to a policy conceived in haste and executed in an atmosphere of fear and anger at Japan" (Commission on Wartime Relocation and Internment of Civilians, 1982, p. 18). A well-documented case to the contrary is argued by Michelle Malkin in her book *In Defense of Internment* (Malkin, 2004).

Issei, Nisei, and *Sansei*

Japanese Americans were criticized because they maintained their Japanese culture and language, and resisted assimilation into mainstream American life. Many Japanese Americans, indeed, did not want to become integrated into the American melting pot. But there were also legal barriers. The U.S. Immigration Act of 1924 was intended to curb migration of Japanese and Chinese. Japanese Americans who had migrated to the U.S. were prevented from becoming naturalized citizens, which effectively kept them from owning land. These *Issei*, first-generation migrants, mainly older individuals born in Japan, understandably felt snubbed by the United States. Their children, the second generation, or *Nisei*, were educated in the United States and considered themselves 100 percent Americans, although some were fluent in Japanese as well as English, and they shared Japanese values with their parents (Figure 4-3). The third generation, or *Sansei*, typically small children at the time of World War II, were completely assimilated. After the war, many *Sansei* married non-Japanese, as many third-generation American Jews intermarried with non-Jews.

Figure 4-3. Evacuation of Japanese Americans from San Francisco in April 1942.
This family was among the first group of 664 Japanese Americans who were transferred to WRA relocation camps. While the child and the mother appear to be smiling, notice the bitter look on the father's face. He is an *Issei* (born in Japan), and his children are *Nisei* (born in the United States).
Source: Washington, D.C., U.S. Library of Congress, WRA Collection, Dorothea Lange, LC-USZ62-34565.

The Munson Report warned against thinking of all Japanese Americans as a homogeneous category. Munson described the three generations, and drew conclusions about the loyalty of each. He pointed to a subgroup of the *Nisei*, *Kibei*, who were second-generation migrants and U.S. citizens, but who had returned to Japan for at least part of their education, and who had absorbed nationalistic values there.[5] The *Kibei* constituted 13 percent of the *Nisei*. Munson predicted that the *Kibei* might pose a loyalty risk, depending on how the government treated Japanese Americans. Munson urged President Roosevelt to issue a reassuring message about the loyalty of Japanese Americans, but he did not do so.

A cultural gap existed between the *Issei* and the *Nisei* due to their different citizenship and contrasting cultural values. A wide age gap existed because the first generation of immigrants had delayed in starting their families (Spicer & others, 1969). Often a young man would migrate to the United States, get established over a period of several years, and then get married (perhaps in his thirties) to a "picture-bride" (who was selected by a matchmaker in Japan, and whose photograph was then mailed to the prospective bridegroom in the United States, with the bride following if the man agreed to the choice). Thus, the typical family in a relocation camp during World War II consisted of a 50-year-old father, a 40-year-old mother, and teenage (or younger) children.

Some Japanese Americans, especially the *Issei* (who were Japanese citizens), expressed their pride in, and support for, the 1930s Japan military conquests in Manchuria and China. Thousands of care packages were sent from America to Japanese soldiers fighting in Asia (Ng, 1996; Hayashi, 1995). Support for Japanese military aggression in China in the 1930s, however, was quite different from disloyalty to the United States during World War II.

The roundup of all Japanese Americans into the WCCA assembly centers in spring, 1942, regarded the *Issei*, *Nisei*, *Kibei*, and *Sansei* as simply "Japs."[6] This tendency for gross classification illustrates one aspect of ethnocentrism, defined as the tendency to regard all members of an out-group as a homogeneous mass, and as inferior to one's own culture. So to the prejudiced American officials in charge of the relocation process, the loyalty, or lack of it, by different individuals did not matter. All Japanese Americans were treated as disloyal (Figure 4-4). The hatred of Japanese Americans was expressed by a sign displayed in California in 1942: "Jap Hunting Licenses Issued Here. Open Season—No Limit."[7]

Figure 4-4. Evacuation of Japanese Americans from the West Coast in April 1942.
These children and their parents wait with their luggage at the Los Angeles Train Station for evacuation to one of the ten WRA relocation camps. Each family was only allowed to bring the few belongings that they could carry.
Source: Washington, D.C., U.S. Library of Congress, Farm Security Administration, Russell Lee, LC-USF33-13289-M.

The Media as Guard Dogs

An analysis of newspaper coverage of Japanese Americans during the period from Pearl Harbor to February 19, 1942, (when President Roosevelt signed Executive Order 9066) shows that the media originally stressed the patriotism of Japanese Americans and their loyalty to the United States. Soon the *San Francisco Chronicle* and the *Los Angeles Times* began to report the FBI arrests of several thousand "dangerous enemy aliens" in the days following Pearl Harbor. The California newspapers stopped using Japanese Americans as sources, instead quoting law enforcement officials and U.S. Army officers. Journalists essentially accepted the U.S. government policy in framing the issue of West Coast Japanese Americans (Bishop, 2000). California newspapers became pawns of the government's efforts to construct a perception of Japanese Americans as spies and saboteurs. For example, when U.S. Secretary of the Navy Frank Knox returned on December 15, 1941, from inspecting the disaster at Pearl Harbor, he was quoted as saying that "the most effective fifth column work of the war was done there." This remark was widely quoted by California newspapers.

In late January 1942, the *San Francisco Chronicle* carried a headline "Subversive Elements Will Be Crushed," while the *Los Angeles Times* published an inflammatory headline, "Eviction of Jap Aliens Sought" (Bishop, 2000). Unsubstantiated reports of fifth column activity were disseminated. The public was urged by the media to leave the solution of the "Japanese problem" to the government, who "possessed all the facts." The media declared that the distinction between American-born and foreign-born Japanese Americans did not matter; both were equally dangerous and should be interned. Thus the media accepted the government's definition of the situation, molding public opinion in support of the government's February 19 evacuation order.

Here the media played what is called a "guard dog" function in championing the dominant political structure without questioning its perspective on the issue. In contrast, the media might have been "watchdogs," gathering facts through investigative reporting (as occurred in the case of Watergate) and seeking a more balanced view of the West Coast Japanese Americans (Donahue, Tichenor, & Olien, 1995). But in December 1941, and early 1942, the press abandoned the Japanese Americans, and sided wholeheartedly with the U.S. government, thus contributing to a flawed policy decision. Thanks to media coverage of this issue, public opinion, one factor that might have prevented internment of the Japanese Americans, was instead prejudiced against them.

THE RUTH HASHIMOTO STORY

The wartime experiences of the 120,000 Japanese Americans is illustrated by one relocatee, Ruth Hashimoto (1999). She was born Satoye Yamada (her maiden name) in Seattle in 1913. Her father, Asataro Yamada, ran away from his Hiroshima home at age 16 to work as a cabin boy on an American ship. Ruth's mother, a teacher, was introduced to her father, when he returned to Japan, by a relative who served as a matchmaker. Ruth's father started Nippon Plumbing Electric Works in Seattle's Japantown, mainly selling to U.S. Navy ships. Yamada was a successful businessman, and was well on the way to becoming somewhat wealthy.

Ruth and her young brother accompanied their mother to Japan, and then lived for five years in a Buddhist temple, while their mother returned to Seattle to rejoin her husband. Ruth returned in 1919 (thus she is a *Kibei*), and completed her public schooling in Seattle. She took "Ruth" as her American first name after a movie star that she admired. Her father became very ill and was hospitalized, but recovered when a Japanese minister prayed for him. Impressed with the minister's religion, Konkokyo (an international religion with Japanese roots), her father sold his Seattle businesses, attended a seminary in Japan, and then became a minister in San Jose, California.

Ruth worked as a secretary/translator for another minister, Reverend Yoshiaki Fukuda,[8] in the San Francisco Konko Church until she married her husband, Denichi Hashimoto, a pressman for a

Japanese language newspaper. Their first daughter was born, and then a second. Her husband was hospitalized with tuberculosis, and they moved to San Jose in 1939, to be nearer her family.

Suddenly, their pleasant life was interrupted on Pearl Harbor Day. That afternoon at 2:00 P.M., two FBI agents came to Reverend Yamada's Konko Church in San Jose, where he was preaching. The FBI agents took Ruth's father away in handcuffs. He was transported to a U.S. Army camp for prisoners-of-war in Lordsburg, New Mexico, and then transferred to the Santa Fe Internment Camp. He was 64 years old and experienced stomach problems, perhaps due to stress and to the camp diet.[9] Later, he was transferred from the Santa Fe Internment Camp to the Heart Mountain Relocation Camp to rejoin his family in summer, 1944. Meanwhile his son (Ruth's brother) was serving in the U.S. Army.

Ruth, her husband, and children reported to a designated gathering point in San Jose in May 1942, and then were transported to a WCCA assembly center at the Santa Anita Race Track near Los Angeles, where they were assigned to live in a newly-built barracks. For bedding, they stuffed straw into bags made from old sheets. After several months, in September 1942, Hashimoto and her family were moved by train to the Heart Mountain Relocation Camp in Wyoming. Today Ruth remembers the blizzards, 35 degrees below zero weather, and walking in knee-deep snow. Ruth's family huddled around a pot-bellied stove in their one-room barracks apartment. They built their own furniture out of scrap lumber. Ruth's two daughters, aged three and 5, suffered, along with her husband, from being cramped in the small space of their one-room barracks apartment. Her mother and husband argued constantly. The mess hall food, which the Japanese Americans called "slop-suey," was despised.

The Japanese American National Museum in Los Angeles displays one-half of a barracks from the Heart Mountain Camp.[10] The stark wooden structure, covered with black tarpaper, is a symbol of the dismal life in the relocation camps. Visiting this display brought tears to Ruth's eyes. She was deeply affected by a 55-gallon oil drum filled with thousands of small rocks, each painted with a single *kanji* character like *mu* (emptiness) or *chikara* (strength). These mysterious rocks were hand-painted by individuals in the Heart Mountain Camp, and then buried. Leslie and Bora Bovee discovered the barrel a few years after the war, and later donated it to the Japanese American National Museum.

Ruth worked as secretary to her block manager at the Heart Mountain Camp, and a year later she became the block manager. In October 1943, after about a year in Heart Mountain, Ruth was appointed as a language instructor at the Army Intelligence Japanese Language School at the University of Michigan. Her husband opposed her taking this position, as he predicted Japan would win the war, and that Ruth would then be lined up and shot. He remained at Heart Mountain. In Ann Arbor, Ruth taught both brilliant young language recruits and retired U.S. military officers to speak Japanese, so that they could serve as mayors and other officials in the occupation forces in Japan after the end of the war. Ruth almost divorced her husband, but in 1946, after working in Chicago at various jobs, he rejoined the family.

After the war, Ruth worked for the U.S. Navy at Moffett Field, near San Jose. In 1951, Ruth and her family moved to Albuquerque, where she worked at Kirtland Air Force Base, until her retirement in 1973. Then Ruth could work at what she loved best: Various community activities to improve U.S./Japan relationships. She taught English language and American citizenship classes to *Issei* in New Mexico, so they could become naturalized citizens. Ruth taught conversational Japanese to 100 people from Albuquerque in order to prepare them for a visit to their sister city, Sasebo, Japan. In 2002, at age 89, Ruth worked part-time (as a dollar-a-year volunteer) as an international relations consultant for the University of New Mexico's Alliance for Transportation Research Institute (Figure 4-5).

In 1990, when Ruth received the $20,000 paid by the U.S. government to all living refugees of the relocation camps, she donated it to help improve U.S./Japan relationships. Ruth returned to Heart Mountain at age 86 in 1999, with Norman Mineta, her fellow campmate, a former U.S. Congressman from San Jose, and the U.S. Secretary of Transportation. The occasion was a ceremony to recognize the Japanese Americans who had spent the war years beside Heart Mountain.

Figure 4-5. Ruth Hashimoto's Mother, Fusako (Iriye) Yamada; Ruth; Her Eldest Daughter, Ada Jane Noriko Akin; David Evans, a Former University of Michigan Army Intelligence Student of Ruth's, En Route to His Home in Kansas after Serving in Occupied Japan; and Ruth's Father, Reverend Asataro Yamada.

This Japanese American family is standing in front of the Konko Church in San Jose, CA, in late 1945, after Ruth's parents returned from the Heart Mountain Relocation Center. Reverend Yamada spent part of the World War II period in the Santa Fe Internment Camp. Evans brought news of Ruth's younger sister, who lived in Japan.

Source: S. Ruth Y. Hashimoto, Albuquerque, New Mexico.

THE RELOCATION CAMPS

One of the first problems in talking about the wartime Japanese American camps is what to call them. The U.S. government officially referred to them as "relocation centers" or "relocation camps." This terminology implied that the Japanese Americans were simply being relocated from the West Coast to other parts of the country. This euphemistic label, however, would not call for barbed wire, armed guards, and searchlights. The guns pointed *inside*, to keep the Japanese Americans in the camps, not toward the outside in order to protect them from racially prejudiced Americans.

Many people, including President Roosevelt on various occasions (Weglyn, 1976), referred to the relocation centers as "concentration camps."[11] The Japanese American concentration camps were certainly unlike the Nazi death camps, although there were certain similarities (forcible removal of all citizens classified in a racial categorization, and imprisonment in camps without trial). Today many scholars and others writing about the 1942–1946 relocation camps refer to them as "concentration camps."

Internment Camps

The ten relocation camps should be distinguished from the several "internment camps" in which 7,000 Japanese enemy aliens (that is, *Issei*) were imprisoned during World War II (Figure 4-1). These individuals were considered as high-risk by the U.S. government. Some 1,800 were seized by the FBI immediately after Pearl Harbor, many, like Ruth Hashimoto's father, on December 7, 1941. The FBI and Naval Intelligence had been compiling dossiers on them over previous months and years. Most were teachers, newspaper editors, or leaders of a Japanese religious or cultural organization.

Four main internment camps were operated by the Immigration and Naturalization Service (INS) of the U.S. Department of Justice (rather than by the War Relocation Authority, the government agency responsible for the ten relocation camps): (1) Fort Missoula, near Missoula, Montana, (2) Fort Lincoln, near Bismarck, North Dakota, (3) Santa Fe, New Mexico, and (4) Crystal City, Texas. The federal government's original plan, worked out during the year before World War II began, was for the FBI to arrest all Japanese American enemy aliens who were considered to be potentially dangerous. These individuals were then to be placed in custody at one of the four Immigration and Naturalization Service camps (Figure 4-1). They were considered "detainees" until hearings could be held to determine whether each individual should be imprisoned (that is, interned) for the duration of the war. If not so interned, the enemy aliens were to be transferred to one of the ten WRA relation camps to be reunited with their family members.

If an enemy alien were classified as a dangerous risk, he was sent to one of the several prisoner-of-war camps administered by the U.S. Army, such as the facilities at Lordsburg (located in the southwest part of New Mexico, about 22 miles from the Arizona state line) or at Fort Stanton (in western New Mexico, 45 miles southwest of Santa Rosa). These Army POW camps also held captured enemy troops, whose numbers swelled after May 1943, when the German and Italian armies in North Africa surrendered, and 170,000 POWs were transported to camps in the U.S. The Japanese Americans were then moved to the Santa Fe or Crystal City Internment Camps. The Santa Fe camp held only men, with a peak population of 2,100. The Crystal City held families (and thus was somewhat similar to a WRA relocation camp), and had a peak population of 3,326 in May 1945.

Legally, the individuals in the internment camps had certain rights guaranteed by the Geneva Convention, and were treated as equivalent to prisoners-of-war. The Japanese Americans in the relocation camps, however, had no legal rights, as the Geneva Convention did not apply to them (many were American citizens, rather than foreign nationals). The Geneva Convention Relative to the Treatment of Prisoners of War was signed by 46 nations in 1929, including the United Sates and Japan. The Convention specified such details as the amount of food to be provided (5.298 pounds per prisoner per day), that POWs could not be required to work, and so forth. Prisoners were to be housed, clothed, and fed in ways similar to military personnel of the nation that held the POWs. The provisions of the Geneva Convention were enforced by a protecting third power that was a neutral in the particular conflict. This nation was Spain in the Japanese/American conflict of World War II; the Spanish Consul in San Francisco monitored the Santa Fe Internment Camp.

Many people then, and now, referred to the relocation camps as "internment camps," and to the residents as "internees." To make the terminology even more confusing, many Japanese Americans in the relocation camps referred to their "evacuation," and to themselves as "evacuatees," implying the government had removed them from their West Coast homes to save them from danger (which may have been in part correct, given the strength of anti-Japanese prejudice in California in 1941-1942). More than 100 books and reports have been written about the ten relocation camps, but little has been published about the four internment camps. Even the Japanese American Museum in Los Angeles has very little information about the Santa Fe Internment Camp. The internment camps have been all but erased from the American memory.

Where Were the Relocation Camps?

The ten relocation camps were situated in barren, isolated areas, on federal land on which barracks and other structures could be quickly constructed (Figure 4-1).

1. Manzanar, in the southeastern part of California.

2. Tule Lake, at Newell, in the northeast corner of California, a particularly troublesome spot for the WRA. Eventually dissidents from other camps were sent to Tule Lake. Several hundred of the Tule Lake troublemakers were transplanted to the Santa Fe Internment Camp in the last year of the war, where they caused a minor revolt.

3. Poston, on the Colorado River, in southern Arizona near the California state line.

4. Gila, near Sacaton, Arizona, located on Indian reservation land 20 miles south of Phoenix.

5. Minidoka, located 15 miles north of Twin Falls, Idaho, on government land.

6. Heart Mountain, located 13 miles northwest of Cody, on federal reclamation project land in northern Wyoming (Figure 4-6).

7. Amache, near Granada, 130 miles east of Pueblo, in southeastern Colorado.

8. Topaz, located on the salt flats of Utah, 140 miles south of Salt Lake City.

9. Rohwer, near McGehee in southeast Arkansas, on land purchased by the U.S. Department of Agriculture for future subsistence farmer homesteads.

10. Jerome, located 10 miles south of Dermott, AR, and like Rohwer, located on government land intended for homesteaders in southeastern Arkansas.

All ten relocation camps were situated in particularly isolated, godforsaken places, characterized by unpleasant weather, physical isolation, and difficult living conditions. The Poston Camp was typical of the "sand and cactus" relocation centers, with almost constant winds that blew desert sand into the barracks homes, to the dismay of the cleanliness-minded Japanese Americans. Scorpions, rattlesnakes, and sidewinders inhabited the camp grounds. Temperatures at the Poston Camp reached one hundred-twenty-five degrees in the shade for several months each year. Jokingly, the relocation camp residents referred to their community as "Poston, Toastin', and Roastin'."[12] The Rohwer and Jerome relocation camps were situated in a mosquito-infested swampy delta in Arkansas (Thomas & Nishimoto, 1946). The Heart Mountain Relocation Camp was in a deep freeze.

Figure 4-6. Under the Heart Mountain.
  Some 11,000 Japanese Americans lived in this desolate location during World War II, making the Heart Mountain Relocation Camp Wyoming's third largest city. Heart Mountain looms at the end of P Street, the main thoroughfare of this WRA Camp.
  Source: Washington, D.C., National Archives, Photographer Tom Parker, RG 210-G-8E-61.

Why did the WRA choose these "devil's islands" as camp sites? The Japanese Americans had been accused of being spies and saboteurs, so the U.S. government thought it was necessary to locate the camps far from military facilities and manufacturing plants. Further, governors of the Western states resisted having the relocation camps in their state unless they were securely guarded and located far from populated areas. The governors feared that the Japanese Americans might purchase property in their state, and live there after the war.[13] Finally, the U.S. government located the camps on unused federal land, which tended to be in remote areas.

Camp Facilities

The camp inmates were assigned to live in tarpaper-covered wooden barracks, each about 100 feet long and 20 feet wide. Four families lived in a barracks, so each family had a space of about 20 feet by 24 feet. Each "block," the foundation of community organization, consisted of from 12 to 24 barracks, and housed 300 to 600 residents. The block elected one *Issei* representative, the "block head," to the community council for the camp, and the camp administrators appointed a block manager (a *Nisei*). Each block had latrines, mess halls, a laundry, recreation hall, schools, and other facilities.

One result of these living conditions for the camp inmates was to reduce the respect for the father of the family, and to provide the children with much greater freedom. Some young males formed gangs, which beat up camp policemen, suspected FBI informers, or *Nisei* leaders. Gambling, a favorite sport of many Japanese American men before Pearl Harbor, flourished in the relocation camps, even though it was opposed by churches and by community leaders.

The industrious Japanese Americans, after arrival in the bleak camps, cleaned up the grounds until they were spotless. They scrounged scrap wood to build furniture for their barracks homes (Figure 4-7). Neat vegetable gardens were laid out, in order to supplement the mess hall food, which the Japanese Americans regarded with bitter disdain (in part, because it consisted of dishes like sauerkraut and sausages which they did not customarily eat). Boy Scout and Girl Scout troops were organized, along with schools and a camp newspaper. The American war effort was aided by such projects as making camouflage nets and growing guayule for rubber. Camp residents who were employed in a camp, or who worked outside the camp for local farmers, were paid from nine to 19 dollars per month (about 10 cents an hour).

Figure 4-7. Many of the Industrious Japanese American Families Converted their Tarpaper Barracks into Cozy Homes.

M. Imafuji, a Japanese American veteran of World War I, utilized scrap lumber and other materials to decorate his family's barracks home in the WRA Relocation Camp at Heart Mountain, Wyoming. This photograph was taken on January 7, 1943, after the Imafuji family had lived in this tarpaper barracks for about six months.

Source: Washington, D.C., National Archives, Photographer Tom Parker, RG 210-G-8E- 620.

Racialization

At a casual glance the relocation camps appeared to be an attempt to reproduce an American community in a bleak landscape. Below the surface, however, was seething dissatisfaction and anger. The Japanese Americans deeply resented being treated as a single category by the U.S. government. It did not matter whether they were Japanese citizens (*Issei*) or American citizens, loyal or disloyal. The result was racialization, the belief that all Japanese Americans constituted one race, whose members were regarded as inferior by other Americans (Nishimoto, 1995). As General DeWitt, the military commander who rounded up the West Coast Japanese Americans to begin the relocation process, stated, while testifying before a Congressional Committee: "A Jap is a Jap."

The result of the relocation process was to strengthen the inmates' self-identification as Japanese and to create greater loyalty to Japan. In the camps, as time went on, the inmates typically organized Japanese language classes and held training sessions in Japanese flower arranging and the tea ceremony. Japanese flags were sewn and displayed. At the Poston Relocation Camp, inmates shouted "*Banzai* to the Emperor of Japan!*"* (Hayashi, 1995, p. 15). At the unruly Tule Lake Camp, the *Kibei* campaigned against anything Western. They broke up dances in which the dance style was not Japanese (Smith, 1995). Some *Kibei* in the Tule Lake Camp marched and drilled, shouting "*Washa! Washa!*", sounded bugle calls, and played the Japanese national anthem. The dissidents performed early morning calisthenics, and acted like Japanese soldiers to the extent possible. Each month, they celebrated the anniversary of the Japanese attack on Pearl Harbor. The Tule Lake troublemakers wore rising-sun emblems on their shirts and jackets, and flouted rising-sun sweatshirts (Culley, 1991). They shaved their heads in the manner of Japanese soldiers (Clark, 1980), and wore headbands. Further, they intimidated, coerced, and attacked Japanese Americans who cooperated with the camps' administrators.

In each relocation camp, a political struggle occurred between the *Issei*, who tended to be more loyal to Japan, versus the America-born *Nisei*. Because the FBI interned many of the Japanese American community leaders (who were *Issei*) in separate internment camps, *Nisei* rose to leadership positions in the relocation camps (Thomas & Nishimoto, 1946). The leadership shift in 1941-1942 from *Issei* to *Nisei* gave greater power to the Japanese American Citizens League (JACL), which mainly represented the *Nisei*. JACL leaders believed that Japanese Americans should accept what was inevitable, and help the relocation camps function smoothly.

Some relocation camp inmates chose to be repatriated to Japan during the war. The repatriates were exchanged for a shipload of American prisoners-of-war on the SS *Gripsholm*, which sailed from New York on September 1, 1943. Some 4,742 camp residents were repatriated to Japan by 1946, including 1,949 *Nisei* who renounced their U.S. citizenship and moved to Japan after the war.[14] In late 1944, when several hundred *Kibei* renounced their U.S. citizenship (which made them Japanese aliens in the United States), they were transferred to the Santa Fe Internment Camp. Most of the interns in the Santa Fe Camp, however, were older *Issei* (they averaged 52 years of age).

The Japanization process in the relocation camps was encouraged by broadcasts from Radio Tokyo, which conveyed such messages as instructions not to work as sugar beet harvesters.[15] Rumors about the progress of the war and other topics spread within the relocation camps, and from camp to camp. Letters were smuggled by placing them inside balloons, which were hidden inside jars of homemade pickled vegetables, which were then sent as gifts to a relative in another camp (Nishimura, 2001). For example, a letter to Satashi Yoshiyama in the Santa Fe Internment Camp from his mother at the Tule Lake Relocation Camp was smuggled to him inside a package addressed to a Mr. Keisuka, sent via the Gila Relocation Camp by mutual friends (the censors at the Santa Fe Camp discovered this letter when searching through the package)(Yoshiyama, 1945).

The degree of bitter anti-American feeling is illustrated by the following paragraph, deleted by camp censors, in a letter from Miye Ichiki (August 27, 1945) at Tule Lake Relocation Center to a relative at the Santa Fe Internment Camp: "All I hear and see nowadays is Atomic Bomb, relocating from Center, helping the United States industries, and Japanese American soldiers in the United States uniform, and it makes me sick. I am glad to hear that a couple of United [States] soldiers whom I know have been killed in action. I understand Kurokawa's son is also killed in action. It served them right for fighting for the United States. When I see any Japanese Americans in United States uniform visiting this camp, I feel like killing them."

The Japanese as a people do not bear shame lightly, and the relocation camp experience was socially constructed by them as very shameful. They felt that they were treated without respect, which led to strong resistance against the WRA administrators and their camp policies.

EFFECTS OF THE RELOCATION CAMPS

By August 7, 1942, five months after the relocation process began, all West Coast Japanese Americans had been confined in either WCCA assembly centers or WRA relocation camps. Three months later, a year after the Pearl Harbor attack, all 110,000 Japanese Americans were in the ten relocation camps, with an additional 7,000 *Issei* in the four main internment camps.

Research on the Relocation Camps

Much of what we know today about the relocation camp experience of the Japanese Americans comes from anthropological and sociological studies at each of the camps, carried out by more than 30 professional scholars in collaboration with several hundred Japanese American field researchers in the camps.[16] These clandestine field researchers, who made observations and transmitted their reports to the social science scholars, feared that their role would be discovered by their fellow camp inmates. They were suspected of serving as FBI informers, and were called *inu* (dogs) in camp slang. In Poston, a crude drawing of a dog that had been hanged served as a somber warning to the Japanese Americans researchers (Hirabayashi, 1999).

Richard Nishimoto, an *Issei* who migrated to the United States and earned an engineering degree at Stanford University before the war, served as a field researcher while at the same time functioning as a community leader in the Poston Relocation Camp in Arizona. He insisted on being referred to as "X" by the University of California at Berkeley sociologist with whom he collaborated in studying camp life. Eventually, in June 1945, the WRA camp administrator discovered Nishimoto's clandestine research role, and discharged him from Poston.

The process through which the Japanese Americans were psychologically whipsawed by the relocation camp experience is illustrated by Nishimoto's (1995, pp. 5-6) self-statement, made in concluding an analysis of his national identification: "Now you can understand what I mean when I say I am loyal to both Japan and the U.S. . . . Evacuation finished what was going on with me . . . . My girls grew up here. They have to be American. But I know what I am now. I am [an] enemy alien . . . here."

The Agony of the Two Questions

One of the most traumatic experiences for the camp residents was a questionnaire that each individual over age 17 was required to complete. The U.S. Army in early 1943 needed manpower, and sought to recruit military volunteers from the relocation camps and from Japanese Americans in Hawaii. The two crucial questions were:

#27. Are you willing to serve in the U.S. armed forces on combat duty? (This question was asked of all males).

#28. Will you swear unqualified allegiance to the United States of America, and faithfully defend it, and foreswear any allegiance or obedience to the Japanese emperor? (This question was asked of all adults.)

The questionnaire was entitled "Application for Leave," which was puzzling to elderly *Issei*. Anyway, they were far too old to serve as combat troops. Question #28 was especially puzzling to the *Issei*, who were Japanese citizens; if they answered "yes" to this question, they would be individuals without a country. So the WRA officials rewrote the question for the *Issei*: "Will you swear to abide by the laws of the United States and to take no other action which would in any way interfere with the war effort of the United States?" (Daniels, 1971, p. 113).

Of the 70,000 individuals who filled out the questionnaires, 65,000 said "yes" to Question #28. The remainder, who said "no" or who qualified their answer were classified as disloyal, and shipped to the Tule Lake Camp (Daniels, 1971). Some 5,000 of the 20,000 young men of military age were "No-Nos," or gave qualified answers to Question #28 (Spicer and others, 1969). Many of the eligible young men who qualified their answer insisted that their Constitutional rights be restored before they would fight to defend their country. But eventually 2,355 *Nisei* volunteered for military service from behind the barbed wire of the relocation camps.

The Purple Heart Regiment

At the beginning of the war, the Pentagon doubted the loyalty of Japanese American soldiers, but soon *Nisei* GIs overcame this prejudice by proving themselves on the battlefield.

In all, 33,000 Japanese Americans served in the U.S. Armed Forces during World War II.[17] Most famous was the "Pineapple Army," the 100th Battalion, originally composed of Japanese Americans from Hawaii, which fought in the bloodiest battles in Italy: Rapido River, Monte Cassino, and the Anzio Beachhead. The 100th Battalion was joined in June 1944, by the 442nd Regimental Combat Team, composed of volunteers and draftees from the relocation camps. These troops experienced 225 days of combat, including rugged conflict as they fought north through Italy and into southern France. They boasted that they never gave up an inch of territory, always moving forward. The 442nd Regiment was the most-decorated unit in U.S. military history, receiving more than 18,143 individual medals, including 3,600 Purple Hearts for being wounded in action (Takaki, 1993).[18] This Purple Heart Regiment had one of the highest rate of casualties of any Army unit, some 314 percent of the original strength of the battalion. The regiment's *Nisei* felt they had something to prove about loyalty and bravery.

A proud moment occurred for Japanese Americans at the end of the war in Europe when President Harry S. Truman welcomed the Japanese Americans home: "You fought not only the enemy, you fought prejudice - and you won" (Takaki, 1993, p. 384). The Japanese Americans' combat record was featured in the 1951 Hollywood film "Go for Broke," named after the 100th Battalion's slogan, which derived from their addiction to playing dice.

The battlefield success of the Purple Heart Battalion was one of the important media stories of 1944-1945, and it had a strong impact on U.S. public opinion about Japanese Americans (Smith, 1995). Abner Schrieber, deputy administrator at the Santa Fe Internment Camp, stated, "I remember one guy who came to the camp to visit his father. He had been in the Army, the U.S. Army, and was pretty badly shot up. It made quite an impression on me." Many of the *Issei* in the Santa Fe Internment Camp had *Nisei* sons fighting in World War II.

THE INTERNMENT CAMPS

The four internment camps were operated by the Immigration and Naturalization Service (INS) of the U.S. Department of Justice, the federal government agency responsible for the internal security of the United States. The INS internment camps were relatively peaceful Japanese communities, at least in contrast to the often turbulent relocation camps (Clark, 1980).

Most of the *Issei* (about two-thirds or so) accompanied their families to one of the ten WRA relocation camps; only some 7,000 individuals that the FBI considered as dangerous enemy aliens were sent to the four internment camps, where each individual case was reviewed by a three-person board from the individual's home community. The *Issei* men classified as "dangerous" were to be transferred to Army POW camps, such as those at Lordsburg and Fort Stanton.[19] But due to the overpopulation of these and other Army POW camps, mainly caused by the 1943 surrender of Germans in the Afrika Corps (and after the Normandy invasion of June 1944, in France), many *Issei* were held in the INS internment camps for the duration of the war. In other words, what were intended to be temporary screening camps actually became prisoner-of-war camps for the Japanese nationals considered to be dangerous security risks.

The Santa Fe Camp was for men only (Figure 4-8). The *Issei* community leaders were put into one of three categories on the basis of their security risk (Okada, 1975):

1. Group A, categorized as "known to be dangerous," were mainly fishermen, Shinto and Buddhist priests, and influential businessmen (Ruth Hashimoto's father was placed initially in Group A).

2. Group B were considered "potentially dangerous."

3. Group C, classified as "pro-Japanese," were mainly language teachers, *Kibei*, and newspaper editors.

Figure 4-8. The Possessions of Mamoru Ike, a Newly-Arrived Internee at the Santa Fe Internment Camp, Are Searched by INS Officers.

The camp guards were recruited locally, and wore military-style uniforms. Note the guard holding a billy club or nightstick (these weapons were made of light wood, and many broke when used in the "minor revolt" on March 12, 1945). A twelve-foot-high wire mesh and barbed wire fence surrounded the camp.

Source: Used with permission of Mrs. Abner Schreiber, Los Alamos, New Mexico.

The "dangerous enemy aliens" often were so classified on little more than a whim. For example, one internee sold rope in his small store in Stockton, CA. The FBI found a carved ceremonial archer's bow in the home of another Japanese American. Another *Issei* had been an expert in *kendo*, an ancient kind of fencing with bamboo sticks; unfortunately he had the bamboo poles in his home when the FBI searched his residence.

Both Fort Missoula (in Montana) and Fort Lincoln (near Bismarck, North Dakota) held several hundred *Issei* in the early months of the war, but then mainly housed German prisoners after 1942.[20] The two other INS internment camps, at Santa Fe and at Crystal City, differed in their function. The Crystal City Internment Camp, located 110 miles southwest of San Antonio in an isolated area near the Mexican border, was a family camp, where women and children could volunteer to join their husbands and fathers.

Most of the internees in the four camps came from the West Coast of the United States, but there were also a few Hawaiians. In addition, both the Santa Fe and Crystal City Camps held many of the 2,100 Japanese Latin Americans (80 percent of whom were Peruvians), whom the United States had had arrested and shipped to the U.S. internment camps. The Japanese Peruvians were forcibly escorted to the United States, and were then charged with illegal entry (Mangione, 1978). The misguided policy for this bizarre move was the mistaken idea that these Japanese citizens could then be exchanged for Americans interned in enemy countries (Clark, 1980). This strategy failed completely. The Japanese Peruvians spoke some of the best Japanese (Yamashita, 1978). Many of the tailors in the Santa Fe and Crystal City Internment Camps were Peruvians. Camp authorities allowed them to establish sewing shops, and charge a small fee for their work. After the war, most of the Japanese Peruvians moved to Japan, rather than returning to Peru, where anti-Japanese prejudice was intense.

Each of the four internment camps was run like a high-security federal penitentiary, with the prisoners treated like prisoners-of-war, as governed by the Geneva Convention. Each internee was photographed, and identification numbers were stenciled on the back of the internees' shirts and jackets (Figure 4-9). In addition to barbed wire and guard towers, the internment camps were equipped with searchlights and guard dogs.

Figure 4-9. The Funeral for Dr. Sadakazu Furugochi on November 12, 1943, in the Santa Fe Internment Camp.
   A large number of individuals attended this funeral service. Many wear identification numbers on their jackets. A Shinto priest stands to the left of the casket, and a Christian minister on the right. In front of them stand 34 men, facing the crowd, who may be friends of the deceased. Beyond the guard tower in the upper left are the Sangre de Cristo Mountains.
   Source: Los Angeles, Japanese American National Museum.

The Santa Fe Internment Camp

   The Santa Fe Internment Camp was located on the site of an abandoned Civilian Conservation Corps (CCC) camp on the western outskirts of the city, within the city limits but about a mile from the center of Santa Fe. This 80-acre area is now known as the Casa Solana neighborhood, near the present site of the Radisson Hotel. The old CCC camp consisted of eight barracks and a mess hall, and housed about 400 persons. It was expanded to a capacity of 2,000 internees. Additional housing was constructed for the Japanese Americans in March 1942, and later, after several barracks and the mess hall burned in a June 23, 1943, fire of unknown origin (Clark, 1980). The Army-style barracks buildings were 20 feet by 140 feet, and were planned to provide 80 square feet per person. Toward the end of World War II, in 1945, when the Internment Camp was heavily populated, the space per person dropped to only 48 square feet, well below the Geneva Convention standard of 60 square feet (Melzer, 1994).

Security was provided by a 12-foot high woven wire and barbed wire fence, fastened on both sides of posts that were six inches in diameter, with a two-foot barbed-wire overhang on top. Sixteen strands of barbed wire were strung on each side of the posts. Spotlights and guard towers were located every 100 yards and on each corner of the 28-acre barracks area. The administrative buildings were located outside the main gate of the barracks area. Some 100 Immigration and Naturalization (INS) officers guarded the camp (one of the guards was Slim Pickens, later to be a Hollywood actor in "Doctor Strangelove" and other films). The entire area sloped down from the fenced barracks compound toward the Santa Fe River (Figure 4-10).

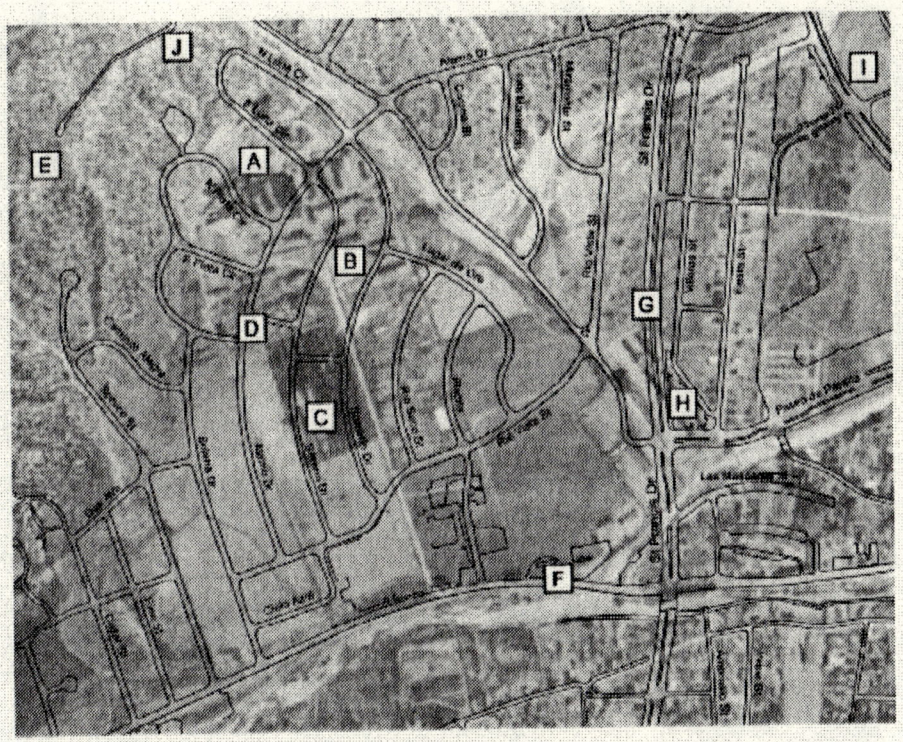

Figure 4-10. A 1951 Aerial Photograph of the Santa Fe Internment Camp.
This photo was taken in about 1950, several years after the last Japanese American internees were released from the camp, but prior to construction of the Casa Solana housing development. Note: (A) the 28-acre fenced barracks area, (B) the several administrative buildings, lying just outside of the camp's fence, (C) the orchards, planted and cared for by the internees, (D) a large cottonwood tree, believed to have been planted at the site of Bataan survivor Manuel Armijo's first post-War house in Casa Solana, (E) the outer borders of the Internment Camp, (F) the present-day West Alameda Street, which here parallels the Santa Fe River, (G) present-day St. Francis Drive, (H) the six stables and the parade grounds of the New Mexico National Guard 200th Regiment (when it was still a cavalry unit), where Dr. George Kistiakowsky from the Los Alamos project rode horses, (I) Rosario Cemetery, where stone monuments mark the burial of two Japanese American internees, and (J) site of the Santa Fe Internment Camp marker, dedicated in 2002.
Source: Santa Fe, New Mexico, Planning Division, City of Santa Fe.

Adjoining the barracks area, a 40-acre fenced plot was used for hiking and for a small golf course that the *Issei* constructed. The camp site also included a 20-acre vegetable garden, a chicken house, baseball fields, and a theater. In all, the Santa Fe Camp was perceived by the local townsfolk as a rather cushy place. Why, they asked, were the Japanese Americans provided with plenty of food, including meat and sugar, which were rationed for everybody outside of the camp? The diet was certainly adequate, as described by an internee, Masaru Ben Akahori (1944), in a letter to his wife: "For breakfast, I have enough toast and butter, plenty of milk, hot coffee, as many cups as I want, scrambled eggs, oatmeal, and fruit of course. For lunch, boiled beef, mash potatoes, rice, and bread, coffee, cake or prunes, tea, soup (bean or vegetable). For supper, rice, meat, and cabbages, pickled vegetables, all in the Japanese fashion."

The first trainload of 425 *Issei* arrived from California on March 14, 1942, only 12 days after construction of the expanded camp facilities had begun. The internees were trucked from the railhead to the camp with their hands tied behind their backs. No announcement was made by government authorities, but Santa Feans noticed that large supplies of rice were purchased for the camp, so it was assumed that the internees were Japanese. At first, the internees were housed in 200 tents, later to be replaced by 24 barracks.[21] Soon the camp's inmates numbered 826 people. Six months later, in September 1942, the Santa Fe Internment Camp was temporarily abandoned when 523 internees were transferred to WRA relocation camps (after a decision was reached by the review board for each individual), and 302 internees were sent to Army-administered camps at Lordsburg and Fort Stanton (which was called Japanese Segregation Camp #1) in New Mexico.[22]

Six months later, on March 23, 1943, as the Army POW camps filled with captured German and Italian soldiers from North Africa, 357 *Issei* were shipped back to the Santa Fe camp, and its population continued to grow thereafter. A total of 4,555 Japanese Americans passed through the Santa Fe Internment Camp, with a peak population of 2,100 in June 1945, shortly before the end of World War II. The local population of Santa Fe was only about 20,000 during World War II, so the camp inmates constituted 10 percent of the city's total population. The Santa Fe Internment Camp continued for a year after the war; in December 1945, the camp population was 1,697, although 900 internees were released that month. Finally, the Santa Fe camp closed in May 1946, with the last 12 internees transferred to Crystal City, Texas, the final INS internment to close down (this in February 1948).

The Internment Process

One function of the INS internment camps was to determine whether or not the internees were indeed the dangerous security risks that they had been classified by the FBI. This decision was made by Alien Enemy Hearing Boards, each constituted of three civilians, at least one of whom was a lawyer. As many of the internees at the Santa Fe camp were from San Francisco or San Jose, several boards from these cities were constituted at Santa Fe to review each individual's file and to conduct an interrogation. The civilian boards conducted the 1942 loyalty hearings through interpreters and guards who utilized various means to obtain information. For example, at the Fort Lincoln Internment Camp, several staff members were reprimanded and punished by the U.S. government for pushing, shaking, and shouting at the Japanese American internees, and for making them stand for long periods or for confining them in a guardhouse without reason. One camp interpreter was suspended from duty for knocking out two of an internee's front teeth during an interrogation (Van Valkenburg, 1995).

The hearing boards often rushed through the interrogations so as to be able to return to their home communities. For example, one hearing board heard cases from early morning until 10:00 p.m., hardly providing careful decisions about the internees' lives (Clark, 1980). Many *Issei* were surprised at the details about their personal affairs that had been gathered by the FBI in the years prior to World War II. For example, one internee was amazed to learn that his file showed that he had played a round of golf with a Japanese consular official in Los Angeles several years previously (Clark, 1980). The internee could hardly remember that particular golf game.

Under the flawed processes of the hearings boards, it is not surprising that many *Issei* disputed the resulting decisions that they were to be kept in the Santa Fe Internment Camp, rather than reunited with their families in a WRA relocation camp.

Most of the *Issei* in the Santa Fe camp were middle-aged or older, with an average age of 52 (Culley, 1991) (Figure 4-11). Their primary concern was to be reunited with their families who were in the WRA relocations. Under these circumstances, time wore heavily on the Santa Fe internees, as they fretted endlessly about how to keep occupied. Boredom, or "barbed-wire sickness," was the biggest problem (Mangione, 1978, p. 328). The Japanese had been accustomed to working long hours, so their adjustment to camp life was especially difficult. As Tom Yamamoto (1976, p. 163) explained: "My experience was of working hard when I started out my business [a hardware store] - no holidays, no Sundays. Just a few days a year would we rest. Most days and nights, we worked hard. When the war broke out, we were put into the camps and there was nothing to do." Yamamoto (1976, p. 171) continued: "I think I spent a very quiet time at Manzanar [WRA Relocation Camp] and at Santa Fe, reading books, playing *go* (a Japanese board game), playing golf, and having recreation just to keep out of trouble.

One prisoner, in a letter to his wife, begged her to release their pet canary from its cage. "No living thing should be caged," he wrote. "When I am free, I want to live in a house without locks, even without doors" (Mangione, 1978, p. 329).

Figure 4-11. Japanese American Leaders of the Santa Fe Internment Camp Pose with Abner Schrieber, Deputy-in-Charge of the Camp (seated to the right of the internee with a walking stick).
Note the internee near the right end of the second row, who is wearing a "Lordsburg" sweater. Presumably he was transferred from the Lordsburg camp, operated by the U.S. Army. The INS internment camps were generally relatively peaceful, compared to the rather tumultuous WRA relocation camps, especially Tule Lake. Note the older age (averaging 52 years) of the internees.
Source: Mrs. Abner Schrieber, Los Alamos, New Mexico. This photo was taken by Parkhurst Studios of Santa Fe.

Kenko Yamashita (1978, p. 191), who spent one year at the Santa Fe camp, and was then transferred to Crystal City, noted that "Japanese farmers couldn't sit and just watch it [the barren soil], so they put gardens in front of their houses [in Crystal City]. They grew eggplant and cucumbers." In fact, a Santa Fe camp administrator, Abner Schrieber (1979) joked: "It seemed like every other week or so, we had to dig another root cellar to store the vegetables and one thing and another that they were able to grow."

The Santa Fe internees wore old Army uniforms, operated their own poultry farm for fresh eggs[23] and chickens, and grew vegetables in their irrigated garden (the inmates joked about their "millionaire gardener," who was a wealthy California *Issei*). The camp's truck farm was so productive that surplus vegetables were traded to Bruns General Hospital for fish, to the New Mexico State Penitentiary for canned fruits and vegetables, and to a local supermarket in exchange for various foodstuffs (Melzer,1994). The internees constructed Japanese-style *ofuro* bathtubs in the camp's shower rooms. They carved wooden objects, polished and painted stones, and made other crafts. The *Issei* made pets out of wild birds. They viewed lots of movies.[24] Anything to keep occupied.[25]

With plenty of time on their hands, many *Issei* gambled incessantly. The camp inmates organized *sumo* wresting and a string orchestra, built a Japanese theater,[26] and a miniature five-hole golf course. They organized softball and baseball leagues (Figure 4-12). The names of the baseball teams are revealing: "Rising Sun," and "Zero Fighters," for example (Okada, 1995, p. 41). The inmates at the Santa Fe camp published their own daily newspaper, the *Santa Fe Jiho* (Times), a mimeographed sheet which operated with the approval of the camp administration and with a minimum of censorship. A report by the Spanish Consul, a Señor F. de Amat (1944), who inspected the camp, showed 171 internees working as cooks, dishwashers, bakers, etc. in the camp, and 160 internees volunteering to work outside the camp (they were paid 80 cents per day). So about one-third of the camp population worked.[27] However, after March 1945, when the first New Mexican POWs returned to Santa Fe (these prisoners were liberated from Cabanatuan in the Philippines) with accounts of Japanese atrocities, local public opinion became strongly anti-Japanese and the internees were no longer allowed outside of the camp (Melzer,1994).

Figure 4-12. Guard in the Watchtower Became a Spring Baseball Fan at the Santa Fe Internment Camp.
    Enemy aliens were not allowed to have cameras, but they could make drawings and watercolors like the above, which was drawn by Kango Takamura in 1942. The caption under this drawing says "When the ball is hit over the fence, the guard retrieves it for us." The writing on the side translates as "The Santa Fe Internment Camp provides a baseball comic," and a poem appears at the top: "Spring baseball, the sentry looks around, boos, a very good catcher says the pitch is a strike, scares the batter."
    Source: Los Angeles, UCLA, Charles E. Young Research Library, Department of Special Collections.

    The revitalization of Japanese values in the camps is suggested by an entry in Reverend Taisho Tana's diary: "Being treated by the U.S. as enemy aliens, we should be reborn as Japanese, and realize that the U.S. is our enemy" (quoted in Okada, 1995, p. 60). About

1,000 internees at the Santa Fe camp chose voluntary deportation to Japan after the war (Okada, 1995).

Mutual Accommodation

The *Issei* in the Santa Fe Internment Camp were trapped in an illogical bureaucratic web. They were imprisoned by the American government during World War II because they were aliens; they were aliens because the U.S. government had prevented them by law from becoming citizens. This Catch-22 led to anger and frustration. The internment process served to isolate the *Issei* further from American society. The result was an uninhibited expression of Japanese culture, mainly in the form of non militant patriotism. For example, the internees at the Santa Fe camp, with the tacit permission of the camp's authorities, celebrated the Emperor's birthday by painting a red circle in the center of a white sheet, to make a huge Japanese flag.

Several events illustrate how the guards and administrators accommodated to the internees' frustration and heightened Japaneseness. For instance, Kenko Yamashita (1978, p. 193) explained: "The watchmen [guards] and sergeants knew how we felt. They tried to avoid anything that might upset us . . . . They gave us sake on New Year's Day because they knew that's a special day for the Japanese." Yamamoto (1976, p. 163) noted that the guards occasionally came down from their towers to play catch with the internees. Usually, they tossed a baseball back and forth in the space between two barracks, where they were unlikely to be seen. On at least one occasion, the camp administrator provided a special treat for the more cooperative internees by organizing a picnic for them outside of the camp grounds (Mukaeda, 1975).

Head counts were made at night while the *Issei* slept, rather than in daylight, which would be more demeaning to the internees (Melzer, 1994). Tom Yamamoto (1976, p. 177) pointed out that at first, the camp guards checked on him and the other sleeping internees with flashlights three times each night. It disturbed their sleep. The internees' spokesperson told the guards: "None of us would escape or try to escape even if you paid us [to do so]." The nightly flashlight inspections promptly stopped.

The camp's administrators (Loyd Jensen from April 19, 1943, to October 26, 1944, and then Ivan Williams) were seasoned INS officers, highly experienced in handling large numbers of aliens. Their general approach was to treat the internees with as much respect as possible under the circumstances. Abner Schrieber (1979, p. 91), the second-in-command, explained: "The Geneva Convention was the Bible . . . . If we gave the internees more than what they usually were entitled to as to food, space, and other things under the Geneva Convention, we would have something to take back as a punitive measure if they got out of line." One illustration of Schrieber's carrot-and-stick policy is the camp's visiting hours, which were six hours per week, well over the Geneva Convention's two hours per week. When two internees charged that the camp did not meet the provisions of the Geneva accords, the camp administrators retaliated by reducing visiting hours to two hours per week. After the internees' complaint to the Spanish Embassy, visiting hours were increased to 12 hours per week (Culley, 1991).

Many of the internees reciprocated the generally positive treatment that they received from the camp staff. Certain *Issei* at the Santa Fe camp referred to their truck farm as a "Victory Garden," a direct reference to *American* wartime patriotism. Further, some of the internees saved and collected scrap iron for the U.S. war effort, as part of a national scrap metal drive! There could not have been much scrap metal inside the Santa Fe camp, except for small items like razor blades and nails.

Masaru Ben Akahori (1944) was a small businessman in Seattle until December 7, 1941, when the FBI arrived at his home to arrest him as a dangerous enemy alien. He was detained for several months at Fort Missoula, Montana, and then transferred to the Lordsburg Internment Camp, where he encountered rattlesnakes, scorpions, and Gila monsters. Some 18 months later, Akahori was moved to the Santa Fe Internment Camp, where he spent most of the rest of the war years.

Hundreds of letters to his wife and daughter, who were in the Minidoka Relocation Camp, display his strong American loyalty. He enrolled in English language classes, and became a journalist on the camp newspaper. Akahori saved the money that he earned and purchased U.S. War Bonds for his daughter, who he encouraged to sing "God Bless America" in her school, and to be a good citizen. His wife Kikuko wrote to him on April 10, 1943: "I am determined to become a part of American soil in order to bring up a new American generation, am willing to take part in patriotic duties such as school PTA. My one point is to make an American of our child and a true one."

Akahori continued to admire the U.S. judicial system, even while his hearings and rehearings went against him, and while his pleas to be reunited with his wife and daughter at the Crystal City Internment Camp went unheeded. As his months and years in the internment camps went by, Akahori became increasingly religious. He joined a Christian church, was christened, and urged his family members to do the same. He consistently crossed out the word "Prisoner" in "Prisoner of War," which was stamped on the letterhead envelopes which he was provided at Santa Fe, and defiantly wrote in "Internee" (Akahori, 1944).

The internees evaded certain camp rules. For example, they manufactured homemade sake from rice, raisins, and sugar that they stole from camp supplies. Later, the camp administrators allowed the *Issei* to buy beer. After the camp was vacated in 1946, workmen found underground caches of knives, hatchets, and other homemade weapons, although no serious fighting occurred among the internees or with the camp guards (except for the minor revolt by several hundred *Kibei* in March 1945). Disputes occurred among the internees, but were settled without involving camp staff, so that no record appeared in the internees' files (which might affect release of the *Issei* to join their families in a relocation camp). On November 14, 1945, Otomatsu Kimura scaled the camp's fence near a guard tower in broad daylight, demanding that the guard shoot him. Kimura had mental problems, and had made several previous suicide attempts at another camp (Melzer, 1994).

Some of the Santa Fe internees were so pro-Japan that they refused to believe that the war was over, even when they were shown the famous *Life* magazine photograph[28] of General MacArthur with the Japanese Emperor (Mukaeda, 1975). A letter from an internee at the Santa Fe camp, Kazuo Kodoni (August 21, 1945), stated, "There has been various rumors going around this camp since the war ended. All the publications of the United States are false and propaganda. Japan is victorious in this War, and that is positive, so do not worry." Another letter, this from Miye Ichiki (August 21, 1945), said: "Regardless of what the newspapers and radio say, Japan has positively won this War. They have defeated the inhuman nations of United States and Britain. With the great object to be accomplished such as creating a great East Asia for Prosperity, our nation will be never surrender."

Minor Revolts

Two violent events occurred during the five years of the Santa Fe Internment Camp. The first happened when news of the Bataan Death March initially reached Santa Fe in spring, 1942; many New Mexico families had relatives in the 200th Regiment in the Philippines (see Chapter 2). An angry mob of townspeople, armed with shotguns and hatchets, marched on the Santa Fe camp (Mangione, 1978). The camp commander convinced the crowd that any violent action would only result in retribution by the Japanese against the New Mexican POWs in the Philippines and in Japan (Okada, 1995). After the mob dispersed, the Japanese American internees petitioned the camp administrators to raise the height of the perimeter fence by an additional foot (Mangione, 1978).

A more violent affair involved 366 *Kibei* troublemakers who transferred to the Santa Fe camp from the Tule Lake Relocation Camp. They led a minor revolt, involving ten minutes of violence, on the morning of March 12, 1945. Several months previously, these Japanese

American dissidents had renounced their American citizenship at the Tule Lake Relocation Camp, the center at which troublemakers from all ten WRA relocation camps were concentrated. By renouncing their U.S. citizenship, the Tuleans legally became enemy aliens and thus were moved to the Santa Fe Internment Camp. They wore white headbands on their shaved heads, blew bugles, and behaved in a militantly Japanese manner. They were organized in two groups: (1) *Sokuji Kikoku Hoshi-Dan*, the Organization to Return Immediately to the Homeland to Serve, and (2) *Hokoku Seinen-Dan*, the Young Men's Organization to Serve Our Mother Country.

Abner Schrieber (1979, p. 94), who was in charge of security at the camp, described the *Kibei* leaders in his report of the incident as "surly." The Tule Lake dissidents were markedly unlike the older *Issei* at the Santa Fe camp, and the two groups of Japanese Americans did not mix. Some isolated beatings of *Issei* leaders occurred in the camp, and a strong-arm Suicide Squad threatened the camp's censors with death (Clark, 1980; Culley, 1991). On March 10, 1945, a complete search of the 366 Tulean internees was made by camp guards, and several dozen white sweatshirts adorned with a rising sun were confiscated. These sweatshirts, which served as a kind of uniform for the dissidents, had been banned at the Santa Fe camp. Anticipating trouble, Schrieber brought in 30 Border Patrol inspectors from El Paso, to reinforce his cadre of local guards. The number of guards in each tower was doubled, and submachine guns and riot guns were issued (Culley, 1991).

Schrieber felt that "something was ready to pop." On the morning of March 12, three Tulean ringleaders learned that they would be moved to another camp. A crowd of 250 to 300 gathered at the wire fence in front of the administration building. "We asked them to 'Break it up'" (Schrieber, 1979, p. 94). He then repeated the order four or five times, and asked a secretary to take notes on what transpired, so that he could document what happened in his official report on the incident.

After these repeated warnings, Schrieber ordered tear gas canisters fired into the crowd, and then led 16 of the Border Patrol officers into the barracks area, armed with night sticks. They had borrowed the night sticks from the Military Police at Bruns General Hospital in Santa Fe. Schrieber (1979, p. 95) said that the dissidents had "a heck of a lot of iron pipe," as well as crowbars and rocks. His guards hit the *Kibei* with the night sticks, but they were made of "some kind of balsa wood," and many of the sticks broke (Schrieber, 1979, p. 95).

Schrieber and his men formed a wedge-like phalanx, which they drove into the U-shaped group of *Kibei* shaveheads, who were throwing stones at them from three sides. The guards shortly put the Tule Lake dissidents under control: "We broke it up. There were a few guys lying around there after it was over (Schrieber, 1979, p. 95). Some 30 internees suffered bruises from being beaten with the night sticks; four injured Tuleans were treated at the camp hospital. The 366 dissidents were placed in the camp's stockade; some were held for up to one month. The 17 leaders of the rock-throwing incident were transferred to Japanese Segregation Camp #1 at Fort Stanton (Clark, 1980). In a March 15, 1945, letter to each internee, Ivan Williams, the Officer-in-Charge of the Santa Fe camp, said that the rising sun sweatshirts became, "as a result of the acts of hoodlumism and worse that have been carried out by at least some of the more rabble-rousing members of this group, a symbol of such intolerable activities." Williams (March 15, 1945) concluded: "I wish to make it clear that no internees have anything to fear from the 'Suicide Squad.' Its members will not be here very long. And where they are going, they will not be together." The 17 Tulean leaders, after exile to Fort Stanton, were repatriated to Japan (Culley, 1991).

Eventually, the Santa Fe camp settled back to its usual slow routine, although the Tuleans continued to be an unruly element in the camp. They kept to themselves, not mixing with the older *Issei*. Abner Schrieber, on orders from INS headquarters, told his camp staff to observe a "press blackout" about the minor revolt (Schrieber, 1979, pp. 97-98).

The above account is the official government record of the March 12, 1945, incident, filed by the camp's administrators. A quite different perspective is provided by Bill Nishimura (2001), one of the Tulean *Nisei* in the Santa Fe Internment Camp. A truck farmer in Southern California before the war, Nishimura was sent to the Poston Relocation Camp, where he "did a lot of farm work, and also plenty of fishing" in the nearby Colorado River. When confronted with the famous two questions, Nishimura declared himself to be a "no-no." He insisted that he would not serve with the U.S. Army until his human rights were restored. Shortly thereafter, in January, 1944, he was transferred to Tule Lake, where he joined the *Hoshi-Dan*, enrolled in Japanese language classes, and began planning to become a Japanese citizen. In early 1945, Nishimura was transferred to the Santa Fe camp with the other Tulean "troublemakers," where he was reunited with his father, also interned at Santa Fe.

On the morning of March 12, Nishimura says that he and the other Tuleans lined up against the camp fence to say "Sayonara (goodbye) to several of their *Hoshi-Dan* friends. Border Patrol officers ordered them to disperse, and fired tear gas at them, which blew back on the officers. A melee ensued when the officers entered the camp gate and charged the Tuleans with their night sticks. The conflict was short-lived and inconsequential, as Nishimura remembers it. Thereafter, his possessions were inspected and he was forced to cut out the rising sun symbols on his sweaters and teeshirts. He spent several months in the camp stockade with his fellow Tuleans. He requested exchange to Japan, but could not go with the other repatriatees because his father became very ill. Abner Schrieber arranged for Nishimura to work as a hospital orderly, so that he could be at his father's side. Nishimura began to feel that the U.S. government had a human side after all. Nishimura reconsidered his request to renounce his U.S. citizenship.

In November 1945, Nishimura and his father were moved to the Crystal City Internment Camp, and finally, after more than five years in internment, Nishimura (2001) was released. He returned to Gardena,

CA, where he has spent his life as a quiet gardener. When the present authors interviewed Nishimura in April 2001, he said that he was still working as a full-time gardener, although he sometimes had to rest for an hour in midday. The former *Hoshi-Dan* activist is now a congenial older man.

The Santa Fe Internment Camp closed on May 1946, when the dozen remaining internees were transferred to the internment camp at Crystal City, Texas. Nothing remains today of the Santa Fe Internment Camp, except for the graves of two of the *Issei*, N. Sudo and D. Yoshikawa, who are interned forever in Rosario Cemetery. Small concrete headstones mark the two graves, which are at some distance from the other graves.

In 1997, a movement began to construct a memorial to the Japanese Americans who had been interned at the Santa Fe camp. After considerable conflict with the Bataan survivors, in October 1999, the Santa Fe City Council voted to proceed with a marker (Chapter 2), which is located on a site overlooking the former internment camp (see Figure 4-11). The marker, consisting of a bronze plaque on a huge boulder, was dedicated in 2002.

Bill Nishimura recollected, "'The government really starved us in Santa Fe. We got enough to eat, but this was an all-male camp so we were starved for female companionship'" He continued, "'I always thought I would be deported . . . . To my surprise, Uncle Sam said, "If you wish to stay here, you may do so." So, I felt Uncle Sam still has a warm heart in him.'" Subsequently, Nishimura chose to reinstate his citizenship (Sharpe, 2002) and declared, "I just love this country" (Ando, 2002).

Table 4-1.
Time-Line of the Santa Fe Detention/Internment Camp.

Date	Event
1942	
February 19	President Roosevelt signs Executive Order #9066.
March 14	425 *Issei* arrive (1,212 Japanese Americans out of 1,771 "enemy aliens" were rounded up right after the bombing of Pearl Harbor).
April	401 more *Issei* arrive; 826 detainees in camp.
April-Aug.	Release or parole of 523 of 826 detainees decided by Alien Enemy Hearing Boards (16-17 residents of Los Angeles; 9 residents of Santa Fe comprise board).
September 24	Last detainee departed; camp closed (temporarily abandoned).
1943	
March 23	357 *Issei* internees arrive.
June 16	Camp totals 1,257 male internees.
August	Camp totals 1,783 male internees.
1944	
Late & '45 and	366 *Kibei* males from Tule Lake "Segregation Center" Relocation Camp were transferred to Santa Fe, NM, Ft. Lincoln, ND (Fort Missoula, MT).
1945	
March 12	Minor revolt (366 persons put in stockade). 17 sent to Ft. Stanton, NM.
June	Maximum camp population totaled 2,200 or about 10% of Santa Fe population of 20,325.
September 2	World War II ends; Japan signs surrender documents.
1946	
April 18	Camp closes permanently.

The Lordsburg Army Camp

Both the WRA and the INS operated specialized facilities for the hard-core resistors who refused to go along with the relocation/internment process. The WRA channeled their protesters initially to a camp at Moab, Utah, which was opened in December 1942, and continued for several months. Then, on April 27, 1943, the individuals from Moab were transferred to the Leupp Isolation Center, in Arizona. There a former boarding school on the Navajo Reservation was outfitted with barbed-wire and guard towers.[29] Some 150 Military Police guarded 80 prisoners, who were considered "difficult" Japanese Americans from Tule Lake and other WRA camps.

The INS internment camps at Santa Fe and at Crystal City also identified their "troublemakers," individuals who refused to go along with the internment process. Perhaps they tried to escape their camp, went on a hunger strike to protest against the food service, or organized some other protest. These "troublemakers" were shipped to the Army POW camp at Lordsburg, which mainly held German and Italian POWS, or to Fort Stanton. As Abner Schrieber (1979, p. 92), the second-in-command at the Santa Fe Internment Camp, explained, Fort Stanton was the "stinker camp," that is, for the worst troublemakers. As mentioned previously, Fort Stanton was officially identified as Japanese Segregation Camp #1.

At the beginning of World War II, the Lordsburg Camp experienced a host of internal troubles due to inept leadership. Lieutenant Richard S. Dockum served as adjutant (that is, second-in-command) at Lordsburg from June 1942, for about one year.[30] The base commander was Lieutenant Colonel Clyde A. Lundy, a regular Army officer who had worked his way up from enlisted man (Fukuda, 1990). Lt. Dockum (1977, p. 52) described his boss as "the typical Army officer, wearing his boots and carrying a riding crop . . . . He liked very much the old, formal entertaining that the Army had always had in peacetime. He wanted a party every Saturday night at the Officers' Club."

Dockum (1977, p. 57) described one of these parties: "We fixed up the Officers' Club with bales of hay and so forth. We had the old artillery horses and wagons . . . . We had these wagons meet the guests at the camp gate. They came to the building in hay-filled wagons. Then they had to crawl through a tunnel of hay going into the Officers' Club. Some local musicians, cowboys who played the fiddle and all, furnished the music. We had some cages with chickens and pigs all around to give it an authentic look. I was dressed as the old black mountaineer, barefoot, with a beard, hat, shotgun, and a jug . . . . A lieutenant's wife . . . weighed about two hundred pounds. She had on a regular apron affair with sunbonnet, a corncob pipe, and GI shoes. Colonel Baker was the doctor who ran the hospital. He dressed as one of the Japanese internees, and he would say, 'So solly, please' . . . . They fixed a 'well' over in one corner with buckets, you know, that you draw up. One bucket had Manhattans and another had martinis . . . . Finally, the fiddler became drunk enough to fall off a bale of hay and that put an end to the dancing."

Colonel Lundy kept his office safe stocked with liquor. Each day as the sun went down, the safe was opened and "after that, the sky was the limit" (Dockum, 1977, p. 53). Lundy was eventually charged with such irregularities as (1) transferring funds from the Japanese Americans' post exchange (store) to the Officers' Club, (2) diverting food from the Japanese Americans' rations to the Army mess halls, and (3) assigning musical instruments provided to the Japanese Americans by the International Red Cross, to the Officers' Club. Colonel Louis Ledbetter, who replaced Colonel Lundy as camp commander, investigated these and other administrative irregularities. Lundy was let off of the charges in exchange for his agreement to retire immediately.

A serious problem occurred under Colonel Lundy's leadership, the shooting of two Japanese Americans by a camp guard on July 27, 1942. Some 147 *Issei* from the Bismarck (North Dakota) Internment Camp arrived at the train station at Plateau, near the Lordsburg camp. Twenty-five guards met the new arrivals at 3:30 in the morning, and escorted them to the Lordsburg camp, a distance of two miles (Pressler,

2000). Two of the Japanese Americans, Toshihiro Kobata and Isomura Hirata, sixty-year-old invalids, could not keep up with the march. Kobata had suffered from tuberculosis and Hirata had a spinal injury from working on a fishing boat. The two *Issei* lagged behind the others, accompanied by one guard, Private Clarence A. Burleson. They walked a ways, rested, and then walked some more. As they neared the front gate of the camp, the two *Issei* requested permission to urinate against the fence alongside the road. The guard claimed that the two internees tried to escape. He shouted for them to halt, and then fired his 12-gauge Stevens sawed-off riot shotgun.

The Japanese Americans in the Lordsburg camp heard the shots, and noted that the two elderly men failed to appear. Later, camp administrators informed them that the two *Issei* had been killed while trying to escape. People in Lordsburg took up a collection for the guard, promising him free meals and drinks (Dockum, 1977). Private Burelson was court martialed but cleared of the charges because it was decided that he shot the two internees in the line of duty. It seems dubious that the two invalids, barely able to walk, could have escaped. The Army transferred Burelson to a combat unit in North Africa (Pressler, 2000).

On another occasion during 1942, 20 American convict soldiers were interned with the Japanese Americans in the Lordsburg camp, despite complaints to Colonel Lundy from the internees. While under the influence of alcohol, on Thanksgiving Day, one of the convicts jumped astride a Japanese American, Dr. Uyehara, and stabbed him repeatedly. The American convict was subsequently court martialed, the camp Commander was reprimanded, and then removed from command (Clark, 1980). Clearly, the Army POW camp at Lordsburg was out-of-control in 1942, until Colonel Lundy was replaced.

Finally, during the last year of the war, the Japanese Americans were moved out, and the Lordsburg Camp held 4,000 German prisoners-of-war captured in Normandy, and 3,500 Italian POWs captured in North Africa. Many of these prisoners at Lordsburg were "incorrigibles" who were transferred from other Army POW camps.

Today, artifacts of the former Lordsburg camp can be observed just east of Lordsburg. Hundreds of huge concrete blocks, used as tie-downs for the barracks, litter the area. One block has *"Viva Italia"* scratched on its surface. Several tarpaper barracks remain on the flat alkali fields, a forlorn reminder of the prison community that once bustled along POW Road.

RESTITUTION

After the war, when the Japanese Americans returned to their homes, stores, and farms, they often found that their personal property had been seized by their former neighbors. Most of their goods stored privately were rifled, stolen, burned, or sold (Weglyn, 1976). After the war, some 43,000 (39 percent) Japanese Americans scattered to Illinois (15,000), Colorado (6,000), Utah (5,000), Ohio (3,900), Idaho (3,500), and other non-West Coast states.

Most *Nisei* were reluctant to discuss their relocation camp experience, as they sought to blend into American society. The third-generation Japanese American *Sansei* had little interest in the wartime relocation of their people, even though some of them were born in the camps. They excelled at getting a university education, and many entered the professions of law, medicine, and business. Eventually Japanese Americans gained political power, and several were elected to the U.S. Congress.

In the 1970s, as a result of the civil rights movement in the United States, Japanese Americans became increasingly interested in the World War II mistreatment of their people. The admission of Hawaii to the Union in 1959 meant that several Asian American legislators were elected to Congress (Daniels, 1991). Japanese American politicians like U.S. Senators Daniel K. Inouye and Spark Matsunaga of Hawaii and Congressman Norman Y. Mineta of San Jose and Robert T. Matsui of Sacramento led this political process (Hatamiya, 1993). In 1981 a federal commission was appointed to investigate; it recommended a government apology and a cash payment. In 1988 with passage of the

Civil Liberties Act, a formal apology was made. Each of the 80,000 evacuatees still living was sent a letter of apology from U.S. President George H. Bush and awarded $20,000, with the first payments made in October 1990, to the oldest Japanese Americans. The total compensation amounted to $1.65 billion. In his letter of apology, President Bush stated, "We can take a clear stand for justice and recognize that serious injustices were done to Japanese Americans during World War II" (quoted in Takezawa, 1985, p. 28). Unfortunately, very few of the 4,500 Japanese Americans who had been in the Santa Fe Internment Camp were alive in 1990 to benefit from the restitution payments.

A Japanese American Memorial is located in Washington, D.C., between the Capitol and Union Station on Louisiana Avenue, to honor citizens of Japanese ancestry who were persecuted during World War II. The $10 million monument is a statue of two cranes, one of whose wings are tied with barbed wire. The names of 800 *Nisei* soldiers who died for their country, and the names of the ten relocation camps are inscribed on plaques. Former Congressman Norman Mineta, who wrote the legislation for the memorial, remembers when his family was ordered to leave their San Jose home for a relocation camp in 1942. Mineta, wearing his Cub Scout uniform, took his bat, ball, and glove with him. A U.S. Army military policeman confiscated his baseball bat as a lethal weapon (Wheeler, 1999). In the days following the September 11, 2001, terrorist attacks on the United States, Mineta, the U.S. Secretary of Transportation, urged President George W. Bush not to discriminate against Arab-Americans solely on the basis of their ethnicity.

❖ ❖ ❖

Finally, almost 60 years after it began, this sad chapter in American history was closed for most Japanese Americans, but not for the Japanese from Latin America and South America.

5

LOS ALAMOS

> " . . . we can propose no technical demonstration likely to bring an end to the war; we see no acceptable alternative to direct military use."
> —(J. Robert Oppenheimer, "Memorandum for the Secretary of War," June 26, 1945, quoted in Herken, 2002, p. 134.)

The early end of the Pacific War resulted (1) from the development, and the testing, of the atomic bomb, which took place in New Mexico, at Los Alamos and at Trinity, respectively, and (2) from its use, shortly thereafter, to destroy Hiroshima and Nagasaki. The first of these events was located in New Mexico because the state had vast areas of relatively uninhabited space. Remoteness was an important requirement for the super-secret Manhattan Project. Neither the Germans nor the Japanese knew that the United States had developed an atomic bomb until President Truman's 1945 radio announcement of the destruction of Hiroshima, although Russian leaders had been well-informed through their spies in Los Alamos.

Development of the atomic bomb was one of the greatest scientific achievements of all time. The Manhattan Project represented a huge investment, $2.2 billion (worth many times this amount in today's dollars), and the work of 129,000 people over a period of several years. At the time, the Manhattan Project was the largest scientific project in history (Goodchild, 1985). In fact, not even a rich nation like the United States would have made this vast investment in developing an atomic bomb unless in desperate straits, such as in a world war of uncertain outcome.[1]

BACKGROUND OF THE ATOMIC BOMB

During the 1920s and 1930s, the main centers of academic excellence in theoretical physics were the Cavendish Laboratory at Cambridge University in England, the University of Göttingen in Germany, the University of Copenhagen, Denmark, and several other European laboratories. German scientists dominated the ranks of Nobel laureates during the decades until the 1930s. Nearly all of the American physicists who later became well known for developing the atomic bomb had traveled to Europe, especially to Göttingen, to earn their Ph.D. degrees (Jungk, 1956). One of these young Americans was J. Robert Oppenheimer, who was to serve as the scientific director of Project Y, the Los Alamos Project to develop the atomic bomb.

"Oppie" (as he was called by those who knew him well), the son of wealthy Jewish parents in New York, was educated at a private school, and at Harvard, where he graduated *summa cum laude* in chemistry in three years. He was brilliant and multi-talented, a kind of Renaissance individual. Oppie wrote poetry, studied languages (like Sanskrit), read widely, and loved hiking and outdoor life. He was also a whiz at science, although his friends at Harvard noticed that he never seemed to study very much. A college friend said that Oppenheimer "intellectually looted Harvard," taking the maximum of six courses per term the University regulations allowed, while auditing four more (Rhodes, 1986, p. 121). While a freshman, Oppenheimer petitioned the physics department for graduate standing, so that he could enroll in graduate-level courses. He did not have a single date during his three years at Harvard (Goodchild, 1985).

As Oppenheimer approached graduation, he decided to pursue a career in physics. The late 1920s were an exciting time for scholars in this field, with new theoretical breakthroughs like Einstein's theory of relativity pointing to new directions. Supported by fellowships from the U.S. government and from private foundations, Oppenheimer attended the University of Göttingen. He typically worked all night, and then slept most of the day (Schweber, 2000). Oppenheimer conducted research on applications of quantum mechanics to the changes in the paths and the velocity of atomic particles when they collide (Smith & Weiner, 1995). Oppenheimer's research with Max Born, Director of the Institute of Theoretical Physics at Göttingen, led to his Ph.D. degree (with distinction) in 1927. Oppenheimer completed his Ph.D. degree in one year.

Göttingen at this time represented an intellectual crossroads of continental physics. The physicists leading the new paradigm of quantum wave mechanics engaged in a collaborative problem-solving process of research conferences, correspondence, and criticism (Smith & Weiner, 1995). Hans Bethe remembered the 1920s and 1930s as a golden age: "The physicists of all countries knew each other well and were friends. And life at the centers of the development of quantum theory, Copenhagen and Göttingen, was idyllic and leisurely, in spite of the enormous amount of work accomplished" (Schweber, 2000, p. 100).

Oppenheimer's personal relationships with leading European scholars of the New Physics were a crucial resource that he brought back across the Atlantic. His study on the Continent gave him membership in a personal network with the greatest minds in physics.[2] This network would later prove crucial when Oppenheimer was recruiting for the Los Alamos Project.

The Discovery of Fission

Given the preeminence of German science in the 1920s and early 1930s, it is not surprising that the key breakthrough in setting off the race to the atomic bomb occurred in Berlin in 1938, with the discovery of fission by Otto Hahn and Fritz Strassman. They demonstrated that the nucleus of uranium, one of the heaviest of elements, when bombarded with neutrons, could be split into two or more parts, releasing tremendous energy. The sum of the masses of the fission fragments (including that of the neutrons) was *less* than that of the uranium nucleus. Thus the fission process transferred mass into energy in accordance with Einstein's famous formula, $E = mc^2$.

Realization that an atomic bomb was feasible had occurred five years previously, to Leo Szilard, an eccentric Hungarian theoretical physicist and friend of Albert Einstein (they both had taught at the University of Berlin). Of Jewish heritage and a refugee from Hitler's fascism, Szilard had temporarily alighted in London. He remembers when the idea of a chain reaction hit him. It was September 1, 1933, and Szilard was staying at the Imperial Hotel.[3] He was waiting on a red light to cross Southampton Row, "As the light changed to green and I crossed the street, it . . . . suddenly occurred to me that if we could find an element which is split by neutrons and which would emit *two* neutrons when it absorbs *one* neutron, such an element, if assembled in sufficiently large mass, could sustain a nuclear chain reaction" (quoted in Rhodes, 1986, p. 28). With this profound realization, humankind was on its way to developing a nuclear chain reaction. Over the next dozen years, Szilard was to be a leading advocate for England and America to develop an atomic bomb before Germany did.

Otto Hahn and Fritz Strassman worked in the Kaiser Wilhelm Institute of Chemistry in Dahlem, a suburb of Berlin. Lise Meitner, Hahn's long-term research partner, had suggested to him that they bombard uranium, element 92 in the periodic chart of the elements, with neutrons (an ideal tool because neutrons do not carry an electrical charge), thus following a procedure pioneered by Enrico Fermi in Rome. When Hahn and Strassman performed this experiment on December 16, 1938, to their amazement, they found traces of *barium*, with an atomic weight of 56, half the periodic table away from uranium! This result seemed completely bizarre. The two German scientists conveyed their puzzling results to Meitner, who, as an Austrian Jew, had fled from Hitler to Sweden. On December 19, 1938, Otto Hahn wrote to his colleague Meitner in Stockholm: "The thing is: There is something so ODD about the 'radium isotopes' that for the moment we don't want to tell anyone but you . . . . Our RA [radium] isotopes behave like BA [barium] . . . . Perhaps you can suggest some fantastic explanation" (quoted in Rife, 1999, pp. 182-183).

Table 5-1.
Time-Line for the Development of the Atomic Bomb.

Date	Event
1938	
December	Discovery of fission in Berlin by Otto Hahn and Fritz Strassman, and the identification of this process by Lise Meitner and Robert Frisch.
1939	
March	Germany occupies Czechoslovakia, and stops uranium exports.
July 16	Hungarian refugees Leo Szilard, Eugene Wigner, and Edward Teller visit Albert Einstein, who writes a letter to President Roosevelt about the possibility of a German atomic bomb.
September 1	World War II begins with the German invasion of Poland.
October 11	Alexander Sachs takes Einstein's letter to Roosevelt, who establishes the President's Advisory Committee on Uranium.
1940	
	Germany conquers most of Europe and bombs Britain.
1941	
March 1	Glenn Seaborg and his colleagues discover plutonium.
December 7	The Japanese bomb Pearl Harbor, and the United States declares war on Japan, and shortly on Germany and Italy.
1942	
June	Robert Oppenheimer leads a summer conference at Berkeley to explore the feasibility of making an atomic bomb.

September 17	General Leslie Groves becomes director of the Manhattan Project.
November	Los Alamos is selected as the laboratory site to develop the atomic bomb.
December 2	First self-sustaining nuclear chain reaction in the Met Lab at the University of Chicago by Enrico Fermi.

1943

March	Oppenheimer and a few staff arrive in Los Alamos, soon to be followed by several thousand others.

1944

June 6	D-Day landings in Normandy, France.

1945

May 8	Germany accepts surrender on 7th; War in Europe ends (V-E Day).
July 14	Little Boy is transported from Los Alamos to the B-29 base on Tinian in the Pacific.
July 16	First atomic explosion of a plutonium implosion-type bomb, Fat Man, at Trinity Site, New Mexico.
July 26	The Allies issue the Potsdam Declaration, calling for Japan's unconditional surrender.
August 6	A uranium-235 gun-type bomb, Little Boy, is dropped on Hiroshima.
August 8	USSR declares war on Japan.
August 9	Fat Man is dropped on Nagasaki.
August 14	Emperor Hirohito proclaims in a nationwide radio broadcast that Japan surrenders.
September 2	Official surrender ceremonies are held on board the USS *Missouri* in Tokyo Bay.
October 16	Oppenheimer resigns as Director of the Los Alamos Laboratory.

1946

June	Bikini atomic bomb tests held.

1949

August 29	The Soviet Union tests an atomic bomb.

Meitner was a brilliant scientist; Einstein called her "our Madame Curie" (Cassidy, 1992, p. 310).[4] Meitner discussed the Hahn/Strassman scientific conundrum with her nephew, Otto Robert Frisch, a German physicist 34 years her junior, who came to visit her over the December holidays from Copenhagen, where he was studying with Niels Bohr. He and Meitner met in the small Swedish town of Kungaelv, near Goeteborg (Frisch, 1979, p. 114). Meitner and Frisch developed the theory of fission while taking a walk in the woods on Christmas Eve, 1938 (Wheeler, 1998). Frisch skied while Meitner walked, as they discussed the puzzling results just in from Berlin. Finally he unstrapped his skis and they sat on a snow-covered log. Meitner pulled a pencil and paper out of her winter coat pocket.

They imagined the uranium nucleus as a wobbly and unstable drop of liquid, not as a solid, and calculated that about 200 million volts of energy would be required to divide it (Frisch, 1979). Then, using, Einstein's formula of $E = mc^2$, they calculated the energy released by such fission as equivalent to one-fifth the mass of a proton, which was 200 million volts! Frisch exclaimed, "It all fit!" (Rife, 1999, p. 190). The energy released by splitting one atom was enough to split another, which would set off a chain reaction. After Christmas, Frisch returned to Bohr's lab in Copenhagen to test their theory; by January 13, 1939, he had evidence that uranium emitted energy when it split (Rife, 1999). Frisch named the process of splitting the uranium atom "fission." Meitner and Frisch concluded that barium had been produced as a result of splitting uranium, with the combined mass of the fission products totaling slightly less than the parent material. The difference in weight released a tremendous amount of energy.

Uranium is a dense, blue-purple metal. Its main use had been as a coloring agent for pottery glaze and for painting luminous numbers on watch dials. Suddenly, with news of the Hahn/Strassman discovery of fission, uranium came to be regarded as a very precious commodity. Ominously, Hitler would invade Poland only nine months later, in September 1939, and World War II would begin. It was not too difficult to imagine that a uranium fission bomb might play a key role in the rapidly approaching war.

The Race to the Atomic Bomb Begins

News of the Hahn/Strassman discovery of fission in December 1938, followed a complicated trail of personal network relationships from Berlin to America. Frisch, Lise Meitner's nephew, returned to Copenhagen from visiting his aunt in Sweden in order to continue his research with Niels Bohr, just before Bohr departed on the SS *Drottningholm* to cross the Atlantic. Bohr was to take up a visiting professorship at Princeton University in January 1939. John Wheeler, who had been a postdoctoral student with Bohr in Copenhagen in 1935, was teaching at Princeton in 1939. He greeted Bohr at dockside in New York Harbor on January 16, 1939. The welcoming committee also included Enrico Fermi and his wife (Fermi, an Italian, had fled Mussolini's fascism two weeks earlier, and was teaching at Columbia University). Bohr told them of the recent fission experiment by Hahn and Strassman in Berlin.

Once settled at Princeton, Bohr collaborated with Wheeler on a theory of nuclear fission. Niels Bohr was 53 and world-famous, while Wheeler was 27 and an assistant professor of physics, but they worked well together, in part because of their previous collaboration in Copenhagen. Bohr's news about fission caused an instant turmoil of scientific excitement at the Conference on Theoretical Physics on January 26, 1939, in Washington. Some physicists bolted from the meeting, rushing to their laboratory or telephoning distant colleagues. Oppenheimer, who was teaching at University of California Berkeley in 1939, heard the news from Berlin. A faculty colleague said: "I do not recall ever seeing Oppie so stimulated and so full of ideas" (Smith & Weiner, 1995, p. 207).

Otto Frisch and another German physicist, Rudolf Peierls, arrived as refugees in England, where they alerted the British government about the possibility of a German atomic bomb project. The British, moving with greater speed than their American counterparts, established the "Tube Alloys" Project, their atomic bomb project, which later joined forces with the Manhattan Project at Los Alamos.

The 1930s were the beginning of the United States' rise to scientific eminence. The shift in the center of science across the Atlantic was mainly due to Adolf Hitler. His persecution of the Jewish people in Germany led to a vast intellectual migration, beginning in 1933 when Hitler became the German chancellor. The non-Jewish atomic physicists who remained in Germany, like Werner Heisenberg, were hampered in their research and teaching by the politicization of science. Hitler and his followers forbad German physicists to mention Einstein's name (which made it awkward to lecture about the theory of relativity). Theoretical physics, which the Nazis called "Jewish physics," went into a steep decline. Hitler's atomic bomb project also floundered because Germany lacked the vast industrial resources for production of the uranium and plutonium for an atomic bomb.[5]

Einstein's Letter

Albert Einstein was at the Institute for Advanced Study at Princeton University in 1939, having led the great migration of European brainpower across the Atlantic in 1933. Einstein had developed the theory of relativity, won a Nobel Prize, and was the most famous scientist of his time. In July 1939, Einstein was approached by three Jewish refugee scientists from Hungary, Leo Szilard, Eugene Wigner, and Edward Teller. Old friends, they met with Einstein at his summer home on Long Island, at Old Grove Pond, on Nassau Point, to implore him to write a letter to U.S. President Franklin Delano Roosevelt alerting him to the threat posed by the German capability to create an atomic bomb. It was a half year after the Hahn/Strassman discovery of fission. Szilard, in a one-man campaign to raise the alarm about the threat of a German atomic bomb, called himself a "meddling foreigner." The idea of a nuclear chain reaction was his obsession (Rhodes, 1986, p. 203).

It was Sunday, July 16, 1939. The three Hungarians got lost en route to Einstein's vacation house, and had to ask a small boy for directions.[6] Finally, they found Einstein's summer place, and sat with him on his porch. Einstein and the three Hungarians drafted and redrafted the letter. On September 1, 1939, Germany invaded Poland, and World War II began. President Roosevelt was now extremely occupied with international affairs, and Einstein could not contact him. Finally, on October 11, 1939, the letter was conveyed to President Roosevelt in the White House by Alexander Sachs, another European émigré and a personal friend of the President. Einstein's letter stated: "Sir: Some recent work by E. Fermi and L. Szilard . . . leads me to expect that the element uranium may be turned into a new and important source of energy in the near future . . . . Extremely powerful bombs of a new type may thus be constructed . . . .Yours Very Truly, A. Einstein."

As a consequence of Einstein's letter, President Roosevelt established the Advisory Committee on Uranium, headed by Lyman Briggs, but the effort languished for the next two years. Then in June 1940, Vannevar Bush, an electrical engineer from MIT who had become director of the government's Office of Scientific Research and Development (OSRD), took over leadership of the Uranium Committee. Bush was convinced by American and British intelligence reports[7] that the Germans were working on an atomic bomb (they were indeed, under the direction of Nobel Prize winner Werner Heisenberg).[8] Bush kick-started the Manhattan Project, placing it under the U.S. Corps of Army Engineers, the agency that he thought best equipped for the huge construction task that the Project would demand.

The Italian Navigator

Enrico Fermi, the leading Italian physicist, left Rome in 1938 to receive the Nobel Prize in Stockholm. His wife was Jewish, and Mussolini's fascist dictatorship pursued anti-Semitic policies. So the Fermis traveled to Stockholm and then kept on going, to a faculty appointment at Columbia University in New York, where Fermi continued his uranium research. Soon, his work on a controlled nuclear reaction was moved to the University of Chicago's Metallurgical Laboratory (the Met Lab). There he created the world's first self-sustained nuclear chain reaction on December 2, 1942, and thus became "the Prometheus of the Atomic Age" (Frisch, 1979, p. 22) (Figure 5-1).

Figure 5-1. Enrico Fermi, Nicknamed the "Italian Navigator," Created the First Self-Sustained Nuclear Chain Reaction at the University of Chicago.
Fermi headed an important physics research institute in Rome until he won the 1938 Nobel Prize. He migrated to Columbia University, then to the Met Lab at the University of Chicago, and finally to Los Alamos. On December 2, 1942, Fermi and his colleagues at the Met Lab created the world's first nuclear reaction to go critical.
Source: College Park, MD, Vemilio Segre Visual Archives, Niels Bohr Library, Center for History of Physics, American Institute of Physics.

Fermi and his Met Lab research team built a large pile of uranium bricks. The ominous black beehive was 25 feet wide by 20 feet high, and cost $1 million. "Neutrons were its bees, dancing and hot" (Rhodes, 1986, p. 439). The rate of fission was controlled by inserting or removing cadmium rods (cadmium absorbs neutrons). Fermi operated the pile for 28 minutes, gradually withdrawing the cadmium rods, while carefully measuring the reactivity of the uranium as radiation levels built up. Then Fermi shut down the pile by reinserting the cadmium rods (Segré, 1970). Neutrons from fission created further fission, releasing tremendous amounts of energy. The experiment was conducted beneath the West Stands of Stagg Field, an unused football stadium. This building was razed in 1957, and the location of the world's first self-sustaining chain reaction is marked today by a Henry Moore statue, *Nuclear Energy.*

Arthur Compton, Director of the Met Lab, sent the following coded message to James Conant at Harvard, the Associate Director of the OSRD, the U.S. program funding uranium research: "The Italian navigator [Fermi] has just landed in the new world." Conant asked, "Were the natives friendly?" Compton assured Conant that "Everybody landed safe and happy" (Groves, 1983, p. 54; Segré, 1970, p. 129). Fermi and his research team celebrated their accomplishment by drinking a bottle of Chianti out of paper cups.

Now the way was clear to develop an atomic bomb. And the United States was off to a good start in the race, thanks in large part to its European refugee scientists.

The Manhattan Project

In September 1942, President Roosevelt established the Manhattan Project (full name: the Manhattan Engineering District, U.S. Army Corps of Engineers) of the U.S. War Department. It was hoped that this strange name might deceive America's enemies as to the Project's real purpose. The Corps of Engineers constructed government buildings, dams, and other facilities, so it was logical for the Corps to be in charge of the atomic bomb project, which involved building a secret research and development laboratory, and two huge factories, all in remote locations, in Washington and Tennessee.

Colonel Leslie M. Groves was appointed to head the Manhattan Project on September 23, 1942 (Figure 5-2). Groves had just completed construction of the Pentagon, the vast building that served as the headquarters of the U.S. Department of the Army. He did not want to direct the Manhattan Project, instead demanding a combat assignment. Groves was one of the older Army colonels, and a promotion to brigadier general helped convince him to accept the Manhattan Project assignment (Goodchild, 1985). Groves was aggressive and blunt by nature, with a can-do attitude. Dr. Vannevar Bush originally felt that Groves lacked the tact needed to coordinate the diverse organizations and individuals that would be involved in the Manhattan Project. After his first meeting with Groves, Bush wrote to a colleague: "I fear we are in the soup." Later events showed just how wrong Bush had been in his initial assessment. The tough, brutally direct Groves turned out to be a good choice.

The Manhattan Project initially consisted of a loose network of physicists, chemists, mathematicians, and other scientists conducting research at several U.S. universities. Two large facilities were created to produce the uranium and the plutonium that would be needed. They were located at Oak Ridge, TN (originally called Site X, the Clinton Engineer Works), which concentrated on producing uranium, and at Hanford, WA, Site W, which produced plutonium. Both were given innocuous names, so as to attract minimum attention.

Figure 5-2. Major General Leslie Groves in the Washington, D.C., Office of the Manhattan Project.
Groves had just completed construction of the Pentagon in 1942, when he was assigned to direct the Manhattan Project. Colonel Groves preferred a combat assignment, and only reluctantly accepted leadership of the U.S. atomic bomb project. He was highly efficacious, with a reputation for accomplishing difficult tasks for the Army Corps of Engineers. Groves soon decided that U.S. research on the atomic bomb should be concentrated at one place, and chose Los Alamos as the secret site.
Source: Washington, D.C., National Archives, Photograph by J. E. Westcott of the Manhattan Project, NWDNS-208-PU-83S-2.

The Manhattan Project needed a critical mass of scientists at one place, rather than at scattered university locations. A headquarters site would serve as a central node for the dispersed network of atomic scientists, and would provide a location at which an atomic bomb could actually be assembled. The ordnance and engineering aspects of delivering an atomic bomb meant that engineers and other technicians would need to be involved, in addition to the physicists and chemists. If the combined efforts of the engineers and the atomic scientists were to be effective, they would have to work together at one, secret place. It would be at Site Y, Los Alamos, New Mexico.

J. ROBERT OPPENHEIMER

The Manhattan Project was centered in New Mexico because this state was a favorite of J. Robert Oppenheimer.

Perro Caliente

In 1922, at the request of his parents, one of Oppenheimer's high school teachers from New York led him and several of his friends on a trip to the Pecos River basin in northern New Mexico, a pristine area of trees and mountains. A sickly boy, Oppenheimer felt that his visit to New Mexico improved his health. The young New Yorker fell in love with the Land of Enchantment.

In 1928, when Oppenheimer was about to begin teaching at Berkeley, he was diagnosed with tuberculosis. Oppie and his brother Frank rented a small ranch cabin in the Sangre de Cristo Mountains east of Santa Fe, near Cowles, New Mexico. Oppenheimer jokingly called the cabin "Perro Caliente" because he exclaimed "Hot Dog!" when told that the property was available. Oppenheimer's father purchased the cabin, and in later years Oppenheimer arranged to spend a month or more each summer at the family's ranch house. With his brother and friends, Oppie went horseback riding and hiking in the mountains, greatly enjoying outdoor life.

Oppenheimer sometimes traveled on horseback the 40 miles to the Los Alamos Ranch School, located atop a mesa on the Pajarito Plateau, 35 miles northwest of Santa Fe (Figure 5-3). The school had been established in 1917 by Ashley Pond, Jr., a Detroit businessman and a firm believer in vigorous outdoor life. The 50 or 60 students, mainly the sons of elite East Coast families, wore Boy Scout-type uniforms year around (all were required to join Troop 22). They slept in unheated sleeping porches. Each student was responsible for a horse. The Ranch School stressed a Spartan, outdoor life that was intended to toughen up the students, who came from sheltered homes. The masculine ideology of the Los Alamos Ranch School was inspired by

Teddy Roosevelt; Ashley Pond had been one of Roosevelt's Rough Riders in the Spanish-American War (Chambers & Aldrich, 1999).[9]

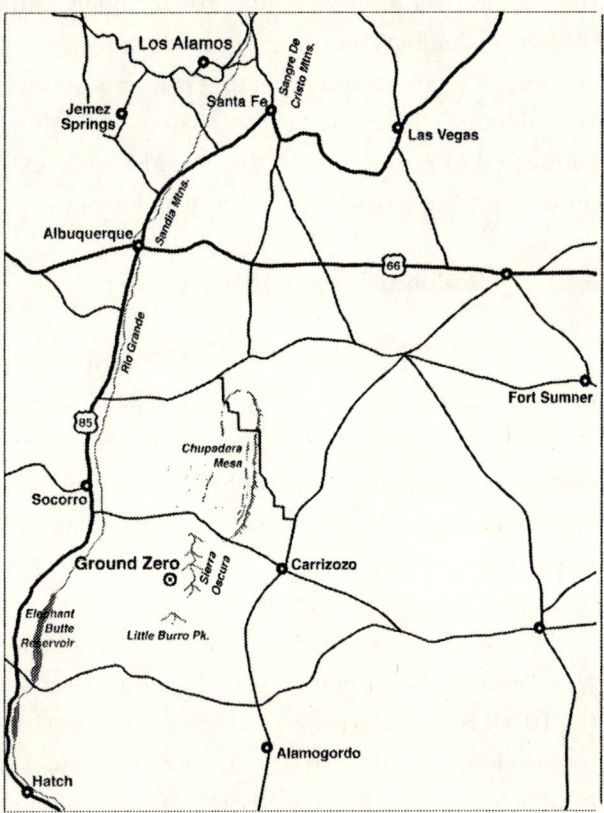

Figure 5-3. Map of New Mexico Showing the Location of Los Alamos and Ground Zero for the Trinity Site.

Los Alamos was chosen as the R&D center for the Manhattan Project because of its remote location 35 miles northwest of Santa Fe. Robert Oppenheimer influenced General Groves to consider Los Alamos because he had previously visited the Los Alamos Ranch School, from his summer cabin in the Sangre de Christo Mountains. Trinity Site is located in the bleak Jornada del Muerto in Southern New Mexico, about 120 miles south of Albuquerque, and 210 miles from Los Alamos. The present-day I-40 closely parallels old Route 66, and I-25 follows the former Route 85. Trinity was chosen for testing the plutonium bomb on July 16, 1945, because it was a relatively uninhabited area, which was fortunate, given that the explosion (equivalent to 20,000 tons of TNT) was many times more powerful than the atomic scientists had predicted.

In the center of the school grounds was a good-sized pond, irreverently named "Ashley Pond." Nearby stood the main building of the Los Alamos Ranch School, Fuller Lodge, constructed of giant logs placed vertically. The Lodge remains today in downtown Los Alamos, serving as a community meeting hall and as the headquarters of the Los Alamos Historical Society. The Los Alamos Ranch School was connected to Santa Fe and the outside world by means of a dirt track down from the mesa on which it was located.

Oppenheimer's Academic Career

After returning from study in Europe, Oppenheimer became a professor of physics at the University of California at Berkeley, which, until Oppenheimer, had no one who specialized in the new quantum mechanics. Oppenheimer spent spring term each year at Cal Tech in Pasadena, which had an excellent research program in physics. Oppie was an intellectual leader, writing important scholarly papers and becoming an influential teacher of graduate students. During his Berkeley years, Oppenheimer's favorite clothes were jeans, a blue work shirt, and a silver-buckled belt. This outfit was an uncommon look in the 1930s, particularly for a college professor. Oppenheimer had picked up his clothing habits in New Mexico, along with a taste for spicy food. Haakon Chevalier, a leftist Berkeley professor of French literature, said of Oppenheimer: "He looked like a young Einstein, and at the same time like an overgrown choir boy" (Rhodes, 1986, p. 443).

Both of Oppenheimer's universities, Berkeley and Cal Tech, became leading centers of American physics during the decade of the 1930s. Berkeley became particularly famous, due to Oppenheimer's theoretical work, coupled with the experiments of Ernest O. Lawrence, who invented the cyclotron that bombarded nuclei with highly accelerated atomic particles. When Lawrence converted his cyclotron to extract uranium-235 for an atomic bomb, he called in Oppenheimer to calculate the amount of U-235 that would be needed to reach critical mass (Goodchild, 1985). Thereafter Oppenheimer had a growing involvement with the Manhattan Project.

A Pull to the Left

During the late 1930s, Oppenheimer became interested in world problems of maintaining peace, in response to the threat posed by the rising fascist dictatorships in Europe. His relatives in Germany suffered under Hitler's anti-Jewish policies, and his graduate students could not find jobs in the Depression era.[10] Oppenheimer considered communism as an alternative to fascism. He became involved in civil liberties, antifascist politics, and Marxism. Through a girlfriend, Jean Tatlock, a member of the Communist Party, Oppenheimer joined various left-wing organizations, and contributed funds (about $1,000 a year) to radical causes (Goodchild, 1985).[11] Oppenheimer's wife Kitty, whom he married in 1940, had previously been a member of the Communist Party, although not an enthusiastic one; she dropped out before marrying Oppie. Oppenheimer drifted away from communism when the Party's "flip-flopping" line made no sense to him. He read Marx, and was not impressed.

Oppenheimer's personal associations with the Left during the 1930s at Berkeley were known to General Groves when he selected Oppenheimer to head the Los Alamos Project. Oppie stated on a security questionnaire on joining the Manhattan Project that he had belonged to, or contributed to, just about every communist front organization on the West Coast (Goodchild, 1985). Groves had the highest admiration for Oppenheimer's scientific counterpart: "He's a genius . . . Why Oppenheimer knows about everything . . . [but] he doesn't know anything about sports" (quoted in Rhodes, 1955, p. 17). Groves ordered the security officers to clear Oppenheimer to work on the Manhattan Project. They did, although reluctantly, in July 1943 (Bacher, 1999). Later, during the Cold War in the 1950s, Oppenheimer's 1930s communist connections at Berkeley would destroy his career as an advisor on U.S. atomic energy policy.

Oppenheimer's Selection as Director

Oppie became increasingly involved in the Manhattan Project during the several months prior to his appointment as scientific director of the Los Alamos Project. The fall of France to Hitler's army in June 1940 was a watershed for Oppenheimer; thereafter he began to oppose Germany more strongly, and joined the Manhattan Project (Schweber, 2000). Oppenheimer estimated the amount of uranium-235 required for a bomb. He was responsible for fast neutron research at the University of California at Berkeley, working closely with physicists at the University of Chicago's Metallurgical Laboratory. A chief concern was whether or not an atomic explosion could be contained, so that it would not run away to destroy the earth's atmosphere. Calculations by Oppenheimer and other theoretical physicists at Berkeley indicated that a bomb could be contained. Oppie's important research in developing the atomic bomb made him a natural choice to head the Los Alamos Project, once General Groves decided to concentrate the research at one site (Figure 5-4).

The selection of Oppenheimer as the scientific director of Project Y turned out to be equivalent to choosing Los Alamos as the site for the Project. Oppenheimer may have had this site in mind all along. Further, the University of California at Berkeley was chosen to manage the Los Alamos Project (as it continues to do so to this day) mainly because Oppie was a faculty member there. At the time of his selection, Oppenheimer had no real experience in directing a large scientific enterprise, nor had he been awarded the Nobel Prize (as had four of the atomic scientists who worked under him at Los Alamos).[12] A further problem was his leftist connections at Berkeley. Groves (1983) said that he chose Oppenheimer to direct Project Y because he was so highly respected and well-liked by his fellow physicists. Oppenheimer's secretary at Los Alamos, Priscilla Duffield (1980), notes: "It's a real mystery that he rose to this position [Director at Los Alamos] so fast, considering that he was a very diffident, shy person to begin with."

She says: "Like many people, I found Dr. Oppenheimer unbelievably charming and gracious. He had a marvelous voice."

Figure 5-4. J. Robert Oppenheimer, Scientific Director of the Manhattan Project at Los Alamos.
Oppenheimer earned his Ph.D. degree in theoretical physics at the University of Göttingen in Germany in 1922, and then taught at the University of California at Berkeley and at Cal Tech, before moving to Los Alamos in March 1943. Although only 41 years of age at the time and lacking the Nobel Prize, Oppenheimer had the brainpower, the social network connections, and the personal charm to lead the U.S. atomic bomb project. Nevertheless, the administrative burdens and the time pressures of the race to an atomic bomb created great stress, and Oppenheimer, already of spare build, dropped to only 117 pounds at the time of the Trinity test.
Source: Washington, D.C., National Archives, NWDNS-434-OR-7(44).

SELECTION OF LOS ALAMOS

A first step for the Manhattan Project was to choose its location. General Groves was headquartered in a small office in Washington, D.C., his main location during the war. Groves and Oppenheimer visited several possible sites for the new R&D laboratory during the fall of 1942. They were in a hurry to get the project underway, so one selection criteria was to be able to acquire the needed land quickly.

Groves rejected sites in California, Utah, and Nevada. New Mexico appeared to be an ideal state in which to site the new facility, given its wide-open spaces. Further, as Groves (1983, p. 65) noted, "Because a New Mexico National Guard regiment had been captured in the Philippines, we could count on a population and a state government intensely interested in continuing the war effort. The support we received was superb." On November 16, 1942, the site selection team, consisting of Oppenheimer and several others traveled to Jemez Springs, New Mexico, about 60 miles north of Albuquerque (see Figure 5-3). When the General arrived at the site around noon, he immediately rejected Jemez Springs. Groves quickly noted that the steep walls of the canyon were too narrow. If the project were to grow to large size, as he suspected that it would (Oppenheimer was planning on only 30 scientists at this point), Jemez Springs lacked room to expand. Further, Oppie did not like the site because he wanted an expansive view so as to make it easier to recruit scientists. Jemez Springs looked depressing to him (Goodchild, 1985).

Oppenheimer said, "Well, a little further up this road there is a boys' school, and we might go look at that" (McMillan, 1980). They drove by vehicle from Jemez Springs to the Los Alamos Ranch School. A light snowfall slowed their travel. When they arrived at the boys school in the late afternoon, Oppenheimer and Groves saw the students and their teachers playing football in the snow. At an altitude of 7,200 feet, it was bitterly cold. But the boys wore shorts. Immediately impressed by this Spartan display, Groves said: "This is it."

The Los Alamos Ranch School was in financial difficulty due to declining enrollment, because of the transportation difficulties connected with the war and due to problems in finding suitable instructors (who were being drafted). Much of the surrounding area was federally-owned National Forest. Groves immediately began government action to condemn the school land in order to acquire it for Project Y. Students at the boys school finished the school year on a speeded-up schedule, so that the four seniors graduated in January 1943. Then the Los Alamos Ranch School closed forever. In its place grew "the city that never was."

INSIDE BOX 1663

When Oppenheimer's new scientific recruits and their family members arrived in Santa Fe, they reported to the Project's Office at 109 East Palace Avenue, just off the Plaza (a metal plaque marks this building today).[13] Dorothy McKibbin greeted the newcomers in a friendly manner and sent them up the Hill by jeep, truck, or bus (Figure 5-5).

One day in March 1943, McKibbin, recently out-of-work when her Santa Fe company closed down, was talking to an acquaintance in the lobby of the La Fonda Hotel. He offered her a job as a secretary, but was very vague about the nature of the duties. Just then, she observed a tall, lean man crossing the lobby; he was wearing a porkpie hat and a trench coat, with a pipe in his hand. He walked in an unusual way, on the balls of his feet. McKibbin was introduced to him, but did not catch his name. He exchanged a few words, and then said goodbye. When the man (it was Oppenheimer) got about six feet away, McKibbin blurted, "I'll take the job."

Figure 5-5. Dorothy McKibbin Greeted New Staff Members of the Los Alamos Project at Her Office at 109 East Palace Avenue, Santa Fe.

McKibbin, called "the First Lady of Los Alamos," met newcomers at this office, located just off of the Plaza, marked only by a red-and-blue sign reading "United States Engineer Office No. 3." McKibbin, a graduate of Smith College, arrived in Santa Fe in 1926 as a tuberculosis patient. In March 1943, she began work for the Manhattan Project, issuing security passes to new arrivals, helping them find housing, and arranging transportation to the Hill. McKibbin is shown here a few years after the war.

Source: Los Alamos, New Mexico, Los Alamos Historical Museum.

McKibbin (1982) recalled: "I thought to be associated with that person would be *simply great*, and I never met a person with a magnetism that hit you so fast and so completely.... I just wanted to be allied.... with a personality such as his."[14] McKibbin went to work at eight o'clock the next morning, greeting newcomers at 109 East

Palace Avenue. She issued security passes, soothed jangled nerves, cared for babies, made housing arrangements, kept secrets, and relayed messages. At the end of each day, she was required to destroy all papers with notes or typing, except for a file card on which each civilian's arrival and departure were noted (Steeper 2003).

Atop the mesa, new arrivals at Los Alamos were greeted by the sight of Army bulldozers creating a secret scientific lair, with laboratories, a cyclotron, warehouses, homes, and the other facilities that a rapidly growing city of several thousand people would need. A newcomer to the Los Alamos Project noticed the nine and one-half foot high woven wire fences topped with barbed wire, and the guardhouse at the entrance. Several European scientists objected strongly to the barbed wire, which reminded them of Hitler's concentration camps (Rhodes, 1986). The top scientist-leaders at Los Alamos lived on "Bathtub Row," so-called because the dozen homes located near Fuller Lodge had been used by masters at the boys school, and had tubs instead of showers. Many military staff at Project Y lived in Army barracks, rather similar to those in the Japanese Internment Camp down the Hill in nearby Santa Fe.

As the population at Los Alamos doubled and then doubled again, living conditions became increasingly difficult. Many individuals resided in relatively primitive housing. Mud was everywhere. General Groves, in order to cut costs, decided to forego paved sidewalks and streetlights (Figure 5-6). Priscilla Duffield (1980), Oppenheimer's secretary, describes her initial impression of Los Alamos: "It was a pretty appalling place. It was windy, dusty, cold, snow . . . . At that point [March 1943], nothing was finished. It looked kind of amazing, not as if one were going to be able ever to move into it."[15] People worked long hours, but Sunday was a day of rest. The isolated boomtown lacked recreation facilities, so people provided their own diversion: Hiking, horseback riding,[16] skiing, sports, and parties. Los Alamos was the kind of place that "once you got in, you could not get out." You knew too much information that was essential to the war effort.

Figure 5-6. General Groves Resisted Constructing Paved Roads and Sidewalks at Los Alamos, Which He Regarded as a Temporary Site.
The springs had been removed from this jeep, which may have been the vehicle used by General Groves on his visits to Los Alamos, so that riding over rutted roads would convince the General to improve the road.
Source: Los Alamos, New Mexico, Los Alamos Historical Museum.

The organizational culture at Los Alamos during World War II was something like a "democratic commune" (Schweber, 2000), with a high degree of collaboration. The threat of Hitler's atomic bomb project was an unmitigated horror, driving the atomic scientists to intense effort. Oppenheimer orchestrated the spirit of Los Alamos, creating a climate for scientific productivity. Here was a unique opportunity for physicists and other scholars to work directly in developing an atomic weapon. As Oppenheimer noted after the war, in 1946, little of fundamental discovery occurred at Los Alamos; there was no great new insight (Schweber, 2000). But the highly applied work on the Pajarito Plateau represented a direct contribution to ending the war. This realization was very motivating. When an experiment was underway, scientists and their technicians slept on cots in their laboratory, often for days at a time (W. Dabney, 2000).

The Hill was a kind of virtual prison in which people vanished for years. Jokingly, some referred to Los Alamos as "Lost Almost" (Melzer, 2000, p. 15). Staff members at Project Y were not allowed to travel beyond Santa Fe, except on official business or to take care of personal emergencies. The desk clerk at La Fonda Hotel in Santa Fe was a government security agent, as were the waiters and bartenders in La Cantina, the hotel bar (Figure 5-7). Telephone calls from Los Alamos could only be made in English, and were censored. If a speaker's voice trailed off a bit, the censor would testily cut in "Speak louder, please" (Melzer, 2000, p. 29). Key scientists were assigned a bodyguard, who also served as an intelligence agent watching the scientist. The homes and offices of the scientists contained concealed microphones (Melzer, 2000).

Figure 5-7. The La Fonda Harvey Hotel, on the Southeastern Corner of the Santa Fe Plaza, Where Manhattan Project Staff Members Spent Leisure Hours.
Bartenders, waiters, and desk clerks at the La Fonda Hotel were undercover FBI employees during World War II, in order to listen for loose talk about the Manhattan Project. Although mail and telephone calls were censored and despite many other security precautions, three Los Alamos employees were passing secret information to the Soviet Union during World War II.
Source: Los Alamos, New Mexico, Los Alamos Historical Museum.

About 10 babies were born per month in Los Alamos, a total of 260 during the two and one-half year wartime period, including a daughter, Katherine, to Robert and Kitty Oppenheimer.[17] Birth certificates listed the home address as Box 1663. Groves railed at Oppenheimer for the explosion of births, which the General felt must somehow be Oppenheimer's fault. The General sent a telegram to Oppenheimer, "Please, can't you do something about the birth rate at

Los Alamos?" Oppenheimer cabled back: "What do you expect when you pen them up like rabbits?" (Howes, 1972).

Recruiting Scientists

Oppenheimer knew many scientists from his graduate student days in Europe and from teaching at Berkeley and Cal Tech. He was well connected in the network of relevant experts, respected as a scientist, and liked as a human being. But his recruiting task was difficult. Oppenheimer could not tell an individual much about the secret project until he or she signed on. Oppenheimer was inviting leading scholars to give up the comfort of their university position in order to move to a remote site and live under primitive conditions for an uncertain number of years, the duration of the war. The area was surrounded by a fence, and protected by armed guards. Any way one looked at it, this treatment translated into very restricted personal freedom. Further, Project Y was getting underway relatively late in the war, and many top scholars were already involved in other military research by the time they were approached by Oppenheimer.

Oppenheimer argued that he was only inviting a select list of top scientific people to join the New Mexico Project. He told each recruit that the scientific project was so important that it might shorten the war, saving many lives. His persuasive task got easier as he went along, especially once famous scientists like Hans Bethe[18] from Cornell University signed on, as is the nature of a critical mass. A three-day conference of top physicists, which included Isidor Isaac Rabi and Enrico Fermi, held at Los Alamos, was a key turning point. During the first day of the conference, jokes were made about the remote location, but by the second day, the charm of Los Alamos' blue skies and high mountain air had their expected effect. By May 1943, Oppenheimer had commitments from 150 individuals, the cream of American and European science.

Harold Agnew, who was later to become the third Director of the Los Alamos Laboratory, jokes that he was recruited so that

Oppenheimer could hire his wife. Beverly Agnew was a secretary at the University of Chicago Met Lab, where her husband worked on the Manhattan Project before his transfer to Los Alamos. Beverly knew how to handle security procedures, payrolls, and the secrecy classification of documents. As Project Y got underway, it needed these exact skills. Harold Agnew arrived at Los Alamos a week before his wife, and went bubbling up to Oppenheimer: "Here I am." Oppenheimer replied, "Well, where is Beverly?" (Agnew, 1980), anticipating the arrival of his first secretary.

Most of the 700 scientists at Los Alamos were white males, which reflects the characteristics of those who had earned graduate degrees in scientific fields by the early 1940s. Among the most famous atomic scientists at Los Alamos were the several dozen European refugees, but the majority were Americans.

Richard Feynman

One of the greatest characters at Los Alamos was the youthful Richard Feynman, who later was awarded the Nobel Prize in Physics, and who served on the Rogers Commission probing the causes of the 1986 Challenger disaster. He wrote a best-selling book about his experiences as a theoretical physicist called *"Surely You're Joking, Mr. Feynman!"* (Feynman, 1985). The title derived from his days at Princeton University, when he was invited to tea at the weekly Dean's hour. As a new doctoral student, Feynman was not sure how to act. The Dean's wife asked him, "Would you like cream or lemon in your tea, Mr. Feynman?" Faced with uncertainty, he blurted out, "I'll have both, thank you." She snickered, "Heh-heh-heh-heh-heh. Surely you're *joking*, Mr. Feynman" (Feynman, 1985, p. 48).

As an extra, unassigned duty, the irreverent Feynman assumed responsibility for security at the Los Alamos Project in 1943-1945. The mischievous Feynman made a habit of breaking into his colleagues' office safes, in order to demonstrate the inadequacy of their locks (Figure 5-8). Their file cabinets were filled with secret papers about the uranium and plutonium bombs under development. Feynman would leave a note "Feynman was here!" Then, at the next staff meeting, Feynman would plead for better padlocks and more attention to security measures.

Figure 5-8. Richard Feynman, the Contrarian of Los Alamos.
Feynman is shown here in middle age, a few decades after his work at Los Alamos, in his office at Cal Tech. Feynman became involved in the Manhattan Project at Princeton University, while earning his Ph.D. in physics, and then transferred to Los Alamos. One of his self-appointed duties uncovering security violations by picking locks and calling to attention a hole in the fence around the Los Alamos Project.
Source: College Park, Maryland, Vemilio Segre Visual Archives, Niels Bohr Library, Center for History of Physics, American Institute of Physics.

Military/Scientist Relationships at Los Alamos

At first, the research staff at Project Y consisted only of civilians. But in fall, 1943, a detachment of WACs (Women's Army Corps) arrived, to perform secretarial and other support tasks, setting off a rumor among the townspeople of Santa Fe that the Hill was a clandestine camp for pregnant WACs.

Later, scientists and engineers who had been drafted into the Army joined Project Y. These military researchers, termed "SEDs" (for Special Engineer Detachment) eventually played a very important technical role at Los Alamos, such as by operating the desk calculators to make the complicated estimates for the theoretical physicists, and machining the precision components for Little Boy and Fat Man (Sparks, 2000).

By July 1945, half of all the people at Los Alamos were military personnel. The total number of scientists and support personnel jumped from 500 at the end of 1943, to 1,700 in late 1944, and to 2,500 in mid-1945. With dependents, military guards, etc., the total population of the secret city reached 6,000 (Melzer, 2000).

U.S. Navy Captain William "Deak" Parsons[19] brought in other Naval personnel, especially to the Ordnance Division that he headed at Los Alamos. The arrivals of these Navy people led to a rumor in Santa Fe that Los Alamos was developing windshield wipers for submarines! Twenty-two British scientists from the Tube Alloys Project joined the Los Alamos Laboratory in December 1943.[20] The address on drivers' licenses and birth certificates simply stated "Box 1663, Sandoval County Rural." For the first several years of its existence, Los Alamos was not marked on maps. Personal mail, after it was censored, was flown daily to Chicago and mailed from there (this during the first year of the Los Alamos Laboratory) (Sparks, 2000).

Oppenheimer as a scientist-leader played a very important role in the success of the Los Alamos Project. So did General Groves, Director of the Manhattan Project of which Los Alamos was one part. They talked daily, often four or five times a day, by telephone if not in person.

The general and the scientist did not agree on all matters, although they held each other in high regard. Oppenheimer and Groves represented two different worlds, one a scientific system that valued open information-exchange and the other a military system of strict censorship and discipline in which orders were to be obeyed. Behind his back, the scientists at Los Alamos called General Groves "His Nibs." The contrasting world views collided on certain important matters.

One early conflict dealt with whether the civilian scientists should become military officers. General Groves insisted that the scientists have military rank, and Oppenheimer actually was fitted for an Army uniform (Goodchild, 1985). But many civilian scientists that he was trying to recruit to Los Alamos absolutely refused to join the Army. Finally, Groves gave up on this issue. The atomic scientists remained in civilian clothes.

Censorship

Another bone of contention for the atomic scientists was censorship. They chafed under a system in which even personal letters written to family members underwent military censorship. The censors at Los Alamos had no legal right to inspect the mail of people inside the United States, so they asked laboratory staff to mail their letters unsealed. If the censors, who occupied the second floor of the Post Office in Santa Fe, found a violation, they would return the letter with a polite note. Norris Bradbury (February 1971), later to become the Laboratory's second director, explained how the tight security caused frustration at Project Y: "The existence of Los Alamos was classified [and] the fact that one was at Los Alamos was classified . . . . The fact that the mail was censored was itself classified."

The irrepressible Richard Feynman mentioned in a letter to his wife, who was in an Albuquerque hospital with tuberculosis, that if you divide one by 243 you get .004115226337, a set of numbers that then repeat themselves endlessly. This letter was returned with a censor's note informing Feynman that letters could be written only in

English, Russian, German, and so forth. Feynman sent his letter back to the censors with a polite note requesting permission to write in Arabic numbers. Permission was granted (Feynman, 1985).

Oppenheimer's Crisis

In mid-1943, Oppenheimer experienced a crisis in self-confidence, becoming depressed by the magnitude of the director's position. He suffered from administrative overwork, which prevented him from devoting his time and attention to the scientific research that he loved. Oppenheimer was six feet tall, but was rail thin at only 125 pounds. Now he became even thinner. His morale slumped on June 12, 1943, when he visited his former fiancée, Jean Tatlock, on a trip to San Francisco. FBI agents tailed him, and reported that the couple had drinks at the Top of the Mark, and that he stayed the night at her apartment on Telegraph Hill (Melzer, 2000). Oppenheimer regarded this event as a personal matter, but security officers persistently questioned him about his relationships with Tatlock and other suspected communists, fearing a leak of technical information about the atomic bomb to the Russians. Seven months after their rendezvous, Tatlock committed suicide (Schweber, 2000).

Oppenheimer was persistently questioned by security agents about his relationship with Haakon Chevalier, a professor of Romance languages at Berkeley who had met Oppenheimer in 1937. They had become close friends, with Chevalier regarding him in a way that "bordered on hero worship" (Goodchild, 1985, p. 32). In early 1943, before Oppenheimer moved to Los Alamos but while he was employed on the Manhattan Project, Chevalier and his wife came to dinner at the Oppenheimers' home in the Berkeley Hills (Oppenheimer, 1954). Chevalier followed Oppenheimer into the kitchen, while the host mixed martinis, Chevalier told Oppenheimer that he had talked with George Ellenton, a British engineer who had worked in Russia, and who could convey technical information to the Russians.[21] Oppenheimer told

Chevalier that he would have no part in such dealings, and that the idea "sounded terribly wrong to me" (Oppenheimer, 1954).

When interrogated later about his communist friends, Oppenheimer admitted that he had been approached about conveying secret information to the Russians, but refused to disclose by whom. Oppenheimer was caught between his friendship for Chevalier and his responsibility as the scientist-leader of the Manhattan Project. Finally, on December 12, 1943, while driving with Groves from Los Alamos to Santa Fe, the General demanded to know who had approached him. Oppenheimer finally told Groves that it had been Haakon Chevalier (Melzer, 2000). Later, in 1944, as a result of Oppenheimer's disclosure, Chevalier was dismissed by the University of California at Berkeley (Melzer, 2000).

So Oppenheimer had much on his mind, in addition to his immense responsibilities in leading the scientific side of the Manhattan Project. General Groves forbad Oppenheimer (1) to fly in airplanes (Groves doubted their safety), or (2) to travel by automobile unless driven by a chauffeur/guard (Oppie was a notoriously bad driver). Los Alamos, a beautiful land of mesas and mountains, was fast becoming a kind of prison for Oppenheimer (Smith & Weiner, 1995). In this sense, Los Alamos was not unlike the Santa Fe Internment Camp at the bottom of the Hill, 35 miles away, where several thousand Japanese Americans were imprisoned.

Compartmentalization Versus Cross-Fertilization

Oppenheimer believed that cross-fertilization of ideas was essential in solving scientific problems. Groves insisted that each individual unit of the Los Alamos Project should be a watertight compartment, so that each scientist would only know the small portion of the total problem on which he or she worked. Oppenheimer eventually won this battle with Groves, and weekly colloquia were held at which the 100 key atomic scientists presented their progress and discussed their research problems (this colloquium series continues at Los Alamos

National Laboratory to this day) (Figure 5-9). Oppie began each of the Wednesday night sessions with remarks on scientific progress and new problems encountered during the past week. Then Fermi, Bohr, or some other notable scientist would present. These colloquia added to the espirit de corps of the Los Alamos researchers (Hammel, 2000a). Klaus Fuchs, the spy who was leaking secret information to the Soviet Union, had a white security badge which allowed him to attend the weekly meetings.

Dr. James Tuck, British researcher at Los Alamos, recounted: "At the very start, Oppenheimer killed the idiotic notion prevalent in other laboratories that only a few insiders should know what the work was about and that everyone should follow them blind. I, an almost unknown scientist, came here and found that I was expected to exchange ideas with men whom I had regarded as names in textbooks. It was a wonderful thing for me, it opened my eyes. Here at Los Alamos I found a spirit of Athens, of Plato, of an ideal republic" (Davis (1968), pp. 186-187).

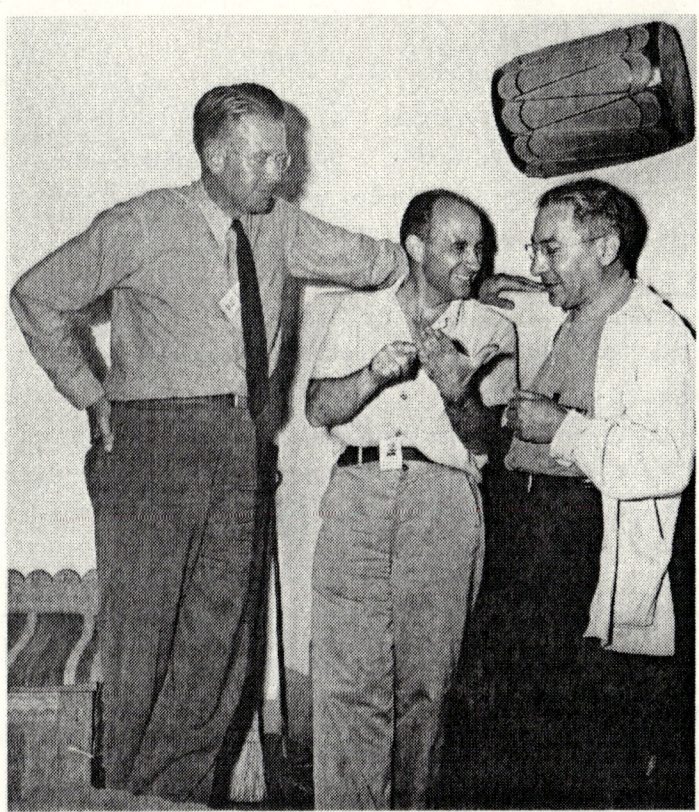

Figure 5-9. Three Nobel Prize Laureates, Ernest Lawrence, Enrico Fermi, and Isidor Rabi, Chat Informally at the Los Alamos Laboratory during World War II.

Lawrence, an experimental physicist at the University of California at Berkeley, pioneered in building atom-smashing cyclotrons. Fermi, a refugee from Italy, led the first controlled nuclear fission at the University of Chicago in 1942. Rabi, a refugee from Austria, won the Nobel Prize in Physics in 1944 for his research on the magnetic properties of atomic nuclei. Los Alamos during World War II represented one of the world's greatest concentrations of scientific talent. General Groves initially ordered the Manhattan Project staff at Los Alamos to work in compartmentalized units without sharing secret information on the atomic bomb's development. This security precaution was overturned by Robert Oppenheimer, who insisted that open information exchange among the top 100 scientists was essential for the success of the Manhattan Project.

Source: Washington, D.C., National Archives, NWDS-434-RF-Folder 32-1, Miscellaneous History.

FAT MAN AND LITTLE BOY

The Los Alamos Project produced two different atomic bombs, one a uranium bomb and one a plutonium bomb. Two types of bombs were developed, given the uncertainty that they would function properly. Originally, the two bombs were labeled "Fat Man" and "Thin Man." These labels were for cryptographic purposes, in hopes that they would be confused as code names for British Prime Minister Winston Churchill and U.S. President Roosevelt. "Fat Man" was a round, squat plutonium bomb, to be exploded by the implosion method. In 1945 it was tested at Trinity Site in New Mexico, and its twin dropped on Nagasaki. "Thin Man," as originally designed, did not work and had to be scrubbed, to be replaced by "Little Boy," a uranium-235 gun-type bomb. Little Boy was the atomic bomb dropped on Hiroshima.

Designing the Bombs

The main logistical problem facing the Manhattan Project was to obtain enough fissionable material. Huge facilities were constructed at Oak Ridge, Tennessee and at Hanford, Washington. The two plants employed 120,000 workers, more than the entire U.S. automobile industry (Takaki, 1993). About two years were required to produce adequate amounts of U-235 and Pu-239. Meanwhile, from 1943 to 1945, the mission of the Los Alamos Project was to design the pair of atomic bombs, including how to explode them in wartime situations. By 1945 an adequate supply of uranium and plutonium would be available for producing the atomic bombs.

The atomic bomb rested on the notion of a critical mass, the minimum amount of fissionable material to sustain a chain reaction (Figure 5-10). By surrounding a mass of fissionable material with a protective envelope of some other material, escaping neutrons could be made to bounce back into the active material, reducing the amount of fissionable material needed for a chain reaction.

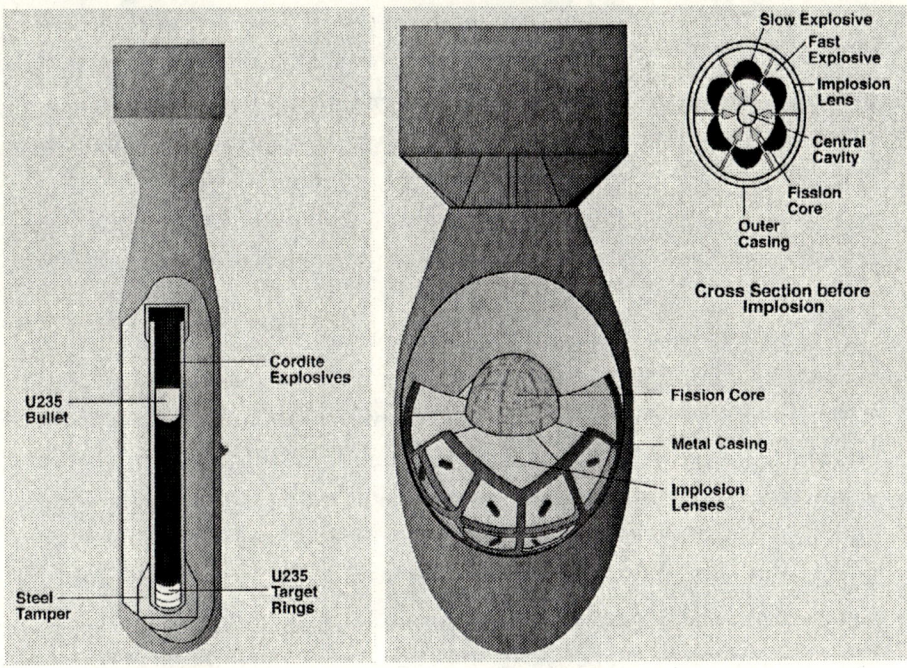

Figure 5-10. The Functioning of Little Boy and Fat Man.
   Little Boy was a gun-type weapon in which an explosive charge propelled a "bullet" of uranium-235 into a "target" of almost-critical uranium-235, creating a powerful explosion.
   Manhattan scientists at Los Alamos were so confident of Little Boy's successful functioning that it was not tested prior to being dropped on Hiroshima on August 6, 1945. Fat Man, the plutonium bomb, was exploded by the implosion method. The fission core of plutonium-239 was surrounded by "fast" and "slow" explosives which were detonated so as to compress the core, creating a critical mass and setting off the explosion. Fat Man was tested at Trinity Site on July 16, 1945, and then its twin dropped on Nagasaki on August 9.
   Source: Drawings based on Rhodes (1986) and Goodchild (1985, pp. 114-115).

How could this chain reaction be set off at just the right time, so as to explode an atomic bomb? Needed was an internal source that would instantly deliver millions of neutrons. One solution was the so-called "gun" method of the uranium bomb in which a sub-critical mass of fissionable material was fired like a projectile at a target of another sub-critical mass of fissionable uranium. This gun mechanism was placed inside the bomb casing of Little Boy. When it was fired, a chain reaction occurred.

The gun method was unsuitable, however, for a plutonium bomb, because of the presence of Pu-240, an unwanted companion of Pu-239, an isotope which tended to spontaneous fission, releasing neutrons. This process meant that the detonator of the plutonium bomb would have to be lightning fast, much faster than the gun method. So an "implosion" device was created in which a sub-critical mass of fissionable plutonium was surrounded by high explosives. When they were set off, they compressed the fissionable material, increased its density, and made it go critical, thus setting off a chain reaction.

Early research on the implosion method for the Fat Man bomb faced many problems, and Oppenheimer almost decided to scrub further work. Seth Neddermeyer, an experimental physicist trained at Berkeley, doggedly kept on with the research. Deak Parsons realized that the Los Alamos design team needed the help of John von Neumann, the famous Hungarian refugee mathematician at Princeton University. Parsons wrote a "Dear Johnny" letter to von Neumann, who agreed to work on the mathematics of the implosion device. He did some of the work at Princeton, and made several month-long trips to Los Alamos. Success was finally achieved.

The Race with Time

The German atomic bomb project was directed by Werner Heisenberg, a world-class theoretical physicist. Various clues suggested to the Allies that the Germans were developing an atomic weapon. For example, when the Germans occupied Norway in 1940, they directed the Norsk Hydro plant to increase its production of heavy water, which could be used in the fission process (Williams, 1987, p. 38).

Although the Germans had an early lead in the race to develop an atomic bomb, Hitler and his leaders decided that an atomic bomb was an economic impossibility, and downgraded the priority of the project on June 4, 1942.[22] Allied intelligence services gradually picked up clues that the Germans were losing the race to an atomic bomb. Moe Berg, a professional baseball catcher for the Boston Red Sox who served in the Office of Secret Services (now the CIA) and who was proficient in German,[23] was sent to a physics conference at Zurich in neutral Switzerland in December 1944, to meet Heisenberg. Berg gave himself a crash course in theoretical physics, so that he could talk intelligently to Heisenberg. Berg reported that the German atomic bomb project was lagging, and that it posed no threat to the Allies.[24] If it had, Berg was ordered to assassinate Heisenberg (Dawidoff, 1994).

The Manhattan Project's information-gathering in Europe was conducted by its Alsos (Greek for "grove") team, in order to track the progress of the German counterpart to Los Alamos. Teams of expert atomic scientists were assigned to closely follow the invading Allied armies, in order to learn about Germany's progress. In November 1944, the Allies captured Strasbourg, and the Alsos team found the scientific papers left behind by Carl Friedrich von Weizsächer, a leading atomic scientist, in his research institute (Cassidy, 1992). This evidence indicated that the German atomic project had stalled since 1942 (Goodchild, 1985). Rather, they focused on rocket research. Finally, late in the European War, in April 1945, the Alsos team captured the supply of German uranium ore at Hechingen (Rhodes, 1986).[25] After Germany's surrender on May 8, 1945, it was understood that the atomic bombs being prepared at Los Alamos would be dropped on Japan.

Uranium and Plutonium

The Manhattan Project utilized a telescoping strategy in which each of the major components was developed more or less simultaneously, so that each component would be ready to be utilized when it was needed. Time, the scarcest resource of all, was thus telescoped. For this strategy to work, deadlines for each component task had to be strictly met.

Separating the uranium and plutonium in the quantities needed to create the two atomic weapons was a major and expensive task facing the Manhattan Project. The United States had 1,250 tons of very high-grade uranium ore stored on Staten Island; unfortunately, the President's Advisory Committee on Uranium did not know about this ore for several years. When Belgium was overrun by the German Army in 1940, Edgar Sengier, an astute official in the Union Miniére, the Belgian Mining Company which operated a large uranium mine in the Belgian Congo, shipped uranium ore to New York, so as to keep it out of Germany's clutches.

Sengier then repeatedly notified the U.S. Department of State about the huge stash of rich uranium ore. State Department officials were unaware of the U.S. government's top-secret development of an atomic bomb, and took no action. Finally, in 1942, General Groves learned about the invaluable ore, stored in 2,000 steel drums on Staten Island. This acquisition meant that the Manhattan Project would not run out of uranium ore during World War II (Groves, 1983).

The main difficulty with uranium was that uranium-238 and uranium-235, the material utilized in an atomic bomb, are almost identical substances, and cannot be separated by chemical processes. U-235 has 143 neutrons on each nucleus and U-238 has 146; this difference had to be used somehow to make uranium-235 atoms go one way and uranium-238 atoms go another. A centrifuge process was tried and it worked, but not very well. A more promising approach was gaseous diffusion, in which the difference in mass was used to separate the two substances by converting uranium to a gas form, and then passing it through many porous barriers, with each one increasing the concentration of uranium- 235. This gas separation plant was put in operation at Oak Ridge.

Then a second method of separation was used, the electromagnetic process, in which a beam of uranium ions is passed through a magnetic field. More of the U-235 ions change direction than do the U-238 ions. Using these two processes in sequence, gaseous diffusion and electromagnetic separation, enriched uranium was produced at Oak Ridge, TN, in kilogram quantities by late 1944 (Los Alamos Historical Society, 1997). This uranium would be used in Little Boy.

Obtaining enough plutonium for Fat Man was also a limiting factor for the Manhattan Project. In this case the purification process was carried out in reactors at the Hanford, Washington plant, and at Oak Ridge. The plutonium was obtained by a process in which the molten metal was spun in a centrifuge. By mid-1945, the needed amounts of plutonium began to arrive at Los Alamos. Once a week, a high-security courier carried that week's output of plutonium from the Hanford plant in an ordinary suitcase. The amount was rather minuscule; the plutonium core ultimately used in Fat Man was only the size of a baseball.

It was a lucky break that adequate supplies of both the uranium and the plutonium became available at the same time, within a few days of each other (Hammel, 2000a).

The Unsung Role of the SEDs

The SED (Special Engineer Detachment) consisted of young Army personnel who possessed design, metal-working, data-analysis, and other technical skills needed to construct the atomic bombs. Typically, the SEDs were selected on the basis of their Army intelligence test scores. A typical example was Gordon Knobeloch, who was drafted just after graduation from Washington University in St. Louis, where he studied chemistry. He was assigned to an Infantry replacement unit in Texas in 1944. He scored very high on an Army intelligence test, and was thus selected to attend Ohio State University for a few months while an FBI security check was run. Then he was sent to Santa Fe, where he reported to 109 East Palace Avenue. His housing at Los Alamos consisted of an 8 foot by 8 foot plywood hutment, in which he lived with six other enlisted men and a pot-bellied stove. Bathroom facilities were next door in a barracks. The hutment was located near the present day Los Alamos Hospital. The crowded conditions did not matter, as Knobeloch often slept on a cot in the lab where he worked (Knobeloch, 2002).

Knobeloch worked in the Chemical Metallurgical Research Lab, located near Ashley Pond, where the Los Alamos Inn now stands. His job was to assist with experiments to test the shape of explosive charges around the plutonium core, so as to make a uniform "squeeze" on the core from all sides. A pea-sized sphere of radioactive lanthanum was used in the tests. Once the spheres were prepared, each was tested in a simulated plutonium bomb with actual explosives in nearby Bayo Canyon. The explosions were observed from a sealed Army tank. It was dangerous work, involving radioactivity, and Knobeloch's white cell count was checked regularly. He was 21 years old at the time, and felt that he was doing very important work, aiding the war effort. In fact, the *Manhattan District History: Project Y, the Los Alamos Project* describes the radioactive lanthanum firing tests as "the most important single experiment affecting the final bomb design." When he arrived at Los Alamos as an Army private, Knobeloch was paid $50 a month. This handsome wage jumped to $75 a month when he was promoted to technical sergeant (Figure 5-11).

Figure 5-11. The Staff of the Chemical Metallurgical Research Lab, Mainly SEDs, in 1945.
Technical Sergeant Gordon Knobeloch (in uniform) is in the center of the front row. This Lab conducted some of the most important experiments on exploding the plutonium bomb. One of the women shown was the group's secretary, and the other was the wife of a civilian researcher. The research group's leader and assistant leader were civilians.
Source: Gordon Knobeloch, Los Alamos, New Mexico.

Jay Wechsler, an SED who came from New Jersey, was 21-year-old Army private when he arrived at Los Alamos in early 1944. He was assigned to work as a lab technician for a physicist with an Austrian accent. It was Otto Frisch. Sergeant Wechsler looked up Frisch's entry in *Who's Who* in the Library of the Los Alamos Project, and was surprised to learn that his boss was a famous scientist. Wechsler (2000) remembers that when something went wrong in one of their experiments, Frisch would curse in German. Both Knobeloch and

Wechsler, after the war, became career employees at Los Alamos, where they live in retirement today.

Following are excerpts from a letter, held by the Los Alamos Historical Museum, written to his parents by Ed Doty, an SED, on August 7, 1945, the day after explosion of the Hiroshima bomb.

> Dear Mom and Dad:
> Now you know why I was sent to this oasis in the desert.... Sitting on top of this thing for so very long has been quite something.... About two days after I got to Los Alamos, I went to the Technical Library, and got a copy of White's "Classical and Modern Physics."[sic] I was astounded.... the book was replete with names that had been coming over the PA system ever since I came here. Kistiakowsky, Enrico Fermi, Lawrence, Bohr, Oppenheimer, Sir James Chadwick.... It was just unbelievable.... That dorm party I went to a week ago was full of such men. Fermi did one of the best jitterbugs I have ever seen.
>
> When I first came here, there were about 100 SEDs. Virtually all were college graduates, many had master's degrees, and there was a very liberal sprinkling of Ph.D.s. Informality is unparalleled in any other organization.... I would answer the phone with 'Doty;' the voice at the other end would say, 'This is Oppie.'
>
> This last 24 hours has been quite exciting. Everyone has been keyed up to a pitch higher than anything I have ever seen on such a mass scale before.... It was the first radio announcement of the dropping of the bomb.... This announcement came over the PA system: "Attention please. Attention please. One of our units has just been successfully dropped on Japan." It was electrifying.... It is high time to get to work. I haven't really done a thing since that word came through yesterday morning.
> With love,
> Ed

The Cowpunchers

The time-schedule for the Manhattan Project called for a test of the plutonium bomb on July 4 (this was Trinity, later rescheduled for July 16), and then to drop the new weapon on Japan about a month later. The Trinity test was timed to precede (1) the forthcoming Potsdam Conference in Berlin, at which the U.S. President needed to know if the bomb would work, and (2) the planned invasion of the Japanese mainland in fall, 1945. If the atomic bomb were not operational by then, its value in shortening the war would be lost.

In February 1945, the prospects of the Los Alamos Project meeting this ambitious timetable looked gloomy. Design decisions for The Gadget went through endless changes, with one or more influential scientists' holding out stubbornly for his favorite approach. For example, George Kistiakowsky, a Ukrainian-born Harvard chemist before the war, insisted on developing a lens-type device to explode the plutonium bomb, despite repeated failure in making such an approach work. The various alternative designs of the weapon splintered scientific talent, causing bickering and conflict. Meanwhile, deadlines were slipping by.

Finally, Deak Parsons sent a memo to Oppenheimer about their alarming situation entitled "Home Stretch Measures." Parsons insisted that strong medicine was needed. Oppenheimer reacted by freezing such design details as having a solid plutonium core for Fat Man, using electric detonators, and exploding the plutonium bomb by a lens that focused the force inward. He appointed a "Cowpunchers Committee" of six tough-minded individuals at Los Alamos, including Parsons, to ride herd over the on-time development of the two bombs. The Cowpunchers were to be ruthless in keeping the Manhattan Project on schedule. Oppenheimer also formed two teams, one for the Trinity test, and the other, code-named the Alberta Project, which was to deliver the bomb in combat.

As the atomic scientists at Los Alamos neared the foreseeable end of their efforts to create The Gadget, it was decided that a test of the implosion method of detonating the Fat Man plutonium bomb was necessary. There were too many unknowns in dropping the plutonium bomb on Japan. What if it were a dud? Further, data were needed about the explosive power of the atomic bomb, which could not be gathered if it were first used over enemy soil. Thus was the July 1945, Trinity test of Fat Man planned in southern New Mexico.

SELECTING TRINITY

One of the criteria for choosing the test site was that it should be relatively flat land, preferably in an area with very few people. Secrecy was a high priority, so it should be in a very remote location. Ideally, the test should be within a fairly convenient distance from Los Alamos. An 18-by-24-mile square section in the northwest corner of the Alamogordo Bombing Range (now the White Sands Missile Range) in New Mexico was selected (Figure 5-3). It was code-named "Trinity." The nearest human inhabitant was 12 miles away, and very few people, mainly ranchers, were within a 50-mile radius.[26] The site in the White Sands Desert was about 130 miles south of Albuquerque, and thus 228 miles from Los Alamos, a reasonable distance.

Trinity is situated in the Jornada del Muerto (Journey of Death) in the south-central part of New Mexico. This particularly desolate area earned its grim name several centuries ago when the wagon trains on El Camino Real, the royal road connecting Mexico City with the Spanish settlements in northern New Mexico, found no water during their three or four-day traverse of this 90 miles of desert. El Camino Real could not follow the Rio Grande River for this stretch, due to its steep canyon walls and gorges. The road through the Jornada was the straightest distance between El Paso and Santa Fe. Many Spanish travelers died while trying to pass through the Jornada del Muerto, hence its morbid reputation. No wonder that few people inhabited the Jornada.

Constructing the Base Camp

A Base Camp was constructed as a local headquarters, along with a control bunker at some distance from Ground Zero. Thousands of miles of wire had to be strung along the desert floor in order to connect the base camp, the control bunker, and Ground Zero with hundreds of measurement instruments that were placed at various distances from Ground Zero. All of the instruments near Ground Zero would have to relay their information instantly, before they were incinerated (Szasz, 1984). Meanwhile military police were brought in to protect the security of the test site. The men toiled through the particularly hot summer of 1945, preparing for the test explosion, originally scheduled for July 4. That date slipped by, and the explosion was rescheduled for July 16, 1945.

Today, Trinity Site, a national landmark, is open to the public two days per year, the first Saturday in April, and the first Saturday in October. The chief attractions for visitors to this historic site are Ground Zero, marked by a stone monument, and Jumbo, a huge steel bottle. What function did this monstrous cylinder perform? The Trinity test in 1945 used up America's supply of plutonium. Oppenheimer and his fellow scientists worried that if the test failed, many months would be required to build up a new supply of this rare material. Thus they concocted the notion of exploding the bomb inside a strong container, so that most of the plutonium would still be concentrated in the immediate area, and thus could be recovered. Accordingly, Jumbo was built to Manhattan Project specifications by a steel company in Ohio, and transported with great difficulty[27] to the Trinity site. Jumbo was 12 feet in diameter and 25 feet long, with walls 14 inches thick. It cost half a million dollars and weighed 214 tons (Szasz, 1984). The name Jumbo was indeed appropriate (Figure 5-12).

Figure 5-12. Jumbo at Trinity Site.
    Jumbo was a huge steel vessel, weighing 214 tons, and costing half a million dollars. Because the supply of plutonium was so limited in mid-1945, Los Alamos scientists initially planned to explode Fat Man inside Jumbo. But as the date for the Trinity test approached, the atomic scientists became more certain of Fat Man's reliability, and so Jumbo was mounted on a tower near Ground Zero in order to determine the effects of the explosion. Jumbo can be seen at Trinity site today.
    Source: Los Alamos, New Mexico, Los Alamos Historical Museum.

    By the time Jumbo was built and transported to Trinity, further theoretical calculations by the atomic scientists at Los Alamos convinced them that the likelihood of a successful explosion was so high that Jumbo was unnecessary. Anyway, exploding the bomb inside Jumbo would interfere with the sought-after measurements of the bomb's effects. That left the practical problem of what to do with a 214-ton bottle in the middle of the New Mexico desert. The ever cost-conscious General Groves was especially troubled by this seeming extravagance. So Jumbo was put to another use, that of testing the bomb's explosive power. It was raised on a 70-foot tower, located a half mile from Ground Zero (Szasz, 1984). The tower was destroyed, but Jumbo survived the explosion. It remains today as a behemoth relic at Trinity Site.

The control bunker was located two miles from Ground Zero, which was expected to be a safe distance. Slit trenches were dug for observers who would come to Trinity in order to experience the expected fireworks. Among the observers were Vannevar Bush, the President's science advisor and Director of the Office of Scientific Research and Development (OSRD), and James B. Conant, Bush's deputy. General Groves and Oppenheimer were also present, along with Enrico Fermi, Isidor Rabi, and various other scientists involved in the Los Alamos Project. Groves knew that Oppenheimer would be very nervous during the test, so he arranged for several of Oppenheimer's scientific friends to accompany him to Trinity (Goodchild, 1985).

THE TEST

The Gadget was placed in a metal shed atop a 100-foot tower, without the detonators in place. Fat Man's outward appearance was brutish, a bulbous weapon with a ganglia of wires protruding. It was five feet in diameter, and so heavy that it had to be lifted with a massive industrial winch (Figure 5-13).

Figure 5-13. The Plutonium Bomb Was Hoisted to the Top of a 100-Foot Tower at Trinity Site.
Fat Man was a huge ball, five feet in diameter, and so heavy that it had to be lifted up the tower with an industrial winch. Army mattresses were heaped under Fat Man during its ascent in order to cushion a possible fall. Once atop the tower, the plutonium bomb weathered a severe rainstorm during the night before the explosion on July 16, 1945, with lightning striking all around.
Source: Los Alamos, New Mexico, Los Alamos Historical Museum.

The key figure in designing the Trinity bomb's firing mechanism was George Kistiakowsky, a Harvard chemist and explosives expert. If The Gadget were a dud, "Kisty" would likely be blamed. Oppenheimer, now down to only 115 pounds and a bundle of intense energy, became extremely nervous as July 16 approached. He snapped at Kistiakowsky over unexpected snafus in preparing Fat Man's firing mechanism.

During the last few days before the Trinity test, Kistiakowsky (1975) said: "I had a lot of very acrimonious and bitter arguments with

... Oppenheimer, and even [Vannevar] Bush and [James] Conant, and General Groves, all of whom were accusing me of malfeasance and incompetence . . . . 24 hours or 48 hours before the actual test, news came from Los Alamos that an identical charge (minus the plutonium) . . . failed to perform properly. That's what started the real emotions running wild at Trinity Site." Kistiakowsky reassured Oppenheimer that the test back on the Pajarito Plateau at Los Alamos was flawed and thus its results could be disregarded.[28] Kistiakowsky could not soothe Oppenheimer's anxieties, however, so he said, half-jokingly, "Look Oppie, I bet you a whole month's salary of mine against ten dollars that it's going to work." Oppenheimer agreed to the bet.

The bomb was assembled in the small house at the George MacDonald Ranch, a nearby ranch home. The final assembly of the plutonium core of the bomb took place on July 12 in the bedroom of the ranch house. Located two miles from Ground Zero, the building survived the blast, and can be observed today.

The Countdown

The detailed and carefully rehearsed plans for the Trinity test unfortunately had not adequately considered the weather. July is the rainy season in New Mexico, a time of frequent flash floods and lightning storms. The explosion was originally scheduled for 4:00 A.M. on the morning of July 16, 1945, but a heavy rain was falling the night before. Lightning split the desert skies while 200 men watched the weather and cursed. The 100-foot tower was a huge lightning rod. Would a lightning strike set off the weapon? At 11:00 P.M., Oppenheimer had to order a delay. At 2:45 A.M., the rain seemed to be stopping, and Oppie decided to proceed with the test, now rescheduled for 5:30 A.M. (Szasz, 1984). It was the latest possible time, as darkness was essential for observing the explosion properly. Oppenheimer was so nervous that General Groves maneuvered him out of the command bunker into the dark night, where he could talk with him calmly. Oppenheimer told Groves: "If we postpone, I'll never get my people up to pitch again"

(Lamont, 1965, p. 212). Fortunately, at 4:00 P.M., the rain let up.

The countdown (the world's first) began at 5:10 A.M., with the announcement, "It is now zero minus 19 minutes." The countdown proceeded, first at five-minute intervals, and then by seconds. The detonators were inserted in The Gadget at the top of the 100-foot tower by explosives experts, who then fled to a safe distance in a convoy of several jeeps. The back-up jeeps were just in case the lead jeep had engine trouble (as had happened in an earlier dry run). The final switch was thrown, activating the arming system for the explosion to occur 60 seconds later. The public address system announced, "Ten, nine, eight, . . . three, two, one, ZERO!" The explosion occurred at 5:29:45 A.M. on July 16, 1945.

The Explosion

Observers were instructed to lie down on the ground, with their feet toward the blast. They were told to close their eyes, and cover them. After the flash, they could look at the explosion through darkened welders' glasses. The blast was spectacular, a brilliant flash seen in three states (Szasz, 1984). It rattled windows in Gallup, New Mexico, 300 miles away. Geiger counters near Ground Zero began to click at a furious rate. A huge mushroom cloud shot upward, reaching 38,000 feet in seven minutes (Szasz, 1984).

The contrarian Richard Feynman ignored the instructions to watch the explosion through dark glasses. "Dark glasses! Twenty miles away, you couldn't see a damn thing through dark glasses. So I figured the only thing that could really hurt your eyes (bright light can never hurt your eyes) is ultraviolet light. I got behind a truck windshield, because the ultraviolet can't go through glass . . . and I could *see* the damn thing" (Feynman, 1985, pp. 116-117). Feynman observed a tremendous flash of white light changing into yellow and then into orange. "Clouds form and disappear again - from the compression and expansion of the shock waves. Finally, a big ball of orange, the center that was so bright, becomes a ball of orange that starts to rise and billow a little bit and get a little black around the edges, and then you see it's a big ball of smoke with flashes on the inside, with heat of the fire going outwards. I am about the only guy who actually looked at the damn thing - the first Trinity test" (Feynman, 1985, p. 117).

Feynman stumbled out of the truck's cab, a bright purple splotch dancing in front of his eyes (Lamont, 1965). After about a minute and a half, Feynman heard a tremendous noise, a BANG, followed by a rumble like thunder. "That's what actually convinced me . . . . But this sound released everybody - released me particularly because the solidity of the sound at that distance meant that it had really worked" (Feynman, 1985, p. 117).[29]

Jay Wechsler, the SED who worked with Otto Frisch at Los Alamos, was at Trinity, about ten miles away from Ground Zero. He heard the countdown on a loudspeaker, and then saw a sudden bright light. The shock wave felt like a powerful earthquake. Then the mushroom cloud expanded in the sky. "It was amazing to watch! It looked like the cloud was boiling, luminous, growing larger. Unlike an explosion that makes a sharp report, the sound from the Trinity explosion rumbled continuously, like heavy traffic. It was eerie, unnerving" (Wechsler, 2000).

Jean Dabney, the WAC lab assistant, was not allowed to go to Trinity, so she and some friends walked to the top of the ski run at Los Alamos. It was raining in the morning darkness when they saw a flash to the south that was as bright as the sunrise. A physicist friend calculated when the shock wave would arrive; they had walked halfway down the hill when the ground shook (J. Dabney, 2000).

Kistiakowsky had bet a month of his salary against Oppenheimer's $10 that The Gadget would work. He was thrown to the ground by the blast, and covered with mud (Szasz, 1984). Immediately after the explosion, the emotional Kistiakowsky threw his arms around the Director's shoulders and hugged him. He said: "Oppie, Oppie, you owe me $10." Oppenheimer reached for his wallet and said, "It's empty, you'll have to wait" (Lamont, 1965, p. 237). The bet was paid off a few days later, at Los Alamos, when Oppenheimer briefed the atomic scientists on the results of the Trinity test.

In the quiet after the explosion, Ken Bainbridge told Oppenheimer, "Well, now we're all sons of bitches" (Los Alamos Historical Society, 1997, p. 54). His remark suggested the gravity of the moral and political problems that would arise from mastering nuclear power (Schweber, 2000). The mood, at first, was elation as the atomic scientists exulted in relief that the bomb worked. This initial euphoria, however, was soon followed by a reflexive soberness at base camp, as the realization set in as to what they had done.

Effects of the Bomb

One of the main questions to be answered by the Trinity test was the power of an atomic explosion. Enrico Fermi made a rough calculation by dropping bits of paper from a height of six feet (Szasz, 1984). The shock wave blew the paper scraps several feet away from where he stood. By this rough method, calculated in the first minutes after the explosion with his slide rule, Fermi figured the power of the bomb as equivalent to 19,000 tons of dynamite, an estimate that turned out to be remarkably accurate (Groves, 1983).[30]

The power of Fat Man was *much* greater than had been expected, exceeding estimates by many times (Jungk, 1956). Other indicators of the bomb's tremendous explosive power were evident. The earth was scorched black for a one-fourth mile radius around Ground Zero, which was now marked by a saucer-shaped crater depression some 1,200 feet across, and 25 feet deep at the center. No blade of grass was left within one mile of Ground Zero. The desert surface was covered with a new material that the Los Alamos scientists called "Trinitite," a green glasslike material of radioactive melted sand which then solidified. The steel tower was vaporized by the explosion, except for the concrete stumps of its four legs. The huge cloud from the Trinity explosion was blown, fortunately, over largely uninhabited areas, so that few people were exposed to radiation. However, hundreds of cattle in the area later developed strange white blotches on their backs, and their hair fell out (Szasz, 1984). At this time, not much was known about the effects of radiation on human or animal life.

The explosion was so powerful that many people, some at a considerable distance from Trinity Site, called newspapers and other media to inquire as to what had happened. A cover-up story was needed. So the commander of the nearby Alamogordo Army Air Base (now Holloman AFB) was asked to release the following explanation to the local press: "A remotely located ammunition magazine containing a considerable amount of high explosives and pyrotechnics exploded. There was no loss of life or injury to anyone, and the property damage outside of the explosives magazine itself was negligible. Weather conditions affecting the content of gas shells exploded by the blast may make it desirable for the Army to evacuate temporarily a few civilians from their homes" (Los Alamos Historical Society, 1997, p. 56).

The Trinity test was a success in that the implosion-type plutonium bomb, Fat Man, had worked, and was much more powerful than had been expected. Oppenheimer sent a telegram to Arthur Compton, Director of the Metallurgical Laboratory in Chicago: "You'll be interested to know we caught a very big fish" (Lamont, 1965, p. 254).

THE POTSDAM CONFERENCE

After Germany surrendered on May 8, 1945, the Allied leaders planned to meet in Berlin in order to redraw the boundaries of European nations, and to discuss next steps in conducting the war with Japan, the remaining Axis power. U.S. President Harry Truman delayed the Potsdam Conference until the Trinity test was conducted. He arrived in Berlin on July 15, 1945.

Later on the day of the Trinity explosion, July 16, 1945, General Groves' secretary in Washington, at his instructions, sent the following message to U.S. Secretary of War Henry Stimson in Berlin: "Operated on this morning. Diagnosis not yet complete but results seem satisfactory and already exceed expectations. Local press release necessary as interest extends a great distance. Dr. Groves pleased. He returns tomorrow. I will keep you posted" (Los Alamos Historical Society, 1997, p. 57). In the evening of the same day as the Trinity test, July 16, President Truman was told the news from New Mexico.[31]

The next day, Groves sent a coded message to U.S. Secretary of War Stimson at Potsdam via George Harrison, Stimson's deputy: "Doctor has just returned most enthusiastic and confident that the little boy is as husky as his big brother. The light in his eyes discernible from here to Highhold and I could hear his screams from here to my farm" (Los Alamos Historical Society, 1997, p. 57). The meaning? The plutonium bomb was as potent as the uranium gun-type bomb, its flash could be seen for 250 miles (the distance from Washington, D.C., to Henry Stimson's Long Island estate), and its bang heard for 50 miles (the distance from the Pentagon to Harrison's farm in Upperville, VA) (Rhodes, 1986, p. 688; Weintraub, 1996, p. 117). Truman told Josef Stalin about the atomic bomb after a working session at Potsdam on July 24, 1945. Stalin did not seem surprised, which puzzled Truman. Later, the United States learned that Stalin was already fully informed about the Manhattan Project, thanks to Klaus Fuchs and two other Russian spies at Los Alamos.

U.S. President Harry Truman issued the Potsdam Ultimatum on July 26, 1945, which called for immediate and unconditional surrender by Japan, or else its complete destruction. The Declaration from the United States, England, and China demanded that Japanese military forces be disarmed. Japan would be occupied, and war criminals would be tried. But the Japanese people would have freedom of speech and religion, and, it was finally decided, they could retain their Emperor.[32] B-29s showered Japan with leaflets about the Potsdam Declaration. Two days later, on July 28, Premier Kantara Suzuki announced that Japan would ignore the Potsdam Declaration.[33]

The way was now clear to drop an atomic bomb on Japan in order to end the Pacific War. Within 17 days of the Trinity test, the Manhattan Project had an operational bomb ready to drop in combat. Would destroying a Japanese city with the bomb force Japan's military leaders to surrender?

JAPAN AS A PUNCH-DRUNK FIGHTER

The U.S. strategy in the Pacific War was to invade a string of Japanese-held island strongholds, moving north across the Pacific from Australia while bypassing the majority of Japanese troop strength in Indonesia, Burma, China, and Korea.

B-29s Over Japan

One Allied goal in the Pacific War was to secure airfields from which the Japanese mainland could be bombed by B-29s and other long-range bombers. This bombing began in 1944, once the Marines had captured Guam and Tinian. From the air, Tinian looked like a giant aircraft carrier 6 miles wide and 13 miles long, made of limestone (Knebel & Bailey, 1960). Tinian resembles Manhattan in size and shape, and its roads were labeled Fifth Avenue, Madison Avenue, and so forth. At the time, Tinian's North Field was the world's largest airport (Alvarez, 1987). The island had six runways, each a ten-lane highway two miles long (Rhodes, 1986). Hundreds of silvery B-29s were parked at their hardstands. Two of the big bombers would fill a football field, and the plane's tail was three stories high. The B-29 flew at such high altitude that Japanese antiaircraft fire could not reach it.

In the first months of bombing Japan, however, the effects were disappointing. At that time the United States followed a policy of precision bombing, that is of dropping bombs on military and industrial targets. Late in the European war, precision bombing had given way on certain occasions (like the fire bombing of Dresden, Germany) to pattern bombing. The key difference was a shift to bombing civilians, and thus to destroying entire cities. The logic was that the workers whose homes were destroyed (perhaps along with the workers) labored in the factories. So, the argument went, bombing the workers' homes was practically equivalent in its effects to bombing the factories. General Curtiss LeMay, who directed the B-29 bombing of Japan, claimed that factory production in Japan was decentralized to workers' homes, with a drill press in each house.[34]

The fire bombing of Tokyo on March 9 and 10, 1945, and the subsequent use of incendiary bombs on 65 other Japanese cities, implemented the policy of pattern bombing.[35] General LeMay devised the strategy of dropping incendiary bombs from a relatively low altitude in a concentrated section of the Japanese capital. After takeoff, the B-29s were strung out for 63 miles from their base in the Marianas (Ross, 1985). Just after midnight, pathfinder bombers came in low over Tokyo at 500 feet, and made a big fiery "X" with napalm bombs. Then a massive force of 334 B-29s dumped their loads of magnesium cluster bombs. High winds of up to 80 miles per hour blew the flames across 16 square miles of the city (Frank, 1999). A towering firestorm resulted, in which the wood and paper homes of Tokyo residents went up in smoke. The updraft tossed the huge bombers around like paper airplanes (Sayle, 1995). An estimated 100,000 people on the ground were killed. Many died gasping for air because the towering fire consumed all of the available oxygen. One million people were left homeless in this single night of pattern bombing. The destruction was greater than the combined damage at Hiroshima and Nagasaki. In a few months, about all that remained of Japan's five main industrial cities (Tokyo, Nagoya, Osaka, Kobe, and Yokohama) were burned-out ruins and piles of ashes. Eventually, the B-29s burned out 100 square miles of Japanese homes and factories (Frank, 1999). Some 40 percent of all urban housing in Japan was destroyed.

By spring, 1945, Japan was a defeated nation, although the top Japanese military and government leaders refused to surrender. Despite attacks on U.S. warships by Japanese *kamikazes* (planes loaded with explosives that were flown by suicide pilots),[36] the U.S. Navy's shelling of Japan's coastal cities continued relentlessly. Japan was like a punch-drunk fighter, a nation with no fuel and little food, cut off from the resources of its Asian empire. Japan stood alone, as Germany and Italy had already surrendered. Not a single oil tanker reached Japan after March 1945 (Frank, 1999). Yet no military or political leader could mention the possibility of surrender, or they would have been assassinated. The *bushido* spirit of the Japanese leaders, derived from the *samurai* code of feudal times, demanded that Japan fight onto the death, as indeed Japanese soldiers had done in defending Guadalcanal, Iwo Jima, Okinawa, and the other Pacific islands invaded by U.S. forces as they marched toward Japan.

The Cost of Invading Japan

The U.S. invasion of Okinawa, located only 350 miles from the Japanese mainland, involved a long and costly campaign, with 36,000 American casualties, including 12,000 dead. Another 21,000 casualties were involved in conquering the tiny island of Iwo Jima, which was needed as an emergency landing base for B-29s returning from bombing runs over Japan. The island leapfrogging policy in the Pacific was becoming very expensive. Nevertheless, the next logical step was to invade the Japanese mainland. Operation Olympic was to be an amphibious assault against Kyushu, the southern island of Japan, scheduled for November 1945. Nine divisions (three more than the Normandy landings in France) were to hit the beaches while three airborne divisions would be dropped inland. Three-quarters of a million American troops would invade the southern Japanese island. Some 14 Japanese divisions were on Kyushu to defend against the invasion. Troops were withdrawn from Manchuria, Korea, China, and elsewhere in order to prepare for the expected American invasion. As many as 10,000 *kamikazes* were waiting for the American ships (Frank, 1999). The Japanese high command planned to cause staggering losses in the Kyushu invasion, so many casualties that the American public would demand peace. Indeed, at the time the atomic bombs were dropped on Japan, the Pentagon was questioning whether Operation Olympic, the invasion of Kyushu, had a reasonable probability of success (Frank, 1999).

The American invasion plans called for Operation Coronet to take place north of Tokyo in March 1946. Two million men would invade the largest Japanese island, Honshu. The Pentagon estimated that the planned invasion of Japan would entail one million American casualties,[37] and the invasion planners were counting on hospital facilities for this number of casualties (Cave, 1996). A half-million Purple Hearts, awarded for receiving wounds as the result of enemy action, were stockpiled by the U.S. for the invasion, so many that after all the intervening wars, some were still left in 2002.

The casualty estimates for the invasion of Japan were based on projections from the fighting for Iwo Jima and Okinawa, 33 percent and 36 percent, respectively. Three months of fierce fighting were required to overcome the Japanese defense of Okinawa; it was expected that resistance in Japan would continue until 1947. A conservative estimate called for the total cost of the invasion to include 300,000 deaths among the Americans invading Japan, approximately 100,000 POWs whom the Japanese planned to kill, and at least 600,000 Japanese soldiers and civilians who would fight to the death. The 1,000,000 expected deaths represented a million reasons to drop the atomic bomb on Japan, in order to force the Japanese to surrender. Dropping the bomb would also send a strong message to the Russians; top American leaders expected that the Soviet Union would be their enemy in the post-World War II Cold War.

HIROSHIMA

Ultimately, U.S. President Harry S. Truman decided not to interfere with plans already made by his predecessor, Franklin Delano Roosevelt, who Truman succeeded after FDR's death in April 1945. However, as the date for using the bomb approached, certain of the atomic scientists began to question how, and whether, it should be used.[38] They had been recruited to the Manhattan Project by Oppenheimer in order to beat Hitler's Germany in the race to build an atomic bomb. But by this time, in mid-1945, Hitler was dead and Germany had surrendered, so the German atomic bomb project was no longer a threat.[39] Ending the war in the Pacific was a priority goal, of course, but was dropping an atomic bomb on a Japanese city the best way to end the conflict? The Manhattan Project represented a considerable cost to the United States, and the government was heavily committed to using the bomb. The argument really came down to: "We have it, so why don't we use it?" As Oppenheimer stated: "The decision was implicit in the project" (quoted in Szasz, 1984, p. 152) (Figure 5-14).

Figure 5-14. Niels Bohr and J. Robert Oppenheimer in 1950.
　　Bohr, the eminent European theoretical physicist, carried the news of the 1938 Hahn/Strassman discovery of fission in Berlin to the United States in January 1939. Bohr escaped from German-occupied Denmark to join the British Tube Alloys Project and then moved to Los Alamos, where he was given the code name of Nicholas Baker. As use of the atomic bomb against Japan neared, in 1945, Bohr met with President Roosevelt and Winston Churchill to plead for international control of nuclear power, but to no avail. Here, Bohr and Oppenheimer discuss nuclear policy five years after the war.
　　Source: College Park, Maryland, Vemilio Segre Visual Archives, Niels Bohr Library, Center for History of Physics, American Institute of Physics.

In May 1945, a high-level Interim Committee was assigned by President Truman to select a handful of target-cities. The Committee decided that the atomic bombs should be dropped on inhabited areas of Japan without prior warning. The B-29s were pounding Japanese cities with so many incendiary and high-explosive bombs, that by May 1945, most large cities were practically obliterated. The Interim Committee had reserved a handful of cities which the B-29s were forbidden to bomb, in order to preserve them as targets for the atomic weapons that would be dropped. An undamaged background was needed on which to assess the destructive power of the atomic bombs. Among the virgin target-cities were Hiroshima and Nagasaki, along with Kokura, Niigata, and Kyoto.[40] Hiroshima was the main embarkation port for Japanese soldiers going overseas. Nagasaki was the site of an important steel plant that manufactured torpedoes. Both were military targets. They also were cities inhabited by several hundred thousand civilians. For instance, Hiroshima was Japan's eighth-largest city.

When General Groves presented the target-list to his superiors in Washington, however, U.S. Secretary of War Henry Stimson intervened, and insisted that Kyoto be eliminated as a target. Stimson had visited this beautiful city in the 1920s, and argued that it had such great religious and historical significance for the Japanese that it should not be destroyed (Groves, 1983).[41] Kyoto was founded in 793, and was a center for the Buddhist and Shinto religions, with hundreds of historic temples and shrines. It was spared from Allied bombing.

Engineering the Bomb

Deak Parsons came to Los Alamos in May 1943 from extensive experience in testing naval weapons, where he had become a "nut" about repeated testing of any new device under field conditions. Parsons ordered three complete "kits" of everything needed to prepare the B-29 bomber and its weapon for the mission to Japan. Each "kit" included air-conditioned buildings in which to assemble the bomb, personnel, and all the needed equipment, down to the right screwdriver. One of the kits was shipped to Muroc, CA (where B-29 crews were training to drop the atomic bomb) and assembled there, just to be sure that every problem had been anticipated.

A second kit was transported to Tinian, and preparations were made for its use in bombing Hiroshima. A third kit was sent to Iwo Jima and assembled there, just in case a back-up B-29 might be needed. Such redundancy came at a price, adding to the total cost of the Manhattan Project. But Parsons' painstaking planning meant that most operations went off without a hitch. In fact, the last-minute pre-Hiroshima preparations on Tinian were almost leisurely, as Parsons directly supervised the assembly of the bomb's components, mounted Little Boy in the bomb bay of the *Enola Gay*, and briefed Lieutenant Colonel Paul Tibbets and his crew (Figure 5-15). Finally, it had long been understood that Parsons would fly along on the mission, sharing decisions with the pilot on any last-minute technical problems.

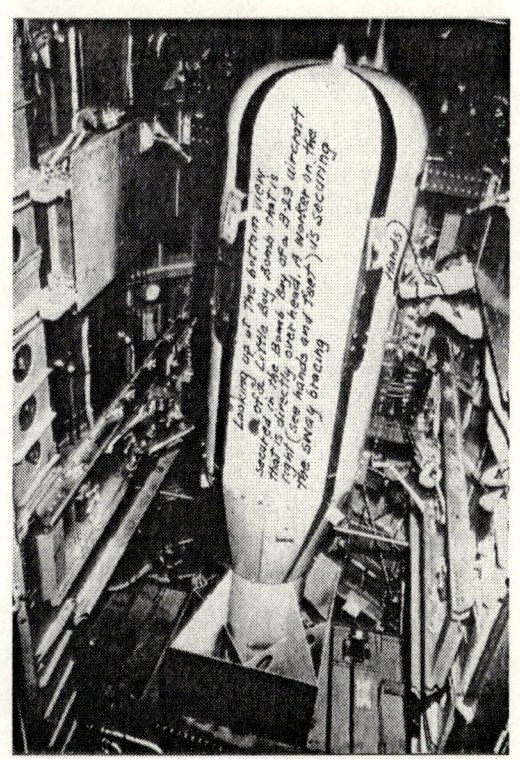

Figure 5-15. Little Boy Is Secured in a B-29 Bomb Bay.

This view looks up through the bomb bay door at the uranium weapon as it was secured by a technician standing to the right of the bomb, in the fuselage of the B-29. Little Boy weighed 9,700 pounds, and was 10 ½ feet long and 29 inches in diameter.

Source: Los Alamos, New Mexico, Los Alamos Historical Museum.

Tinian

Lieutenant Colonel Tibbets commanded the 509th Composite Bombing Group, which had been training for a year to drop the atomic bomb. This Group was a miniature air force, with its own mechanics, transport planes, and everything else that a stand-alone unit needed to drop an atomic bomb on a Japanese city. Tibbets had a priority codeword, "Silverplate," that got him anything he needed from other units. Some wags called the 509th "Tibbets' Air Force."

It was originally planned that the atomic bomb would be finally armed on the ground just prior to take off. But after Captain Parsons, the Navy ordnance expert, arrived on Tinian, he observed B-29s taking off to bomb Japan. A B-29 started down the runway every 15 seconds for an hour and a half. Heavily loaded with fuel and bombs, some planes could not get airborne. Parsons noted with alarm that four bombers in a row crashed while taking off. The night sky was ablaze with exploding fuel and ammunition. Crashing during take off with an atomic bomb could take out all 20,000 people on Tinian (Russ, 1984). So Parsons decided to arm the atomic bomb while en route to Japan, a tricky procedure due to the cramped space in the *Enola Gay*'s bomb bay.

First, however, the components of the atomic bomb had to be transported to Tinian Island. The first leg of the trip was from Los Alamos to San Francisco Bay, where a cruiser, the USS *Indianapolis*, the fastest ship in the American Navy, was assigned to carry the bomb across the Pacific. Four days after delivering the goods to Tinian on July 26, 1945, as the *Indianapolis* headed for the Philippines, she was sunk by a Japanese submarine and the lives of 779 of the 1,196 crew members were lost. Most died in the water from exposure or were eaten by sharks during the four days before help arrived. The location of the cruiser was secret, and the U.S. Navy did not realize she had been sunk. In memory of this tragic event, Tibbets' crew members scrawled on their bomb, "From the boys of the *Indianapolis*."

The 9,700-pound bomb hung on hooks in the B-29's bomb bay. There were 11 steps in the procedure of arming the bomb. Parsons practiced them all day before the *Enola Gay* took off from Tinian's North Field (Figure 5-16).

Figure 5-16. Deak Parsons and Paul Tibbetts Brief the B-29 Crews Prior to Take-Off for Hiroshima.
The crew of the *Enola Gay* and of the other B-29s involved in dropping the atomic bomb on Hiroshima were unaware of the purpose of their previous year of training until just prior to the mission.
Source: Los Alamos, New Mexico, Los Alamos Historical Museum.

Dropping Little Boy

Very careful preparations were made prior to the *Enola Gay*'s trip to Hiroshima, in typical Deak Parsons style. For example, several standby planes were ready and their crews trained, in case they were needed. Three B-29s served as weather planes; they each flew to one of the three target cities (Hiroshima, Kokura, and Niigata), one hour in advance of the *Enola Gay*, in order to radio back the weather conditions at each target.

The 509th Squadron had their own area on the northwest side of Tinian, fenced off from the rest of the airfield with special passes required to gain entrance, even if a general were demanding to see what Tibbets' airmen were up to (Figure 5-17).

Figure 5-17. The *Enola Gay*, Parked at North Field on Tinian, on the Day after Dropping Little Boy on Hiroshima.
One of the propellers of the B-29 Superfortress is being replaced. The B-29 bombers were so large that two of them were the size of a football field. The *Enola Gay* weighed 65 tons at take off on August 6, 1945, even after all the machine guns (except the tail guns) were removed in order to save weight and thus extend the range of the bomber, and to increase air speed immediately after dropping the bomb. The plane was still 8 tons overweight.
Source: Los Alamos, New Mexico, Los Alamos Historical Museum.

Hiroshima as a Military Target

One last-minute consideration in selecting a target for Little Boy was the POW camps in Japan, in which captured American and Allied soldiers were imprisoned. Kokura was originally the number one target for the first atomic bomb. But at the last minute, U.S. intelligence reported a POW camp nearby, Kokura Number 17, where POW Manuel Armijo was working in a coal mine (see Chapter 2). So Hiroshima moved up to become their primary target. Was there a POW camp in Hiroshima? Not according to the official list in the hands of the U.S. military. However, as we know from the New Mexican Bataan survivors, several of them were close by (see Chapter 2).

Pumpkins from the Sky

Tibbets and his crew had spent months of special training in preparation for their mission. Bombs that were the size, shape, and weight of Fat Man, but filled with conventional explosives, were dropped on a bombing range at Muroc, CA (now Edwards Air Force Base). These "pumpkins" were painted a bright orange, at the order of General Groves, so as to distinguish them from their nuclear look-alike.

Unlike Fat Man, Little Boy dropped much more like a conventional bomb. When one of the first Little Boys (filled with concrete to simulate the weight of the uranium) was dropped at a U.S. bombing range, it penetrated the earth to the depth of a four-story building. Parsons insisted that the dud be dug up in order to determine whether the bomb's mechanism would still operate. If Little Boy were a dud when dropped over Japan, a probability that Oppenheimer had estimated at 1 in 10,000, Parsons wanted to know whether the Japanese could retrieve it and learn its secrets.

NAGASAKI AND SURRENDER

In the days following the Hiroshima explosion on August 6, U.S. planes dropped six million surrender leaflets on the 47 largest Japanese cities. The Americans planned to drop the second bomb, Fat Man, five days after the destruction of Hiroshima, so as to convey to the Japanese that nuclear bombing would continue until surrender. Expected bad weather, however, pushed the date of the second bombing up to August 9, just three days after Hiroshima. In retrospect, the United States underestimated how long it would take for the Japanese government to understand the destruction at Hiroshima, given that the damage was so complete that lines of communication to Tokyo were cut off (Weintraub, 1996). Military commanders on Tinian, however, felt that the sooner the second bomb was dropped, the more likely the Japanese would be to feel that the U.S. had a large quantity of atomic bombs.

Major Charles W. Sweeney was selected as the pilot to drop the second bomb from a B-29 named *Bock's Car*. He had flown alongside the *Enola Gay* in order to drop measurement instruments on Hiroshima. Fat Man was 10 feet 8 inches long, and 5 feet in diameter (Figure 5-18).

Nagasaki was selected as the target for Fat Man after the primary target, Kokura, was weathered in. Nagasaki was Japan's largest shipbuilding and repair center, and was important for its production of naval ordnance.

On Tinian, his commanding general asked Sweeney, "Young man, do you know how much that bomb cost?" Sweeney replied: "About $25 million." The general said: "See that we get our money's worth" (Groves, 1983). Carrying out this order would not be easy for Sweeney and his crew. Everything possible went wrong during the entire Nagasaki mission. Just before take off from Tinian, a defective fuel pump was discovered; this meant that 800 gallons of desperately needed fuel could not be used by the plane's engines, although it would have to go along for the ride. The *Bock's Car* made three bomb runs over Kokura, using up a precious 45 minutes of fuel, before deciding that the cloud cover precluded visual bombing. More scarce fuel was used to fly on to Nagasaki. By this time, Sweeney and his crew only had enough fuel remaining for one bomb run over Nagasaki. Fat Man generated a sustained humming sound, indicating it was armed, when the bomb bay doors opened (Craig, 1967). The overcast cleared just enough to drop Fat Man, but it missed the intended target by one and one-half miles.

Figure 5-18. Harold Agnew in Front of the Instrumentation Lab on Tinian in Mid-1945, Holding the Core of the Plutonium Bomb Dropped on Nagasaki.
Agnew, a physicist at the Manhattan Project at Los Alamos when this photograph was taken, was assigned to Project Alberta, the task force on Tinian that prepared the atomic bombs for delivery. When U.S. Air Force General Carl (Tooey) Spaatz arrived on Tinian in order to see the working parts of an atomic bomb, he refused to believe that the plutonium core, about the size of a baseball, could have destroyed an entire Japanese city.
Source: Los Alamos, New Mexico, Los Alamos Historical Museum.

Bock's Car had to land on Okinawa, rather than return directly to Tinian, due to lack of fuel. But the B-29 could not get tower clearance to land, despite several distress calls of "Mayday, Mayday," and by dropping colored flares (Knebel & Bailey, 1960, p. 266). Finally, in desperation, the big bomber just barrelled down through the congested air traffic and landed. On the ground, the dipstick showed only seven gallons of fuel remaining, not even enough for *Bock's Car* to taxi off the runway. The bomber had to be towed. After refueling on Okinawa, Sweeney flew the B-29 on home to Tinian. Because of the lateness of the hour (it was midnight), there was no celebration for *Bock's Car*.

But the mission was successful in that Sweeney's bomber indeed dropped Fat Man. An estimated 35,000 people were killed immediately in Nagasaki. A total of 70,000 people died by the end of 1945, and 140,000 by the end of five years. Fat Man was a more powerful explosion than Little Boy (with an estimated TNT equivalent of 50,000 tons, compared to 15,000 tons for Little Boy at Hiroshima), but there was less damage and loss of life at Nagasaki than at Hiroshima due to the steep hills in the city. The Mitsubishi plant at Ground Zero in Nagasaki was obliterated. It had manufactured the torpedoes used at Pearl Harbor (Alvarez, 1987).

Another bomb, a Fat Man, was ready to be shipped to Tinian, waiting in the wings to be dropped on Japan. Seven more atomic bombs would be available by late October 1945.

Japan Surrenders

Japanese Emperor Hirohito intervened at the war Cabinet of Japan, to demand surrender. The agony of the final days of the war ended on August 15, 1945, six days after the second bomb was dropped on August 9, and a week after the Soviet Union entered the war against Japan. Russian troops were already racing across Manchuria, en route to occupying northern Korea. Japanese leaders had great fear of a Russian occupation of at least part of the Japanese home islands (Sayle, 1995).

On August 15, the Emperor broadcast a surrender message to the Japanese people and to military forces over NHK radio, the government broadcasting network. Most Japanese people had never heard the Emperor's voice. Vehicle traffic halted all over Japan in order to listen to the surrender message. Military leaders were still reluctant to lay down their arms. A small military force took over the Imperial Palace in Tokyo, and tried (unsuccessfully) to stop the Emperor's radio broadcast. General Korechika Anami, head of the military war council, acquiesced to the Emperor, and then committed ritual suicide. Some 2,000 Japanese Army officers followed his lead. On August 16, the Imperial Navy was ordered to obey the Emperor, and two days later the Japanese Army of over a million men in China was ordered to lay down their arms. At surrender, Japan had 4.3 million men in uniform.

The final act was signing the surrender documents on board the USS *Missouri* in Tokyo Bay on September 2, 1945. Finally, World War II was over. Peace at last!

WINNING THE RACE

The Manhattan Project was successful in its race with time, in that atomic bombs were developed before the end of World War II. Could these weapons have been readied even earlier? America dawdled for several years in getting its atomic project underway, in comparison to Germany and England. John Wheeler (1998), the theoretical physicist who worked with Niels Bohr at Princeton University in 1939 to formulate a comprehensive theory of fission, estimated that if the United States had started the Manhattan Project one year sooner, an operational weapon could have been developed by mid-1944 instead of mid-1945. During that crucial last year of World War II, 3 million lives were lost in battle and 12 million civilian deaths occurred as the result of bombing cities, the Holocaust, and so forth. One of those 15 million deaths was John Wheeler's brother, Lieutenant Joe Wheeler, who was killed in the fighting in northern Italy soon after sending his physicist brother a postcard that stated simply, "Hurry up!

6

CONCLUSIONS

> "Shall we put an end to the human race; or shall mankind renounce war? . . . There lies before us, if we choose, continued progress in happiness, knowledge, and wisdom. Shall we, instead, choose death, because we cannot forget our quarrels?"
> (The Bertrand Russell-Albert Einstein Manifesto of 1954, quoted in *Rotblat*, 1967, pp. 77–79.)

The previous chapters of this book show how a sparsely-populated state made a big difference in World War II, arguably the most important event of the 20th Century. What general lessons can be derived from New Mexico's role during these four years?

Wars are bizarre happenings. By their very nature, they are filled with paradoxes of conscience, contradictions, culture clashes, chance connections, heroism, villainy, violations of individual rights, and unsound choices. This final chapter points to these qualities as they relate to the circumstances of World War II, and, even more, to the particular circumstances of New Mexico. We stress that "That's always how war is," not by portraying war as "oddities" of World War II in New Mexico, but as illustrative instances.

In World War II, the timeless truths of war stood out in uncommonly sharp relief in the case of New Mexico because of the unique characteristics of the state: A large, empty land of appealing climate and natural beauty, remote from the centers of science and industry of the nation, and sparse of population, among which Hispanics and Native Americans played uncommonly large roles. The qualities of war stood out clearer in New Mexico than elsewhere because New Mexico was a kind of uncluttered canvas, yet one with unique qualities that laid forth the special nature of war in bold lines.

AFTERWARDS

In the Matter of Robert Oppenheimer

Robert Oppenheimer resigned as director of the Los Alamos Project in October 1945. Later he became director of the Institute for Advanced Study at Princeton University, where he finished out his career (Figure 6-1). Oppenheimer traveled frequently to Washington, advising government nuclear policymakers. In the late 1940s, he strongly opposed development of the hydrogen bomb, which was a thousand times more powerful than the Hiroshima atomic bomb. Oppenheimer regarded certain individuals, including Washington officials, as incompetent. He treated them with cold disdain, and criticized them publicly. Accordingly, he made enemies in high places.

Figure 6-1. Albert Einstein and Robert Oppenheimer at the Institute for Advanced Study at Princeton University, after World War II.
Oppenheimer was Director of the Institute and Einstein was its most famous member. After resigning as Director of the Los Alamos laboratory in October 1945, Oppenheimer moved to Princeton, and served as a top government advisor on nuclear policy until his Q clearance was cancelled by the Atomic Energy Commission in 1954. After Hiroshima, Einstein, a peace advocate, regretted that he had written to President Roosevelt in 1939, urging the creation of an American atomic bomb project.
Source: College Park, MD, Vemilio Segre Visual Archives, Niels Bohr Library, Center for History of Physics, American Institute of Physics.

Oppenheimer's "Q" security clearance was withdrawn on June 29, 1954, by the Atomic Energy Commission, the successor agency to the Manhattan Project. Oppenheimer's leftist associations at Berkeley in the late 1930s surfaced again in the Atomic Energy Commission's investigation "in the matter of J. Robert Oppenheimer." This month-long, quasi-legal hearing concerned whether his security clearance should be reinstated. Especially damaging to Oppenheimer was the 1942 approach by his Berkeley friend, Haakon Chevalier, offering to pass on information about the Manhattan Project to the Russians. Oppenheimer only disclosed this kitchen conversation with Chevalier to General Groves under pressure and then only many months after the event (Bacher, 1999). On December 23, 1954, the Atomic Energy Commission decided not to reinstate Oppenheimer's security clearance, which meant the end of his advising government policymaker on nuclear issues. This decision was a tremendous setback to Oppenheimer, and he took the vote of no-confidence very hard. A play "In the Matter of J. Robert Oppenheimer," first written in German by Heinar Kipphardt, describes the trial.

On February 18, 1967, Oppenheimer died from throat cancer.

The Future of Los Alamos National Laboratory

After the two atomic bombs were dropped on Japan, a profound depression settled over Los Alamos (Goodchild, 1985). Once the race to an atomic bomb was won, no further compelling scientific objective was immediately evident. In 1945, no plans had been made as to the future of the Los Alamos laboratory. Oppenheimer's final act was to appoint Norris Bradbury as his successor. Bradbury was a Navy commander on leave from Stanford University's Physics Department. He continued as Director at Los Alamos for the next 25 years, guiding the Lab through its difficult post-War years.

Many of the key scientists and their families left the Pajarito Plateau soon after the war, usually to return to their university posts.[1] By October 1945, a month or so after the Japanese surrender, only 1,000 of the 3,000 civilian employees at Los Alamos remained. Should research at the Los Alamos Project be continued? Some observers urged that the Lab be abandoned, or moved to California, or that its research should be converted to peaceful purposes. American policymakers eventually decided that Los Alamos should be continued in order to protect the huge investment already made in nuclear weapons research. The United States was involved in a Cold War struggle with the Soviet Union, and continuing nuclear weapons research was justified for national security reasons.

In 1946, Los Alamos provided technical support for the Bikini tests in the Marshall Islands. The Lab came under the Atomic Energy Commission in 1947. Edward Teller proposed the idea of a thermonuclear bomb, commonly called the hydrogen bomb, which required extremely high temperatures, obtainable only with a fission device, to cause fusion to occur. The hydrogen bomb reproduces the interior of the sun where the fusion of very light nuclei occurs.[2] The concept of the hydrogen bomb originated with Fermi and Teller with key assistance from Stanislaw Ulam, a Polish mathematician at the Los Alamos Laboratory. The "Super," as it was called, was tested on Eniwetok, a South Pacific atoll, in 1952. The fusion bomb represented a major escalation of the arms race.

The Soviet Union Gets the Bomb

Josef Stalin was not surprised at the 1945 Potsdam Conference when Harry Truman told him that the United States was about to utilize a secret weapon in the Pacific War. Moscow had started developing an atomic bomb in the early 1940s, even prior to being alerted by its spies that America was developing an atomic weapon.

Klaus Fuchs, a German communist, became a British citizen in 1942, and came to Los Alamos with the Tube Alloys research team (Figure 6-2). Fuchs was in the inner circle of scientists at Los Alamos, and he possessed almost complete information about the plutonium bomb. He passed this secret information to the Soviet Union from 1942 to 1945. Fuchs eventually betrayed the details of the plutonium bomb in his seventh meeting with Harry Gold, a Soviet spy from New York, on June 2, 1945, at a meeting on Alameda Street at Castillo Street Bridge (now Paseo do Peralta) in Santa Fe, located near the present Inn of Loretto (Dillon, 2000).

Figure 6-2. Pass Identification Photograph of Klaus Fuchs, the Soviet Spy Who Worked on the Plutonium Bomb at Los Alamos.

Fuchs was born and educated in Germany, where he became a member of the Communist Party. He migrated to England, became a British citizen, and worked on the Tube Alloys Project until he was transferred to Los Alamos. Despite the intensive security precautions at Los Alamos, Fuchs leaked secret information to the Soviet Union on seven occasions, and was not apprehended until 1950. His espionage helped Russian scientists in developing their atomic bomb, exploded in 1949, which was virtually a copy of the Fat Man plutonium bomb.

Source: Los Alamos, New Mexico, Los Alamos Historical Museum.

Fuchs was perceived by his colleagues at Los Alamos as a rather blank personality, as someone who kept his own company, and who seldom said much. Fuchs "left absolutely no impression," said George Kistiakowsky (1975). "He was an extremely withdrawn character . . . . I couldn't even tell you what he looked like anymore. Just a pale shadow." Hans Bethe (1979) remembers Fuchs as "perhaps the hardest-working member of our entire division. He worked day and night . . . . He contributed very greatly to the success of the Los Alamos Project. Unfortunately, . . . every month or so, he went down to Santa Fe and met another man and told all the results [of the Los Alamos research] to the Russians." Bethe points out that Fuchs believed very strongly that nuclear weapons should be under international control, rather than an American monopoly. Fuchs was acting from his conscience, but he was still a traitor.

Sergeant David Greenglass, an Army SED technician at Los Alamos and brother to Ethyl Rosenberg, sold plans for Fat Man's implosion lens triggering mechanism to Gold on June 3, 1945, in Albuquerque, for $500 (Lamont, 1965).[3] A third Russian spy, Theodore Hall, had been recruited to Los Alamos while a student at Harvard University. The FBI security check had not detected that Hall's Harvard roommates were members of the Communist Party. Hall passed secret information about the implosion experiments for Fat Man to his former roommate, Saville Sax, and to Lona Cohen, a Soviet courier, on the University of New Mexico campus in Albuquerque, in August 1945 (Albright & Kunstel, 1997; Melzer, 2000). The three defectors at Los Alamos, Fuchs, Greenglass, and Hall, "carried out the greatest theft of the twentieth century, the secret to the atomic bomb" (Melzer, 2000, p. 78). Fuchs was the most important.

The three Soviet spies at Los Alamos easily penetrated General Groves' security wall, stole the secret of the atomic bomb, and conveyed it to the Russians with powerful consequences. KGB espionage shortened the time required for the Soviets to explode their first atomic bomb, perhaps by 18 months.[4] Further, Klaus Fuchs, Theodore Hall, and David Greenglass escaped detection by U.S. authorities until several years after the war. All three had white security badges, which meant that they attended the weekly colloquia at Los Alamos. Due to the lack of compartmentalization, these spies (especially Fuchs) possessed rather complete information about the atomic bomb. Money was not an important motivation for the three spies, although the KGB payments to Greenglass allowed him to rent an apartment in Albuquerque, in order to see his wife on weekends. The Los Alamos security leaks were mainly motivated by political/ideological factors.

Profiting from their spies inside Los Alamos, the Soviet Union tested an atomic bomb on August 29, 1949, only four years after the Manhattan Project had done so.[5] The Russian bomb was almost an exact replica of the plutonium bomb dropped on Nagasaki, suggesting how important the spying at Los Alamos was to the Russians (Rotblat, 1998).[6] The American public was shocked when the security leaks at Los Alamos were disclosed. After 1949, the Cold War turned frigid, as the American public feared that the Soviet Union sought to impose its totalitarian system on the entire world, as they had done in Eastern Europe. This deep fear translated into an anti-Communist hysteria in America, leading to excessive questioning of the loyalty of certain individuals, investigations by the House Un-American Activities Committee (HUAC), the blacklisting of Hollywood actors and directors, and the firing of professors.[7]

Both Cold War adversaries possessed nuclear weapons, and a confrontation occurred in the 1962 Cuban Missile Crisis. For several weeks that October, the world teetered on the brink of nuclear war. The Nuclear Club today includes the United States, the Soviet Union (after the 1992 breakup of the USSR, Russia, Belarus, the Ukraine, and Kazakhstan have the bomb), Britain, France, China, Israel, India, Pakistan, and South Africa. Does this club make world peace more, or less, stable? On one hand, nuclear weapons have not been used since 1945. On the other hand, the U.S. fears that a terrorist group might gain access to a nuclear weapon. One assignment for Los Alamos National Laboratory in the post-Cold War era is to study means of detecting and preventing nuclear proliferation. Earlier, the mission of

LANL was to design and test nuclear weapons; today, the mission is to reduce global nuclear danger by means of stockpile stewardship, non proliferation, and nuclear cleanup.

Los Alamos National Laboratory Today

Much of the important scientific work on the atomic bomb was originally conducted in Tech Area 1 of the Los Alamos Project, located on one side of Trinity Drive. Parts of the first atomic bomb were assembled in the Ice House, a small stone building originally built to store ice blocks cut from the Pond. Most of the buildings in Tech Area 1 have been removed, but Fuller Lodge and the original homes on Bathtub Row still stand.

Los Alamos is now a city of 18,000 people. The conversion of a secret government laboratory into a New Mexico community was a gradual process. Los Alamos became a county in 1949, so that its residents would no longer be living on federal land, and thus could vote in state and local elections. In 1957, the gates of the Los Alamos Project were opened, allowing people to enter the city without passing through a checkpoint (most areas of the Laboratory, however, are still heavily guarded).

The end of the Cold War in the early 1990s, with the fall of the Berlin Wall and the break up of the Soviet Union, meant the end of an era for Los Alamos National Laboratory (LANL). No longer was the Laboratory's R&D on nuclear weapons so essential to U.S. national defense. Nevertheless, total funding of the Los Alamos National Laboratory continued at more than $1.5 billion per year. LANL today supports about 30 percent of the economy of Northern New Mexico. The total workforce is about 13,000 people (including contractors).

New Mexico is an extremely poor state, ranking almost last among the 50 states in per capita income in the midst of the richest country in the world. New Mexico is characterized by high unemployment, relatively poor health, low levels of education, and many other social problems. The Manhattan Project brought high-salaried brainpower to New Mexico, and in significant numbers compared to the rather sparse population of the state. The real pay off from Los Alamos, however, may lie in its potential for creating a northern New Mexico technopolis (a technology city, like California's Silicon Valley) through high-tech spin-off companies from the federal weapons' laboratory. In the post-Cold War era, Los Alamos National Laboratory increasingly focused on technology transfer, by converting technological innovations resulting from weapons R&D into useful consumer products that could be sold in the marketplace. During the late 1990s, LANL began to encourage its employees to spin-off new high-technology enterprises, and thus to create a New Mexico technopolis.

An important partner in this vision is Sandia National Laboratories (SNL). Back in 1945, Oppenheimer and Groves felt that they were running out of room on the mesa. The Army had taken over a civilian airfield in Albuquerque, Oxnard Field, renamed it Kirtland Field, and used it for dismantling old airplanes (Truslow & Smith, 1947). It became known as Sandia Air Base because of its proximity to the Sandia Mountains, which border Albuquerque on the east. At first, this new R&D unit was designated as the Z-Division of the Los Alamos Project, and began with the transfer of 145 people from Los Alamos. Sandia was assigned responsibility for the conventional explosives used in atomic bombs. Sandia's work focused on the engineering of weapons delivery, particularly on the non nuclear portion of nuclear weapons.[8] By 1949, it had grown to large size and was named the Sandia Corporation, later changed to Sandia National Laboratories (SNL). This R&D organization originated as the remnants of Deak Parsons' wartime Ordnance Division at Los Alamos, and it has more of an engineering orientation than do the people on the Hill. Splitting off Sandia National Laboratories allowed Los Alamos National Laboratory to concentrate on more basic research. Today, Sandia National Laboratories is about the same size as Los Alamos National Laboratory in budget and number of staff.

The 1940s Manhattan Project was originally established to beat the Germans in developing an atomic bomb, at a remote laboratory site in northern New Mexico where Oppenheimer expected to assemble 30 fellow theoretical physicists for the duration of World War II. Five decades later, Los Alamos National Laboratory has become an important force for economic development in New Mexico.

HEROES

The bravery of ordinary people–soldiers in the New Mexico National Guard, Navajo Code Talkers, and *Nisei* in the Purple Heart Regiment–influenced the outcome of World War II. The atomic scientists at Los Alamos were not ordinary people in their intelligence. The events at Los Alamos and Trinity and Hiroshima were the work of a few hundred key people, supported by 129,000 other employees of the Manhattan Project. What the atomic scientists accomplished in 28 months ended the war, saving a possible million American and Japanese lives, but also posing ultimate questions for the future of humanity.

The two thousand New Mexicans on Bataan, the 420 Navajo Code Talkers, the several thousand Japanese Americans in the Purple Heart Regiment, and dozens of key atomic scientists at Los Alamos were heroes, individuals who made personal sacrifices for the common good of their society. As many photographs in this book suggest, most were boyishly young in the early 1940s. The accomplishments of New Mexicans during World War II were not just the result of individual effort. For example, developing the atomic bomb required a telescoping of activities carried out by different organizations at various locations (Los Alamos, Hanford, Oak Ridge, Trinity, and Tinian, for example), working in unison toward a common goal. Little Boy and Fat Man could not have been dropped on Japanese cities had not the U.S. Marines captured the Marianas, Iwo Jima, and Okinawa just months previously, and had not the B-29, an advanced bomber, been developed in time to transport the bombs to their targets.

Further, the Manhattan Project at Los Alamos developed the atomic bomb through a multi disciplinary team approach, including physicists, chemists, mathematicians, engineers, and specialists in other fields. Theoretical physicists like Oppenheimer, Hans Bethe, Enrico Fermi, and Niels Bohr were dominant intellectual forces at Los Alamos, and were in the top administrative positions. But if one starts with the Fat Man and Little Boy bombs, and asks who contributed the integrated technologies and mechanisms that produced these sophisticated weapons, the answers include many others, such as Glenn Seaborg, George Kistiakowsky, John von Neumann, and Deak Parsons. Creating the atomic bombs at Los Alamos was a joint effort, involving numerous scientific fields. The SED machinists and other skilled technicians at Los Alamos actually fabricated the measuring instruments, and tested explosives. The SEDs, Army enlisted men, provided the skilled hands that helped make the bombs.

Teamwork won World War II, which often involved collaboration among very unlike individuals. General Groves, commandingly autocratic and bulging, worked closely with Robert Oppenheimer, rail-thin, intense, and ethereal (Figure 6-3). They were the original odd couple. But each brought something essential to the Manhattan Project; both counterparts knew that collaboration was necessary for success.

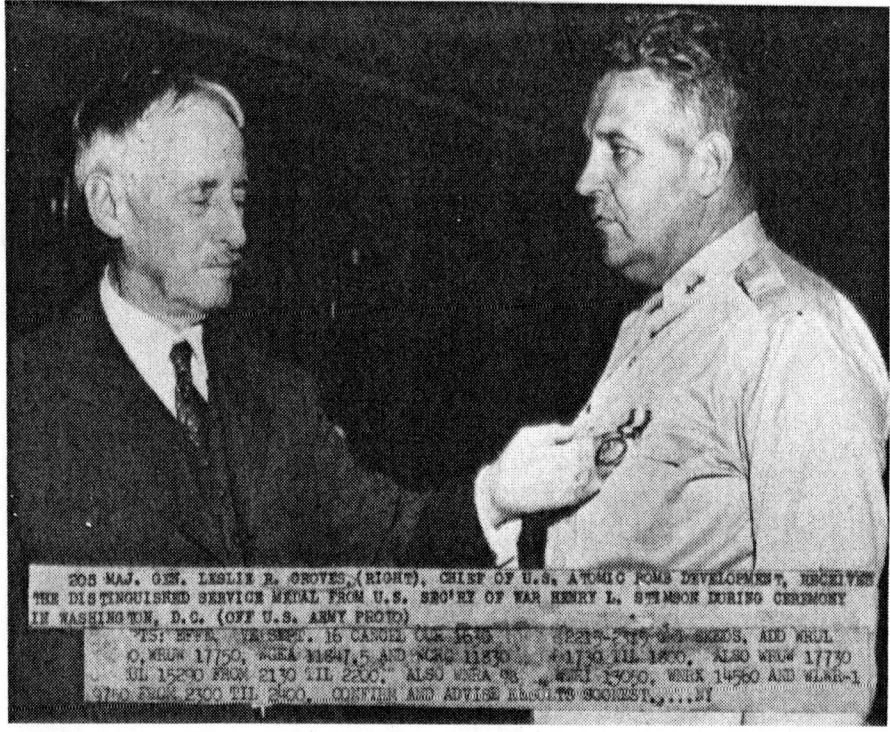

Figure 6-3. U.S. Secretary of War Henry Stimson Awards the Distinguished Service Medal to Major General Leslie Groves in a Ceremony in Washington, D.C. after World War II.

Groves added weight during the period in which he led the Manhattan Project. Despite the efforts of Mrs. Groves, the general had difficulty in following a diet. He kept a box of chocolates locked in his office safe in Washington, which he ate in order to maintain his energy level while working long hours.

Source: Washington, D.C., National Archives, NWDNS-208-PU-83S-5.

THE QUALITY OF POLICY DECISIONS

Several of the key policy decisions of World War II described in this book were made by chance or by ignoring available evidence. West Coast Japanese Americans were ordered to relocation and internment camps by the federal government, in part, on the basis of racial prejudice and wartime hysteria, while ignoring the government's own Munson

Report and information from the broken Japanese Purple Code. The decision to locate the atomic bomb project at the Los Alamos Ranch School was equally capricious, decided mainly by J. Robert Oppenheimer's love for northern New Mexico, in turn a chance result of his sickly childhood. Seeing the Ranch School students playing football in the snow, in shorts, seemed to have made a strong impression on General Groves. The New Mexico National Guard's 200th Regiment was ordered to the Philippines a few months before December 7 because the U.S. Army thought there would be good "chemistry" between Hispanic New Mexicans and Filipinos.

World War II was a conflict decided by intelligence, secret codes, and by science, as well as by brutal fighting. The outcome of this conflict was settled, in part, by cracking the enemy's code, and by maintaining the secrecy of the American communication system. The Navajo Code Talkers in the Pacific War represented a cryptographic system that was unbreakable by the Japanese. This triumph greatly aided the U.S. Marines in their invasion of Pacific islands, so as to provide airfields for the B-29s to bomb Japan. U.S. Navy Admiral Chester Nimitz knew the approximate locations of the four Japanese aircraft carriers sunk in the Battle of Midway in June 1942, because American intelligence had broken the Japanese Purple Code.

The development of the atomic bomb by the physicists and other scientists at Los Alamos was a supreme scientific achievement. But the government decision to launch the Manhattan Project was one of bungled decisions, an early do-nothing committee (the President's Advisory Committee on Uranium), and the almost accidental discovery of a huge stockpile of high-quality uranium ore from the Belgian Congo, stored in New York City. Here we see how extreme secrecy, while necessary from a security viewpoint, also worked against the success of the project it was intended to assist.

Many of the policy decisions discussed in this book were made in the rush of war (for example, General Groves was under extreme pressure to get the Manhattan Project underway when he selected Los Alamos as the site), and available evidence was often not fully considered. Once made, these policy choices (like the relocation and internment of the West Coast Japanese Americans) had long-term unanticipated consequences. For example, the four years that the Japanese Americans spent in the camps influenced many to become more loyal to Japan. Several hundred *Nisei* renounced their U.S. citizenship, and demanded repatriation to Japan. After the war, their relocation and internment camp experience led many Japanese Americans to disperse from their West Coast ghettos, and to spread out across the United States, exactly what many state governors had feared would happen.

NETWORKS

Person-to-person networks provided channels for rapid information dissemination, and for social support during World War II. For instance, Leo Szilard was a friend of Albert Einstein from their prewar teaching at the University of Berlin. So when Szilard wanted to call the potential danger of a German atomic bomb project to the attention of U.S. President Franklin Delano Roosevelt, he approached Einstein to help him compose the letter and to give it credibility with the nation's chief executive.

Network relationships were also important to J. Robert Oppenheimer in recruiting atomic scientists to the Los Alamos Project. Fortunately, as a result of his having earned a Ph.D. degree at the University of Göttingen, Oppenheimer was widely acquainted both with top European physicists and their American counterparts.

News of the 1938 Hahn/Strassman discovery of fission in Berlin spread via a complicated chain of human relationships: Hahn and Strassman to Lise Meitner, their Jewish refugee colleague in Sweden, through her nephew Otto Frisch to Niels Bohr in Copenhagen (where Frisch was studying on a postdoctoral fellowship), and then across the Atlantic with Bohr to New York and Princeton, where the Danish physicist alerted American physicists about the fission process and the prospects for developing an atomic weapon. Papers in scholarly journals also played a role in spreading this news, but the interpersonal networks got there first.

Networks also provide social support to individuals in times of stress. Navajo Code Talker Bill Toledo enlisted in the U.S. Marine Corps with his uncle Frank Toledo, a cousin, and two other high school classmates. They went through boot camp and code talker school together. During the fighting on Iwo Jima, Bill and Frank Toledo met in a foxhole for a chat about the folks back home and their own wartime adventures. Then they put down their coffee cups and returned to battle. This rendezvous was the only occasion that the two met in the Pacific, and it meant a great deal to Bill Toledo.

Evidence of the effects of social support is provided by the relatively higher survival rates of the New Mexicans of the 200th Regiment in Japanese POW camps and on the Death Ships to Japan. Their strong group solidarity helped them live through starvation, beatings, and overwork at the hands of their Japanese captors.

PARADOX

The events of World War II in the Pacific illustrate numerous paradoxes and contradictions. People of Japanese descent were involved with New Mexicans in each of the events in previous chapters. Japanese cruelty was evidenced in their mistreatment of the New Mexican POWs captured in the Philippines. The stubborn fighting skills of Japanese soldiers were illustrated in the Pacific island-hopping warfare in which the Navajo Code Talkers were involved. Clearly, the Japanese fought by a different cultural code than the Americans. For instance, the Japanese soldiers believed that their fighting spirit was enough to overcome all odds. They treated anyone who would surrender, including the 200th Regiment, with disgust and contempt.

Sympathy is evoked for the Japanese Americans relocated and interned by the United States for the duration, while their American born sons in the Purple Heart Regiment fought with unusual bravery in Europe. The U.S. atomic bombs, originally designed as a necessary defensive weapon to counter a Nazi possible atomic bomb, by 1945 were used as an offensive weapon to end World War II by destroying two Japanese cities.

Thus was World War II a matter of a paradox, of contradictions, and of connections or networks, points amply illustrated by the role of New Mexico in the Second World War.

THE ROLE OF RELIGION

Warfare usually is a matter for governments, without religion being involved (except, of course, in the case of religious wars), but religion influenced the outcome of World War II in several important ways.

Many of the key scientists in the Manhattan Project were Jews who fled Hitler's fascism in Europe: Hans Bethe, Leo Szilard, Niels Bohr, Edward Teller, I.I. Rabi, and John von Neuman. Others, like Enrico Fermi, migrated because his wife was Jewish. Certain key Americans involved in the Manhattan Project, like J. Robert Oppenheimer and Richard Feynman, were Jewish. The German/American race to develop an atomic bomb (which turned out to be no race at all) was a scientific and intellectual competition. The nation with the best brains won. Due to religious persecution, the United States had not only its own best brains, but also considerable European scientific brainpower.

Religion was a factor in several of the other events described in this book. For example, the Catholicism of the New Mexicans on Bataan, especially Hispanics, helped pull them through as prisoners of the Japanese. Navajo religious ceremonies helped the former Marine code talkers survive and to recover, mentally and spiritually, from their battlefield experiences in the Pacific. In Los Alamos, for a time, the various religions shared the same facility. In the Santa Fe Internment Camp Buddhist, Shinto, and Protestant priests also were internees.

THE ROLE OF WOMEN

Women played a limited role in the events of World War II described in the present volume. In the 1940s, especially in wartime, men were dominant. Women were expected to stay home, and out of the limelight. Many did. This homebound role did not mean they did not suffer also, or that they were not involved in the war. Some 6.5 million women workers in the U.S. were employed to replace the men who went off to fight. And 350,000 women were in uniform.

What role did women play in the scientific development of the atomic bomb? Madame Marie Curie of France had done important research on radioactivity (for which she won the Nobel Prize). Lise Meitner collaborated with Otto Hahn and Fritz Strassman in the Berlin research group that first created fission, and she led in identifying the fission process. Many hundreds of women were at Los Alamos, including the Women Army Corps (WACs). The spouses of the atomic scientists, secretaries, laboratory assistants, and other support staff were hired to help. Perhaps the title of a monograph about women at Los Alamos during World War II aptly describes their role: *Standing By and Making Do* (Wilson & Serber, 1988). The patriarchal gender division at Los Alamos was in part due to the small number of female physicists in the early 1940s, although Elizabeth Graves, Ph.D., was an exception. Photographs of various physics conferences in the 1930s show only men.

The New Mexican Bataan survivors were all men, although a dozen or so American nurses were captured by the Japanese on Corregidor, and were held in a POW camp in Manila. The New Mexican survivors from Bataan were surprised after they were liberated in 1945 to see WACs, WAVEs, and WAFs. The Bataan survivors had not known that women were in uniform during World War II.

No wives or children were assigned to the Santa Fe Internment Camp, although mail and packages were exchanged between internees and their families assigned to other camps.

TRAMPLING INDIVIDUAL LIBERTIES

Individual liberties were limited in various ways during all wars, including during the main wartime events analyzed here. For example, the civil rights of Japanese American citizens were violated by the Presidential Executive Order of February 1942. The Bataan survivors were mistreated by their Japanese conquerors, tortured, starved, and worked to exhaustion. Even the atomic scientists, while lauded for their scientific success, were essentially prisoners on the Pajarito Plateau, almost as much as the relocated and interned Japanese Americans or the Bataan POWs. Individual freedoms were severely restricted in fighting a war that was intended to guarantee freedoms to the world.

In wartime, people are often asked to give up certain of their freedoms for the common good. During World War II, the United States was fighting to preserve individual freedoms. But throughout the chapters of this book, we have seen how wartime conditions meant that the personal freedoms of Americans were curtailed such as censorship and the fencing of the atomic scientists at Los Alamos, and Japanese Americans in the Santa Fe Internment Camp. A means/ends paradox is apparent: The means used by the United States to prosecute the war often represented what the U.S. opposed in Axis fascism.

CONSCIENCE

Ethical concerns of conscience were raised by the wartime events described in this book. Leo Szilard acted as the "conscience" of the Allied efforts to develop an atomic bomb, initially motivated by the possibility that Hitler might develop this weapon first. Later, near the end of World War II, Szilard, along with many of his fellow atomic scientists, became concerned with how the United States would use atomic bombs on Japanese cities, and with the issue of the postwar civilian and international control of atomic energy. The Association of

Los Alamos Scientists unsuccessfully lobbied to have atomic energy available to all nations.

Ethical issues were also involved in battlefield conflict with the Japanese in the Pacific War. The Japanese Imperial Army did not abide by the Geneva Convention; they often killed battlefield prisoners and mistreated POWs. American Marines also killed Japanese prisoners. So neither side behaved in ways consistent with the approved rules of warfare. Such is the inherent nature of war, which leads to an escalation of cruelty and violence.

INTERSECTIONS

The main events chronicled in this book are connected by a strange variety of intersections which involve New Mexico and New Mexicans. An example is the torturing of Joe Kieyoomia, a New Mexico National Guard survivor of the Bataan Death March, by the Japanese in order to extract the Navajo Code Talkers' cryptographic system (which, although a Navajo, he did not know because he had not been trained as a code talker).

Another intersection is the Bataan Death March survivors, some of whom, as POWs imprisoned in Japan, were killed by Fat Man and Little Boy at Hiroshima and at Nagasaki, respectively. Yet, for other POWs, the bombs saved their lives because their prison conditions ended and, because U.S. troops did not invade Japanese soil before the surrender, the POWs were not exterminated as Japanese commanders were ordered to do.

Ernie Pyle, who loved his adopted Albuquerque home, included many New Mexicans in his columns. He promoted the Bataan Relief Organization and war bond campaigns. New Mexicans posthumously honored him by naming an Ernie Pyle Day, awarding him an honorary university degree, and maintaining a library for children in his home (Melzer, 1996).

After returning from the Pacific, code talker Bill Toledo spent his career working in uranium mining in New Mexico, an industry created by wartime Los Alamos. Ruth Hashimoto, a West Coast Japanese American, who had been relocated to the Heart Mountain Camp in Wyoming, worked at Sandia National Laboratory in Albuquerque after the war.

An ultimate irony was the 4,555 "dangerous enemy aliens" who were interned in Santa Fe, only 35 miles from Los Alamos, America's top secret laboratory of World War II. Paradoxically, Enrico Fermi and his wife's visas listed them as "enemy aliens" since the U.S. was at war with Italy.

In a state with a sparse population like New Mexico, perhaps it is inevitable that the individuals involved in the events described here would intersect in a variety of ways.

❖ ❖ ❖

Some 58 years after these narrated events of World War II, what happened to certain of the important sites at which these events occurred?

Leupp, Arizona, where Philip Johnston grew up at the Presbyterian Mission while gaining fluency in *Diné* (and where 80 *Nisei* dissidents were detained in 1943 at the Leupp Isolation Center, a former boarding school for Navajo children), is now a deserted crossroads. Ruins of the old trading post remain, with goats and ducks roaming through the former Presbyterian church, whose front door swings forlornly in the desert wind.

Navajo Code Talkers meet monthly in Gallup, New Mexico. Bataan survivors gather in Santa Fe and Albuquerque to reminisce, while they live out their halcyon years. About 100 Bataan veterans are still alive. Almost all of the Japanese Americans interned in the Santa Fe camp are gone, as is most evidence that the camp ever existed. A marker was erected on the hill overlooking the former internment camp site, now a middle-class suburb where several Bataan veterans live. Nearby, Los Alamos National Laboratory continues on the Pajarito Plateau.

On the opposite side of the world, Hiroshima is a bustling city of 1.1 million people, on the surface at least rejuvenated from its 1945 destruction. The postwar constitution of Japan precludes its participation in any future war.

As is often the case, fragments of the history are told by various people and in different settings. The pieces taken together tell a more enduring story. Perhaps, the important lessons learned will live on.

ADDENDUM A

FURTHER RESOURCES AND POINTS OF INTEREST

New Mexico National Guard (from all areas of the state, including Indian reservations)

Albuquerque. Bataan Park at Lomas and Carlisle. Memorials are engraved slabs with the history and names of the 200th and 515th Battalions. Commemoration service is held around April 9th.

Deming. Luna Mimbres Museum and original home of the 111th Cavalry, predating the 200th Battalion. A "LEST WE FORGET" Memorial is in Veteran's Park.

Las Cruces. Statue commemorating 60 years since the Bataan surrender is located on Veterans Highway.

Santa Fe. Bataan Memorial Building, former state capitol, Galisteo Street and Santa Fe Avenue. Site of April 9th commemoration sponsored by Bataan Veterans, the NM National Guard, State of NM, and the City of Santa Fe. New Mexico Veterans Memorial. Bataan Military Museum and Library (exhibits, books, photo, and video library).

Taos. Plaza Memorial. Bataan building nearby is where men signed up for the National Guard.

White Sands. Veterans, military, and interested people march part of 65 miles in the desert in late April to respect those who were in the Bataan Death March.

Medals. U.S. Army medals and the Bataan Medal awarded by the State of New Mexico.

Navajo Code Talkers (Navajo Reservation overlapping both New Mexico and Arizona)

Gallup. Meeting room and exhibits in the Chamber of Commerce Building.

Window Rock, Arizona. Navajo Museum and Navajo Code Talkers Association.

Medals. U.S. Marine Corps, Congressional Gold and Silver Medals, awarded in 2001.

Ernie Pyle (popular war correspondent killed on Ie Island off Okinawa in April, 1945).

>**Albuquerque**. Ernie Pyle Branch Library, 900 Girard SE.

Santa Fe Internment Camp (on the outskirts of Santa Fe) (The U.S. Department of Justice camp operated by the U.S. Immigration Service.)

>**Frank S. Ortiz Park**. Stone marker with plaque overlooking Casa Solana Sub-division, built on the site of the Internment Camp.
>
>**Lordsburg**. Museum of POW camp that once held some Japanese Americans.
>
>**Santa Fe**. New Mexico State Archives, official government papers and photos; Palace of the Governors Archives, personal papers.

Manhattan Project (Los Alamos (Santa Fe as entrance), Albuquerque, and White Sands).

>**Albuquerque**. The National Atomic Museum, associated with Sandia National Laboratories.
>
>**Los Alamos**. Los Alamos Historical Museum, Book Shop, and Archives at Fuller Lodge. Los Alamos National Laboratory's Bradbury Science Museum; Los Alamos National Laboratory Archives. Namesake places and events: Oppenheimer Drive, Oppenheimer Study Center at the Laboratory, Oppenheimer home, Oppenheimer annual lecture and science scholarships.
>
>**Medals**. Manhattan Project U.S. 4th Army patch; "E" Awards to civilians.
>
>**White Sands Memorial Site**. Trinity Test Site. Open to the public on the first Saturday in April and October.

ADDENDUM B

			ADDENDUM B COMPARISON OF MAIN EVENTS 1941-1945		
Who?	NM National Guard	Navajo Code Talkers	Japanese-Americans– living in Am.	Manhattan Project	Trinity Site Testing
Where From?	All areas of NM; of various backgrounds.	NM & AZ.	West Coast (CA, OR, WA), AL, Hawaii & Peru	European émigrés, Allies, U.S.	European émigrés, Allies, U.S.
Where Sent?	Philippines	Pacific islands	Lordsburg, Ft. Sumner, Santa Fe Internment Camps	Los Alamos means "the cottonwoods" in Spanish.	Alamogordo means "fat cottonwood" in Spanish.
Under which US Dept.?	U.S. Army	U.S. Marine Corps.	FBI/U.S. Justice Dept.	Civilian Scientists/ U.S. 4th Army & U.S. Navy/Army Air Forces	Civilian Scientists/ U.S. Army & U.S. Navy
Language	Spanish/Native American/English	Navajo-Diné/ English	Japanese/ English	Physics/Mathematics/ English	Physics/ Mathematics English
Secrecy	No letters for POWs until end of war. Only Red Cross postcards sent.	Letters allowed but code remained secret during and after the war.	Letters censored, Internees required to write in English while in camp.	Letters censored. Secret places and mission until end of War. Guards on horseback patrolled entire fenced community.	Secret test within the Manhattan Project.
Living Condition	Mud & jungle; barracks, foxholes, imprisoned, slave laborers, starvation rations, enemy fire.	Mud & jungle; barracks, foxholes, ships, enemy fire.	Mud & unpaved roads, barracks, imprisoned (garden & rice diet), fenced, sports, educational classes.	Remote, mud, barracks, passes to get in and out, only six telephone lines, fenced, restricted movement outside, area patrolled by guards on horses.	Desert, camping, temporary quarters.
Women's Role	No wives, WAVES, WACS, or nurses were with POWs in Japanese camps.	No females. Wives, if any, at home in U.S.	No wives, except at Baca Ranch, NM, for Clovis families.	Some female scientists. WACS, WAVES, and wives were secretaries and assistants; computed data.	Women not allowed at site. A few watched from distance.
Ave. Ages All Men	18-35 years	17-36 years (15-35)	52 years	27 years for scientists; 32 years for entire town.	
How Many in Total?	Approx. 1,800 men	Approx. 430 men (350-450)	4,555 men held; 2,100 maximum at one time.	In LA–scientists 700; SEDs 1,823; total 6,000 by end of war.	
How Many Returned?	Approx. 900 men came back.	All but about 11; records are incomplete.	Most remained in U.S.; some returned to Japan, but many came back.	Project staff reduced to 1,600 under second Director Norris Bradbury.	All (a one time experiment).

ADDENDUM C

ADDENDUM C TIME-LINE

	NM National Guard	Navajo Code Talkers	Japanese-Americans	Manhattan Project	Trinity Site
1939				Einstein letter to FDR.	
1940				In New York and at 11 U.S. universities.	
1941 -- Japanese attack Pearl Harbor on December 7 and the Philippines on December 8; U.S. and England declare war on Japan on December 8; Germany and Italy declare war on U.S. on December 11.					
1941	In Jan. 200th departs for Philippines.				
1942	On April 9 the 200th & 515th were surrendered.	In April recruitment begins; trained for 2 months, then sent to Guadalcanal for first assignment.	Santa Fe Detention Camp opens Feb. Closed in Sept.	Sept. 17--General L. Groves heads atomic project; Nov. 7--Los Alamos selected for Manhattan Project.	
1943		Bougainville landing on Nov.1; Tarawa landing on Nov. 20.	Santa Fe Camp reopens. 2,100 men at highest peak.	Feb. LA Ranch School closes; new buildings for 30 scientists initially, increasing "for the duration."	
1944	News of POWs prison conditions angers U.S. and New Mexico.	Saipan--June 15; Guam--July 21; Tinian--Aug. 1; Peleliu--Sept. 15.	Tule Lake, CA dissidents sent to Santa Fe Camp.		
1945	Philippines recaptured on Feb. 5; General Douglas MacArthur returns to Manila.	Iwo Jima--Feb. 19; Okinawa--April 1; Ie Shima--April 21.	Sons of internees served bravely in U.S. military.	Culmination of plutonium research; uranium understood earlier; Bradbury succeeds Oppenheimer.	Plutonium test of Fat Man prototype-- July 16th.
1945 -- Germany surrenders May 2-8; Japan surrenders August 14. WWII ends on September 2.					
1946	POWs return to New Mexico. Bataan Death March surrender date commemorated every year in Santa Fe on April 9.	Code Talkers forbidden from telling about secret code even after discharge.	Santa Fe Camp closed late April or early May; Internees leave for Japan or stay in U.S. Land reverts to NM Penitentiary, then developed for housing.	Atomic Energy Commission formed; Los Alamos Scientific Lab, then National Lab, continues as nuclear defense & non-defense research laboratory.	Area remains military testing ground.
To present		Later honored by several U.S. presidents when their special service is revealed.	Santa Fe Camp marker dedicated.		Open twice a year, first Sat. in April and October.

ILLUSTRATIONS

Maps

Figure 1-2. The Farthest Advance of the Japanese Empire in Mid-1942 (heavy arrows), and the Main Island-Hopping Battles with the United States (lighter arrows), p. 31.

Figure 2-3. The 75-Mile Bataan Death March from Various Surrender Points in Southern Bataan to the Railhead at San Fernando, Where the 75,000 Prisoners, Including 12,000 Americans, Were Transported to Camp O'Donnell, p. 48.

Figure 3-1. Map of the Navajo Nation in Arizona, New Mexico, and Utah, p. 88.

Figure 4-1. Location of the Ten WRA Relocation Camps and the Four U.S. Department of Justice Internment Camps, p. 142.

Figure 4-10. A 1951 Aerial Photograph of the Santa Fe Internment Camp, p. 173.

Figure 5-3. Map of New Mexico Showing the Location of Los Alamos and Ground Zero for the Trinity Site, p. 209.

Photographs

Figure 1-1. The Crew of the Enola Gay on Tinian with Their B-29 in the Background, p. 21.

Figure 2-1. Patriotic New Mexicans Volunteered for Military Service Early in World War II, p.39.

Figure 2-2. Private Art Smith with "Frenchy," the Range Finder, at Fort Stotsenberg, Near Clark Field, in the Philippines, p. 41.

Figure 2-4. Three American Prisoners-of-War on the Bataan Death March Rest Briefly Enroute to Camp O'Donnell, p. 49.

Figure 2-5. Manuel Armijo (with blanket ends tied) on the Bataan Death March, p. 54.

Figure 2-6. Vicente Ojinaga (the POW wearing the Hat) in Camp O'Donnell, p. 56.

Figure 2-7. The Daily Burial Detail at Camp O'Donnell, p.57.

Figure 2-8. Two Americans Liberated from a POW Camp in Japan, p. 68.

Figure 2-9. POW Art Smith Sent a Postcard Home that Contained a Code Word Indicating He Was Alive, p. 73.

Figure 2-9a. Smith marries Bessie, p. 74.

Figure 2-10. Master Sergeant (retired) Manuel Armijo in Santa Fe, in 2001, p. 79.

Figure 3-2. The First 29 Navajo Code Talkers at the Completion of Their Boot Camp Training in San Diego, p. 93.

Figure 3-3. Private First Class Preston Toledo and His Uncle, Private First Class Frank Toledo, Relay Military Orders Over a Field Radio in Diné, p. 103.

Figure 3-4.Two Navajo Code Talkers on Bougainville in December 1943, p. 112.

Figure 3-5. These Three Code Talkers Were in the First Wave of Marines to Fight their Way Ashore in Saipan in June, 1944, p. 116.

Figure 3-6. Marines of the 2nd Division, 3rd Battalion, 6th Regiment on Saipan, Resting Behind the Front Lines, Just after Fighting Off a Japanese Banzai Attack, p. 117.

Figure 3-7. Ernie Pyle, the Famous War Correspondent, at Home in Albuquerque, p. 126.

Figure 3-8. Four of the Five Surviving Members of the First 29 Code Talkers, Who Received Gold Congressional Medals in Washington, D.C., in 2001, p. 136.

Figure 4-2. The U.S. Army Ordered All Japanese Americans to Report to Assembly Centers in 1942, p. 145.

Figure 4-3. Evacuation of Japanese Americans from San Francisco in April 1942, p.149.

Figure 4-5. Ruth Hashimoto's Mother, Fusako (Iriye) Yamada; Ruth; Her Eldest Daughter, Ada Jan Noriko Akin; David Evans, a Former University of Michigan Army Intelligence Student of Ruth's, En Route to His Home in Kansas after Serving in Occupied Japan; and Ruth's Father, Reverend Asataro Yamada, p. 154.

Figure 4-6. Under the Heart Mountain, p. 159.

Figure 4-7. Many of the Industrious Japanese American Families Converted their Tarpaper Barracks into Cozy Homes, p. 161.

Figure 4-8. The Possessions of Mamoru Ike, a Newly-Arrived Internee at the Santa Fe Internment Camp, Are Searched by INS Officers, p. 169.

Figure 4-9. The Funeral for Dr. Sadakazu Furugochi on November 12, 1943, in the Santa Fe Internment Camp, p, 171.

Figure 4-11. Japanese American Leaders of the Santa Fe Internment Camp Pose with Abner Schrieber, Deputy-in-Charge of the Camp (seated to the right of the internee with a walking stick), p. 177.

Figure 4-12. Our Guard in the Watchtower Became a Spring Baseball Fan at the Santa Fe Internment Camp, p. 179.

Figure 5-1. Enrico Fermi, Nicknamed the "Italian Navigator," Created the First Self-Sustained Nuclear Chain Reaction at the University of Chicago, 204.

Figure 5-3. Major General Leslie Groves in the Washington, D.C., Office of the Manhattan Project, p. 207.

Figure 5-4. J. Robert Oppenheimer, Scientific Director of the Manhattan Project at Los Alamos, p. 213.

Figure 5-5. Dorothy McKibbin Greeted New Staff Members of the Los Alamos Project at Her Office at 109 East Palace Avenue, Santa Fe, p. 216.

Fig, 5-6. General Groves Resisted Constructing Paved Roads and Sidewalks at Los Alamos, Which He Regarded as a Temporary Site, p. 218.

Figure 5-7. The La Fonda Harvey Hotel, on the Southeastern Corner of the Santa Fe Plaza, Where Manhattan Project Staff Members Spent Leisure Hours, p. 220.

Figure 5-8. Richard Feynman, the Contrarian of Los Alamos, p. 223.

Figure 5-9. Three Nobel Prize Laureates, Ernest Lawrence, Enrico Fermi, and Isidor Rabi, Chat Informally at the Los Alamos Laboratory during World War II, p. 229.

Figure 5-10. The Functioning of Little Boy and Fat Man, p. 231.

Figure 5-11. The Staff of the Chemical Metallurgical Research Lab, Mainly SEDs, in 1945, p. 237.

Figure 5-12. Jumbo at Trinity Site, p. 242.

Figure 5-13. The Plutonium Bomb Was Hoisted to the Top of a 100-Foot Tower at Trinity Site, p. 244.

Figure 5-14. Niels Bohr and Robert Oppenheimer in 1950, p. 255.

Figure 5-15. Little Boy Is Secured in a B-29 Bomb Bay, p. 257.

Figure 5-16. Deak Parsons and Paul Tibbetts Brief the B-29 Crews Prior to Take-Off for Hiroshima, 259.

Figure 5-17. The Enola Gay, Parked at North Field on Tinian, on the Day after Dropping Little Boy on Hiroshima, p. 260.

Figure 5-18. Harold Agnew in Front of the Instrumentation Lab on Tinian in Mid-1945, Holding the Core of the Plutonium Bomb Dropped on Nagasaki, p. 263.

Figure 6-1. Albert Einstein and J. Robert Oppenheimer at the Institute for Advanced Study at Princeton University, after World War II, p. 268.

Figure 6-2. Pass Identification Photograph of Klaus Fuchs, the Soviet Spy Who Worked on the Plutonium Bomb at Los Alamos, p. 271.

Figure 6-3. U.S. Secretary of War Henry Stimson Awards the Distinguished Service Medal to Major General Leslie Groves in a Ceremony in Washington after World War II, p. 278.

LIST OF TABLES

Table 1-1. Time-Line of the Main Events in World War II, 28

[no Table 2-1.]

Table 3-1. Time-Line for the Navajo Code Talkers, 96

Table 4-1. Time-Line of the Santa Fe Detention/Internment Camp, 188

Table 5-1. Time-Line for the Development of the Atomic Bomb, 198

NOTES

1

1. A similar watch to Nihawa's, also stopped at 8:15 a.m., was picked up by Ed Bemis of the Los Alamos Laboratory a few weeks after the explosion. This watch is in the Los Alamos Historical Museum today.
2. Because the United States is on the other side of the International Date Line, August 7th in Japan was August 6th in America.
3. "*Banzai*" literally means "10,000 years."

2

1. She was Winifred Watkins, who later became Chintis' wife.
2. The New Mexicans noticed that every B-17 was destroyed by the Japanese bombers, while not a single one of the dummy B-17s at Clark Field was bombed. Vicente Ojinaga (2000) and Manuel Armijo (2000) are convinced that Japanese spies had alerted the Japanese bombers as to which planes were dummies. Otherwise, it would have been difficult to distinguish between them from an altitude of 23,000 feet (4 ½ miles).
3. Ralph Rodriguez (2000) saved some *lugao* (watery rice dish) from breakfast, which was served at 5:00 A.M., until midmorning. In the daylight it looked so awful that he could not eat it. After that, he ate the *lugao* when it was still dark.
4. The *Tattori Maru*, one of the Hell Ships that transported 1,993 American POWs from the Philippines to Japan, also carried Japanese soldiers who had been captured by the American troops during the fighting on Bataan. The Japanese were in chains (Knox, 1981).
5. A few of the Japanese guards were fluent in English, but did not disclose this ability.
6. During their several years in the Cabanatuan Prison Camp, an estimated 2,632 (43 percent) of the 6,200 American died (Ashton, 1985).
7. Joe Bergstein still enjoys killing flies. Sometimes, he swats one fly, and then opens the door of his Los Alamos house to let other flies come inside (Bergstein, 2000).
8. Only about one-third of all American prisoners in the Philippines were alive at the end of World War II. The New Mexicans had a higher survival rate because of their group solidarity, which led them to look out for each other during their POW experience.
9. "*Maru*" is the Japanese designation for merchant ship.

10. In 2002, Tony Martinez, the son of Eduardo Martinez, produced a documentary on the Bataan Death March, "Colors of Courage."
11. Agapito ("Gap") Silva (1999) was working in the coal mine at Camp 17 when the roof of the mine collapsed. He suffered four broken ribs, a fractured pelvis, and an injured back. Fortunately, a pile of large rocks prevented him from being completely crushed.
12. After the war, the One-Armed Bandit, along with the commander of Camp 17 and another guard known as The Sailor, were tried for war crimes committed against Allied prisoners-of-war and executed in January, 1946 (Knox, 1981).

3

1. We write "code talker" without a hyphen in this chapter, as is the most common convention.
2. On April 13, 1943, Admiral Isoroku Yamamoto, Commander-in-Chief of the Japanese Fleet, and planner of the Pearl Harbor and Midway attacks, visited Japanese military forces in the Solomon Islands. American cryptoanalysts learned his itinerary, and 18 P-38 fighters met his plane. His death removed one of the most influential Japanese military leaders in World War II (Singh, 1999, p. 191).
3. Johnston (1944) recalled that he yearned for combat in early 1942: "Office work became a nightmare; I hated the inaction, and longed for a chance to sneak over to Bataan . . . . Then right out of the blue plummeted an idea which I picked up, layed carefully on a silver platter, and offered to the Marine Corps."
4. This government policy reflected the "melting pot" belief, then prevalent in the United States, that everyone should learn to speak English and become thoroughly Americanized, gradually losing their original language and culture.
5. Gorman was attending a Christian school, the Rehoboth Mission School in Gallup, New Mexico, but this school pursued the same assimilation policies as the BIA schools (Greenberg & Greenberg, 1996).
6. Later, Shinn said that he seriously doubted Gorman's claim that he was 28, but that he was so impressed by Gorman's personal abilities that he allowed him to enlist anyway (Z. Gorman, 1999).
7. The First 29 were assisted by three Navajo Marines (Wilson Price, Les Hostee, and Felix Yazzie) who were already at Camp Elliott, and who did not become code talkers (M. Gorman, 1999). Philip Johnston was not at the code talker training session, and did not participate in building the code. During this period, he was designing storm sewers for the city of Los Angeles (Johnston, 1970).

8. Several code talkers stated that extemporaneous code words were developed in the field. For instance, the code talkers in one Marine division came to understand that a message stating "Squaw Dance tonight" meant "military action tonight." Back on the Big Res, a Squaw Dance was often held in conjunction with the Enemy Way Ceremony; women chose their dance partners, with the males expected to pay at the end of the dance (M. Gorman, 1999).
9. Later in the war, two Anglos who had grown up in trading posts and had a high level of fluency in *Diné*, were recruited as code talkers, but flunked out of the Navajo Communication Course. Philip Johnston (1970) felt they lacked adequate motivation in learning the code. Code talker Jack Jones (2000) said that the two Anglos in his training batch were quite fluent in *Diné*, but they could not make the rapid translations between English and *Diné* that were required. However, one non-Navajo, Stephen P. Wallace, who had attended an all-Navajo elementary school in Newcomb, New Mexico, and worked in trading posts on the Navajo Reservation, enlisted in the Marine Corps because he had heard about the code talkers. Wallace did not go through the code talker training in Camp Pendleton, but was ordered to participate in code talker training on Okinawa, preparatory to the planned invasion of Japan (Wallace, 2002). Wallace's discharge papers classify him as a Navajo Code Talker, and he was awarded a Congressional Medal as a code talker in November, 2001. So there was one non-Navajo Navajo Code Talker.
10. By the end of the war, the code was expanded with duplicate words for all but the eight least-used letters: Q, S, U, V, W, X, Y, and Z (Durrett, 1998).
11. Toledo was not in an all-Navajo training platoon, of which there were only two: The 382nd (these code talkers were the First 29), and the 297th, whose members graduated in April, 1943 (Billey, 2000).
12. Five brothers serving on the same Navy ship, the USS *Lexington*, were killed in 1942, and thereafter no two family members were allowed to serve in the same military unit.
13. The code talkers' school was moved in early 1943 from Camp Elliott to Camp Pendleton, 30 miles north of San Diego. Camp Elliott later became the U.S. Navy's Miramar Field.
14. Johnston put together an application package which included letters of recommendation from his World War I commander and others. He sent the application directly to the Marine Corps commandant in Washington. Eleven days later, he was a Leatherneck (Johnston, 1970).
15. Two men were usually required to operate the TBX radio. One individual typically sat in the "idiot seat" and cranked the TBX, while the other Marine sent and received messages.
16. Paul Blatchford related how he had instructed a young Marine replacement in his platoon not to pick up souvenirs because they might be booby-trapped. The platoon was advancing under enemy fire with

the new Marine following Blatchford: "Here was this kid. He'd got off my trail and picked up something, I guess it was that booby trap, and when I saw him he was going 50 feet up in the air, and when he came down he was nothing but hamburger" (Blatchford, 1971).

17. It is unclear whether or not the bodyguards were also ordered to kill their Navajo Code Talker if there were danger of capture by the Japanese. Years later, when Toledo met Bonham at a Marine reunion, he could not get him to answer a question on this point (Toledo, 1999). Whether or not the bodyguards were also ordered to be assassins of the code talkers became an issue in the 2002 MGM movie "Windtalkers." The Navajo Code Talkers Association, as consultants to MGM, insisted that the film was inauthentic when actor Nicholas Cage, playing a bodyguard, throws a hand grenade in order to kill a code talker captured by the Japanese.
18. The Navajo Code Talkers noticed that relatively few of their number were promoted to sergeant during the Pacific War.
19. It had been translated by Jimmy King at Camp Elliott in 1943, at the suggestion of Philip Johnston (King, 1971).
20. Billey and other code talkers were believed by their fellow Marines to have some mysterious means of direct contact with high military authority, and thus to know what was going on in the war. Billey (2000) would jokingly tell his buddies, "Now I have just talked to FDR, and he says that . . . ."
21. The code talkers had difficulty getting passports for this trip because they did not have birth certificates (M. Gorman, 1999).

4

1. We use the term "Japanese American" in the present chapter to mean anyone of Japanese descent living in the United States, thus including both citizens born in America and individuals who were born in Japan but were living in the United States at the time that World War II began. The total population of 121,313 imprisoned Japanese Americans included 112,700 individuals from the West Coast, 1,100 from Hawaii, 2,100 Japanese Peruvians, and some 5,413 individuals who were born in the camps during World War II.
2. The 600,000 U.S. residents of Italian descent were classified as enemy aliens in 1941, required to carry a special identification document, and forbidden to travel more than five miles from their home. Some 230 Italian Americans were interned as "dangerous enemy aliens."
3. The sixteen assembly centers were at Fresno, Manzanar, Marysville, Merced, Pinedale (near Fresno), Pomona, Sacramento, Salinas, Santa Anita, Stockton, Tanforan, Tulare, and Turlock, all in California; Mayer, Arizona; Portland, Oregon; and Puyallup, Washington. Most of the WCCA

assembly centers were racetracks, fairgrounds, and other large facilities that were immediately available to house the Japanese Americans.
4. The Japanese Americans in California occupied only one percent of the cultivated land of the state, but produced 10 percent of the total value of California produce (Van Valkenburg, 1995).
5. The Japanese government had encouraged the *Kibei* to return to Japan for their schooling (Smith, 1995).
6. As Colonel Karl Bendetsen (1942) claimed: "In the stress of necessity for immediate action, it was impossibly difficult to sift the loyal from the disloyal."
7. This sign is today in the Japanese American National Museum in Los Angeles.
8. Fukuda (1990) kept a diary during his six years in internment camps, which was eventually translated and published as a book. Fukuda told how he obtained a copy of the Geneva Convention while in the Lordsburg Internment Camp, translated it into Japanese, and published 1,200 copies.
9. Many of the *Issei* in the Santa Fe Internment Camp complained of what the medical staff called "imaginary diseases" that were traceable to their confinement and to worry about their family members who were in relocation camps or in the U.S. Army.
10. This building belonged to rancher Ron Morrison in Wyoming, who used it as a storage shed until 1994 when it was dismantled and trucked to Los Angeles.
11. The term "concentration camp" was originated by Lord Kirchner during the Boer War in South Africa to refer to imprisoned civilians that the British feared might engage in espionage or sabotage.
12. However, daily life at the Poston Camp had some redeeming features. Bill Nishimura (2001), who spent two years there, remembers slipping through the camp's fence to go fishing in the nearby Colorado River.
13. This point was made forcibly at a conference of Western governors and WRA officials, held on April 7, 1942, in Salt Lake City. The governors insisted that the Japanese Americans be kept under strict guard and be treated as prisoners (Smith, 1991).
14. Almost all of these *Nisei* who renounced their U.S. citizenship and went to Japan, eventually returned to the United States and regained their American citizenship (Smith, 1995).
15. Radio Tokyo broadcast a daily talk by Masao Dodo, an *Issei* who had lived in California, graduated from the University of Southern California, and returned to Japan in 1938 (Hayashi, 1995).
16. Much of this research was conducted by the Japanese American Evacuation and Relocation Study (JERS), directed by Dorothy Swaine Thomas at the University of California at Berkeley. The Bureau of Sociological Research (BSR) at the Poston Camp, directed by an

anthropologist, Edward H. Spicer, and a psychiatrist-anthropologist, Alexander H. Leighton, was also important in our understanding of the camp experience.

17. Some 3,700 Japanese Americans served with the Military Intelligence Service in the Pacific and Asia as Japanese language specialists during World War II, coaxing Japanese soldiers to surrender, interrogating Japanese prisoners-of-war, and translating captured documents. The *Issei* father of Technical Sergeant Henry ("Horizontal Hank") Goshu, so nicknamed because of his bravery in combat in the Pacific War, was in the Santa Fe Internment Camp.

18. This number of individual decorations is all the more impressive, given that the Purple Heart Regiment never numbered more than 4,500 men at any given time during World War II.

19. Ten Japanese railroad workers and their families living in Clovis, New Mexico, were evacuated by the U.S. government in late January, 1942. These Santa Fe Railway employees had been housed in a rent-free compound provided by the company. New Mexicans had strong anti-Japanese attitudes at the time, related to the New Mexico 200th Regiment fighting on the Bataan Peninsula, and there were dark suggestions that the Japanese railroad workers might meet with "accidents." The Japanese families were relocated to the Baca Ranch Camp (also called the Old Raton Ranch Camp, essentially a satellite camp of the Fort Stanton Army Camp) for about a year. Then, when the camp was disbanded in September, 1942, they were transferred to Poston, Gila River, Topaz, and other WRA camps (Culley, 1982).

   Japanese Americans in Gallup, Grants, and Belen, New Mexico, were treated quite differently than their counterparts in Clovis, perhaps in part due to their longer residence and to their closer integration into the community. The Gallup City Council voted a resolution of support for the city's Japanese American families when the United States entered World War II.

20. Except that Fort Lincoln received 650 Japanese Americans in 1945 (Clark, 1980).

21. One of the barracks buildings from the Santa Fe Camp is presently located at 3419A Agua Fria, near the San Isidro Crossing.

22. The Fort Stanton Camp held 410 German seamen from the ship *Columbus*, which was captured off Cuba by the British Navy in 1939.

23. The inmates at the Santa Fe Internment Camp were provided with a standard Army ration, which included more red meat than the Japanese preferred. So the Santa Fe Internment Camp swapped beef for fish with Bruns General Hospital.

24. The records of the Santa Fe Internment Camp now held in the National Archives show that movies were shown several nights per week. These films included "Get Hep to Love," "Doin' the Town," "Tarzan Triumphs,"

"Steeds and Steers," and "In Old Santa Fe." Evidently the camp administrators did not consider how cryptic the title of this last film appeared to be.

25. Including writing letters. The camp's censors read an average of 2,000 pieces of mail per day (Melzer, 1994).
26. One play, performed in the camp theater and observed by Mangione (1978), seemed to have a cynical theme: The war is over and two Japanese Americans are returning from an internment camp to their wives. They lug heavy bags, filled with presents for their wives. But when the wives open the bags, they are filled with rocks that their husbands collected while in the internment camp. As the curtain falls, the disgusted wives throw the stones at the two men. The Japanese American men in the Santa Fe Internment Camp gave this play a boisterous reception.
27. The Spanish Consul reported that the religious breakdown of the camp's 701 internees in April, 1944, included 500 Buddhists, 120 Shintoists, 80 Protestants, and 1 Catholic (de Amat, 1945).
28. This photograph, taken on September 27, 1945, shows MacArthur, dressed in his Army uniform, towering over Emperor Hirohito, who wore a formal cutaway (Dower, 1999).
29. Leupp is where Philip Johnston, who initiated the idea of Navajo Code Talkers, gained fluency in *Diné* while growing up at the Presbyterian mission (see Chapter 3).
30. Dockum said that initially he tried every available means (unsuccessfully) not to be stationed at the Lordsburg camp, although after the war he settled in Lordsburg. One reason for Dockum's original apathy to Lordsburg was the weather. It was so windy that each of the camp's barracks had to be lashed to the ground with large cables tied to huge concrete blocks that were buried in the ground (Clark, 1980). A large number of these concrete blocks can be observed today at the former site of the Lordsburg POW Camp, about three miles east of Lordsburg.

5

1. The $2.2 billion cost of the atomic bomb was fairly minor, however, as a part of the total cost of World War II. The United States spent $9.6 billion per week on the war.
2. For instance, Oppenheimer met Werner Heisenberg, who was later to head Hitler's atomic bomb project during World War II, when Heisenberg gave a lecture at Göttingen. Oppenheimer also became friends with John von Neumann, the Hungarian mathematician who later would help develop the implosion method of detonating the Fat Man plutonium bomb at Los Alamos.

3. A year previously, Szilard had read H.G. Wells' (1914), The World Set Free, a book predicting he development of atomic bombs that would destroy cities. That morning, Szilard had read a newspaper article in which the highly respected English physicist Ernest Rutherford called atomic energy "moonshine" (Weart & Szilard, 1978, p. 16). Ed Hammel (2000) of Los Alamos National Laboratory doubts that Szilard's eureka could have happened as early as 1938.
4. Referring to Marie Slowdowska Curie of France, who, with her husband Pierre, was awarded two Nobel Prizes for her research on radium and on radioactivity (Howes & Herzenberg, 1999). Their daughter Iréne Joliet-Curie and son-in-law Frédéric Joliet-Curie continued this research at the Radium Institute in Paris.
5. Germany's failure to win the race to produce an atomic bomb was probably not due to Heisenberg and other German physicists withholding crucial scientific information on moral principle, in light of what Hitler would undoubtedly do with such a weapon (Cassidy, 1992).
6. Szilard asked a seven-year-old boy: "Do you know where Einstein lives?" The youth answered: "Of course I do. I can take you there if you wish" (Jungk, 1956, p. 84).
7. A major influence in activating the Americans was a British committee report, conveyed across the Atlantic by Henry Tizzard in summer, 1941 in a black-enameled metal steamer trunk full of military secrets; this was the original "black box" (Rhodes, 1986).
8. A fateful conversation occurred between Heisenberg and his physics "father figure," Niels Bohr, as they walked and talked in Copenhagen on the evening of September 16, 1941. Heisenberg asked Bohr if he felt it was ethically appropriate for physicists to work on their nation's atomic bomb project. He thus implied that Germany's project was underway. Heisenberg may have been fishing for whatever Bohr knew about the Allies' atomic project (Cassidy, 1992). Bohr, very shaken by the conversation, concluded that the Germans were working on an atomic bomb (Bernstein, 1996). Bohr shortly thereafter slipped out of German-occupied Denmark for Sweden in order to escape the Nazi crackdown on Jews, then joined the British Tube Alloys Project, and eventually the Manhattan Project in Los Alamos.
9. Roosevelt recruited many Rough Riders in New Mexico, and the present-day Rough Riders Museum is located in Las Vegas, New Mexico.
10. Oppenheimer (1954, p. 150) said that he moved to the left because: "I had had a continuing smoldering fury about the treatment of Jews in Germany. I had relatives there, and was later to help in extricating them and bringing them to this country. I saw what the Depression was doing to my students. Often they could get no jobs or jobs which were inadequate."

11. Oppenheimer inherited $392,602 when his father died in 1937; this inheritance provided a dividend income of $10,000 to $15,000 per year. His university salary at this time was $6,000 (Schweber, 2000).
12. Another ten of the Los Alamos scientists were awarded the Nobel Prize after the war.
13. The original doorway of 109 East Palace Avenue, complete with ornate metal bars, is now in the Los Alamos Historical Museum, in Los Alamos, New Mexico.
14. Others who knew Oppenheimer also spoke of his charisma. For instance, Jean Dabney (2000), a WAC who worked as a laboratory technician at Los Alamos, recalls, "Oh, Oppie had *wonderful* eyes."
15. Despite the discouraging living conditions at Los Alamos, most of the women who were there, when interviewed later, remembered the experience as very happy, commenting on the camaraderie with interesting people, the beautiful countryside, and the feeling that they were contributing to the war effort (Manley, 1990).
16. George Kistiakowsky, a chemist from Harvard, often rode horses from the stables of the former New Mexico National Guard's 200th Cavalry Regiment (McKibbin, 1982). These stables (see Figure 4-10) were located near the Japanese Internment Camp in Santa Fe, across the street from the present Gonzalez Elementary School.
17. An official report to General Groves from the chief medical officer at Los Alamos in 1944 estimated that 20 percent of the married women were at some stage of pregnancy (Manley, 1990).
18. Oppenheimer's secretary, Priscilla Duffield (1980), remembers the regular meetings of the Director with the division heads at Los Alamos as "just fascinating because they didn't have any calculators. Bethe and Oppenheimer would have contests about who could figure the numbers fast enough when somebody brought up a problem. Sometimes they missed on the zeros, which can happen to anybody."
19. Parsons' nickname was also spelled "Deke" by some, but "Deak" was more common. The nickname (for Deacon) was given to Parsons at the Naval Academy, as a play on his surname.
20. The British team included Klaus Fuchs, who became the most noted spy at Los Alamos in leaking the atomic bomb secrets to the Soviet Union. Fuchs, a German, had joined the Communist Party while a student at the University of Kiel in 1933. He later became a British citizen and joined the Tube Alloys Project, and thus did not undergo an American security check (Melzer, 2000).
21. Chevalier (1965) says that he had expected Oppenheimer to reject Ellenton's approach, and he had already told Ellenton "No."
22. The German atomic bomb project would have required a massive industrial effort in order to produce the needed uranium-235 and plutonium-239. However, Werner von Braun's V-2 rocket program in

Germany during World War II did receive a top priority and utilized huge resources.

23. Berg had originally come to the attention of the OSS when he was making U.S. propaganda broadcasts to Japan in the Japanese language (Cassidy, 1992). Berg had an unusual ability with languages. While playing shortstop for the Princeton baseball team, he exchanged signals with the second baseman in Latin, so that opposing base runners could not understand them (Dawidoff, 1994).

24. Berg did determine from Heisenberg that the German atomic bomb project had moved from Berlin to the small town of Hechingen in the Black Forest in order to escape Allied bombing, and Berg directed the Alsos team there to capture evidence that the project was no threat to the Allies' race to an atomic bomb (Cassidy, 1992, p. 492).

25. The Alsos team captured Heisenberg, von Weizsächer, Otto Hahn, and seven other German atomic scientists, and transported them to Farm Hall, a manor near Cambridge, England, where they were imprisoned for some months after World War II. When news of Hiroshima reached Farm Hall, hidden microphones recorded the German scientists' extreme surprise and disappointment (Cassidy, 1992, p. 499). For example, Otto Hahn could not believe that the Allies had beaten the Germans in the race to an atomic bomb (Bernstein, 1996).

26. Some ranchers were unwilling to vacate their property for the Trinity test. The last holdouts were convinced to leave when Army personnel shot holes in their livestock water tanks.

27. Jumbo was "an enormous, enormous headache," Oppenheimer's secretary, Priscilla Duffield (1980) remembers: "It involved taking down bridges and finding a route that it could go over. Transporting it across the country was just . . . , it simply became a white elephant that was so big and enormous."

28. A "blank shot" consisting of the Fat Man explosive lens, without the plutonium, had failed. Hans Bethe showed that the failure was due to the instrumentation. Unfortunately, this test did not guarantee that the explosives would function correctly at Trinity, although Kistiakowsky insisted they would.

29. Despite the tight security precautions concerning the Trinity test, two young scientists at Los Alamos had invited Dorothy McKibbin to go on a picnic with them on July 15th. Strangely, they picked her up in the evening. They drove to Albuquerque, and climbed to the peak of Sandia Mountain. They watched toward the south. "At five-thirty, we saw the flash that illuminated a fourth of the horizon, and the flash was so bright that even the green leaves on the trees would shake. It was uncanny; it was a new world . . . . This was a great secret, my going, because we would all have been shot at sunrise . . . ." (McKibbin, 1982).

30. The official TNT equivalent for the Trinity test was 20,000 tons; for Hiroshima, 15,000 tons; and for Nagasaki, 50,000 tons (Truslow & Smith, 1947).
31. When President Roosevelt died on April 12, 1945, in Warm Springs, Georgia, Vice President Harry Truman was sworn in as President of the United States. Secretary of War Stimson then told Truman about the Manhattan Project; it was the first that he knew about the secret project.
32. The Allied leaders decided that if the Emperor were kept in power, he could order the surrender of the Japanese military forces scattered throughout Asia.
33. Susuki used the word "*mokusatsu*," meaning either to ignore or to treat with silent contempt, two rather different meanings. He meant to state that he would wait to respond to the Potsdam Ultimatum until results of Japan's peace feelers through Moscow were known. "*Mokusatsu*" was translated by the Americans as rejection (Craig, 1967, p. 68).
34. Immediately after the war, American observers indeed saw drill presses standing in burned-out homes (Frank, 1999).
35. The shift from precision bombing to pattern bombing helped change the ratio of civilian to military deaths from 5 percent civilian and 95 percent military (with 10 million killed) in World War I, to 48 percent civilian and 52 percent military (with 80 million killed) in World War II (Born, 1964).
36. The potential of the *kamikaze* attacks was ably demonstrated on April 6, 1945, a day when 24 U.S. ships supporting the invasion of Okinawa were sunk or destroyed (Craig, 1967, p. 9).
37. General George Marshall, the Army Chief of Staff, however, did not buy the estimate of one million casualties; he calculated the figure as low as 40,000 Americans killed (Goodchild, 1985).
38. Late in the war, most of the research and development on the atomic bomb was being conducted at Los Alamos, allowing the atomic scientists at the University of Chicago to ponder the issue of the bomb's consequences (Hammel, 2000). A petition that the atomic bomb not be dropped on an inhabited city was drafted by Leo Szilard and circulated among scientists in the Met Lab at the University of Chicago. Some 70 physicists signed it (the chemists and biologists generally did not). The petition was submitted through channels, but did not reach President Truman until after the first atomic bomb had been dropped (Lamont, 1965, p. 146; Weart & Szilard, 1978, p. 188).
39. Actually, the Allies knew that the German atomic bomb was not a threat after the capture of Strasbourg, on November 15, 1944, when Alsos agents found key German documents (Lamont, 1965). The Germans were at least two years behind the U.S. Manhattan Project (Jungk, 1956).

40. Tokyo was not on the target-list because it had already been so heavily bombed that it would not allow the U.S. or Japan to gauge the effects of the atomic bomb. Further, if Tokyo were destroyed, there would be no one left to make peace with.
41. Groves then ensured that Kyoto was not bombed with conventional weapons in the final months of World War II, even though it was a military and industrial target of importance.

6

1. By the end of January, 1946, five months after World War II, Enrico Fermi, Hans Bethe, George Kistiakowsky, Richard Feynman, and Edward Teller had left Los Alamos.
2. Hans Bethe first explained the sequence of nuclear reactions causing the energy produced by the sun, for which he received the Nobel Prize.
3. Greenglass was sentenced to 15 years in federal prison, in 1951. Julius and Ethel Rosenberg, relatives of Greenglass and also Soviet spies, were found guilty of treason, and given the death sentence (Lamont, 1965). Fuchs was arrested in England in 1949, after U.S. cryptographers decoded messages from the Soviet Embassy in New York to Moscow that had been sent during World War II. A report from Fuchs on the Los Alamos research was included in the Soviet message transmissions (Williams, 1987). After Fuchs confessed to being a spy, he was sentenced to jail, but not death, because Russia was an ally when he provided the secret information. When Fuchs was released from prison in 1959, he fled to East Germany.
4. This estimate was made by Hans Bethe (Palevsky, 2000).
5. The cover of each monthly issue of the *Bulletin of the Atomic Scientists* contains a clock face with the minute hand indicating the probability of the end of the world. In 1949, when it became known that the Soviet Union had an atomic bomb, the minute hand ominously moved to only three minutes before midnight (Jungk, 1956).
6. Russian scientists told Ed Hammel (2000a) that the Soviet Union had developed their own version of the atomic bomb, but they chose to copy the American design because Stalin would have killed them if their design did not work.
7. One of these university faculty members, Bernard Peters at the University of Rochester, was investigated by HUAC. Oppenheimer, who had been Peters' doctoral advisor at Berkeley before the war, testified to HUAC against him, much to the disappointment of Oppenheimer's fellow physicists (Schweber, 2000).
8. One important contribution by Sandia National Laboratories is the laminar air-flow cleanroom, which removes dust and other impurities from the air, a technology used in all semiconductor cleanrooms today.

REFERENCES

Harold M. Agnew (February, 1980), Oral history interview conducted by Mario Balibrera, File 82.652, Los Alamos Historical Museum.

Adelberto Aguirre, Jr. & Jonathan H. Turner (1995), *American Ethnicity: The Dynamics and Consequences of Discrimination*, Second Edition, New York, McGraw-Hill.

Masaru Ben Akahori (1944), Correspondence with his wife and daughter, Collection 2010, Box 9, Folders 6-11, Japanese American Project, Department of Special Collections, Charles E. Young Research Library, UCLA, Los Angeles, CA.

Joseph Albright & Marcia Kunstel (1997), *Bombshell: The Secret Story of America's Unknown Spy Conspiracy*, New York, Times Books.

Dorothy Cave Aldrich (April 9, 2000), Personal interview, Santa Fe, New Mexico; and lecture on November 14, 2000, in Los Alamos, New Mexico.

Luis W. Alvarez (1987), *Alvarez: Adventures of a Physicist*, New York, Basic Books.

Maya Angelou (1970), *I Know Why the Caged Bird Sings*, New York, Random House.

Manuel A. Armijo (February 1, 2000), Personal interview, Santa Fe, New Mexico.

Ruth W. Armstrong (1969), *New Mexico: From Arrowhead to Atom*, South Brunswick, NY, A.S. Barnes.

Paul Ashton (1985), *Bataan Diary*, Santa Barbara, CA, Ashton Publications.

Paul Ashton (1990), *And Somebody Gives a Damn*, Santa Barbara, CA, Ashton Publications.

David Axelrod (2003), "Bataan Rescue," American Experience, video, Corporation for Public Broadcasting.

Robert F. Bacher (1999), *Robert Oppenheimer, 1904-1967*, Los Alamos, New Mexico, Los Alamos Historical Society, Monograph 2.

Nancy Reynolds Bartlit (1998), *A Communication Analysis of Visitor Comments after Observing an Antinuclear and a Veterans' Exhibit in the Bradbury Science Museum of the Los Alamos National Laboratory*, MA Thesis, Albuquerque, University of New Mexico.

Fred Begay (April 11, 2002), Personal interview, Los Alamos, New Mexico.

Jimmy Begay (December 29, 1999), Personal interview, Window Rock, Arizona.

Karl R. Bendetsen (November 3, 1942), "An Obligation Discharged: The Army Transfer to War Relocation Authority, a Civilian Organization, Japanese Evacuated from the Pacific Coast," Speech to the Personnel of the Wartime Civil Control Administration; Berkeley, CA, University of California, Berkeley, Bancroft Library, BANC MSS Collection 67/46.

Karl R. Bendetsen (July 8, 1952), Personal interview by Jacobus tenBroek, Berkeley, CA, University of California, Berkeley, Bancroft Library, BANC MSS Collection 67/46.

Joe Bergstein (February 28, 2000), Personal interview, Los Alamos, New Mexico.

Jeremy Bernstein (1996), *Hitler's Uranium Club: The Secret Recordings at Farm Hall*, Woodbury, NY, AIP Press.

Hans A. Bethe (November 9, 1979), Personal interview conducted by Mario Balibrera, File 82.652, Los Alamos Historical Museum.

Fred Billey (August 22, 2000), Telephone interview, Farmington, New Mexico.

Sam Billison (December 29, 1999), Personal interview, Window Rock, Arizona.

Ronald Bishop (2000), "To Protect and Serve: The 'Guard Dog' Function of Journalism in Coverage of the Japanese American Internment," *Journalism and Mass Communication Monographs*, 2(2): 65-103.

Herbert P. Bix (2000), *Hirohito and the Making of Modern Japan*, New York, Harper Collins.

Margaret T. Bixler (1992), *Winds of Freedom: The Story of the Navajo Code Talkers in World War II*, Darien, CT, Two Bytes.

Paul Blatchford (July 10, 1071), Personal interview conducted by Benis M. Frank, Marine Historian, at Window Rock, Arizona; Salt Lake City, University of Utah, Marriott Library, Manuscripts Division.

David Bodanis (2001), $E = mc^2$: *A Biography of the World's Most Famous Equation*, London, Pan Books.

Max Born (April, 1964), "What Is Left to Hope for?" *Bulletin of the Atomic Scientists*, pp. 2-5.

Norris Bradbury (February, 1971), Personal interview, File 72.208, Los Alamos Historical Museum.

Norris Bradbury (February 27, 1975), Talk at the University of California at Santa Barbara, File 75.343, Los Alamos Historical Museum.

James Bradley (2000), *Flags of Our Fathers*, New York, Bantam Books.

Casey Stanley Brown (1977), Oral history interview and lecture, in Keats Begau, Agnes R. Begay, Cozy Stanley Brown, Dan S. Benally, Gernard Tracy, Walker J. Norcross, Peggy Jane Chee, Claude Hatch, Myrtly Waybenais, Chester Hubbard, & Murray Lincoln, *Navajos and World War II*, Tsailo, Arizona, Navajo Community College Press.

David C. Cassidy (1992), *Uncertainty: The Life and Science of Werner Heisenberg*, New York, Freeman.

Dorothy Cave (1996), *Beyond Courage: One Regiment against Japan, 1941-1945*, Las Cruces, New Mexico, Yucca Tree Press.

Dorothy Cave (1997), *Four Trails to Valor: From Ancient Footprints to Modern Battlefields: A Journey of Four Peoples*, Las Cruces, New Mexico, Yucca Tree Press.

Marjorie Bell Chambers (1974), *Technically Sweet Los Alamos: The Development of a Federally Sponsored Scientific Community*, Ph.D. Dissertation, Albuquerque, University of New Mexico.

Marjorie Bell Chambers & Linda K. Aldrich (1999), *Los Alamos, New Mexico: A Survey to 1949*, Los Alamos, New Mexico, Los Alamos Historical Society, Monograph 1.

Guy Claus Chee (December 29, 1999), Personal interview, Window Rock, Arizona.

Haakon Chevalier (1965), *Oppenheimer: The Story of a Friendship*, New York, George Braziller.

Nick Chintis (September 9, 2000), Personal interview, Silver City, New Mexico.

Al Christman (1998), *Target Hiroshima: Deke Parsons and the Creation of the Atomic Bomb*, Annapolis, MD, Naval Institute Press.

Peggy Pond Church (1959), *The House at Otowi Bridge: The Story of Edith Warner and Los Alamos*, Albuquerque, New Mexico, University of New Mexico Press.

Paul Frederick Clark (1980), *Those Other Camps: An Oral History Analysis of Japanese Alien Enemy Internment during World War II*, MA Thesis, Fullerton, California, California State University Fullerton.

Commission on Wartime Relocation and Internment of Civilians (1982), *Personal Justice Denied*, Washington, D.C., Government Printing Office.

Haruko Taya Cook & Theodore F. Cook (1992), *Japan at War: An Oral History*, New York, New Press.

William Craig (1967), *The Fall of Japan: The Last Blazing Weeks of World War II*, New York, Harper.

John J. Culley (1982), "World War II in a Western Town: The Internment of the Japanese Railroad Workers of Clovis, New Mexico," *Western Historical Review*, 8(1): 43–61.

John J. Culley (1991), "The Santa Fe Internment Camp and the Justice Department Program for Enemy Aliens," in Roger Daniels, Sandra C. Taylor, & Harry H.T. Kitano (eds.), *Japanese Americans: From Relocation to Redress*, Revised Edition, Seattle, University of Washington Press, pp. 57–71.

Jean Dabney (October 29, 2000), Personal interview, Los Alamos, New Mexico.

Winston Dabney (October 29, 2000), Personal interview, Los Alamos, New Mexico.

Roger Daniels (1971), *Concentration Camps USA: Japanese Americans and World War II*, New York, Holt, Rinehart and Winston.

Roger Daniels (1991), "Relocation, Redress, and the Report: A Historical Appraisal," in Roger Daniels, Sandra C. Taylor, and Harry H. L. Kitano (eds.), *Japanese Americans: From Relocation to Redress*, Revised Edition, Seattle, University of Washington Press, pp. 57–71.

Roger Daniels (1991), "Relocation, Redress, and the Report: A Historical Appraisal," in Roger Daniels, Sandra C. Taylor, and Harry H. L. Kitano (eds.), *Japanese Americans and World War II*, Revised Edition, Seattle, University of Washington Press, pp. 3–9.

Nuel Pharr Davis (1968), *Lawrence and Oppenheimer*, New York, Simon and Schuster, pp. 186–187.

Nicholas Dawidoff (1944), *The Catcher Was a Spy: The Mysterious Life of Moe Berg*, New York, Pantheon.

Gavan Daws (1994), *Prisoners of the Japanese: POWs of World War II in the Pacific*, New York, Quill.

F. de Amat (1944), *Report of the Spanish Consul on the Santa Fe Internment Camp*, Washington, D.C., National Archives, Record Group 85, Entry 308, Box 1300/C.

Millicent Dillon (2000), *Harry Gold*, New York, Overlook Press.

Richard Dockum (March 18, 1977), Oral History Interview 1612, conducted by Paul Clark and Mollie M. Pressler, at Lordsburg, New Mexico; Fullerton, CA, California State University Fullerton Oral History Collection.

George A. Donahue, Philip J. Tichenor, & Clarence Olien (1995), "A Guard Dog Perspective on the Role of the Media," *Journal of Communication*, 45: 115-132.

John W. Dower (1999), *Embracing Defeat: Japan in the Wake of World War II*, New York, Norton.

Priscilla Greene Duffield (1980), Personal interview, File 82.652, Los Alamos Historical Museum.

Deanne Durrett (1998), *Unsung Heroes of World War II: The Story of the Navajo Code Talkers*, New York, Facts On File.

Hollis Engles (1985), "March of Death," *Santa Fe New Mexican*.

Stanley L. Falk (1972), *Bataan: The March of Death*, New York, Java Books.

Enrico Fermi (1946), "The Development of the First Reacting Pile," *Proceedings of the American Philosophical Society*, 90: 20-24.

Laura Fermi (1954), *Atoms in the Family: My Life with Enrico Fermi*, Chicago, University of Chicago Press.

Rachel Fermi & Esther Samara (1995), *Picturing the Bomb: Photographs from the Secret War of the Manhattan Project*, New York, Harry N. Abrams.

Richard P. Feynman (February 6, 1975), Talk at the University of California at Santa Barbara, File 75.343, Los Alamos Historical Museum.

Richard P. Feynman (1985), *"Surely You're Joking Mr. Feynman"*, New York, Bantam Books.

Harold Foster (November 23, 1992), Personal interview in Window Rock, Arizona by Brittany Nelson; Washington, D.C., Marine Corps Historical Center, Washington Naval Yard.

Tom Foy (September 9, 2000), Personal interview, Bayard, New Mexico.

Richard B. Frank (1999), *Downfall: The End of the Imperial Japanese Empire*, New York, Random House.

Otto R. Frisch (June 19, 1973), Personal interview, File 68.5, Los Alamos Historical Museum.

Otto R. Frisch (1979), *What Little I Remember*, New York, Cambridge University Press.

Yoshiki Fukuda (1990), *My Six Years of Internment: An Issei's Struggle for Justice*, San Francisco, Konko Church of San Francisco.

Evans Garcia (May 1, 2000), Personal interview, Albuquerque, New Mexico.

C. Harvey Gardiner (1981), *Pawns in a Triangle of Hate: The Peruvian Japanese in the United States*, Seattle, University of Washington.

Allison B. Gilmore (1998), *You Can't Fight Tanks with Bayonets: Psychological Warfare against the Japanese Army in the Southwest Pacific*, Lincoln, University of Nebraska.

Peter Goodchild (1985), *J. Robert Oppenheimer: Shatterer of Worlds*, New York, Fromm International.

Mary Gorman (December 28, 1999), Personal interview, Gallup, New Mexico.

Zonnie Gorman (December 28, 1999; and January 27, 2002), Personal interviews, Gallup, New Mexico.

Henry Greenberg & Georgia Greenberg (1996), *Power of a Navajo: Carl Gorman, the Man and His Life*, Santa Fe, New Mexico, Clear Light.

Bob Greene (January 31, 1998), "No One Understands, Enola Gay Pilot Says," *Albuquerque Journal*, p. 1.

Leslie R. Groves (1962/1983), *Now It Can Be Told: The Story of the Manhattan Project*, New York, Harper/New York, Da Capo.

Edward F. Hammel, Jr. (January 11, 2000), "Association of Los Alamos Scientists," Presentation at the Los Alamos Historical Society, Los Alamos, New Mexico.

Edward F. Hammel, Jr. (December 16, 2000), Personal interview, Los Alamos, New Mexico.

Asael T. Hansen (1991), "My Two Years at Heart Mountain: The Difficult Role of an Applied Anthropologist," in Roger Daniels, Sandra C. Taylor, and Harry H.L. Kitano (eds.), *Japanese Americans: From Relocation to Redress*, Revised Edition, Seattle, University of Washington Press, pp. 33–37.

Ruth Hashimoto (July 11, 1999), Personal interview, Albuquerque, New Mexico.

Leslie T. Hatamiya (1993), *Righting a Wrong: Japanese Americans and the Passage of the Civil Liberties Act of 1988*, Stanford, CA, Stanford University Press.

George R. Hawthorne (January 31, 2000), Personal Interview, Santa Fe, New Mexico.

Brian Masaru Hayashi (1995), *'For the Sake of Our Japanese Brethern': Assimilation, Nationalism, and Protestantism among the Japanese of Los Angeles, 1895-1942*, Stanford, CA, Stanford University Press.

Anthony Heilbut (1983), *Exiled in Paradise: German Refugee Artists and Intellectuals in America from the 1930s to the Present*, Boston, Beacon Press.

Gregg Herken (2002), *Brotherhood of the Bomb: The Tangled Lives and Loyalties of Robert Oppenheimer, Ernest Lawrence, and Edward Teller*, New York, John Macrae Book.

John Hersey (1989), *Hiroshima*, New York, Vintage Books.

Lane Ryo Hirabayashi (1999), *The Politics of Fieldwork: Research in an American Concentration Camp*, Tucson, University of Arizona Press.

Eric Hobsbawn (1995), *Age of Extremes: The Short Twentieth Century, 1914–1991*, London, Abacus.

Jane Lee Howes (June 30, 1972), Personal interview, File 68.5, Los Alamos Historical Museum.

Ruth H. Howes & Caroline L. Herzenberg (1999), *Their Day in the Sun: Women of the Manhattan Project*, Philadelphia, Temple University Press.

Mark Hummels (October 28, 1999), "Camp-Marker Vote Sparks Near Brawl," *Santa Fe New Mexican*, p. A-1, A-2.

Miye Ichiki (August 21, 1945), Letter to Telichi Narutomi in the Santa Fe Internment Camp; Washington, D.C., National Archives, Record Group 85, Entry 308, Box 1300/R-1.

Miye Ichiki (August 27, 1945), Letter to Sakaye Ichiki in the Santa Fe Internment Camp; Washington, D.C., National Archives, Record Group 85, Entry 308, Box 1300/R-1.

Philip Johnston (September 4, 1944). Letter to Watson Smith; Flagstaff, Arizona, Museum of Northern Arizona, Philip Johnston Collection, MS 136-5-1.

Philip Johnston (November 7, 1970), Oral history interview conducted by John Sylvester, Doris Duke Collection Number 954, University of Utah, located in the National Archives, Record Group 127, Box 5, Folder 5, College Park, Maryland.

John Pershing Jolly (1964), *History of the National Guard of New Mexico, 1606-1963*, Santa Fe, New Mexico, State of New Mexico, Adjutant-General of New Mexico.

Jack Jones (April 1, 2000), Personal interview, San Juan Pueblo, New Mexico.

Robert Jungk (1956), *Brighter than a Thousand Suns: A Personal History of the Atomic Scientists*, Translated by James Cleugh, New York, Harcourt Brace.

Kenji Kawano (1990), *Warriors: The Navajo Code Talkers*, Flagstaff, Arizona, Northand.

Jimmy King (July 10, 1971), Personal interview conducted by Benis M. Frank, Marine Historian, at Window Rock, Arizona, Salt Lake City, University of Utah, Marriott Library, Manuscripts Division.

George Bogdan Kistiakowsky (January 30, 1975), Talk at the University of California at Santa Barbara, File 82.652, Los Alamos Historical Museum.

Fletcher Knebel & Charles W. Bailey II (1960), *No High Ground*, New York: Harper.

Gordon Knobeloch (March 20, 2002), Personal interview, Los Alamos, New Mexico.

Donald Knox (1981), *Death March: The Survivors of Bataan*, New York, Harcourt Brace.

Kazuo Kodani (August 21, 1945), Letter to Mitsuye Kodani in the Tule Lake Relocation Camp; Washington, D.C., National Archives, Record Group 85, Entry 308, Box 1300/R-1.

Lansing Lamont (1965), *Day of Trinity*, New York, Antheum.

Keith Little (December 29, 1999), Personal interview, Window Rock, Arizona.

Los Alamos Historical Society (1997), *Los Alamos: Beginning of an Era, 1943-1945*, Los Alamos, New Mexico, Los Alamos Historical Society.

Michelle Malkin (2004), *In Defense of Internment: The Case for 'Racial Profiling' in World War II and the War on Terror*, Lanham, Maryland, Regnery Publishing, Inc.

Richard C. Mallonée II (1997), *Battle for Bataan: An Eyewitness Account*, Novato, CA, Presidio Press.

Jerre Mangione (1978), *An Ethnic at Large: A Memoir of American in the Thirties and Forties*, New York, Putnam's Sons.

Kathleen E. B. Manley (1990), "Women of Los Alamos during World War II: Some of Their Views," *New Mexico Historical Review*, 65(2): 251-266.

"Colors of Courage: Sons of New Mexico, Prisoners of Japan" (2002), prod. and dir. Tony Martinez and Scott Henry, 110 min., Albuquerque, New Mexico, University of New Mexico Center for Regional Studies, videocassette.

Eva Jane Matson (1994), *It Tolled for New Mexico: New Mexicans Captured by the Japanese, 1941-1945*, Las Cruces, New Mexico, Yucca Tree Press.

Bill Mauldin (1947), *Back Home*, New York, William Sloane Associates.

Sally McClain (1994), *Navajo Weapon*, Boulder, CO, Books Beyond Borders.

Dorothy McKibbin (January 13, 1982), Oral history interview, File 82.652, Los Alamos Historical Museum.

Edwin McMillan (1980), Oral history interview conducted by Mario Balibrera, File 82.652, Los Alamos Historical Museum.

Stephen M. Mellnik (1981), *Philippine War Diary 1941-1945*, New York, Von Nostrand Reinhold.

Richard Melzer (1994), "Casualties of Caution and Fear: Life in Santa Fe's Japanese Internment Camp, 1942-1946," in Judith Boyce DeMark (ed.), *Essays in Twentieth-Century New Mexico History*, Albuquerque, University of New Mexico Press.

Richard Melzer (1996), *Ernie Pyle in the American Southwest*, Santa Fe, Sunstone Press.

Richard Melzer (1999), *Coming of Age in the Great Depression: The Civilian Conservation Corps Experience in New Mexico, 1935-1942*, Las Cruces, New Mexico, Yucca Tree Press.

Richard Melzer (2000), *Breakdown: How the Secret of the Atomic Bomb Was Stolen during World War II*, Santa Fe, New Mexico, Sunstone Press.

Katsuma Mikeada (May 22, 1975), Oral History Interview 1341b, conducted by Paul F. Clark, at Los Angeles; Fullerton, CA, California State University Fullerton Oral History Archive.

Franklin Ng (November/December, 1996), "America's 'Concentration Camps'," *Christianity Today*,

Richard S. Nishimoto (1995), *Inside an American Concentration Camp: Japanese American Resistance at Poston, Arizona*, Tucson, University of Arizona Press.

Bill Nishimura (April 28, 2001), Personal interview, Torrence, California.

Vicente R. Ojinaga (February 1, 2000), Personal interview, Santa Fe, New Mexico.

Koichiro Okada (1995), *Forced Acculturation: A Study of Issei in the Santa Fe Internment Camp during World War II*, MA Thesis, Las Vegas, New Mexico, New Mexico Highlands University.

Gary Y. Okihiro (1996), *Whispered Silences: Japanese Americans and World War II*, Seattle, University of Washington Press.

John E. Olson (1985), *O'Donnell: Andersonville of the Pacific*, Privately published.

J. Robert Oppenheimer (March 4, 1954), Letter from J. Robert Oppenheimer to General K. D. Nichols, General Manager, Atomic Energy Commission, in *Brief on Behalf of J. Robert Oppenheimer, Filed with the Atomic Energy Commission*, Washington, D.C., U.S. Library of Congress, J. Robert Oppenheimer Collection, Box 200.

J. Robert Oppenheimer (November 18 and 20, 1963), Personal interview by Thomas S. Kuhn; College Park, MD, Archive for the History of Quantum Physics, Niels Bohr Library, Center for History of Physics, American Institute of Physics.

J. Robert Oppenheimer (May, 1964), Talk on Neils Bohr, File 1001-1, Los Alamos Historical Museum.

Mary Palevsky (2000), *Atomic Fragments: A Daughter's Questions*, Berkeley, University of California Press.

Doris A. Paul (1973), *The Navajo Code Talkers*, Pittsburgh, Dorrence.

PBS (2003), "Bataan Rescue," THE AMERICAN EXPERIENCE, (documentary video), History Channel.

Mollie Pressler (September 10, 2000), Personal interview, Lordsburg, New Mexico.

Bob Quick (July 11,1999), "Innocence Was Lost Forever," *Santa Fe New Mexican*.

Aurelio Quintana (January 31, 2000; and November 14, 2000), Personal interviews, Santa Fe, New Mexico.

Edwin O. Reischauer (1986), *My Life between Japan and America*, New York, Harper & Row.

Richard Rhodes (1955), "Introduction," in Rachel Fermi & Esther Samra (eds.), *Picturing the Bomb: Photographs from the Secret World of the Manhattan Project*, New York, Harry N. Abrams, pp. 12-19.

Richard Rhodes (1986), *The Making of the Atomic Bomb*, New York, Touchstone.

Patricia Rife (1999), *Lise Meitner and the Dawn of the Nuclear Age*, Boston, Birkhauser.

Ralph Rodriguez (May 1, 2000), Personal interview, Albuquerque, New Mexico.

Bill D. Ross (1985), *Iwo Jima: Legacy of Valor*, New York, Vanguard.

Joseph Rotblat (1967), *Pugwash, the First Ten Years: History of the Conferences on Science and World Affairs*, London, Heinemann.

Joseph Rotblat (1998), "A Social Conscience for the Nuclear Age," in Kai Bird & Lawrence Lipschultz (eds.), *Hiroshima Shadow*, Stony Creek, Connecticut, Pamphleteer's Press.

Harlow W. Russ (1984), *Project Alberta: The Preparation of Atomic Bombs for Use in World War II*, Los Alamos, New Mexico, Exceptional Books.

"Santa Fe Internment Camp Historical Marker Dedication Ceremony" (April 20, 2002), prod. Joe Ando, 45 min., Albuquerque, NM, videocassette.

Murray Sayle (July 31, 1995), "Did the Bomb End the War?" *The New Yorker*, pp. 40-63.

Elvira Scheich (1997), "Science, Politics, and Morality: The Relationship of Lise Meitner and Elisabeth Schiemann, *Osiris*, 12: 143-168.

Abner Schrieber (March 19, 1979), Oral history interview 1613, via telephone; Fullerton, CA, California State University Fullerton Oral History Archive.

Marge Schrieber, Florence Koontz, Jane Howes, & Jane Wortmann (June 30, 1975), Personal interviews conducted by Margaret Wohlberg, File 68.5, Los Alamos Historical Museum.

S.S. Schweber (2000), *In the Shadow of the Bomb: Bethe, Oppenheimer, and the Moral Responsibility of the Scientist*, Princeton, NJ, Princeton University Press.

Emilio Segré (1970), *Enrico Fermi: Physicist*, University of Chicago Press.

Tom Sharpe (April 21, 2002), "Internment camp remembered," *The Santa Fe New Mexican*, Santa Fe, New Mexico, pp. B1-B4).

Hampton Sides (2001), *Ghost Soldiers*, New York, Doubleday.

Agapito ("Gap") Silva (March 8, 1999), Personal interview by Connie Lowe, as part of the SER/SFFS Career Academy Project, Santa Fe, New Mexico, Bataan Memorial Museum and Library.

Simon Singh (1999), *The Code Book: The Evolution of Secrecy from Mary Queen of Scots to Quantum Cryptography*, New York, Doubleday.

Albert Smith (December 29, 1999; and January 26, 2002), Personal interview, Gallup, New Mexico.

Alice Kimball Smith & Charles Weiner (eds.) (1980), *Robert Oppenheimer: Letters and Recollections*, Stanford, CA, Stanford University Press.

Arthur Smith (January 31, 2000), Personal interview, Santa Fe, New Mexico.

Geoffrey S. Smith (1991), "Racial Nativism and Origins of Japanese American Relocation," in Roger Daniels, Sandra C. Taylor, & Harry H. L. Kitano (eds.), *Japanese Americans: From Relocation to Redress*, Revised Edition, Seattle, University of Washington Press, pp. 78-87.

Page Smith (1995), *Democracy on Trial: The Japanese American Evacuation and Relocation in World War II*, New York, Simon and Schuster.

Ralph C. Sparks (2000), *Twilight Time: A Soldier's Role in the Manhattan Project at Los Alamos*, Los Alamos, New Mexico, Los Alamos Historical Society.

Edward H. Spicer, Asael T. Hansen, Katherine Luomala, & Martin K. Opler (1946/1969), *Impounded People: Japanese-Americans in the Relocation Centers*, Washington, D.C., U.S. Government Printing Office/Tuscon, University of Arizona Press.

Allen Stamm (April 1, 2000), Personal interview, Santa Fe, New Mexico.

Nancy Cook Steeper (2003), *Dorothy Scarritt McKibbin: Gatekeeper to Los Alamos*, Los Alamos, New Mexico, Los Alamos Historical Society.

Sidney Stewart (1956), *Give Us This Day*, New York, Norton.

Ferenc Morton Szasz (1984), *The Day the Sun Rose Twice: The Story of the Trinity Site Nuclear Explosion, July 16, 1945*, Albuquerque, New Mexico, University of New Mexico Press.

Ronald Takaki (1993), *A Different Mirror: A History of Multicultural America*, Boston, Little, Brown/Back Bay Books.

Yasuko I. Takezawa (1995), *Breaking the Silence: Redress and Japanese American Ethnicity*, Ithaca, NY, Cornell University Press.

Dorothy Swaine Thomas & Richard S. Nishimoto (1946), *The Spoilage: Japanese-American Evacuation and Resettlement during World War II*, Berkeley, University of California Press.

Gerald W. Thomas, Monade L. Billington, & Rogers D. Walker (eds.), (1994), *Victory in World War II: The New Mexico Story*, Las Cruces, New Mexico State University, Rio Grande Historical Collections.

Robert McG. Thomas, Jr. (February 1, 1998), "Carl Gorman, 90, Navajo Word Warrior, Dies," *The New York Times*.

Frank Thompson (March 30, 2002), Personal interview, Gallup, New Mexico.

Paul Tibbets (1985), *Mission: Hiroshima*, New York, Stein and Day.

James Tobin (1997), *Ernie Pyle's War: America's Eyewitness to World War II*, Lawrence, Kansas, University Press of Kansas.

Bill Toledo (December 27, 1999; and October 18, 2000), Personal interviews, Laguna, New Mexico.

Edith C. Truslow & Ralph Carlisle Smith (1947), *Manhattan District History, Project Y, The Los Alamos Project, Volume II, August, 1945*, Washington, D.C., U.S. Atomic Energy Commission Report.

Yoshiko Uchida (1982), *Desert Exile: The Uprooting of a Japanese American Family*, Seattle, University of Washington Press.

Carol Bulgear Van Valkenburg (1998), *An Alien Place: The Fort Missoula, Montana, Detention Camp, 1941-1944*, Missoula, MT, Pictorial Histories Publishing Company.

Steve Wallace (January 26, 2002), Personal interview, Gallup, New Mexico.

Bruce Watson (August, 1993), "*Jaysho, Moasi, Dileh, Ayeshi, Hasclishnih, Beshlo, Shush, Gini*," *Smithsonian*, pp. 34-43.

Spencer R. Weart & Gertrude Weiss Szilard (eds.) (1978), *Leo Szilard: His Version of the Facts: Selected Recollections and Correspondence*, Cambridge, MA, MIT Press.

Jay Wechsler (October 29, 2000), Personal interview, Los Alamos, New Mexico.

Michi Nishiura Weglyn (1976), *Years of Infamy: The Untold Story of America's Concentration Camps*, Seattle, University of Washington Press.

Stanley Weintraub (1996), *The Last Great Victory: The End of World War II*, New York, Truman Talley Books.

H.G. Wells (1914), *The World Set Free: A Story of Mankind*, London, Macmillan.

John A. Wheeler (1998), *Geons, Black Holes, and Quantum Foam: A Life in Physics*, New York, Norton.

Linda Wheeler (October 22, 1999), "Memorial to Remind of WW II Segregation," *Washington Post*, p. B3.

Richard Wheeler (1965), *The Bloody Battle for Suribashi*, New York, Crowell.

Alex Williams (July 10), Personal interview conducted by Benis M. Frank, Marine Historian, at Window Rock, Arizona; Salt Lake City, University of Utah, Marriott Library, Manuscripts Division.

Dana Akiko Williams (October 17, 1999), "Museum Keeps Alive Memory of Internment Camps," *Santa Fe New Mexican*, p. G-3.

Ivan Williams (March 15, 1945), Letter to Each Internee in the Santa Fe Internment Camp, Washington, D.C., National Archives, Record Group 85, Entry 308, Box 1300/C.

Robert Chadwell Williams (1987), *Klaus Fuchs: Atomic Spy*, Cambridge, MA, Harvard University Press.

"New Mexico Story: Death March to the Atomic Bomb" (2002), prod. and dir by Aaron Wilson, ~120 min., Las Cruces, New Mexico, McGaffey Productions, videocassette.

Jane S. Wilson & Charlotte Serber (1988), *Standing By and Making Do: Women of Wartime Los Alamos*, Los Alamos, New Mexico, Los Alamos Historical Society.

W. Dean Wilson (July 10, 1971), Personal interview conducted by Benis M. Frank, Marine Historian, at Window Rock, Arizona; Salt Lake City, University of Utah, Marriott Library, Manuscripts Division.

Tom Yamamoto (September 9, 1976), Oral History Interview 1522, by Paul F. Clark, in Los Angeles; Fullerton, CA, California State University Fullerton Oral History Archives.

Kenko Yamashita (April 10, 1978), Oral History Interview 1617, conducted by Makio Yamashita & Paul F. Clark, in Los Angeles; Fullerton, CA, California State University Fullerton Oral History Archives.

Mrs. Yoshiyama (June 13, 1945), Letter to her son Satoshi Yoshiyama in the Santa Fe Internment Camp; Washington, D.C., National Archives, Record Group 85, Entry 308, Box 1300/R-1.

NAMES INDEX (Illustrations are in Bold Type)

Ando, Joe, 187
Agnew, Beverly, 222
Agnew, Harold, 221-22, **263**
Akahori, Kikuko, 182
Akahori, Masaru Ben, 174, 181-82
Akin, Ada Jane Noriko, **154**
Albright, Joseph, 272
Aldrich, Dorothy Cave, See Cave
Aldrich, Linda K., 38, 209
Alex, Steve, 55
Alvarez, Luis W., 251, 264
Anami, Korechika, 265
Anaya-Gorman, Michael, 136
Apodaca, Ramon, 69
Armijo, Frances, 76-77
Armijo, Manuel, 38, 41-42, 53, 60, 65, 71, 75-81, **79**, 173, 261, 293
Ashton, Paul, 50, 58, 71, 293
Asmuth, Walter, 114

Bacher, Robert F., 211, 269
Bahe, Kee, 129
Bailey, Charles W., II, 19-20, 251, 264
Bainbridge, Ken, 248
Baker, Col, 190
Bartlit, Nancy Reynolds, 66
Begay, Fred, 108
Begay, Jimmy, 106, 128-29, 132
Begay, Roy, 129
Bemis, Ed, 293
Bendetsen, Karl R., 141, 297
Berg, Moe, 233, 302
Bergstein, Joe, 47, 52, 55, 57-58, 60, 63-64, 67, 71, 293
Bernally, Johnny, 91, 96, 101-02, 107
Bernstein, Jeremy, 300, 302
Besher, Col., 59
Bethe, Hans, 196, 221, 272, 277, 282, 302, 304
Biddle, Francis, 141, 144
Billey, Fred, 105, 130-31, 295-96
Billison, Sam, 106, 122-23, 132, 135

Bishop, Ronald, 150
Bixler, Margaret T., 19
Blake, Henry, 112
Blatchford, Paul, 123, 295-96
Bodanis, David, 23
Bohr, Niels, 200 01, 228, 238, **255**, 265, 277, 280, 282, 300
Bonham, Richard, 114, 296
Born, Max, 196, 303
Bovee, Bora, 153
Bovee, Leslie, 153
Bradbury, Norris, **216**, 225, 269, 291-92
Bradley, James, 86
Briggs, Lyman, 203
Brown, Cozy S., 91, 129-30
Brown, John, Jr., **136**
Burleson, Clarence A., 191
Bush, George, 193
Bush, George W., 135, 193
Bush, Vannevar, 203, 206, 243, 245

Cage, Nicholas, 137, 296
Caron, George R., 21
Caron, Robert, 21, 24
Carson, Kit, 90
Cassidy, David C., 200, 233, 300, 302
Cave, Dorothy, 36, 38, 43-45, 48, 51, 53, 55, 58, 64, 67, 69, 77-78, 121, 254
Chadwick, James, 238
Chambers, Marjorie Bell, 209
Chee, Guy Claus, 131
Chevalier, Haakon, 210, 226-27, 269, 301
Chibitty, Charles, 109
Chintis, Nick, 40, 42-43, 45-46, 55, 58, 64, 66-67, 69, 71
Chiang Kai-shek, 32
Chintis, Winifred Watkins, 69, 293
Churchill, Winston, 28, 33, 84, 230, 255

Clark, Paul Frederick, 162, 167, 170, 172, 175-76, 184-85, 191, 298-99
Clinton, William Jefferson (Bill), 83
Cohen, Lona, 272
Compton, Arthur, 205, 249
Conant, James, 205, 243, 245
Conner, Howard, 133
Cook, Haruko Taya, 34
Cook, Theodore F., 34
Craig, Bob, 135
Craig, Vincent, 135
Craig, William, 263, 303
Crawford, Eugene, 93
Culley, John J., 162, 181, 184-85
Curie, Marie Slowdowska, 200, 283, 300
Curie, Pierre, 300

Dabney, Jean, 247, 301
Dabney, Winston, 219
Daniels, Rogers, 166, 192
Davis, Nuel Pharr, 228
Dawidoff, Nicholas, 302
Daws, Gavan, 43-44, 71
de Amat, F., 178, 181, 299
Delgado, Larry, 81
De Witt, John L., 141, 162
Dillon, Millicent, 270
Dockum, Richard S., 189-91, 299
Dodge, Henry Chee, 88
Dodo, Masao, 297
Donahue, George, 151
Doty, Ed, 238
Dower, John W., 299
Duffield, Priscilla, 212, 217, 301-02
Durret, Deanne, 295

Einstein, Albert, 23, 195-98, 200, 202-03, 210, 266, **268**, 280, 292, 300
Ellenton, George, 226, 301
Engles, Hollis, 76
Etsicitty, Ken, 97
Evans, Bill, 51
Evans, David, **154**
Ferebee, Tom, 21-22
Fermi, Enrico, 197, 199, 201, 203, **204**, 205, 221, 228, **229**, 238, 243, 248, 270, 277, 282, 286, 304

Fermi, Laura, 203, 283
Feynman, Richard, 222, **223**, 225-26, 246-47, 282, 304
Flores, Ruben, 70
Foster, Harold, 83
Foy, Tom, 38, 52, 66, 70-71
Frank, Richard B., 252-53, 303
Frisch, Otto Robert, 200-01, 204, 237, 247, 280
Fuchs, Klaus, 228, 250, 270, **271**, 272-73, 301, 304
Fukuda, Yoshiaki, 151, 189, 297, 297
Furugochi, Sadakazu, **171**

Gandert, Miguel, 79
Garcia, Evans, 60, 65, 69, 71, 80
Gilmore, Allison B., 35
Gold, Harry, 270, 272
Goodchild, Peter, 194-95, 206, 211, 214, 225-26, 233, 243, 269, 303
Goon, 108
Gorman, Carl, 89, 91-93, 105, **116**, 137, 294
Gorman, Mary, 91, 110, 114, 137, 294-96
Gorman, Zonnie, 89, 91-92, 294
Goshu, Henry, 298
Graef, Calvin, 63
Graves, Elizabeth, 283
Greenberg, Georgia, 89, 92-94, 133-34, 294
Greenberg, Henry, 89, 92-94, 133-34, 294
Greene, Bob, 22
Greenglass, David, 272-73, 304
Groves, Leslie R. (Gen.), 198, 205, **207**, 209, 211-12, 214-15, 217-18, 220, 224-25, 227, 229, 234, 243, 245-46, 248-50, 256, 261-62, 269, 272, 275, 277, **278**, 279, 292, 301, 304

Hahn, Otto, 196-98, 201-02, 255, 280, 283, 302
Hall, Theodore, 272
Hammel, Ed, 228, 238, 300, 303-04
Harrison, George, 250
Hashimoto, Denichi, 151

Hashimoto, Ruth (Yamada, Satoye), 151-52, **154**, 155, 168, 286
Hatamiya, Leslie T., 192
Hayashi, Brian Masaru, 148, 162, 297
Hayes, Ira, 124, 133
Heard, Gayle, 137
Heisenberg, Werner, 202-03, 232-33, 299-300, 302
Herken, Gregg, 194
Hersey, John, 24
Herzenberg, Caroline L., 300
Hewlett, Frank, 36
Hideo, Henry, 139
Hirabayashi, Lane Ryo, 165
Hirata, Isomura, 191
Hirohito, Emperor, 33, 180, 183, 199, 264-65, 299, 303
Hitler, Adolf, 27-30, 125, 139, 197, 200, 202, 211-12, 217-18, 233, 254, 282, 284, 299-300
Homma, Masaharu, 45, 99
Hostee, Les, 294
Howes, Jane Lee, 221
Howes, Ruth H., 300
Hull, Cordell, 144
Hummels, Mark, 81

Ichiki, Miye, 164, 183
Ike, Mamoru, **169**
Imafuji, M., **161**
Inouye, Daniel K., 192
Itow, Sashima, 139

Jensen, Loyd, 181
Johnston, Philip, 85-86, 96, 98, 109, 115, 133, 286, 294, 296, 299
Joliet-Curie, Frederic, 300
Joliet-Curie, Irene, 300
Jolly, John Perching, 36, 42
Jones, Jack, 107, 119, 295
Jones, James E., 86
June, Allen Dale, **136**
Jungk, Robert, 195, 248, 300, 304

Kawano, Kenji, 107, 137
Kawano, Yukio, 137
Kennedy, John F., 135
Kieyoomia, Joe, 107-08, 285
Kirchner, Lord, 297

Kimura, Otomatsu, 182
King, Edward P., 45, 125
King, Jimmy, 296
Kipphardt, Heinar, 269
Kirk, George, **112**
Kistiakowsky, George, 173, 238-39, 244-45, 247, 272, 277, 301-02, 304
Knebel, Fletcher, 19-20, 251
Knobeloch, Gordon, 235-36, **237**, 264
Knox, Donald, 45-46, 52-53, 65-66, 82, 293-94
Knox, Frank, 141, 144, 150
Kobata, Toshihiro, 191
Kodoni, Kazuo, 183
Kunstel, Marcia, 272
Kuribayashi, Tadamichi, 120, 122

Lamont, Lansing, 246-47, 249, 272, 303-04
Lawrence, Ernest O., 210, **229**, 238
Lear, Victor, 82
Ledbetter, Louis, 190
Leighton, Alexander H., 298
LeMay, Curtiss, 251-52
Lithgow, Clarence, 81
Lithma, Oscal, **116**
Little, Keith, 106-07, 110, 127, 130, 132-34
Lundy, Clyde A., 189-91

MacArthur, Douglas, 37-38, 43-45, 61-62, 119, 183, 292, 299
Malkin, Michelle, 146
Mangione, Jerre, 176, 183, 299
Manley, Kathleen E.B., 301
Manuelito, Johnny, 96, 101-03
Marshall, George, 303
Martinez, Eddie, 77, 294
Martinez, Tony, 294
Matsui, Robert T., 192
Matsunaga, Spark, 192
Matthews, Alexander, 81
McClain, Sally, 95, 97-98, 107-09, 111, 113-14, 117, 120, 123-25, 133-34
McDonald, Peter, 131
McKibbin, Dorothy, 215, **216**, 302-03

McMillan, Edwin, 214
Meitner, Lise, 197-98, 200-01, 280, 283
Melzer, Richard, 172,178, 180, 183, 219, 224, 226-27, 272, 285, 299, 301
Mineta, Norman, 153, 192-93
Montoya, Bernie, 78
Morgan, Herbert, 103
Morgan, Ralph, 103
Morgan, Rod, 129
Morrison, Ron, 297
Mukaeda, 180, 183
Munson, Curtis B., 143, 148

Neddermeyer, Seth, 232
Nez, Chester, **136**
Nez, Jack, **116**
Ng, Franklin, 148
Nihawa, Kengo, 23, 293
Nimitz, Chester W., 85, 110, 279
Nishimoto, Richard, 158, 163, 165
Nishimura, Bill, 186-87, 297

Ojinaga, Vicente R., 38-39, 53, 56, 61, 65, 68, 71, 82, 293
Okada, Koichiro, 178, 180, 183
Olien, Clarence, 151
Oliver, Lloyd, **136**
Olson, John E., 52, 58
Omoru, Sgt., 79
Oppenheimer, Frank, 208
Oppenheimer, J. Robert, 20, 23, 194-96, 198-99, 201, 208-12, **213**, 214-15, **216**, 217-21, 224-29, 232, 238-39, 241, 243-45, 247-48, 254, **255**, 261, 267, **268**, 269, 275-77, 279-80, 282, 290, 292, 299, 300-01, 304-05
Oppenheimer, Katherine, 220
Oppenheimer, Kitty, 211, 220
Ortiz, Frank S., 81-82

Pacheco, Bessie, 61, 72, **73-74**, 75
Palevsky, Mary, 304
Palmer, Joe, **136**
Parsons, Deak, 20, 224, 232, 239, 256, 258, **259**, 261, 275, 277, 301
Paul, Doris A., 98, 100, 124-25, 133
Peierls, Rudolf, 201

Peters, Bernard, 304
Pickens, Slim, 172
Pinto, John, 131
Pond, Ashley Jr., 208-09
Pressler, Mollie, 190
Price, Wilson, 294
Pyle, Ernie, 125, **126**, 127, 285, 289

Quintana, Aurello, 38, 42, 56, 58-59, 66, 69-70

Rabi, Isidor Isaac, 221, **229**, 243, 282
Ragsdale, Luther, 51
Reagan, Ronald, 134
Redhawk, Johnny (fictional character), 135
Rhodes, Richard, 195, 197, 202, 205, 210-11, 217, 233, 250-51, 300
Rife, Patricia, 198, 200
Rodriguez, Ralph, 42, 44-45, 52, 55, 71, 78, 293
Roessler, Paul, 77
Roosevelt, Franklin Delano, 28-29, 43, 62, 84, 141, 143, 148, 150, 155, 188, 198, 202-03, 205, 230, 254-55, 268, 280, 292, 296, 303
Roosevelt, Teddy, 26, 33, 85, 209, 300
Rosenberg, Ethel, 304
Rosenberg, Julius, 304
Rosenthal, Joe, 121
Ross, Bill D., 120-22, 252
Rotblat, Joseph, 266, 273
Russ, Harlow W., 19, **257**, 259
Rutherford, Ernest, 300

Sachs, Alexander, 198, 203
Sandoval, Merril, 123
Sandoval, Sandy, 78
Sax, Saville, 272
Sayle, Murray, 252, 264
Schrieber, Abner, 167, **177**, 181, 184-86, 189
Schults, William C., 52
Schweber, S.S., 196, 212, 218-19, 226, 301, 305
Seaborg, Glenn, 198, 277
Segre, Emilio, 205

Sengier, Edgar, 234
Serber, Charlotte, 283
Sharpe, Tom, 187
Shinn, Frank, 87-88, 91, 96, 101, 294
Sides, Hampton, 49, 66
Silva, Agapito ("Gap"), 70, 294
Singh, Simon, 98, 294
Smith, Albert, 105, 115, 131-33, 137
Smith, Alfred, 106
Smith, Alice Kimball, 167, 201, 227,
Smith, Art, 41, 52, 61, 64, 68, 72, **73-74**, 75-78, 137
Smith, Geoffrey, 297
Smith, Holland M., 86, 122
Smith, Page, 167, 297
Smith, Ralph Carlisle, 303
Sousa, John Philip, 87
Spaatz, Carl, 263
Sparks, Ralph C., 224
Spicer, Edward H., 140, 148, 166, 298
Stalin, Josef, 250, 304
Steeper, Nancy Cook, 217
Stimson, Henry, 141, 144, 249-50, 256, **278**, 303
Strassman, Fritz, 196-98, 200-02, 255, 280, 283
Sudo, N., 187
Suzuki, Kantara, 250, 303
Sweeney, Charles W., 262-64
Szasz, Ferenc Morton, 241, 243, 245-49
Szilard, Gertrude Weiss, 300, 303
Szilard, Leo, 197-98, 202-03, 300, 303

Takaki, Ronald, 36, 167
Takamura, Kango, 179
Takezawa, Yasuko I., 193
Tana, Taisho, 179
Tatlock, Jean, 211, 226
Teller, Edward, 198, 202, 270, 282, 304
Thomas, Dorothy Swaine, 138, 163, 298
Thomas, Gerald W., 38, 46, 85
Thomas, Norman, 140
Thomas, Robert McG. Jr., 85

Thompson, Frank, 107, 117
Tibbets, Paul, 19-21, 24, 132, 257-58, **259**, 260-61
Tichenor, Philip J., 151
Tizzard, Henry, 300
Todecheenie, Frank Carl, 131
Tojo, Hideki, 50, 54-55, 125
Toledo, Bill, 89, 98, 100-05, 110, 112-14, 118, 120, 123-24, 127-28, 138, 281, 285, 295-96
Toledo, Frank, 102, **103**, 104, 123-24, 281
Toledo, Preston, **103**-104
Truman, Harry S., 19, 22, 66, 167, 194, 249-50, 254, 256, 303
Truslow, Edith C., 275, 303
Tsuneyoshi, Yoshio, 53
Tuck, James, 228
Turing, Alan, 84

Ulam, Stanislaw, 270
Underhill, James L., 95
Uyehara, Dr., 191

Van Valkenburg, Carol Bulgear, 175, 297
Vogel, Clayton B., 86-87, 96
von Braun, Werner, 302
von Neumann, John, 232, 277, 282, 300
von Weizacher, Carl Friedrich, 233, 302

Wainwright, General Jonathan, 43
Wallace, Stephen P., (Non-Navajo Navajo Code Talker), 295
Watkins Chintis, Winifred, 69, 293
Watson, Bruce, 115
Wayne, John, 106
Weart, Spencer R., 300, 303
Wechsler, Jay, 237, 247
Weglyn, Michi Nishiura, 140, 144, 155, 192
Weintraub, Stanley, 67, 250, 262
Wells, H.G., 300
Wigner, Eugene, 198, 202
Williams, Alex, 125
Williams, Ivan, 181, 185
Williams, Robert Chadwell, 233, 304
Wilson, Dean, 91, 129, 131

Wilson, Jane S., 283
Wheeler, Joe, 265
Wheeler, John, 200-01, 265
Wheeler, Linda, 193
Wheeler, Richard, 120
Woo, John, 137

Yahzee, Carl, 137
Yamada, Asataro, 151, **154**, 168
Yamada, Fusako, **154**
Yamada, Satoye (Ruth Hashimoto), **154**
Yamamoto, Isoroku, (Death of), 294
Yamamoto, Tom, 176, 180
Yamashita, Kenko, 170, 177, 180
Yazzie, Felix, 294
Yazzie, William D., 131
Yoshikawa, D., 187
Yoshiyama, Satashi, 163

SUBJECT INDEX (Illustrations are in Bold Type)

100th Battalion ("Pineapple Army," HI), see U.S. Army
109 E. Palace Avenue, Santa Fe, 216
111th Cavalry, see New Mexico National Guard
200th Coast Artillery Regiment, see New Mexico National Guard
442nd Regimental Combat Team, see U.S. Army
509th Composite Squadron Bombing Group ("Tibbett's Air Force"), see U.S. Army Air Force
515th Regimental Combat Team, see New Mexico National Guard

Afrika Corps, German, 28
Alameda Street, Santa Fe, NM, 270
Alaska, 32, 84, 291
   See Attu
Alberta Project, 239
Albuquerque, 25-26, 71, 75, 78, 92, 125, **126**, 153, 214, 225, 240, 272-73, 275, 285-86, 302
   Albuquerque Indian School, 107
   Alliance for Transportation Research Institute, 153
   Bataan Park, 289
   National Atomic Museum, 290
   Pyle, Ernie, 125, **126**, 127, 289
     Ernie Pyle at home (Figure 3-7), **126**
     Ernie Pyle Branch Library, 289
     Ernie Pyle Day, 285
   Sandia Mountains, 302
   Sandia National Laboratories, see Sandia National Laboratories
Algeria, 28
Alien Enemy Hearing Boards, 175, 188
Alliance for Transportation Research Institute, Albuquerque, 153
Allied Powers, 28-29, 32-33, 84, 199, 233, 249, 251, 291, 300, 303
Alsos Team, 233, 302
Amache Relocation Camp, CO, 158

America, see United States of America (U.S.A.)
Americans, 45-46, 51-52, 55, 60, 90
   See Bataan Death March Survivors
   See Los Alamos
   See Manhattan Project
   See Navajo Code Talkers
   See Santa Fe Internment Camp
Anglo, 123, 132, 295
Apache, 25
Arisan Maru (Death Ship), 62
Arizona, 87, **88**, 90-91, 110, 141, 143, 289, 291, 297
   Arizona State University, 132
   Chinle, 91-92, 116
   Fort Defiance Army Station, see Fort Defiance
   Ganado Mission School (Presbyterian), 106
   Gila Relocation Camp, 158, 163
   Kaiberto, 91
   Leupp, 28, 85, 189, 286, 299
   Leupp Isolation Center, 189, 286
   Museum of Northern Arizona University, Flagstaff, 134
   Pima Indian, Ira Hayes (Iwo Jima flag), 124
   Poston Relocation Camp, 158, 162, 165, 186, 297-98
   Window Rock, AZ (Big Res), **88**, 97, 134, 289
     Map of the Navajo Nation (Figure 3-1), **88**
Arizona Highways, 96, 115
Arkansas, 143
   Jerome Relocation Camp, 158
   Rohwer Relocation Camp, 158
Assembly Centers, 141, **142**, 143, **145**, **147**, 148, 295
Association of Los Alamos Scientists, Los Alamos, NM, 284-85

Atomic Bomb Dome, formerly Hiroshima Prefectural Industrial Promotion Hall, Japan, 24
Atomic bomb, 32, 66, 75, 80, 96, 164, 194-95, 197-99, 201-03, 206-07, 212-13, 218, 226, 230, 232-34, 239-40, 248, 250, 253-59, 261-75, 277, 279-82, 284, 299-03
    Alsos Team, 233, 302
    American research, *see* Manhattan Project
    British research, *see* Tube Alloys Project
    Danish research, *see* British research
    German research, 202-03, 232-33, 302-04
    Russian research, 304
        See spies
        See Fat Man
        See Little Boy
        See Race to atomic bomb
Atomic Energy Commission, 268-70, 292
Attu, Aleutian Island, Alaska, 32, 84
Auschwitz (German Concentration Camp), 29
Australians, 46
Australia, 37, 44, 61, **103**, 110-11
    Field Radio—Preston Toledo and Frank Toledo, 1943 (Figure 3-3), **103**
Austria, 28, 229
    Strasbourg, 233, 303
Axis Powers, 32-33, 249
    Fascism, 284

B-17s, American planes, in Philippines, 40-41, 293
B-29 Superfortress, American, 19-20, 22, 29, 32-33, 119-21, 124, 199, **257**, **259**
    509th Composite Squadron Bombing Group, 19, 258, 260, 289
    Bomb secured in a B-29 Bomb Bay (Figure 5-15), **257**
    Deak Parsons and Paul Tibbetts Brief Crews on Tinian (Figure 5-16), **259**
    Flights over Japan, 66, 75, 80, 250-52, 256, 258-60, 262, 264, 279

Baca Ranch Camp, Clovis, NM (for Japanese Americans), 298
Banzai ("10,000 years"—battle cry), 34-35, **117**, 118, 122, 128-29, 137, 162, 293
    2nd Division, 3rd Battalion, 6th Marine Regiment on Saipan (Figure 3-6), **117**
Bataan, 22, 36, 38, 42, 44-46, 49, 61-62, 72
Bataan Death March, Map, **48**
Bataan Death Marcher Manuel Armijo (Figure 2-5), **54**
Bataan Death Marchers Resting (Figure 2-4), **49**
Bataan Death March/Survivors, 28, 47, **48-49**, 50, 53, **54**, **56-57**, 62-63, 65-66, 70-71, **73-74**, 75, 77, **79**, 82, 90, 105, 108, 183, 187, 284-86, 289, 292-94
    200th Coast Artillery Regiment, 36-38, 44-46, 72, 76, 81, 105, 173, 183, 279, 281, 292, 301
    515th Regimental Combat Team, 42, 44, 289, 292
    Anglo, 123, 132, 295
    Bataan Death Marcher Manuel Armijo (Figure 2-5), **54**
    Bataan Death Marchers Resting (Figure 2-4), **49**
    Bataan Military Museum and Library, Santa Fe, NM, 54, 56, 68, 81, 289
    "Battling Bastards of Bataan," 36-37
    Camp O'Donnell Daily Burial Detail (Figure 2-7), **57**
    Camp O'Donnell Prisoner Vincente Ojinaga (Figure 2-6), **56**
    "Colors of Courage," 294
    Hispanic, 25-26, 36, 38
    Manuel Armijo, Master Sergeant, with pistol (Figure 2-10), **79**
    Map of 75-mile March from San Fernando to Camp O'Donnell (Figure 2-3), **48**
    Ortiz Park Marker, Frank S., Santa Fe, NM, 81-82, 187
    Parachute as wedding dress, Art Smith and Bessie Pacheco (Figure 2-9a), **74**

Postcard, International Red Cross, Art Smith's code to family (Figure 2-9), **73**
See Camps in China for Allied POWs
See Camps in Japan for Allied POWs
See Camps in Manchuria for Allied POWs
See Camps in Philippines for Allied POWs
See Death Ships or Hell Ships
"Spirit of Bataan," 62

Bataan Memorial Building, Santa Fe, NM, 80, 289
Bataan Military Museum and Library, Santa Fe, NM, 54, 56, 68, 81, 289
Bataan Park, Albuquerque, NM, 289
Bataan Peninsula, PI, 28, 35, 43, 45, 49, 76, 298
    Corregidor, 44-45, 48-49, 51, 59
Bataan Relief Organization (BRO), Santa Fe, NM, 62, 285
Bataan Veterans Association, 81
"Bathtub Row," Los Alamos, NM, 217
Battle of Britain, 84
Battle of El Alamein, 28, 84
Battle of Midway, 28, 32-33, 279
Battle of the Bulge, 29
"Battling Bastards of Bataan," 36-37
Bayo Canyon, Los Alamos, NM, 236
Belarus, 273
Belgium, 28, 30, 234
Bento (Japanese box lunch), 65
BIA, *see* U.S. Bureau of Indian Affairs
Bikini Island (Marshalls), 199, 270
Bilagaana (non-Navajos), 85-87, 94, 101, 130
Bill of Rights, 140
Blessing Way Chant, 129-30
Blitzkrieg (German for "lightning war"), 28, 30
Bock's Car (B-29), 262, 265
Body guards (for code talkers), 114, 296
Booby-trap, 113
Boot camp, U.S. Marine Corps, 92, **93**, 95-96, 102, 104, 106-07, 130
    First 29 Navajo Code Talkers at Boot Camp (Figure 3-2), **93**
Bougainville (Solomons), 33, 96, 105, 112, 114, 118, 132, 292

Field Radio—Henry Blake and George Kirk, Bougainville, 1943 (Figure 3-4), **112**
Bradbury Science Museum, Los Alamos, NM, 290
Britain, 28, 30, 183, 198, 228, 300
    Bletchly Park, 84
    Intelligence, 203
British, 28, 46, 84, 226, 228, 301, 297-98, 300
    Scientists, 224
    See Bohr, Niels
    See Churchill, Winston
    See Ellenton, George
    See Fuchs, Klaus
    See Tube Alloys Project
    See Tuck, Jim
British Malaya, 31-32
Brooks General Hospital, TX, 70
Bruns General Army Hospital, Santa Fe, NM, 70, 178, 185, 298
Bulletin of the Atomic Scientists, 304
Burma, 32
Bushido (Japanese warrior spirit), 35, 50, 253

Cabanatuan Prison Camp, Camp #1 and #3, PI, 48, 58-60, 64, 74, 178, 293
    "Water treatment" (torture), 59
Cabcaben Airport, PI, 77
California, 25, 140-41, 143-44, **147**, **149**, 150, 157, 174, 178, 186, 214, 257, 269, 275, 291, 296-97
    Camp Elliott (First Code Talker School), 86, 95-96, 101, 104, 107, 294-96
    Camp Pendleton (Second Code Talker School), 95
    Gardena, 186
    Los Angeles, *see* Los Angeles
    Manzanar Relocation Camp, 157
    Muroc bombing range, Edwards Air Force Base, 257, 261
    Oceanside, 95
    Sacramento, 192
    San Diego, *see* San Diego
    San Fernando, **48**, 49, 53
    San Francisco, *see* San Francisco
    San Jose, *see* San Jose
    Santa Anita Race Track, 143, 152
    Stockton, 169
    Sausalito, 107

California Institute of Technology (Cal Tech), 210, 213, 221, 223
Cambridge University, 195, 302
Camp Cabanatuan, see Cabanatuan Prison Camp
Camp Elliott, CA (First Code Talker School) (later U.S. Navy Miramar Field), 86, 95-96, 101, 104, 107, 294-96
Camp O'Death, PI, 55, 57
Camp O'Donnell, PI, **48**, 49, 52-55, **56-57**, 58, 71, 77, 82, 108
    Camp O'Donnell Daily Burial Detail (Figure 2-7), **57**
    Camp O'Donnell Prisoner Vincente Ojinaga (Figure 2-6), **56**
    Map of 75-mile March from San Fernando to Camp O'Donnell (Figure 2-3), **48**
Camp Pendleton, CA (Second Code Talker School), 95
Cape Glouster, New Britain Islands, 129
Carlson's Raiders (elite U.S. Marine fighting force), 111
Casa Solana Neighborhood, Santa Fe, NM, 171, 173
Castillo Street Bridge, Santa Fe, NM, 270
Cavendish Laboratory, Cambridge University, 195
Ceremony, see Navajo Ceremony
Chemical Metallurgical Research Lab, Los Alamos, NM, 236, **237**
    SED Staff in 1945 (Figure 5-11), **237**
Chicago, 97, 224
"Chief" (nickname for code talker), 118, 122
    Lone Ranger and Tonto, 130
China, 30-31, 43, 50, 63-64, 148, 250-51
    Great Wall, 131, 253, 265
    Nanking, 50
Chinese, 32, 91-92
Chinle, AZ, 91-92, 116
Christian Church, 182
Civilian Conservation Corps (CCC), 171
Civil Liberties Act, 193
Clark Field, PI, 37, 39-43, 49, 76, 293

Clinton Engineer Works (Site X), Oak Ridge, TN, 206
Code
    Enigma (German code), 84
    "Magic" (cracked Japanese "Purple" code), 84-86
    Morse, 95
    Navajo, see Navajo code
    "Purple" cipher machine, 84
    "Purple" code, 84, 144, 279
    U.S. Air Corps, 85
    U.S. Army, 85
        See Comanche code, 109
    U.S. Marine Corps
        See Navajo code
    U.S. Navy, 85, 87
        Shackle cipher machine, 87, 101, 114
Code talkers
    See Comanche Code Talkers
    See Navajo Code Talkers
    See U.S. Army
    See U.S. Marine Corps
Code Talkers, The (pulp fiction), 135
Code Talkers Association, see Navajo Code Talkers Association
Cold War, 273
    Post Cold War, 273
Colorado, 143, 192
    Amache Relocation Camp, 158
    Colorado River, 297
"Colors of Courage," 294
Columbia University, 201, 204
Comanche Code Talkers (U.S. Army Signal Corps), 109
Commission on Wartime Relocation and Internment of Civilians (1982), 140
    "Personal Justice Denied," 146
Communism (Communist Party, Socialism, Marxism), 211, 226-27, 270-73, 301
Concentration camp, 139
    German, Auschwitz, 29
Concentration camp definitions, 297
Conference on Theoretical Physics (1939), 201
Conflict over the Santa Fe Internment Camp marker, 281
    Ortiz Park, Frank S., Santa Fe, NM, 81-82, 187
Congressional Medal (for Navajo Code Talkers), 135, **136**, 289

Congressional Medal of Honor, 135
Copenhagen, Denmark, 200-01, 280, 300
Cornell University, NY, 221
Corregidor, PI, 44-45, 48-49, 51, 59
Crownpoint Indian School, NM, 102, 104
Crew of the Enola Gay (B-29) on Tinian (Figure 1-1), **21**
Crystal City Internment Camp, TX, 156, 170, 175, 177, 182, 186-87, 189
Cuban Missile Crisis (1962), 273
Czechoslovakia, 28, 198
    Sudentenland, 28

"Darkwind," 137
D-Day (landings on Normandy), 199
Death March, Bataan, PI, *see* Bataan Death March
Death Ships (Hell Ships), 38, 47, 61-63, 75, 78, 281, 293
    Moji Harbor, Kyushu, 62
    Pusan, Korea, 62
    Taiwan, 62
    Yokohama, Japan, 62
Denmark, 28, 255
    Copenhagen, 200-01, 280, 300
    Niels Bohr and Robert Oppenheimer in 1950 (Figure 5-14), **255**
Diné (Navajo language), 83-86, 91, 94, 97-04, 106-12, 114, 121, 124-25, 130-31, 135, 138, 291, 295, 299
Distinguished Flying Cross (Tibbetts), 24
Dutch, 46
Dutch East Indies (Indonesia), 32

East Asia, 32
East Germany, 304
Edwards Air Force Base (Muroc, CA, bombing range), 261
Einstein's Theory of Relativity, 195
El Paso, TX, 72, 75, 184, 240
Enemy aliens, 156, 165, 168-69, 179, 181, 184, 188, 286
Enemy Way Ceremony, Navajo, 128, 295
England, 43, 197, 201, 250, 265, 273, 292
    Bletchley Park, 84
    Cambridge University, 195, 302

    Cavendish Laboratory, 195
    Farm Hall, 302
    London, 28, 84, 197
Enigma (German coding system), 84
Enigma machines, 84
Eniwetok (Marshalls), 270
Enola Gay (B-29), 19-20, **21**, 22, 132, 257-59, **259**, **260**, 262
    Crew of the Enola Gay on Tinian (Figure 1-1), **21**
    Deak Parsons and Paul Tibbetts Brief Crews on Tinian (Figure 5-16), **259**
    Enola Gay Parked at North Field on Tinian (Figure 5-17), **260**
Ernie Pyle Day, 285
Ethnocentrism, 34, 47, 148
Europeans, 34, 291
European Americans, 144
European Fascism, 27, 103, 201, 203, 211, 265
    Nazism, 27, 282, 284, 300
Executive Order 9066 (Presidential), 141, 144, 146, 150, 284

Fat Man atomic bomb (plutonium), 29, 65, 108, 199, 224, 230-32, 235, 239-40, 242-44, 248-49, 261-64, 271-72, 276-77, 285, 292, 302
    Functioning of the Bombs (Figure 5-10), **231**
Fiesta at the Plaza, Santa Fe, NM, **39**
    Patriotic New Mexicans Volunteered for Military Service (Figure 2-1), **39**
Filipinos, 36-37, 43, 45, 48, 53
    See Bataan Death March
    See Chapter 2, 36-82
First 29 Navajo Code Talkers, 87-89, 91-92, **93**, 94-99, 101-02, 104, 111, **117**, **136**, 289
    First 29 Navajo Code Talkers at Boot Camp (Figure 3-2), **93**
    2nd Division, 3rd Battalion, 6th Marine Regiment on Saipan (Figure 3-6), **117**
    Surviving Four of First 29 Navajo Code Talkers (Figure 3-8), **136**
Fission, 196, 198, 280
Fort Bliss, TX, 39-40, 72
Fort Defiance, AZ, 87-88, 91-92, 96, 116

Fort Lincoln Internment Camp, ND, 156, 170, 175, 188, 298
Fort Missoula Internment Camp, MT, 156, 170, 181, 188
Fort Stanton, NM, 90, **142**, 156, 168, 174, 185, 188-89, 298
  Baca Ranch Camp, Clovis, NM (Japanese Americans), 298
Fort Stotsenberg, PI, 40-42
Fort Sumner, NM, 90-91, 291
Fort Wingate, NM, 88, 92, 104-05
  Indian School, 105
France, 26, 28, 30, 86, 167, 212, 273, 283
  Normandy, 29, 109, 199, 253
  Paris, 300
  Radium Institute, 300
French, 210
French Indo-China, 32
Fukuoka Camp #17 (Japan) for American POWs, 65, 78, 80
Fuller Lodge, Los Alamos, NM, 210, 217, 274

Gadget, 239, 243-44, 246-47
Gallup, NM, 74, 92, 116, 127, 131, 134, 246, 286, 289, 298
  Chamber of Commerce Building, 289
  City Council support for Japanese Americans, 298
  Rehoboth Mission School, 294
  Ganado Mission School (Presbyterian), AZ, 106
Geneva, Switzerland, 72, 75
Geneva Convention, 34, 50-51, 156-57, 170, 172, 181, 285, 297
Germans, 27, 29-30, 33, 84, 194, 201-03, 232-34, 275, 300, 302-03
  6th Army, 29
  Afrika Corps, German, 28
  Atomic bomb, 302-03
  Kristalnacht Jews, *see* Jews
  Luftwaffe, 29-30
  Names given to Navajos, 92
  Nazi, 28, 54, 139
  Nazi Concentration Camps, 54, 155
  POWs, 141, 156, 170, 174, 189, 191
  See Enigma
Germany, 27-29, 30, 33, 198-99, 211-12, 233-34, 252, 254, 265, 271, 292

Berlin, 196, 198, 200-01, 249, 255, 274, 283
Dresden, 251
Hechingen, Black Forest, 233, 302
Potsdam, 239
Potsdam Conference, 239
Potsdam Declaration, 29, 199, 250, 303
Potsdam Ultimatum, 29, 199, 250, 303
GI Bill, 128, 132
Gila Relocation Camp, AZ, 158, 163
Goeteborg, Sweden, 200
"Go For Broke" (100th Battalion), 167
Gonzales Elementary School, Santa Fe, NM, 301
Ground Zero, 23-24, 131, 209, 241-43, 245-48, 264
  Map of New Mexico showing Los Alamos and Ground Zero (Figure 5-3), **209**
Guadalcanal (Solomons), 28, 33-34, 96, 98, 100-01, 103-05, 110-12, 119, 128-29, 132, 253, 292
Guam (Marianas), 33, 96, 105, 118, 124, 128, 132, 251, 292

Hanford, WA (Site W), 206, 230, 235, 276
Harvard University, 195, 205, 239, 244, 272, 301
Hasebro (toy company which makes G.I. Joe), 34, 38, 127, 135, 140, 144, 165-66, 192
Hawaii, 31, 32, 34, 38, 127, 140, 144, 165-66, 192, 291
  100th Battalion, 166-67
  442nd Regimental Combat Team, 166-67, 192, 276, 281, 298
  Maui, 127
Hayes, Ira (Pima Indian from AZ), flag on Iwo Jima, 124, 133
Heart Mountain Relocation Camp, WY, 152-54, 158, **159**, **161**, 286
  Tarpaper Barracks Made Cozy, WWI Veteran (Figure 4-7), **161**
  Under Heart Mountain (Figure 4-6), **159**
Heavy Water, 233
Hechingen, Black Forest, 233, 302
Hell ships, *see* Death ships
Henderson Field, Guadalcanal, 111

Hiroshima, Japan, 19-25, 29, 33, 66, 75, 96, 138, 151, 194, 199, 230-31, 238, 252, 256-58, **259**, 260-62, 264, 267-68, 276, 285, 287, 302-03
    Aioi Bridge, 21-23
    Deak Parsons and Paul Tibbetts Brief Crews on Tinian (Figure 5-16), **259**
    Hiroshima Prefectural Industrial Promotion Hall (now Atomic Bomb Dome), 24
Hispanic, 26, 36, 38
Hokoku Seinen-Dan (pro-Japan young male internees who renounced U.S. citizenship), 184
Honshu, Japan, 67
Hopi Reservation, 25, **88**, 132
Hospitals, 23, 45, 58-59, 68-71, 75, 80, 87, 108-09, 119, 128, 151, 178, 185-86, 190, 225, 236, 254, 298
    Brooks General Hospital, TX, 70
    Bruns General Army Hospital, Santa Fe, NM, 70, 178, 185, 298
    Indian Health Service Hospital, Fort Defiance, AZ, 87
    Letterman General Hospital, San Francisco, CA, 69, 80
    See Navajo Ceremonies, 128-30, 295
    Shima Hospital, Hiroshima, 23
    Veterans Hospital, Albuquerque, NM, 71

Idaho, 143, 192
    Minidoka Relocation Camp, 158, 182
Ie Shima (Island), Okinawa, Japan, 125, **126**, 127
    Ernie Pyle at home (Figure 3-7), **126**
Illinois, 192
    Chicago, 97, 224
        University of Chicago (Met Lab), *see* University of Chicago
Immigration and Naturalization Service (INS), U.S. Department of Justice, 144, 155, 167, 172, 181, 185, 189
India, 273
Indian Health Service Hospital, Fort Defiance, AZ, 87
Indo-China, 31
Inn of Loretto, Santa Fe, NM, 270

Institute for Advanced Study, Princeton University, 202, **255**, 267, **268**
    Albert Einstein and J. Robert Oppenheimer after World War II (Figure 6-1), **268**
    Niels Bohr and Robert Oppenheimer in 1950 (Figure 5-14), **255**
Interim Committee (advised President Truman of target cities for atomic bombs), 256
International Dateline, 293
International Red Cross, 59-60, 72-73, 190, 291
Internment camps, *see* U.S. Department of Justice
Invasion of Japan, 125, 127, 253
    Operation Coronet, 253
    Operation Olympic, 253
Israel, 273
Issei, 142, 144, 146-48, 153, 155, 160, 162-63, 165-70, 174-76, 178, 180-82, 184-85, 187-88, 190-91, 297-98
"Italian Navigator," Enrico Fermi, Enemy Alien, Created First Self-Sustained Nuclear Chain Reaction (Figure 5-1), **204**
Italy, 29, 167, 198, **204**, 252, 265, 286, 292
    Rome, 197
Iwo Jima (Volcanos), 29, 33, 83, 96, 98, 105, 119-21, 123-24, 127, 129, 132-33, 253-54, 257, 276, 281, 292
    Hayes, Ira (Pima Indian from AZ), 124
    Sunovabitchi, Mount, 119-20
    Suribachi, Mount, 83, 119, 121, 124, 133

Japan (Land of the Rising Sun), 4, 28-32, 96, 123, 138, 143, 188, 194, 198-99, 233, 238-40, 249-56, 258, 262, 265, 269, 279-82, 287, 291-92
    Hiroshima, *see* Hiroshima
    Honshu, 67
    Ie Shima (Island), 125-27
    Invasion of, 127
    Kobe, 75, 252
    Kyoto, 304
    Kyushu, 62, 253
    Mitsui Coal Company, 78
    Nagasaki, *see* Nagasaki
    Nagoya, 69, 80, 252

Niigata, 256, 260
Omuta, 80
Osaka, 64, 252
Sasebo, 153
Sendai, 67
Tokyo, see Tokyo
Yokohama, 62, 64, 252
Japanese 34, 46, 37-38
   See Anami, Koreshika
   See Emperor Hirohito
   See Homma, Masaharu
   See Nihawa, Kengo
   See Sgt. Omoru
   See Tojo, Hideko
   See Tsuneyoshi, Yoshio
   See Yamamoto, Isoroku
   See camp internees (Issei, Nisei, Sansei, Kibei)
   Soldiers, 34-35, 40, 47-48, 50-51, 53, 118-126
Japanese Americans (civilians), 28, 140-144, **145**, 146, **147**, 148, **149**, 150-51, **154**, 155-57, 159-67, 169, 171, 173-74, 177, 184, 187-93, 227, 278, 281, 284, 286, 290-92, 296, 298-99, 301
   Enemy Alien Hearing Board, 175
   Evacuated from San Francisco during 1942 (Figure 4-3), **147**
   Evacuated from the West Coast during 1942 (Figure 4-4), **149**
   Executive Order 9066 (Presidential), 141, 144, 146, 150, 284
   Ordered to Report to Assembly Centers by U.S. Army (Figure 4-2), **145**
   "No, No" Renunciants, 165-66, 186
   Public Law 502, 141
   Questions 27 & 28 to test loyalty to U.S.A., 165-66, 185
   Rising Sun emblems in Japanese American camps, 162, 178, 184-86
   Ruth Hashimoto's Family after the War (Figure 4-5), **154**
   See camp internees (Issei, Nisei, Sansei, Kibei)
Japanese American Assembly Centers, 141, **142**, 143, **145**, **147**, 148, 295
Japanese American Citizens League (JACL), 163
Japanese American Evacuation and Relocation Study (JERS) (see Munson Report), 298
Japanese American, Fort Stanton, NM, Segregation Camp #1, 298
Japanese American Internment Camps, 154
   See U.S. Department of Justice Camps
Japanese American Memorial, Washington, DC, 193
Japanese American National Museum, Los Angeles, CA, 152-53, 157, 297
Japanese American Relocation Camps, see WRA Relocation Camps
Japanese atrocities, 51
Japanese Camps for Allied POWs, 54, 57-58, 62, **68**
   #1 camp
   See Cabanatuan POW Camp
   See Camp O'Donnell
   Americans, 108
   Koreans, 62
   Mainland, 62
   See Fukuoka Camp #17
   Manchuria, 62
   Philippines, 62
   Japanese POW Camp Prisoners Liberated (Figure 2-8), **68**
Japanese code crackers, 85
   See Navajo code
Japanese Empire, **31**, 148
   Map of Japanese Empire's Farthest Advance (Figure 1-2), **31**
Japanese Imperial Army, 22-32, 40, 118-20, 285
Japanese Imperial Navy, 28, 40, 84-85, 265
   Battle of Midway, 28, 32-33, 279
Japanese Latin Americans, 170
   Peruvians, 170, 293
Japanese Military leaders, 230
Japanese POW Camp Prisoners Liberated (Figure 2-8), **68**
   #1 camp
Japanese War Cabinet, 264
Japanese War Ministry, 250
Jemez Springs, NM, 214
Jerome Relocation Camp, AK, 158
Jews, 28, 30, 146, 202, 265, 280, 282, 300
   Hungarian, 198, 203, 232

Refugee, 198, 280
Jumbo (large containment vessel), 241, **242**, 302
    At Trinity Site, NM (Figure 5-12), **242**

Kamikaze (wind of the gods), 137, 252-53, 303
Kazakhstan, 273
Kibei, 148, 151, 162, 168, 182-85, 188, 297
Kirtland Field (formerly Oxnard Field, later Sandia Air Base), NM, 153, 275
Kobe, Japan, 75, 252,
Kokura, Japan, 256, 260-62
Konkokyo Church, 151
Korea, 22, 62, 64, 251, 253, 264
Kungaelv, Sweden, 200
Kyoto, Japan, 304
Kyushu, Japan, 62, 253

La Fonda Harvey Hotel, Santa Fe Plaza, permitted relaxation (Figure 5-7), **220**
    See FBI
Land of Enchantment, *see* J. Robert Oppenheimer, New Mexico
Land of the Rising Sun, *see* Japan
Las Vegas, NM, 300
    Rough Riders, 26, 300
Letterman General Hospital, CA, 69, 80
Leupp, AZ, 85, 189, 286, 299
Leupp Isolation Center, AZ, 189, 286
Life magazine, 51, 72, 183
Little Boy atomic bomb (uranium), 20, 22-23, 29, 75, 199, 224, 230, **231**, 232, 235, **257**, 260-61, 264, 276-77, 285
    Functioning of Bomb (Figure 5-10), **231**
    Secured in a B-29 Bomb Bay (Figure 5-15), **257**
Livestock Reduction Program (Navajo), 90, 105
London, 28, 84, 197
Long Walk, Navajo, NM, 90-91
Lordsburg Internment Camp, NM, 142, 152, 156, 168, 174, 177, 181, 189-92, 297, 291, 299
    Museum of POW Camp, 290
    POW Road, 192

Los Alamos, NM, 71, 191, 194, 199, 207, **209**, 210, 212, 217-222, **223**, 224-31, 235-40, 247, 250, 255, 258, 263, 269-77, 279, 282-84, 286, 290-91, 300-01, 303
    Association of Los Alamos Scientists, 284-85
    "Bathtub Row," 217
    Bayo Canyon, 236
    Fuller Lodge, 210, 217, 274
    Los Alamos Historical Society, 210, 235, 248-50
    Archives and Museum, 290, 293, 301
    Los Alamos National Laboratory (formerly Los Alamos Scientific Laboratory), 25, 269, 273-76, 286, 290, 300
    Archives, 290
    Bradbury Science Museum, 290
    Los Alamos Ranch School, NM, 208-10, 214-15, 279, 290-92
    New Mexico map showing Los Alamos and Ground Zero (Figure 5-3), **209**
    Pajarito Plateau, *see* Pajarito Plateau
    Richard Feynman, the Contrarian of Los Alamos (Figure 5-8), **223**
Los Angeles, 86, 110, 132, 145, **149**, 176, 188
    Japanese Americans Evacuated from West Coast during 1942 (Figure 4-4), **149**
    Japanese American National Museum, 152-53, 157, 297
Los Angeles Times, 150
Louisiana, 86
Lugao (rice gruel), 293
Luxemburg, 28, 30

Magic code, 84-86
Manchuria, 30-31, 62, 148, 253, 264, 273
Manila, PI, 40, 42, 63
    Manila Bay, 40, 44, 63
Manhattan Project, Project/Site Y, 20, 25, 66, 194-95, 199, 202-03, 205-06, **207**, 208-09, 211-12, **213**, 214-15, **216**, 217, **218**, 219, **220**, 221-22, **223**, 224-27, **229**, 230, 233-35, **237**, 239, 241, 243, 250, 254, **255**,

257, 263, 265, 267-69, **271**, 277, **278**, 279-80, 282, 284-85, 300-04
   Alsos Team, 273, 302
   At Trinity Site, NM (Figure 5-12), **242**
     Chemical Metallurgical Research Lab, SEDs in 1945 (Figure 5-11), **237**
     Deak Parsons and Paul Tibbetts Brief Crews on Tinian (Figure 5-16), **259**
     Dorothy McKibbin in 109 E. Palace Avenue, Santa Fe Office (Figure 5-5), **216**
     Harold Agnew with Plutonium Bomb Core Dropped on Nagasaki (Figure 5-18), **263**
     Jeep in the Mud at Los Alamos (Figure 5-6), **218**
     J. Robert Oppenheimer, Scientific Director, Los Alamos, NM (Figure 5-4), **213**
     Jumbo (large containment vessel) at Trinity Sites (Figure 5-12), 241-42, 302
     La Fonda Harvey Hotel, Santa Fe Plaza (Figure 5-7), **220**
     Little Boy Is Secured in a B-29 Bomb Bay (Figure 5-15), **257**
     Major General Leslie Groves in Washington, D.C. Office (Figure 5-2), **207**
     Major General Leslie Groves Receives Distinguished Service Medal (Figure 6-3), **278**
     Niels Bohr and Robert Oppenheimer in 1950 (Figure 5-14), **255**
     Nobel Prize Laureates, Lawrence, Fermi, and Rabi Chat (Figure 5-9), **229**
     Pass Identification Photo of Spy Klaus Fuchs (Figure 6-2), **271**
     Richard Feynman, the Contrarian of Los Alamos (Figure 5-8), **223**
     SED Staff in 1945 (Figure 5-11), **237**
   See Ground Zero
   See Spies
   See Trinity Site
Manzanar Relocation Camp, CA, 157
Marianas, 252, 276
Maru (ship), 294

Massachusetts Institute of Technology (MIT), 203
Mati-Mati Maru (Japanese POW ship), 75, 78
Mexico, 26
Midway Island, 33, 84-85
   Battle of Midway, 28, 32-33, 279
Military Equivalents in *Diné*, 97-01
Military Intelligence Service, 109
Mindanao (Philippines), 40
Minidoka Relocation Camp, ID, 158, 182
MIT, Massachusetts Institute of Technology, 203
Mitsubishi bombers, Japanese, 41-42, 76
Mitsubishi plant, Nagasaki, 264
Mitsui Coal Company, 78
Moab Relocation Camp, UT, 189
Mokusatsu (America interpreted Japanese for "silence" or "contempt"), 303, *see* Surrender
Montana, 25
   Fort Missoula Internment Camp, 156, 170, 175, 188, 298
Morocco, 28
Moscow, 30
Movies, 137, 167, 294, 296, 299, 319
Munson Report (Curtis B. Munson), 143-44, 147-48, 278

Nagasaki, Japan, 24, 29, 33, 65-66, 96, 108, 131, 194, 199, 230-31, 252, 256, 262-64, 273, 285, 303
Nagoya, Japan, 69, 80, 252
Nambu (Japanese pistol), **79**
   Manuel Armijo, Master Sergeant, with pistol (Figure 2-10), **79**
National Guard Armory (now New Mexico Military Museum and Library), Santa Fe, NM, 81
Native American, 26, 38, 134
   Apache, 25
   Comanche, 109
   Hopi, 25, 88, 132
   Navajo, *see* Navajo
   Pueblos, 25, 132
Navajo Ceremonies, 128-30, 295
   Blessing Way Chant, 129-30
   Enemy Way Ceremony, 128, 295
   Squaw Dance Ceremony, 129-30, 295

Navajo Code, 83, 85-86, **88**, 93-96, 99-01, **103**, 107-08, 117, 291-92, 295
    Development of the Navajo code, 95-96, 98-01, 295
        Military Equivalents in *Diné*, 97-01
        Wollachee-Shush-Moasi (Navajo Code Alphabet), 98
Navajo Code Talkers, 83-87, 89-01, **93**, **103**, 105-06, 109-11, **112**, 113, 115, 117-18, 122-25, 130, 132-35, **136**, 137-38, **166**, 276, 279, 281, 285, 287, 289, 291-92, 294-95
    "Code Talkers" (song), 135
    Field Radio—Preston Toledo and Frank Toledo, Australia, 1943 (Figure 3-3), **103**
    Field Radio—Henry Blake and George Kirk, Bougainville, 1943 (Figure 3-4), **112**
    First 29 Navajo Code Talkers at Boot Camp (Figure 3-2), **93**
    First 29 Navajo Code Talkers, *see* First 29
    Four of First 29 Navajo Code Talkers (Figure 3-8), **136**
    Map of the Navajo Nation in Arizona and New Mexico (Figure 3-1), **88**
    Marines in First Wave Ashore in Saipan, June 1944 (Figure 3-5), **166**
    National Code Talkers Day, 134
    Non-Navajo Navajo Code Talker, Steven Walker, 295
Navajo Code Talkers Association, 96, 106, 134-35, 296, 299
Navajo GI Joe, 135
    See Hasebro
    See Sam Billison, 106, 122-23, 132, 135
Navajo language, *see Diné*
Navajo Medicine (*Yataalii*), 128
Navajo Nation, 131, 134
Navajo Reservation (Big Res), 38, 86-87, **88**, 94, 101-02, 104-05, 133-34, 289, 295
    Map of the Navajo Nation (Figure 3-1), **88**
Navajos, 74, 86-91, 97, 100, 125, 132, 134-35, 137-38, 282, 285
Navajo Tribal Council, 85, 88, 131

Navajo Tribal Court System, 131
Navajo Tribal Museum, 289
Nazi, 28, 54, 139, *see* Germany, Nazism
Netherlands, 28, 30
Nevada, 214
New Britain, 129
New Guinea, 129
New Mexicans, 46
    See Bataan Death March/Survivors
    See Japanese
    See Japanese soldiers
    See Manhattan Project
    See Navajo Code Talkers
New Mexicans volunteering for military service during Fiesta (Figure 2-1), **39**
New Mexico (Land of Enchantment), 25-27, **39**, 40, 87, **88**, 90, 110, **209**, 266-67, 275-76, 282, 285-86, 289, 291-92
    Alamogordo Army Air Base, 249
    Alamogordo Bombing Range, 240
    Albuquerque, *see* Albuquerque
    Belen, 293
    Carlsbad, 63
    Clovis, 298
        Baca Ranch Camp, 298
    Cowles, 208
        Perro Caliente, 208
    Crownpoint, 102, 104
    Cuba, 102, 127
    Deming, 289
        Luna Mimbres Museum, 289
    Fiesta at the Plaza, Santa Fe, **39**
    Fort Bayard, 70
    Fort Stanton, see Fort Stanton
    Fort Sumner, 90-91, 291
    Fort Wingate, 88, 92, 104
    Gallup, *see* Gallup
    Grants, 128, 298
    Hot Springs (now Truth or Consequences), 75
    Jemez Springs, 214
    Laguna Pueblo, 128
    Las Cruces, 70
        Statue, 289
        Veterans Highway, 289
    Las Vegas, 300, *see* Las Vegas
    Lordsburg, 168, 290
        Museum of POW Camp, 290
    Los Alamos, *see* Los Alamos
    Newcomb, 295

Map of the Navajo Nation (Figure 3-1), **88**
Map showing Los Alamos and Ground Zero (Figure 5-3), **209**
Pecos River, 208
Rio Grande (river), 240
Sandia Air Base (formerly Oxnard Field, formerly Kirtland Field), 153, 275
San Isidro, 127
Santa Fe, see Santa Fe
Santa Rita, 38, 61
Santa Rosa, 156
Shiprock, 83, 88, 91, 109, 131
Silver City, 38, 40, 69, 71
Taos, see Taos
Torreon, 102, 124
Truth or Consequences (formerly Hot Springs), 75
White Sands, 289-90
New Mexico National Guard, 22, 34, 37-38, 40, 42, 44-46, 72, 75-76, 81, 105, 108, 183, 214, 276, 279, 281, 285, 289, 291-92, 301
    111th Cavalry, 37, 173, 289
    200th Coast Artillery Regiment, 36-38, 44-46, 72, 76, 81, 105, 173, 183, 279, 281, 292, 301
    515th Regimental Combat Team, 42, 44, 289, 292
New Mexico map showing Los Alamos and Ground Zero (Figure 5-3), **209**
New Mexico Military Museum and Library (formerly National Guard Armory), Santa Fe, NM, 81
New Mexico State Archives, Santa Fe, NM, 290
New Mexico State Penitentiary, Santa Fe, NM, 70, 178, 292
New Mexico State Teachers College (now Western New Mexico University), Silver City, NM, 40, 71
New York, 26, 270, 279-80
    Columbia University, 201, 204
    Staten Island, 234
New Zealand, 37, 105
Nichols Field, PI, 42
Nihima (Mother Earth in Navajo), 105
Nihonmachi (Japanese town), 145
Niigata, Japan, 256, 260
Nisei, 144, 146-48, 160, 163, 166-67, 186, 192-93, 276, 280, 286, 297

Nobel Prize, 202-03, 212-13, 222, 229, 283, 300-01, 304
"No, No" Renunciants, 165-66, 186
Normandy, France, 29, 109, 199, 253
Norsk Hydro plant (Norway), 233
North Africa, 28, 191
North Dakota
    Fort Lincoln Internment Camp (near Bismarck), 156, 170, 175, 188, 190, 298
Norway, 30, 232-33
    Heavy water, 233
    Norsk Hydro plant, 233

Oak Ridge, TN (Site X), 206, 230, 234-35, 276
Office of Scientific Research and Development (OSRD), 203, 205, 243
Office of Secret Services (OSS), 233, 302
Ohio, 192
Okinawa (Ryukyus), Japan, 29, 33, 96, 125, 129, 132, 253-54, 264, 276, 301
    Ie Shima (Island), 290, 292
Omuta, Japan, 80
Operation Coronet, 253
Operation Olympic, 253
Oregon, 141, 291, 297
    Portland, 145, 297
Ortiz Park, Frank S., Santa Fe, NM, 81-82, 187
Osaka, Japan, 64, 252

P-40 fighters, American, 44
Pacific islands, 28, 32, 97, 116, 124, 132, 138, 253, 279, 291
    Bikini (Marshalls), 199, 270
    Bougainville (Solomons), see Bougainville
    British Malaya, 31-32
    Dutch East Indies (Indonesia), 32
    Eniwetok (Marshalls), 270
    Guadalcanal (Solomons), see Guadalcanal
    Guam (Marianas), see Guam
    Hawaii, see Hawaii
    Island-Hopping Battles (Figure 1-2), **31**
    Iwo Jima (Volcanos), see Iwo Jima
    Marianas, 252, 276
    Mindanao (Philippines), 40
    New Guinea, 129

Okinawa (Ryukyus), see Okinawa
Pavuvu (Russells), 125
Peleliu (Carolines), 96, 119, 129, 132, 292
Philippines, see Philippines
Rabaul (New Britain), 132
Saipan (Marianas), see Saipan
Solomons, 110
Taiwan, 41, 62-64
Tarawa (Gilberts), 34, 129, 292
Tinian (Marianas), see Tinian
Pacific War, 28, 30-35, 37, 62, 84-86, 95, 101, 105, 111, 113, 122, 130, 132-33, 138, 140, 194, 250-51, 254, 279, 281, 285, 298
Pakistan, 273
Pajarito Plateau, NM, 208, 219, 245, 269, 284, 286
Palace of the Governors, Santa Fe, NM, 39
   Archives, 290
Parachute as wedding dress, Art Smith and Bessie Pacheco (Figure 2-9a), **74**
Paris, France, 300
   Radium Institute, 300
Pavuvu (Russells), 125
Pearl Harbor, 28, 31-32, 34, 36-37, 46, 85-86, 96, 106, 139-41, 143, 150, 152, 155, 160, 162, 164, 188, 198, 264, 292, 294
Peleliu (Carolines), 96, 119, 129, 132, 292
Pentagon, 36, 107, 109, 115, 120, 122, 125, 133-34, 166, 206-07, 250, 253-54
Peru, 170, 291
Petition (from scientists related to use and control of atomic bombs), 284, 303
Philippines, 28-29, 31-32, 35-37, 39-40, **41**, 43, 46-47, 49, 61-62, 64-65, 69, 76-77, 81, 105, 108, 119, 214, 258, 279, 281, 291-93
   Cabcaben Airport, 77
   Clark Field, 37, 39-43, 49, 76, 293
   Corregidor, 48-49
   Filipinos, 36
   Luzon, 49
   Manila, see Manila
      Manila Bay, 40, 65
   Range Finder at Ft. Stotsenberg (Figure 2-2), **41**

Samat, Mount, 48
San Fernando, 48-49, 53
   See Camp Cabanatuan
   See Camp O'Death
   See Camp O'Donnell
"Pineapple Army," 100th Battalion, U.S. Army, 166-67, 276, 281, 298
Plutonium, 198-99, 206, 209, 223, 231-32, 234-35, 237, 239-42, **244**, 245, 249-50, 263, 270, **271**, 273, 292, 300
   Bomb Hoisted to Top of Tower, Trinity Site, NM (Figure 5-13), **244**
   Gadget, 239, 243-44, 246-47
P.O. Box 1663, Santa Fe, NM, 215, 220, 224
Poland, 28, 30, 198, 200, 203
Postcard, International Red Cross, Art Smith's Code to Family (Figure 2-9), **73**
Potsdam, Germany, 239
Potsdam Declaration, 29, 199, 250, 303
Potsdam Ultimatum, 29, 199, 250, 303
Poston Relocation Camp, AZ, 158, 162, 165, 186, 297-98
   U.S. Bureau of Sociological Research, 298
POW Road, Lordsburg, NM, 192
Presbyterian Mission School, Leupp, AZ, 85, 286
Presidential Executive Order 9066, 141, 144, 146, 150, 284
President's Advisory Committee on Uranium, 198, 278
Princeton University, 201-02, 222-23, 232, **255**, 265, 267-68, 280
   Niels Bohr and Robert Oppenheimer in 1950 (Figure 5-14), **255**
   Richard Feynman, the Contrarian of Los Alamos (Figure 5-8), **223**
Prisoners of War (POWs), 157, 168, 170
   American, 178, 183, 254, 261, 281, 285, 291-93, see Chapter 2, 36-82
   American nurses in Manila, 283
   Australian, 46
   Camps, 156, 168, 261
   Dutch, 46
   German, 141, 156, 170, 174, 189, 191

Italian, 141, 156, 174, 189, 191
Japanese, 108, 191, 298
Public Law 503, 141
Pueblo, 25, 38, 132
"Purple" cipher machine, 84
"Purple" code, 84, 144, 279
Purple Heart Medal, 135, 254
Purple Heart Battalion/Regiment, 166-67, 276, 281, 298
Pyle, Ernie, 125, **126**, 127, 285, 289
    Ernie Pyle at home (Figure 3-7), **126**
    Ernie Pyle Branch Library, 289
    Ernie Pyle Day, 285

Quan (stew), 56
Questions 27 & 28 to test loyalty of internees, 165-66,186

Rabaul (New Britain), 132
Race to atomic bomb, 197, 201, 213, 218, 232-34, 265, 269, 300, 302-04
Racialization, 162
Radio Tokyo, 163, 265, 297
Range Finder at Ft. Stotsenberg, PI (Figure 2-2), **41**
Rehoboth Mission School, Gallup, NM, 294
Religion, 282
Relocation camps, *see* War Relocation Authority (WRA) Relocation Camps
Reserve Officer Training Corps (ROTC), 93
Rising Sun emblems in Japanese American camps, 162, 178, 184-86
Rough Riders, 26, 300
    City of Las Vegas Museum and Rough Riders Museum, Las Vegas, NM, 300
Rohwer Relocation Camp, AK, 158
Rome, 197
Rosario Cemetery, Santa Fe, NM, 173, 187
Russia, 28-30, 33, 96, 194, 227, 254, 264, 269-70, 272
    Moscow, 30
    Spies, 194, 250, 270-73, 304

Sacred corn pollen, 125
Saipan (Marianas), 28, 33, 96, 115-116, **117**, 129-30, 132, 137, **166**, 292

2nd Division, 3rd Battalion, 6th Marine Regiment on Saipan (Figure 3-6), **117**
Marines in First Wave Ashore in Saipan, June 1944 (Figure 3-5), **166**
Samurai (warrior code), 35, 65, 253
San Antonio, TX, 170
San Diego, CA, 86, 92-96, 104-07, 110, 124, 127-28, 130
San Francisco, 72, 107, 145, **147**, 175, 226, 258
    Evacuated from San Francisco during 1942 (Figure 4-3), **147**
    Konko Church, 151
    Spanish Consul, 157
San Francisco Chronicle, 150
San Jose, 145, 151-54, 175, 192-93
    Konko Church, 152, 154
Sandia Air Base (formerly Oxnard Field, formerly Kirtland Field), NM, 153, 275
Sandia National Laboratories (SNL), NM, 275, 286, 305
    National Atomic Museum, 290
Sangre de Cristo Mountains, NM, 208, 302
Sansei, 146, 148, 192
Santa Fe, NM, 25-26, **39**, 60-61, 69, 72, 75-76, 80, 82, 175, 188, 209-10, 215, **216**, 219, **220**, 224-25, 227, 236, 270-72, 286, 289-92, 297-99
    Alameda Street, Santa Fe, NM, 270
    Bataan Memorial Building, 80, 289
    Casa Solana Neighborhood, 171, 173, 290, 292
    Castillo Street Bridge, 270
    Dorothy McKibbin in 109 E. Palace Avenue Office (Figure 5-5), **216**
    Fiesta 1942 Swearing In at the Plaza (Figure 2-1), **39**
    Gonzales Elementary School, 301
    Inn of Loretto, 270
    La Fonda Harvey Hotel, Santa Fe Plaza, Permitted Relaxation (Figure 5-7), **220**
    National Guard Armory (now New Mexico Military Museum and Library), 81
    Palace of the Governors, 39
    Rosario Cemetery, 173, 187

Sangre de Cristo Mountains, 208
See Bataan Military Museum and
  Library
Veterans Memorial, 289
Santa Fe Internment Camp, NM, 81-
  82, 139, 152, 154, 156, 163-64, 167-
  68, **169**, 170, **171**, 172, **173**, 174-
  76, **177**, **179**, 180-89, 193, 217,
  227, 282-84, 286, 290, 292, 297-99
  Abner Schreiber, Deputy-in-
    Charge of Camp, and Camp
    Leaders (Figure 4-11), **177**
  Aerial Photograph in 1951 (Figure
    4-10), **173**
  Civilian Conservation Corps
    (CCC), 171
  Funeral for Dr. Sadakazu Furu-
    gochi, 1943 (Figure 4-9), **171**
  Games, 178-79
  Guard in the Watchtower as Fan
    of Spring Baseball (Figure 4-
    12), **179**
  Internee Mamoru Ike Possessions
    Searched by INS Officers
    (Figure 4-8), **169**
  Marker, 187
  Minor revolt, 188
  Movies, 299
  Ortiz Park, Frank S., Santa Fe,
    81-82, 187
  Plays, 299
Santa Fe *Jiho*, Camp newsletter, 178
Sasebo, Japan, 153
SEDs, *see* Special Engineer
  Detachment
Sendai, Japan (POW Camp), 67
Shackle cipher (U.S. Navy), 87, 101,
  114
Shiprock, NM, 83, 88, 91, 109, 131
"Silverplate" (priority code word), 258
  See Tibbetts
Site W (*see* Hanford, WA)
Site Y (*see* Manhattan Project)
Site Z, *see* Oak Ridge, TN)
Smith College, 216
Sokuji Kikoku Hoshi-Dan (pro-Japan
  male internees who renounced U.S.
  citizenship), 184, 186-87
Solomon Islands, 96, 110
  See Bougainville
  See Guadalcanal
South Africa, 273
South Asia, 36

South China Sea, 37
South Pacific islands, 32
Soviet, 29, **271**, 273
  Pass Identification Photo of Spy
    Klaus Fuchs (Figure 6-2), **271**
Spain, 25-26
Spanish Consul, San Francisco, 157,
  178, 181, 299
Special Engineer Detachment (SEDs)
  224, 235, **237**, 238, 247, 272, 277,
  291
  SED Staff in 1945 (Figure 5-11),
    237
Spies
  American
    See Greenglass
    See Hall
    See Rosenbergs
  European
    See Fuchs
  Japanese, 293
  Russian, 250, 271-72, 304
"Spirit of Bataan," 62
SS *Gripsholm*, 163
Stagg Field, Chicago, 205
Stalingrad, 33
Stanford University, 141, 165, 269
Straight Flush (B-29 weather plane), 20
Squaw Dance Ceremony, Navajo, 129-
  30, 295
Stockholm, 198, 203
Strasbourg, 233, 303
Submarine, One-Man, 137
Suicide torpedo, 137
Surely You're Joking Mr. Feynman, 222
Surrender (American, German,
  Japanese), 28-29, 33, 44-46, 96,
  108, 138,168, 188, 199, 250, 303
  Leaflets, 262
Sweden, 280
  Goeteborg, 200
  Kungaelv, 200
  Stockholm, 198, 203
Switzerland, 50
  Zurich, 233

Taos, NM, 289
  Bataan Building, 289
  Taos Plaza Memorial, 289
Taiwan, 41, 62-64
Tarawa (Gilberts), 34, 129, 292
Tattori Maru (Death Ship), 52, 293, *see*
  Death Ship

TBX Radio (used by Navajo Code
   Talkers), 113, 295
Texas, 25, 72, 75, 184, 210
   El Paso, 72, 75, 184, 240
   Fort Bliss, 39-40, 72
   San Antonio, 170
Thailand, 32
The 15 Years War (Japan's name for
   WWII), 31
Time-Line of the Main Events in World
   War II (Table 1-1), 28
Time-Line for the Navajo Code Talkers
   (Table 3-1), 96
Time-Line of the Santa Fe Detention/
   Internment Camp (Table 4-1), 188
Time-Line for the Development of the
   Atomic Bomb (Table 5-1), 198
Tinian (Marianas), 19-20, **21**, 22, 24,
   27, 29, 32, 96, 116, 132, 199, 251,
   257-58, **259**, **260**, 262, **263**, 264,
   276, 292
   Agnew Holds Plutonium Bomb
      Core Before Dropped on
      Nagasaki (Figure 5-18), **263**
   Alberta Project, 239
   Crew of the Enola Gay on Tinian
      (Figure 1-1), **21**
   Deak Parsons and Paul Tibbetts
      Brief Crews on Tinian (Figure 5-
      16), **259**
   Enola Gay Parked at North Field
      on Tinian (Figure 5-17), **260**
Tokyo, 49, 66, 144, 252, 262, 265, 304
   Bay, 29, 199, 265
Topaz Relocation Camp, UT, 158, 293
Tottori Maru (Death Ship), 64
Trinity Site, NM, 29, 194, 199, 209,
   230-31, **242**, **244**, 290-92, 239
   Bomb Hoisted to Top of Tower,
      Trinity Site (Figure 5-13), **244**
   Jumbo (Figure 5-12), **242**
   Test, 240-45, 247-50, 276, 291-
      92, 302-03
   Trinitite, 248
Tube Alloys British research team,
   202, 224, 255, 270-71, 301
Tube Alloys Project, 202, 224, 255,
   270-71, 301
Tule Lake Relocation Camp, CA, 157,
   162-64, 166, 177, 183-86, 188-89,
   189

Ukraine, 273

United States of America (U.S.A.), 25-
   26, 28-29, 33, 36, 44, 46, 84, 90, 96,
   115, 130-40, 146, 150-51, 155-56,
   159-60, 162, 175, 180, 183, 192,
   195-98, 205, 225, 250, 265, 270,
   273, 280-84, 286, 291-92, 304
   GI Bill, 128, 132
   Hawaiian Islands, *see* Hawaiian
      Islands
U.S. Advisory Committee on Uranium,
   203, 234, 279
U.S. Air Corps, 85
   Code, 85
U.S. Army, 37, 76, 85-86, 90, 105-06,
   109, 125, 140-41, 143, **145**, 152,
   156, 165, 167, 186, 193, 235, 237,
   276-77, 279, 281, 290-91, 298
   100th Battalion ("Pineapple Army,
      " HI), 166-67, 276, 281, 298
   442nd Regimental Combat
      Team,166-67, 192, 276, 281,
      298
   Aliens Division, 141
   Code, 85
   Code Talkers, 86, 109
   "Go For Broke," 167
   Japanese Americans Evacuated
      from San Francisco during
      1942 (Figure 4-3), **147**
   Japanese Americans Evacuated
      from the West Coast during
      1942 (Figure 4-4), **149**
   Intelligences, 144, 235
   Major General Leslie Groves in
      Washington, D.C. Office (Figure
      5-2), **207**
   Major General Leslie Groves
      Receives Distinguished Service
      Medal (Figure 6-3), **278**
   Ordered to Report to Assembly
      Centers by U.S. Army (Figure 4-
      2), **145**
   Pentagon, *see* Pentagon
   WACs (Women's Army Corps),
      224, 247, 283
   WAFs (Women's Air Force Corps),
      283
U.S. Army Air Force
   509th Composite Squadron
      Bombing Group ("Tibbett's Air
      Force"), 19, 258, 260, 289
         Distinguished Flying Cross
            (Tibbetts), 24

U.S. Army Signal Corps, 109
U.S. Atomic Energy Commission, 268-70, 292
U.S. Bureau of Indian Affairs (BIA), Education, 89, 91-92, 94, 101-07, 130-31, 294
    Chinle, AZ, 91-92, 116
U.S. Bureau of Sociological Research, 298
U.S. Corps of Army Engineers, **145**, 203, 207, **271, 278**
    Japanese Americans Ordered to Report to Assembly Centers (Figure 4-2), **145**
    Manhattan Engineering District, 205
    See Manhattan Project, Project/Site Y
U.S. Department of Defense, 141
U.S. Department of Justice, 141, **142**, 167, **173**
    Immigration and Naturalization Service (INS), 144, 155, 167, 172, 181, 185, 189
    Internment camps (for Japanese Americans), **142**, 154-56, 168-70, 175
        Crystal City Internment Camp, TX, see Crystal City Internment Camp
        Fort Lincoln Internment Camp (near Bismarck), ND, 156, 170, 175, 188, 190, 298
        Fort Missoula Internment Camp, MT, 156, 170, 181, 188
        Map Location of Four Camps (Figure 4-1), **142**
        Santa Fe Internment Camp, see Santa Fe Internment Camp
        Map of Santa Fe Internment Camp **173**
U.S. Department of State, 234
U.S. Department of War, 62, 141, 144, 194
U.S. Far East Air Force, 40
U.S. Federal Bureau of Investigation (FBI), 144, 150, 152, 155-56, 160, 163, 165, 168-69, 175, 181, 220, 226, 236, 272, 291
U.S. House Un-American Activities Committee (HUAC), 273, 304-05
U.S. Immigration Act of 1924, 146

U.S. Immigration Service
    See U.S. Department of Justice
U.S. Livestock Reduction Program (Navajo), 90-91, 105
U.S. Marine Corps, 19, 28, 34, 85-99, 101-11, 113-15, **117**, 119-27, 289-91
    1st Division, on Okinawa, 96, 125
    2nd Division, 96
    2nd Division, 3rd Battalion, 6th Marine Regiment on Saipan (Figure 3-6), **117**
    2nd Division, on Okinawa, 96, 125
    3rd Division, on Guam 118
        On Iwo, 96, 123-24
    4th Division, on Iwo 96-97, 123
        Chicago, 96, 133
    5th Division, on Iwo 96, 123-24, 133
    6th Division on Iwo, 96, 123
        On Okinawa 125
    Carlson's Raiders, 111
    San Diego Marine Corps Recruit Depot, 128
    See boot camp
    See Camp Elliott
    See Camp Pendleton
    See First 29 Navajo Code Talkers
    See Navajo Code Talkers
U.S. Media, 61
U.S. Navy, 32-33, 76, 84-85, 101, 106, 122, 141, 143, 150, 153, 224, 258, 269, 291, 295
    Code, 85, 87, 101, 114
    WAVEs, 283, 291
U.S. West Coast, 28, 140-45, 149-51, 155, 157, 162, 164, 170, 211, 280, 286
Universities, American,
    Arizona State University, 132
    California Institute of Technology (Cal Tech), 210, 213, 221, 223
    Columbia University, 201, 204
    Harvard University, see Harvard University
    Massachusetts Institute of Technology (MIT), 203
    Northern Arizona State University, Flagstaff, Museum of, 132
    Princeton University, see Princeton University
    Smith College, 216

Stanford University, 141, 165, 269
University of California, Berkeley, 198, 201, 208, 210, 212-13, 221, 226-27, 229, 232, 268, 298, 304
University of California, Davis, 132
University of Chicago, 199, 204-05, 212, 222, 229, 249, 303
   Enrico Fermi, "Italian Navigator," First Chain Reaction (Figure 5-1), **204**
   Metallurgical Laboratory, 199, 204-05, 212, 222, 249
   Petition (related to use of atomic bombs), 284, 303
   Stagg Field, 205
University of Michigan, 153
University of New Mexico, 71, 124, 131, 153, 272
University of Rochester, NY, 304
University of Southern California, 86
Western New Mexico University (formerly New Mexico State Teachers College), 40, 71
Universities, European,
   Cambridge University, 195, 302
   Cavendish Laboratory, 195
   University of Berlin, 197, 280
   University of Copenhagen, 195-96
   University of Göttingen, 195-96, 213, 280
Uranium (and uranium isotopes), 28, 197-00, 203-06, 210, 212, 222, 230, **231**, 233-35, 250, 257, 261, 279, 292, 302
   Functioning of Bomb (Figure 5-10), **231**
   President's Advisory Committee on Uranium, 198, 278
USS *Eldorado*, 83
USS *Indianapolis*, 258
USS *Lexington*, 295
USS *Missouri*, 29, 199, 265
USS *Mount Vernon*, 105
U.S.S.R. (Soviet Union), 29, 30, 199, 220, 226-27, 254, 264, 270, 273-74, 301
   Atomic bomb, 304
   KGB, 272-73
   Leningrad, 30
   Moscow, 30, 303
   Spies, 250, 271-72, 304
Utah, 87, 143, 192, 214
   Moab Internment Camp, 189

Vanderbilt University, 71
V-E Day (Germany surrenders), 199
Veterans Administration, 76
   U.S. Hospitals, *see* U.S. Hospitals
Veterans Highway, Las Cruces, NM, 289
Veterans Hospital, Albuquerque, NM, 71
Veterans Park, Deming, NM. 289
V-J Day (Japan surrenders), 24

Wa (Japanese for "harmony"), 137
WAFs (Women's Air Force Corps), 283, 291
War Dance (Navajo), 125
War Relocation Authority (WRA), **142**, 143, 145-47, 149, 155-57, **159**, **161**, 164-66, 168, 174, 176, 184, 189
War Relocation Authority (WRA) Relocation Camps, 22, 29, **142**, 155, 158, **159**, **161**, 162, 297
   Amache Relocation Camp, CO, 158
   Gila Relocation Camp, AZ, 158, 163
   Heart Mountain Relocation Camp, WY, 152-54, 158, **159**, **161**, 286
      Tarpaper Barracks to Coziness, WWI Veteran (Figure 4-7), **161**
      Under Heart Mountain (Figure 4-6), **159**
   Jerome Relocation Camp, AK, 158
   Location Map of Ten WRA camps (Figure 4-1), **142**
   Manzanar Relocation Camp, CA, 157
   Minidoka Relocation Camp, ID, 158, 182
   Moab Relocation Camp, UT, 189
   Poston Relocation Camp, AZ, *see* Poston
   Rohwer Relocation Camp, AK, 158
   Tule Lake Relocation Camp, CA, *see* Tule Lake
Warriors: The Navajo Code Talkers, 137

Wartime Civil Control Administration (WCCA), 141-42, 148, 152, 164
"Water treatment" (torture), 59
Washa! Washa! (Japanese festival marching cadence), 162
Washington, D.C., 44, 63, 87, 95, 121, 134-35, **136**, 183, **207**, 214, 249-50, 256, 267, **278**
    Arlington National Cemetery, 121
    Japanese American Memorial, 193
    Major General Leslie Groves in Washington, D.C. Office (Figure 5-2), **207**
    Major General Leslie Groves Receives Distinguished Service Medal (Figure 6-3), **278**
    Surviving Four of First 29 Navajo Code Talkers (Figure 3-8), **136**
    White House, 140, 143, 203
Washington, 62, 141, 206, 291, 297
    Hanford (Site W), 206, 230, 235, 279
    Puyallup, 297
    Seattle, 119, 145, 151, 181
WAVES, 283, 291
West Coast (U.S.), 34, 140-45, 149-51, 155, 157, 162, 164, 170, 211, 280, 286
Western University (formerly New Mexico State Teachers College), Silver City, NM, 40, 71
White House, Washington, D.C., 140, 143, 203
White Sands, NM, 289, 290, 292
White Sands Missile Range, NM, 240-41
Window Rock, AZ (Big Res), 88, 97, 134, 289
"Windtalkers," 137, 296
Wollachee-Shush-Moasi (Navajo Code Alphabet), 98
World War I, 27, 86, 303
    Tarpaper Barracks to Coziness, WWI Veteran (Figure 4-7), **161**
World War II, 27-29, 31-33, 35, 37, 40, 96, 98, 104, 188, 198, 266-67, 276-79, 281-82, 284, 286, 302-04
Wyoming, 143, 152, 159
    Heart Mountain Relocation Camp, WY, 152-54, 158-59, 161, 286

    Tarpaper Barracks Made Cozy, WWI Veteran (Figure 4-7), **161**
    Under Heart Mountain (Figure 4-6), **159**

Yeibichai (Navajo war dance), 125
Yokohama, Japan, 62, 64, 252

Zero fighters, Japanese, 42, 44, 112, 119, 129
Zero Ward (in a prison camp), 59-60
Zurich, Switzerland, 233

Printed in the United States
51431LVS00002B/61-105